P9-CDV-009

MY HERO

MY HERO

The Indiscreet Memoirs of an Eventful but Unheroic Life

BY DONALD R. RICHBERG

ILLUSTRATED

G. P. Putnam's Sons
New York

Library of Congress Catalog Card Number: 54-10504

MANUFACTURED IN THE UNITED STATES OF AMERICA

To

F.W.R.

E.R.C.

D.R.C.

Contents

I	WHAT IS IT ALL ABOUT?	3
II	ANCESTORS	8
III	YOUTH	16
IV	LOOKING BACKWARD FIFTY YEARS	26
V	THEODORE ROOSEVELT AND ARMAGEDDON	42
VI	THE "BULL MOOSERS"	60
VII	THE FIRST WORLD WAR	78
VIII	A LEGAL BATTLE FOR "THE PEOPLE"	102
IX	LEGAL BATTLES FOR LABOR	112
X	WHAT WAS CALLED "NORMALCY"	134
XI	PROSPERITY AND THEN THE DELUGE	141
XII	FROM HOOVER TO ROOSEVELT	149
XIII	FRANKLIN D. ROOSEVELT—MY FIRST BOSS	162
XIV	LEARNING TO BE A BUREAUCRAT	170
XV	ON BEING "ASSISTANT PRESIDENT"	177
XVI	LAST DAYS OF THE NRA	184
XVII	THE "SICK CHICKEN" CASE	189
XVIII	RETURN TO PRIVATE LIFE	197
XIX	AN UNHEROIC HUSBAND	207
XX	THE "COURT PACKING" MISADVENTURE	220
XXI	PRELUDE TO THE SECOND WORLD WAR	228
XXII	THE NEW DEALERS IN PEACE AND WAR	234
XXIII	THE MEXICAN OIL NEGOTIATIONS	248
XXIV	AFTERMATH OF MEXICAN OIL	264

XXV	THE SECOND WORLD WAR	269
XXVI	OFF-STAGE GLIMPSES OF F.D.R.	279
XXVII	TRUMAN ARRIVES	296
XXVIII	THE DOUBLE MARTINI CLUB AND OTHER ASSOCIATIONS	309
XXIX	A PERSONAL CRUSADE FOR LIBERTY	317
XXX	LIFE IN CHARLOTTESVILLE, VIRGINIA; TEACHING LAW; ARGUING IN THE SUPREME COURT	328
XXXI	IN CONCLUSION—NO HERO	346
	INDEX	361

Sixteen pages of illustrations will be found following page 182.

MY HERO

CHAPTER I

What Is It All About?

SOME responsibility for the title of this book must go to Frank R. Kent of the Baltimore *Sun*. During the 1930's he quoted me so frequently in his column that, having been joked about it by other newspaper men, he once greeted me at a Gridiron Dinner with a cry: "My Hero!" To this I replied: "That would make a good title for an autobiography!"

But let me give you hasty assurance that this will not be the story of a man who is a hero—even to himself. On the contrary, it will be the story of a man who never became an heroic figure, but who aspired to do so much more than he did and to be so much nobler than he was, that "my hero" was always a remote ideal and never an imminent reality.

To write books of fact and fiction that are never first class, to write verses that deserve no immortality, to pour out streams of articles and speeches that never stir a multitude to action, might have meant a growing sense of frustration to an ambitious man. But, when that same man achieved a measure of success and a conspicuous standing as a lawyer and in various public offices, he escaped the feeling that his life had been futile and developed a certain curiosity to find out why he accomplished as much as he had but had not accomplished any more.

My own conclusion for this exploration is a simple one. There are capacities for judgment and action, combined with self-assurance and courage of a high order, that make for genius. There are capacities for patient intrigue and perpetual compromising that bring to some men high position and shiny honors, despite the lack of greatness in their characters or aspirations. I had neither of these capacities. To have been popularly called "Assistant President" of the United States (even discussed in the press as a presidential possibility), to have an appointment to the Supreme Court of the United States frequently predicted and commonly expected, to have spent many years of public life in intimate association with pre-eminent leaders of politics, education, industry and labor, induced many spurts of vanity and puffs of pride, but no abiding conceit.

Gradually it became apparent to me that the daydreams of childhood would never come true. There was no sense of disappointment to one who had been taught the terrifying cost and strain of exercising power to guide or rule the lives of others. It was a relief to know that it would be wiser to scribble an occasional verse to amuse a few friends than to strive in vain for the immortal poem that would uplift the souls of generations to come. It was a relief to know that the Atlasian responsibilities of lofty public service would never fill every day with the torture of unbearable burdens and every night with a crushing load of care.

Living close for years to men of genius (such as Michelson and Millikan, in science) was enough to convince an earth-bound student that he had no soaring genius.

Working closely for years with great politicians (such as Theodore and, much later, Franklin D. Roosevelt) certainly convinced an ever-tense collaborator that he had neither the admirable qualities, nor the less admirable conceits, nor above all the toleration of unsolvable problems, deceitful expediencies and corrupt associations, that make it possible for a political ruler to sleep well at night and to smile through dangerous days.

Probably it was fortunate that my most extravagant period of national (and international) prominence came in 1934–35 when I was over fifty-three years old. It would have been a heady dose to take ten years before when the ailments of midde age had not begun to impress upon me that I could no longer work day and night for weeks and then recuperate with a few days of relaxation. However, it was a bit bewildering to read in a nation-wide poll of editors that the sixth name in the ten most "newsworthy" persons of the year 1934 was Donald R. Richberg. This temporary ranking near No. 1 Franklin D. Roosevelt, No. 2 Adolph Hitler and No. 3

Benito Mussolini might have created delusions of grandeur, even in a very weary bureaucrat. But happily the arthritis which had begun to plague me eighteen years earlier increased the frequency of its painful warnings that I was no more of a superman in body than in mind. It was less of a wound to vanity to say: "I am not physically strong enough to maintain such a pace," than to concede one's mental incapacity.

This brings me to what is perhaps the only good reason for writing this life story. Not only has it been impossible for me to make a hero of myself, but, despite a wide and close acquaintance with many of the towering figures of half a century, I have been unable to give hero worship to any one of them. Indeed, everyone with whom I have worked, or whom I have studied carefully, has demonstrated such a human incapacity to solve superhuman problems and to carry superhuman burdens that sympathy (not too crudely evident!) instead of adoration has been the keynote of our relationship. There is a vast difference between admiration for the great effort of a conscientious leader to achieve the impossible and admiration for the expedient evasion which, although merely postponing the day of reckoning, is proclaimed a great achievement.

Every man of affairs who has lived through the awesome transformation of the material and spiritual conditions of human life in the twentieth century has been compelled to realize his ever-mounting ignorance of the forces which he must to some extent control in order to meet the responsibilities which follow upon the power which he desires or seems fated to wield. Complex as were the issues through which Americans blundered into a ghastly Civil War, they were simple compared with the tangled, obscure issues through which nation after nation floundered into two World Wars, eventually dragging a reluctant United States into both abysses. Complex as were the economic and social problems of 1900, they were simple indeed compared with the problems of 1950.

Most difficult of all problems of any man of affairs in the 1950's is the maintenance of a simple faith in the reason and purpose of living, a guiding star that, often lost to view yet ever shining, will save him again and again from the emptiness and despair of a struggle that has no meaning and no end. What is that faith that has made it possible for some men to remain passably sane in the seats of the mighty? Sometimes it has seemed to be the tiny hard core of an "old time religion" that survived in the heart, if not in the mind, of a modern sophisticate. Sometimes it has seemed to be only a colossal egotism; sometimes only a mystic instinct animating a fleshly organism.

Deep thinkers in ivory towers or monastic philosophers in quiet cloisters may wrestle cleanly with the issues of faith and the infinite design. But meanwhile, in dirt and sweat and suffering, millions of hard-working people are being guided into better or worse living, into comfort or destitution, into peace or war, by men of affairs who have not yet found the way to simplify and distribute their tasks within their competence, who have not yet rediscovered the old certainties of faith that made objectives clear for centuries when ways and means to attain them were obscure. Now that ways and means to infinite progress are becoming visible the terrible question arises: Progress to what and why?

Perhaps in the last half century—which was such an extraordinary half century—there may be found a tiny trend, hardly long enough to indicate where the curve of human destiny will extend through the next thousand years. But, if we look at it under the microscope, we may see enough of the curve to project it ahead for another fifty years. The only microscope which I can use is in my eyes, reviewing the life I have lived, which has no lasting importance whatsoever unless, as a microcosm, it simplifies the puzzle of the failure of human leadership to guide mankind away from self-destruction in the greatest era of material growth of human power.

In this story of my life my hero must ever be the great man whom I could always visualize but never could be, and never knew. To tell this story usefully it is necessary to include both activities in which I have taken a little pride and those of which I have been deeply ashamed. Weaknesses and mistakes will be recounted—not in a mood of self-flagellation—but in fairness to associates who must be discussed with similar candor. There is something pitiable about the biographer who freely points out the frailties of notables with whom he has labored, but refers with only a veneer of modesty to his own follies, for which there is usually offered some appealing excuse, such as: "being under heavy pressure," or "without adequate information," or "my wife being in the hospital at that time."

It does not seem to be necessary, however, to drag the reader of a biography through all the gloomy cellars, dusty attics or smelly back alleys of one's life. Often it is enough to mention that the meat upon which Caesar fed was very bad, without opening the garbage can to demonstrate that it was full of maggots. If a statesman was unhappily befuddled with liquor at the time of a critical decision, that is a pertinent fact; but an exact description of the debauch which preceded a miserable blunder is a needless impertinence. Being thus courteous to friends may justify me in being equally courteous to myself; and thus I may avoid that wallowing in self-exposure which is a curious form of conceit. Obviously there is enough conceit evident already in writing an autobiography, no matter how carefully one may explain other reasons for doing it.

Since, however, any value which this narrative may have will depend on the mature activities and associations of the author, little time will be wasted on his ancestry, or youth, or the petty details of daily living and working. These should have slight interest except to those who ascribe merit or demerit to a writer's observations in accordance with their analysis of hereditary or environmental influences which are often assumed to be far more determinative than I think they are. It is my purpose to parade across the stage of America 1902–1952 the outstanding leaders of political thought and action in this period, including in their number, of course, some leaders of education and industry who indirectly but powerfully shaped public policies. This personally conducted parade will serve its aim if, as the author proves himself to be clearly incompetent for the role of hero, he demonstrates some competence as a well-informed expositor of the reason why none of the acclaimed heroes of this brief era were able to save their followers from participating in the greatest waste of human life and the greatest destruction of accumulated common wealth ever experienced by mankind.

CHAPTER II

Ancestors

EVERYONE has ancestors. This is sometimes a matter of undue pride. On the other hand, many persons seem impressed with a modern cult to the effect that ancestors are of no particular importance, that race, religion and national origin should be given no consideration in any attempt to understand or to appraise the potentialities of persons. For my part, I do not hold even my father and mother responsible for my shortcomings, but I do think that the inheritance of obvious physical and mental characteristics has some influence upon the life and work of every human being which should not be disregarded in any biography. Happily for my readers, I have no such extensive knowledge on my ancestry as might encourage me to spend several chapters on this subject. All that seems to have any importance can be stated briefly.

My father was born in a small town in southern Germany called Romrod, January 26, 1845. His parents, who were evidently moderately well-off, middle-class Lutherans, emigrated to America in consequence of and not long after the revolution of 1848. After spending a short time in the East, where my grandfather's brother located himself in Brooklyn, Louis Richberg, my grandfather, with wife and children, settled in Chicago where he established a small pork-packing business. Whether this has been accurately reported as the first precursor of the great pork-packing industries of Chicago I do not know. But it was at least one of the pioneers. The business was sufficiently successful so that Grandfather raised a family, which included three daughters and one son, in comparative comfort, and at the age of sixteen my father entered Knox College.

This was the year in which the Civil War began. As a transplanted Virginian in my older years, I suppose I should call it the War Between the States. My father ran away from college and joined the Union Army. His father, exercising some political influence, managed to have him taken out of the Army and sent to the U.S. Naval Academy, where he studied for three years and then became a midshipman in the Navy, serving until 1867, when he was honorably discharged. To my childish questions as to whether he had ever been wounded he assured me this had occurred once, as the result of the explosion of a can of baked beans. One of his proud recollections was having served on the U.S.S. *Constitution* on what was, I believe, her last voyage before being retired as a national memorial.

On his return to civil life my father took up the study of law, which in those days was a comparatively brief education, because in 1868 he opened up his law office in Chicago. From this office he was forcibly ejected by the Great Fire of 1871, in the course of which he managed to pack his books and records, which were probably not extensive, in a handcart which he was able to wheel across the Chicago River into an unburned section of the West Side.

The Great Fire seems to have stimulated an enormous amount of energy in all Chicagoans and certainly in my father. He took an active part in the rebuilding of the city and its enterprises; in fact, so active a part that in the late seventies when still quite a young man he became a member and then president of the Board of Education, being known at the time as one of the close associates of the senior Carter H. Harrison, who was a mayor of outstanding capacity. In many ways Harrison served the city well as a very practical politician, who shrugged off criticisms of some of his dubious political supporters with the remark often quoted by my father: "You have to let the boys steal a little."

Far from subscribing to this political philosophy, my father was quite a militant reformer, and his period of power on the Board of Education was marked by two achievements of a radical nature for that time. In the first place, he managed to get the reading of the Bible discontinued in the public schools, not because of any irreligion but because of his conviction regarding the necessary separation of church and state, a principle which has been receiving intense and favorable consideration in the Supreme Court in recent years.

The second radical reform was bringing the compensation of women teachers up to the level of the men.

My father, who was obviously a Republican during the Civil War, had studied law in a lawyer's office in St. Louis and during that period became so impressed with the evils of Reconstruction so obvious in any Southern or border state, that he turned Democrat and remained a Democrat throughout his life, with the single exception of the period in which his opposition to the "populism" of William Jennings Bryan drove him into a temporary espousal of Republican candidates for national office.

In the course of his service as president of the Board of Education my father became acquainted with a very able school teacher, a Vermont Yankee named Eloise Randall, who had come to Chicago in the seventies and moved up so rapidly in the educational field that at the time when she met my father she was the principal of one of the Chicago schools. She became my mother, about whom I shall write further.

Like many a successful lawyer, my father, although enjoying a very good practice, had an ambition to make more money than was the common lot of most lawyers in those days. After he inherited a small fortune from his father, he left his law business in the hands of a partner and started a zinc mining and smelting operation in East Clinton, Tennessee, where he spent most of his time for a period of two years. He also spent his inheritance. This explains why I happened to be born in Knoxville, Tennessee, which has in my later years permitted Southern hosts to introduce me to audiences as "Southern born." But since my father, after his business adventure, returned to his deserted law practice in Chicago, where I lived until 1933, I cannot claim to be "Southern born and bred."

It has always been a source of great regret to me that my father did not write his memoirs. The story of the successful rebuilding of his practice in Chicago would have been a fascinating tale. Chicago was growing with extraordinary vigor and my father played quite a part in that civic adventure.

Possibly one of the reasons he always hesitated to write his story was that he had such an extraordinary record of large clients gained and large clients lost. He represented great mercantile and manufacturing enterprises, one of the "Big Four" of the Union stockyards, insurance companies and transportation companies. Father was a man possessed of a violent temper and an independence of thought and action quite intolerable to many clients. As a boy at home I listened fearsomely to his accounts of terrific rows with clients, some of whom lasted out the storms but many of whom departed. When I eventually joined my father in practice in 1904, these storms continued; clients came and clients left. I often wondered how we would manage to rebuild a disintegrating clientele. But it was this very intensity of feeling and partisanship which made my father a strong advocate in court and a great persuader of juries and judges whom he somehow managed not to offend. This gave him a reputation which in a rapidly growing city seemed sufficient to provide an incoming stream of new clients to replace the outgoing stream.

I am well aware that there has always been within me that intensity of feeling and violence of convictions which can easily lead one to make far more enemies than friends. But in watching and often suffering from my father's temperamental outbursts I had a liberal education in the desirability of trying to govern one's emotions, in seeking for the soft answer that might turn away instead of arouse wrath. I observed a hundred times in court as well as in the office that it was possible even for a man of my father's intensity to control the outward expression of what might be righteous anger or might be simply inability to understand the other fellow's point of view.

My father felt strongly that his eldest son should have the academic education which he had been denied by war and he was determined that I should go through college and then to Harvard Law School. It was a great satisfaction to him that I managed, even without scholastic honors, to graduate from the University of Chicago, A.B., 1901, and from Harvard Law School, LL.B., 1904, and then, by good fortune, to pass the Illinois Bar Examination and enter into practice and partnership with him in July 1904.

My mother was born in Woodstock, Vermont, November 12, 1849, the daughter of two doctors, Nathaniel and Marenda Randall. But the real doctor was my grandmother. My maternal grandfather was by trade a jeweler, who studied medicine only because my grandmother had graduated from Penn Medical College in 1854 and, returning to her native village to practice most successfully, put her jeweler husband in the shade. But, as my mother used to explain, although he obtained sufficient education to become a licensed physician, he had the unfortunate habit of fainting at the sight of blood, which handicapped him severely in his effort to practice his profession.

My maternal grandmother was, as would be guessed, a very radical woman. Her religious tendencies were strongly spiritualistic. Her belief in equality of rights and opportunities for women was militant. She was a suffragist in the days when a woman who wanted to vote was a generally unpopular character. She entered Penn Medical College as the first woman ever accepted there and it may be presumed that the faculty did not anticipate she would survive the rigors of association with male medical students, who, in that time, were notoriously rough characters. But with her inflexible will she went through the entire course and on her graduation was presented with a special letter of commendation signed by the entire faculty, testifying not only to her strength of character but also to the diligence with which she had absorbed all the medical education then available.

In the course of her invasion of Philadelphia Grandmother carried on a continuous campaign for women's rights and had the distinction of addressing the Pennsylvania legislature on the subject. Her speech on that occasion, preserved in the family archives, is one of the most extraordinary forensic efforts I have ever read. Its flamboyance combined with sledge-hammer logic was typical of most political utterances of the pre–Civil War period—the type of speech which even now is heard occasionally in political conventions, but is not as highly regarded as it was in those early days.

My mother, when only fourteen, graduated from the Woodstock High School and soon began self-support through teaching, particularly "elocution." Her only brother was a captain of Vermont Volunteers, fighting through the Civil War until the Battle of the Wilderness, where he was killed. In Woodstock, Vermont, there is today a small granite shaft in a grassy triangle erected by the George C. Randall Post of the G.A.R.

The tradition of fighting for a great cause was strong in my maternal ancestry. There is a Randall farm four miles south of Woodstock, in the corner of which is a small cemetery with tombstones that go back to the Revolutionary War and on which are engraved the names of the Randalls who fought in that war. Among them is Nathaniel Randall, my great-great-grandfather, the father of Nathaniel Randall, my great-grandfather, who was the father of Nathaniel Randall, my grandfather. Perhaps ancestry is of no importance, but at least it was some satisfaction to me in the years of government service when political opponents (such as William Randolph Hearst) undertook to describe me as a "roistering revolutionary," to be able to say that my lineal ancestors in 1776 were also revolutionaries. When accused of a desire to transform the government of the United States, I pointed out that not only did my lineal ancestors fight to establish that government, but my father and my maternal uncle both fought to preserve it.

My mother came to Chicago in about 1876, I believe, in the hope of earning a better living than she had found first in Vermont and then in New Jersey. She obtained a teaching position in the public schools and at the time when she retired to marry my father she had become principal of what was then called the Clark School. For many years thereafter she was very busily engaged in raising a rather large family. I was her eldest son, followed in a few years by twin brothers, one of whom died in infancy, then followed by a sister and finally by another brother who lived less than two years.

In addition to her own children, Mother had the care of my father's two daughters and a son born of an earlier marriage. This half-brother of mine died when he was only ten years old, but the two half-sisters lived well beyond middle age, as did my own brother and sister.

Although absorbed for so many years with the imperative demands of a housewife and mother she never lost her determination to study medicine and become a physician as her mother had before her. So when the family had grown up and should have been able to take care of themselves, my mother sought the satisfaction of this lifelong ambition. She entered medical college after she was fifty, and completed the prescribed four-year course with such honor that she was then asked to teach in the college, which she did for some time.

Now came a curious throwback, in a way, to an experience of

her mother. My father was intensely proud of his wife's intellect and achievements. He was proud to have her study medicine and graduate. But his German temperament (forgive me if this sounds like racial prejudice) was appalled at the idea that his wife should practice medicine and permit an implication that her husband, a successful lawyer, did not adequately support her. He was so offended that my mother, with that resolute will characteristic both of herself and her mother, decided she would go away and practice somewhere where there would be no reflection upon my father. My father, however, did not regard this apparent desertion as a happy solution of the family problem.

Mother established an office in Springfield, Illinois, which was entirely too near Chicago to meet the supposed needs of the situation, especially since Springfield was the state capital where many of my father's fellow lawyers went to argue before the Supreme Court. So Mother moved again—this time to San Francisco, where she began to build a practice. I do not know how long this exile would have lasted if my father had maintained his apparently robust health. In 1909, however, he took a trip alone to Europe and I fear (once having traveled abroad with him and my mother) that he indulged himself recklessly in rich foods and good wines, even though he never drank "to excess." When he returned he attended simultaneously a meeting of the American Bar Association and a meeting of Commissioners of Uniform State Laws. He was president of the Illinois Commission for many years. The combination of these excitements with physical and mental strain was evidently too much for his hardening arteries. Almost immediately after his return to Chicago he had a stroke, which paralyzed his left side. My mother came back at once from San Francisco, gave up her residence and practice there, and devoted herself for the rest of his life to the care of my father in the joint capacity of wife and doctor.

Within a few months my father was able to return to his office with little evidence of his stroke except a slight drag of the left leg and a minor facial paralysis. He went on practicing vigorously until 1915, when he had another stroke which incapacitated him completely, leaving him substantially helpless, so that from then until his death three years later he had to have constant night and day nurse service. This was finally provided by placing him in a nursing home near an apartment in which my mother took up her residence. My mother continued to practice medicine in a small way after my father's death until her death in 1924.

The foregoing brief survey of my ancestors and the family in which I grew up is utterly insufficient to provide for a psychological analysis of the influences of heredity and environment upon my own development. According to many ideas now advanced by modernistic biologists, anthropologists and sociologists, racial and religious inheritances have little influence upon the individual or, if they have, his value as an associate in work or play should be appraised without any consideration of these factors, because they are "accidents of birth." As an individual I feel powerfully influenced by what seem to me racial and religious inheritances; but, in deference to the pseudo-scientific opinions which inform us that, contrary to our own observation, there are no racial characteristics or inheritances, I will avoid in this philosophic memoir any effort to ascribe responsibility for the good or evil in me to my ancestors.

CHAPTER III

Youth

In the first ten years of my life there was a dreadful possibility that my parents had produced an intellectual prodigy. From subsequent observation I have noted that a young prodigy is generally a great annoyance to his family and sets himself a pace which he cannot possibly maintain in his later years. Happily, my intellectual sprint seems to have exhausted me before I entered high school and only at rare intervals in the succeeding years were any evidences of sprinting ability manifested.

For some reason, possibly because of my small size (in early years), my childish ambitions took an intellectual rather than an athletic turn. With the diligent use of alphabet blocks and illustrated primers I had educated myself by the age of five to read the daily newspaper. I had also become household aid to my mother, learning to cook, to wash and iron, sweep and dust and do errands, particularly in the purchase of food and staples. I shall not emphasize these accomplishments since my wife has always been skeptical of them in view of my apparent incapacity to do many household chores in later life.

However, I distinctly remember one episode of taking the streetcar several blocks to a grocery store, purchasing a week's provender and, on returning home, tendering the usual fare, three cents, to the conductor who, with misplaced generosity, said: "You aren't six years old. You travel free." This well-meant kindness sent me home in unmanly tears.

One may wonder why a five-year-old boy engaged in such activities; but the older children were all in school, our limited household servants were overworked, and what was more natural than that a little boy, anxious to show off, should be permitted to fit himself into vacant tasks?

In those days the first grade of the public school which I entered at the age of six was comparable to the kindergarten of today, the children learning for the first time their alphabet and rudimentary writing and arithmetic. This was quite intolerable to an aggressive youngster who had been playing the part of an advanced Boy Scout, so I proceeded to demonstrate my situation to the teacher before the end of the first week. I brought in the daily paper and rather ostentatiously opened it and began reading. The teacher with intended sarcasm called me to the platform and asked me to read to the class what I found so interesting in the paper, assuming, of course, that my bluff would be called in a most humiliating manner. Instead of which, I began reading from the major crime story of the day on the first page. This resulted in my hasty removal to the principal's office and immediate transfer to the second grade where, as a matter of fact, I still maintained a somewhat arrogant superiority. But at least before the end of the year I found something new to learn.

The pride of these early accomplishments swelled within me and I showed off on every possible occasion, reciting poems on days of celebration, such as "The Blue and the Grey" on Memorial Day, and in general making myself as offensive as possible to the more plodding and athletic students, who took particular delight in running over me in games at recess or after school.

The grade school was, however, regulated to a fairly low mediocrity and by the time sixth grade was ended it was decided to form a special grade of the superior students, to take the seventh and eighth grades together. As a result I graduated from grade school shortly before my twelfth birthday, which was all too young for entry into high school where the average age of entering students was fourteen to fifteen. These were young men and young women, not little boys and girls.

I found myself in high school a somewhat unhappy object of general amusement. Being the only boy in the freshman class who wore short pants, I was an obvious mark for ridicule. So I persuaded my parents to buy me a suit with long trousers before the end of the first year, even though I was only a trifle over five feet. I shall never forget the humiliation of my appearance in my new garments of maturity. The boys promptly gathered round me, put me on my back on top of a desk, elevated my feet in the air, pulled down my long trousers and discovered to their joy and my embarrassment that I still wore long stockings. I was held in this humiliating position for the entrance of our algebra teacher, a very beautiful golden-haired, blue-eyed young lady who was adored openly by all the older boys as well as secretly by myself. When I was over sixty, this charming teacher, still in the public schools, wrote me a letter reminding me of the algebra class and also of our conversation at the end of the year when I came to say a tremulous good-by to her. "Aren't you going to kiss me, Donald?" she asked. And I said: "I don't think I'm quite old enough for that." I can hardly imagine any of my schoolmates having made such a response.

Fortunately, I think, for my future enjoyment of life, I began to grow so rapidly toward the end of high school that when I entered the University of Chicago in the fall of 1897 I was over five feet eight inches tall. I had loose wobbly joints, but an increasing love of athletic games and vacation work on a farm had put some muscle on my scrawny frame so that, to everyone's amazement, I made the track team at the University in my freshman year. My loose joints had permitted me to acquire a curious wiggly rambling gait suitable for a "walker" and I actually won points for the varsity in the mile walk in my first year.

But even a certain amount of athletic ability, which eventually won me my college letter and also the handball championship, was not sufficient to lift the sixteen-year-old boy who entered college to the level of social equality with his older classmates—men and women of obvious maturity, at least in their own opinion. Not until the end of my sophomore year did I really come to participate thoroughly in the life of the campus. From then on, the age disparity was not so obvious and I was accepted as a leader in many activities, such as acting in a campus production of *As You Like It,* and in two comic operas, singing in the glee club, leading cheers at football games, becoming managing editor of the student publication and finally leader of the "senior sing" and an officer of the senior class.

Looking back, I think this was a very healthy emergence of a small boy into adolescent responsibilities. I must admit it had a sad effect on my intellectual achievements. I cut so many classes in pursuit of more interesting things that, although I passed enough courses, the laws of the University required me to take additional courses to make up for my absences. So, despite having five and a half credits more for graduation than the required number, I found myself on the eve of graduation short one-half unit of credit. In desperation I petitioned the faculty to waive this deficiency, setting forth my reasons in a hand-written document of twenty-eight pages to demonstrate that a student who had earned five and a half *extra* credits should not be denied a degree for lack of another half credit. This long screed I handed to the Dean just before he entered a faculty meeting. He looked at it in horror and said, "We are only meeting half an hour. I don't see how we could even read this in that time." I said I realized the difficulty, but didn't think it would be right for them to deny my petition without reading it. The Dean agreed at least to present my plea, and it was my great good fortune that the faculty granted the petition, so I graduated with my class.

This narrow escape from failure finally convinced my parents as well as myself that the prodigy of bygone years had faded away. As a result, the whole family was extraordinarily relieved when I graduated from Harvard Law School in 1904, without honors. To me the graduation in itself was close to a miracle because living for the first time away from home—and being accepted as a man of dubious but possible maturity by faculty, schoolmates and social acquaintances—was a very heady experience.

There was an intoxication in life which I had never known before. A bit of this was alcoholic and nicotinish. Because of athletics I had rarely smoked in college and had had very little even of beer or wine to drink. But the freedom to drink and smoke was only a minor excitement in my law school years. The real intoxication came from feeling that I had finally become a free citizen. This led me to seek a variety of ways of earning money, so that I might free myself from absolute financial dependence upon a really indulgent father. I wrote stories and verses and received rejection slips from almost all the important magazines. I sold advertising briefly and actually made as much as $35.00 in one day, which almost blew me out of a future education. I worked on special assignments for the New York *Journal.* With earnest young men and women I spent many hours working over plots of plays and collaborated in the writing of dramas which we hoped some day would appear on Broadway. None ever did.

Despite all this extracurricular activity, which included an unsuccessful attempt to make the Harvard track team, playing in the finals of the handball championship, singing for a time both with the Harvard Glee Club and as a chorister and soloist of the Pierian Sodality (the oldest musical organization in America), and also a great deal of walking, riding, canoeing, dining and dancing around Boston—despite all these, I did study with fair diligence, took part in moot court hearings, and managed to pass final examinations.

In later years I have taught law myself, and I know what a disappointment it is to a teacher to feel that he is not getting a full response from a student. This has made me realize that I must have been a sore disappointment to some of my eminent teachers. I took sufficient part in class discussions to indicate that I might have a capacity for doing some really good work, but my performances never rose above the level of what I should estimate as something less than average.

From the time I left law school I had to work, and work hard, at not only practicing law but constantly learning law, deepening my understanding of its principles and sharpening my ability to present the fundamental justice of a position or its fortification by precedents so as to win an argument or a case for a client. Without presumption, but with some humility, I must confess that the major part of my education in law, economics, political science, sociology and biology has been acquired since emerging from college and law school.

During my college days I came in contact with two men of totally different characters and activities who had considerable influence on their times: John Alexander Dowie, the evangelist, and William Jennings Bryan. John Alexander Dowie built up a huge congregation in the United States and abroad and founded a city—Zion City—forty-two miles from Chicago and the same distance from Milwaukee. He called it "halfway between beer and babel." He was a man of extraordinary personal force and was most successful in his chosen career until, in his declining years megalomania finally overcame him, and, announcing himself as the reincarnation of Elijah, he drifted into a semi-insanity before his death. He had, however, built a whole city, which he ruled as a theocrat, establishing sumptuary laws, such as the prohibition within the city limits of not only alcohol and tobacco but pork and oysters and many other proscribed commodities.

He started his church in a little tabernacle outside the World's Fair in Chicago in 1893. It grew into a great church edifice and a residence and administration building on Michigan Avenue. He claimed divine powers of healing, and the sick, the halt, the lame and the blind by the hundreds streamed into his church, where abandoned crutches, trusses and such artificial aids hung on the wall in mute testimony to Dowie's healing powers. Every member of his church had to contribute one-tenth of his income, a Scriptural tithe, for the support of the church, its pastor and his family.

Dowie's son was a fellow student of mine at the University of Chicago. He was also a handball expert and through playing with him I came to know him much better than other students did. The combination of his father's reputation, his own beard (the only one in the student body) and some slightly unpleasant habits turned most of the students against him. Since I was a partial outlaw as a child among men, it was natural for me to associate a good deal with this other outlaw upon whom his father had put the unfortunate label of "my unkissed son." I dined at times with the Dowies in their luxurious apartment; and when I asked young Dowie how they could take one-tenth of the income of all parishioners and live in such luxury themselves, he remarked, as though it were a complete answer, "We are not Communists." Apparently they believed that to him that hath shall be given.

The most extraordinary example of the Prophet Dowie's faith in himself and his fanatic devotion to his own law came when their only daughter tipped over an alcohol lamp while curling her hair. The curtains caught fire and in her mad efforts to put out the fire she was burned to death. She was the pride and joy of her parents—their only daughter, of whom they were possibly more fond than of their only son. Yet at the funeral services in the packed church on Michigan Avenue I heard Dowie preach an amazing sermon, with the tears running down his face, to the effect that it was the judgment of the Lord upon his daughter that she had used alcohol despite his prohibition and as a result she had suffered the supreme penalty—death.

Few now remember that, after his tremendous success in Chicago, Dowie planned an invasion of New York City, a crusade to redeem this modern "Sodom and Gomorrah." It was alleged that fifty thousand Zionites descended upon New York—the exact number I do not know. Since I had known the Dowies so well in Chicago, the New York *Journal* employed me to cover the Dowie invasion. I warned them that however I might feel personally I would not take advantage of an acquaintanceship to malign or even to ridicule the Dowies. They assured me they had plenty of reporters who would take care of that part of the program! They only wanted someone with access to Dowie from whom they could get accurate information or statements.

The New York papers put on a terrific campaign of ridicule and, even worse, abuse, such as, in streaming headlines, "Zion Babies Starving." There were, of course, hundreds of babies brought by the pilgrims and they had established a very elaborate nursery system to take care of them while their elders were ringing doorbells throughout the city, bringing the message of Zion.

One night when this campaign was at its height the Reverend Dowie summoned me to his apartment in the Plaza Hotel. The floor was strewn with copies of the New York papers which he seemed to take great delight in trampling underfoot as he marched up and down, raving at their calumnies. Of course the New York *Journal* was one of the worst, so he wanted me to resign and take a job which he assured me he had already arranged for me with a rival newspaper. He also offered me a dozen or more enormous portraits of himself which had never been published and which he was sure the rival newspaper would pay handsomely to obtain.

I tried to explain to him the ethics of the situation, but there were no ethics in it to him, and I will admit that from the rough treatment he was receiving he might have been justified in thinking that there were no ethics in journalism. But when I finally left after midnight, still refusing to transfer my allegiance, he insisted upon forcing on me half a dozen of these enormous photographs, which I kept for some years as a souvenir of the occasion, and also as an example of the inflated egotism which possesses men who find they can exercise great power over their fellow men and women.

I met William Jennings Bryan for the first time when he was a candidate for the Presidency in 1900. The University of Chicago student body invited both candidates to address the students at a time suited to their convenience. Mr. Bryan accepted personally and Chauncey Depew spoke later in behalf of William McKinley.

The student committee to escort Mr. Bryan to the campus was composed of O. L. McCaskill (later professor of law at Illinois) and myself. We waited upon "The Great Commoner" in his rooms at the Auditorium Hotel where he received us in the simple democracy of his undershirt, explaining that his wife was sewing a button on his shirt. We talked briefly and then descended to take the open carriage in which we were to drive the seven miles to the University, no automobiles being available in 1900.

On the drive out the candidate, who was reading a small volume of Lincoln's writings, said he supposed we wanted a nonpolitical speech, which he evidently was in the process of composing. We assured him to the contrary—we wanted a thoroughly political speech. We had invited both candidates and we wanted to hear a partisan speech. Thereupon, he folded his book with a look of contentment, as if realizing that no further preparation was needed, and chatted pleasantly all the way to the University. This preliminary is important because Bryan then spoke for half an hour, delivering one of the best organized and in many ways one of the most appealing speeches I have ever listened to. It was quite obviously not memorized, but was rather a demonstration of how a beautifully trained speaker could organize and deliver a speech out of the masses of material in the back of his mind. We used it during the rest of the term in our public speaking course as an example of excellent speech construction. I should add that it was delivered magnificently, since Bryan was then at the height of his oratorical powers.

I had heard Bryan once before—in 1896 in the old Coliseum, where the Democratic National Convention was being held. My father had obtained a seat for me in the gallery and I sat there expectantly waiting for Bryan's appearance because an usher had given me a warning of what was to come. He was a Nebraska usher and as he showed some people to a seat next to me, he said: "You wait till this young feller Bryan comes in. Then you'll hear something."

There were many candidates before the convention; but it is freely admitted that it was Bryan's speech which made him the nominee. That was before the days of microphones and when he began speaking, far away, a speck on that remote platform, little could be heard of what he said. But gradually the hall quieted and as it did his voice rose. It swelled in volume until, way up in the gallery where I was sitting, every word could be heard, down to the famous conclusion: "You shall not press down upon the brow of labor this crown of thorns, you shall not crucify mankind upon a cross of gold." To me the demonstration which followed was, of course, wholly spontaneous, and in some measure it was; but later I learned from my politically wise father that a combination of silver mine owners and Midwestern politicians with certain definite axes to grind had prepared the way to turn the convention into a Bryan demonstration if he did his part as well as was anticipated.

There are many other men with whom I had associations during the educational years who played great parts in the transformation of the America of the gay nineties into the America of two world wars—men like William Rainey Harper, president of the University of Chicago; Professors Michelson and Millikan, who were Nobel prize winners; Amos Alonzo Stagg, the coach of athletics who made a great profession out of the training of young men not only to win games but for future good living. But the influence of these men extended far beyond the collegiate days, during which I had only a small understanding of their worth. Not until much later did I appreciate fully their services to their fellow men.

So, without having done more than skim the top of a trash barrel of recollections, I enter that period from 1902 to 1952 in which I moved (I will not say progressed) from youth to what I once thought was old age, but which I now recognize as a period when youth is gone but not forgotten.

CHAPTER IV

Looking Backward Fifty Years

As I undertake to review the transformation of American life in the half century from 1902 to 1952 I face the difficulty of writing such a personal narrative that, through my intimate experiences, I can follow the economic, social and political changes which, produced largely by advances of science and invention, made over not only the daily habits but the minds of the American people.

Political leadership is always seeking for some way to use the forces of government to satisfy the ever-developing hungers of a people for what they regard as the better things of life. Meanwhile, the instinct or urge to produce things, to sell and distribute things, so as to make a living or a fortune for men of commerce, drives men and women into cooperative organizations producing great benefits for which politicians always like to take the credit, or resulting in misfortunes and disasters for which politicians are ever ready to promise relief. At the same time the moral instinct, the reforming urge which inspires so many people to selfless endeavors, is always pressing upon politicians to forward some noble cause through which perhaps their names may be engraven on historic tablets, or at any rate they may be elevated to public offices providing fairly good wages and some pleasing notoriety for services of uncertain value.

As I began the practice of law in Chicago in 1904 the city was on the verge of one of its recurrent reform campaigns. In reaction against the extreme aggressiveness of private enterprise, particularly in the so-called "gay nineties" which were far from gay for millions of people, there was a growing trend to invoke the powers of government either to curb or to take away the unrestricted power of private owners to control industries and services upon which the public was dependent. Against the power of the railroads the populist agrarian movement of the Midwest had launched successive attacks, climaxed by the free silver campaign of Bryan in 1896. Despite the Sherman Anti-Trust Law, the steel trust and other great aggregations of capital had arisen. The impoverished farmers and ill-paid, ill-housed city workers were murmuring in a swelling chorus against the social injustice of the building of great fortunes on the foundations of a mean existence of humble and unorganized workers.

Symptomatic of the trend of the times was the development of a campaign for municipal ownership of the streetcar properties in Chicago, out of which financial buccaneers like Yerkes, aided by the venal services of grafting politicians, had taken small fortunes and returned bad service. The campaign of Judge Dunne (a Democrat) for mayor on a municipal ownership platform was supported by a great many very young and very zealous reformers just out of college as well as by the usual following of city politicians interested only in the spoils of office but delighted to march behind the shouting front of young enthusiasts.

Thus I found myself speaking for municipal ownership on the same platform as that graced by much more notable young men, such as Joseph M. Patterson, one of the inheritors of the Chicago *Tribune* power and fortune. Patterson was an announced Socialist in those days and upon the victory of Mayor Dunne he was made commissioner of public works, a position in which he could in fact achieve little and of the petty duties of which he soon became weary.

Concurrently, another *Tribune* inheritor, Robert R. McCormick, ran as a Republican for president of the newly created Sanitary District which was to accomplish the miracle of turning the natural flow of the Chicago River toward Lake Michigan into a reverse flow down to the Illinois River and thence to the Mississippi. By this process Chicago escaped the undesirable practice of dumping its vast sewage into Lake Michigan, from which great body of water

Chicago also drew back into the city mains the drinking water of the city.

The procedure of sending the sewage of a great city down inland rivers to perfume the waters which flowed by other great cities was resented by Chicago's neighbors. The question of the right of Chicago to withdraw vast quantities of water from Lake Michigan involved legal and engineering problems of great complexity and long standing. It must be conceded, however, that under McCormick's leadership the Sanitary District began its career successfully. It took some years before other, more acquisitive politicians were able almost to overcome the stench of sewage with the stench of corruption which quite naturally spread from the misgovernment of Chicago and Cook County to the misgovernment of the Sanitary District.

There was one amusing aftermath of Mayor Dunne's campaign which because of its effect on the fortunes of national figures is worth recounting. Mayor Dunne was an easygoing person who played politics on the theory of offending as few people as possible among his own supporters. There was bitter rivalry for the position of corporation counsel, the chief lawyer for the city, between two rising lawyers with strong labor backing, Daniel Cruice and Clarence Darrow. The Mayor-elect, in his desire to avoid offending either faction, approached his inaugural with this important appointment unsettled. Then he listened to the persuasive voice of an eloquent ex-congressman from the Far West, but Virginia born, who had been the star speaker in his campaign—Colonel J. Hamilton Lewis.

It was Lewis' suggestion that he himself receive a "temporary" appointment as corporation counsel from the new Mayor because, as a new arrival in Chicago, this would permit him to become quickly established in the legal profession and then, as soon as the Darrow-Cruice row was settled, he of course would gracefully retire. Mayor Dunne grasped this attractive straw and made the appointment; and anyone knowing the mucilaginous ability of Colonel Lewis will understand that he was never dislodged from the position acquired.

Many Chicagoans in the early days underestimated the peculiar abilities of J. Hamilton Lewis. But he himself was thoroughly aware of his idiosyncrasies. Meeting my father on the street one day, he observed casually: "You know, there are so many people in this town who think I am just a plain damned fool. But it pays, John, it pays." And I can testify from long acquaintance that he had a positive genius for seeking the exact time and place most propitious for the advancement of his fortunes. Typical of this was his astuteness in obtaining the nomination and running for the United States Senate at the one time when the Republican Party was so hopelessly divided that it was possible for a Democrat to be elected from the predominantly Republican state of Illinois. Equally astute was his delightful campaign against Mrs. Medill McCormick, to whom he always referred with that courtly courtesy which somehow made the voters feel that politics was no place for a gentle lady, although in fact everyone knew that Mrs. McCormick was a woman of extreme firmness and vigor, who was much more interested in presiding over a political caucus than a dinner table.

Many years later, I was to experience personally Colonel Lewis' almost unique ability to flatter inordinately without seeming to ridicule. At a time when I had some prominence in Washington, he urged me strongly to accept an appointment to the U.S. Circuit Court of Appeals, in which he knew very well I was not interested. But he pointed out how that would enable him subsequently to urge the President to appoint me to the Supreme Court. I was quite positive at the time that he knew I could not and would not accept appointment to the Circuit Court; and I was fairly certain that he was one of those who had advised the President *not* to appoint me to the Supreme Court (which the President had definitely under consideration) because of Senate opposition. Yet he was able to convince me that here was a dear friend who had long professed a profound liking for me, and who would do anything in his power to advance my fortunes.

The type of practice in which I was engaged and, to some extent, my social environment, accounted for the fact that I found myself in a few years moving along the lines of reform politics which did not particularly appeal either to the profitable clientage of an established law office or to the approval of conventional and comfortably well-off friends.

Despite my father's early reforming propensities, he was under great pressure, after his disastrous business venture, to put his services as a lawyer at the disposal of both large business clients and those political organizations which in that day, at least in Chicago, were more or less subservient to business interests. When I entered the practice our law office represented a great many big business interests, and my father was counsel for the city treasurer and for the Board of Assessors. In that day the city treasurer was legally permitted to retain the interest on public funds as compensation for his services and presumably also for the risk which he took in maintaining the integrity of those funds. The city treasurer's bond in such a sum as, for example, $20,000,000 could be obtained only with the aid of the banks, among which he distributed the deposits of city money, and in consideration of this service by the banks and his service to them, they paid him a low rate of interest. This arrangement was all around profitable for the politicians and the banks, although it became more and more evident to the public that it was hardly profitable for the people of Chicago. As a result, eventually these emoluments of the city treasurer, through which he might make a tidy sum such as $200,000, were transmuted into public revenues and the treasurer himself paid a reasonable salary. Naturally the guidance of the city treasurer through this era from the time of high private profit to subsequent improved public profit required the combination political-legal service which was the function of the city treasurer's counsel.

In this time also the Board of Assessors had an enormous power of political favoritism which was privately of great profit to the members. The antiquated Illinois Revenue Law imposed such impossible burdens upon the honest scheduling of personal property for taxation that it was simply regarded as a proper subject for evasion rather than enforcement. This was a little difficult, because the law required a sworn schedule of property. But, for example, if property had been assessed and taxed according to the legal rate, every trust estate in the banks and otherwise (to say nothing of private fortunes) would have had so much of its income taken by the state that the small return remaining would in fact have driven private capital to seek refuge in some more kindly state. Under these circumstances there had to be a sort of gentleman's agreement between all large property owners and the taxing officials that if schedules were not filed no undue penalties would be imposed, or if schedules of very dubious veracity were filed they would not be too seriously questioned.

But such a casual way of administering the law was bound to lead to many abuses. Some large property owners seemed to fare better than others and there seemed to be a coincidence between those property interests which contributed heavily to political campaigns (and even made other friendly contributions which benefited the ruling politicians) and the satisfactory adjustment of their taxation problems. Meanwhile the inequities, or one might say iniquities, of the taxing procedures were a constant source of political agitation for reform. Out of these came the creation in Cook County of a Board of Review whose function it was to correct any inequalities of official favoritism evidenced by the Board of Assessors. As might have been assumed, the three members of the Board of Review rose in political and financial power in the community to a place which would have aroused more bitter opposition from the five assessors if the reviewers had not tempered their justice with mercy for their political colleagues whom they allowed to share with them in the dispensation of favors and the reaping of well-earned rewards.

Seeing close at hand the manner in which private interests sought constantly to control the administration of public offices, and being a young man without indoctrination into the virtues of what in that time was commonly referred to as legitimate political graft, I became imbued with an idea that in some manner government and politics should be a cleaner, sweeter thing than it seemed to be.

Perhaps the contrast between my business life and social life emphasized this feeling. Since I had married a sister of one of the professors in the University of Chicago and had many of my personal friends of long standing in the University from which I had graduated, we had made our home in the University neighborhood and my social relations centered in that area. As a member of the Quadrangle Club, the faculty club, and an ardent tennis player, I enjoyed relationships of great intimacy for many years with the great physicists Michelson and Millikan, with classical scholars and with literary lights such as Robert Herrick, Robert Morss Lovett and William Vaughn Moody. Indeed, I could list a page of names of friends notable in the educational world whose thoughts, ideas and aspirations were in startling contrast to those men of the political and business world with whom my day's work was concerned.

At that time, too, there developed a bitter contest between the equally divided owners of a group of German newspapers in which my father and I fought a battle for control for many years. It ended in victory for our side, and then the proposal from the losing side to buy out our clients and establish their unrestrained control of this segment of the power of the press. It so happened that after losing one legal battle for control, I had been able to devise a desperate legal foray which was eventually sustained by the Supreme Court of Illinois, resulting in the sweet taste of sharing for the first time a large fee in addition to the rather generous salary which my father was allowing me as a nominal partner.

My father as usual was quite unrestrained throughout the proceedings in his criticisms of the other side. When it was all over our wealthiest opponent, a brewer who had decided he wanted to have control of the papers, purchased that control. He came to me and to my considerable amazement acknowledged the fact that I had been responsible for their defeat and he wanted to engage me as counsel for the new controlling interest. But he asked me whether I could accept the job without sharing my compensation with my father, because he said on one occasion my father had publicly denounced him as "no gentleman." This I may say was only one of my father's mildest comments, but it seemed to have cut him to the quick. My father was quite agreeable to the arrangement, so I became possessed of a client of my own and one of considerable value both from a money standpoint and from the standpoint of experience.

One of the important duties of an attorney for a newspaper is to protect it as far as possible from needless libel suits or to defend it in the unhappy event that a suit is filed. In this extended service to newspapers I observed at close hand the continuing confusion which must always exist between the exercise of the rights of a free press and the right of the people to obtain from their newspapers adequate uncolored presentation of news. A great editor backed by a good publisher must combine strong personal convictions and political opinions which will give character to his publication. But at the same time he must endeavor to handle the news with sufficient honesty and fairness so that his readers are not alienated by the feeling that they are being made victims of propaganda.

Again, I was able to observe that a publisher and editor must not needlessly offend the advertisers who support them, but at the same time must avoid the kind of obvious subservience to these revenue producers that would subject them to political attack and popular discredit.

In those days of highly competitive newspapers, when there were literally dozens of English and foreign-language newspapers competing for public support in Chicago, the problem of a publisher and editor in maintaining his independence was in some ways more difficult than at the present time. Today, a few great newspapers have such a monopoly that advertisers must utilize even those opposed to their opinions or interests, and readers perforce have a choice of publications no one of which may be in harmony with their ideas. From any one of them, however, they are pretty sure to get at least a sufficiently fair coverage of the news of the day, so that they can curse their favorite newspaper at the breakfast table but go on reading it.

During these early years of a miscellaneous practice of the law I had developed a particular interest in anti-monopoly legislation and had become impressed with the idea that the prevailing penalties for monopolistic controls of commerce were and would be increasingly ineffective. The criminal prosecution of individuals would result only in fines. Thus an attempt at monopoly became only a business risk, because there was no acceptance among either business men or the general public of any criminality inherent in any effort to make money by customary means. As a result, the government was not inclined to seek a jail sentence, or if it did, a jury was not apt to convict and subject a defendant to such a penalty.

For these reasons, way back in 1906–07, I went to work on an idea which would have occurred only to a very young man, without either wide experience or profound knowledge of the law. Anti-trust laws, I was convinced, could be enforced through imposing a really effective penalty upon an offending corporation. If this could be done there would be a powerful influence of investors upon management to make sure that the managers in their zeal for making profits did not impair the entire security of the corporate enterprise.

As this idea developed I wrote an article entitled "The Imprisonment of Criminal Corporations," which set forth the proposition that if a corporation were found guilty of violating the anti-trust laws the appropriate remedy would be to impose a criminal receivership whereby for the period of punishment the government would take the corporation into custody just as it did when it imprisoned individuals. It would then appropriate the revenue of the corporation for public purposes, with no more regard for private interests than was shown to the members of a prisoner's family when he was subjected to continuing regulation of his life and work. This article was published in full in a legal magazine. But for preliminary publication I wanted to reach the audience of an influential newspaper. For this reason I took a condensation of my article to James Keeley, then managing editor of the Chicago *Tribune,* who sought the private opinion of a judge as to whether a corporation could be imprisoned. The judge promptly replied over the telephone, while I was sitting by, that a corporation could not be imprisoned, using the old phrase "no body to be kicked, no soul to be damned." I thought this would squelch any publication; instead of which, Editor Keeley, recognizing that there would be popular interest in such an unorthodox idea, said, "We will publish your article." This he did to the extent of two columns on the editorial page, thus insuring an immediate even though largely hostile interest in my proposition.

Emboldened by this success, I sent a copy of the editorial page to President Theodore Roosevelt who, it may be recalled, was stirring up excitement now and then as a "trust buster." In response, I received a letter stating that the President had referred my letter and article to the Attorney General. An older lawyer, more experienced in politics, might have let the matter drop there; instead of which I telegraphed the Attorney General, asking for an interview, to which he responded graciously, that he would see me.

In Washington I was received by the Attorney General in what was then the Department of Justice, which consisted of a large old-fashioned house at the corner of Vermont Avenue and K Street. Curiously enough, there is now a very modern office building on that corner, the eleventh floor of which has been occupied by my law firm in the last few years.

Like so many of those close to President Theodore Roosevelt, Attorney General Moody was an enthusiastic horseman and, fresh from his regular morning ride, he greeted me in riding clothes. He graciously allowed me to develop my idea at some length. At the end of the interview I pleased him greatly by volunteering the fact that I had not come down for purposes of personal publicity, that I had notified no newspaper men of my engagement and would not embarrass him by giving out any statements, since the most innocuous might carry with it an implication that the Attorney General was seriously considering my proposition. From the standpoint of personal notoriety I undoubtedly overlooked a fine opportunity. But it was an early conviction of mine, which I have tried to adhere to, that when one is seriously endeavoring to interest a public official in any proposition the surest way to gain his confidence is to leave it to him to determine what publicity may or may not be desirable.

As I look back upon my own proposition after some forty-five years of practical experience with the problems of government and business, I can see many flaws in what seemed to me an inspired idea. At the same time, I have seen with the passage of the years my fundamental thought utilized in state and national legislation of a more practical nature than I envisaged. Something in the nature of a government receivership has been found useful in dealing with the problem of how to restrain or how to break up a monopoly. But in 1907 my ignorance of the complicated interdependent structure of society, business enterprise and government permitted me to espouse a simplified solution which has led me often since to understand, even when I disagreed with, the sweeping reforms proposed by young men in a hurry, moved by great ambitions and unrestrained by experience and knowledge of the intricacy of the problems to be solved.

I may add here that in 1913, as Director of the Legislative Reference Bureau of the Progressive Party, when I was working in frequent close association with Colonel Theodore Roosevelt, I drafted, with the counsel of a committee of outstanding Progressives, three bills to provide the Progressive Party program with a solution of the anti-trust problem. In these bills I incorporated my receivership for monopolizing corporations and obtained for these proposals (which were introduced in the House by Congressman Victor Murdock) the approval, first, of an eminent committee headed by Dean William Draper Lewis of the University of Pennsylvania, and second, the approval of Colonel Theodore Roosevelt, to whom I explained the bills in detail personally. Finally and most surprisingly I did not arouse the opposition of George W. Perkins, a partner in J. P. Morgan and Company, and chairman of the Executive Committee of the Progressive Party.

Thus I came to feel that perhaps the visionary idea of a young lawyer in 1907 had in it a bit of actual vision and some elements of practicality. In retrospect, I have been able frequently to see that a radical idea germinated by a young enthusiast may with persistence and good luck be developed into a political program gaining from politicians and then from the general public support which would not be given to more conservative and far better-grounded ideas advanced by men of more mature wisdom. In my later-day exasperation with many reform measures which I am sure will do more harm than good, I try to recall that it is ever part of the function of youth to ferment revolutions, while it is the appropriate function of older men to seek to restrain explosive programs but to aid in evolutionary changes which will permit us to live in social, economic and political structures while endeavoring to improve them.

By the year 1911 the Progressive movement, which had been active in both the Republican and Democratic parties, had developed to the stage where local campaigns, such as that of La Follette in Wisconsin and Wilson in New Jersey, were making their impress upon national politics. Colonel Roosevelt had returned from Africa and was seeking the ideological basis for a campaign against President Taft, who had incurred the antagonism of such Roosevelt favorites as Gifford Pinchot. The La Follette "Wisconsin idea" had captured the imagination of young men in many states. The so-called muckrakers had exposed municipal corruption in "the shame of the cities." Widespread hostility to business autocrats and Wall Street financiers had been developed through exposures such as Ida Tarbell's *History of the Standard Oil Company* and Lawson's *Frenzied Finance*. The extraordinary spectacle of ex-President Wilson of Princeton reforming the notorious government of New Jersey was inspiring hope in young collegians everywhere.

In Chicago a campaign was launched by "progressive Republicans" to capture the Republican nomination for mayor under the leadership of Professor Charles E. Merriam of the University of Chicago, who had been surprisingly effective in the City Council in developing popular understanding of just how bad for the city it was to have it governed by what became widely known as "The Grey Wolves." In a startling primary election Merriam received the Republican nomination by a vote of practically two to one over old-line political rivals. His campaign manager was Harold L. Ickes, then a close friend and later a law partner of mine.

There has always been a question as to whether in the ensuing mayoralty campaign Merriam might have won if his campaign manager had been more willing to play ball with the old-line Republican leaders who were in powerful political positions but whom he distrusted as much as they distrusted him. When reform has obtained its first victories and the defeated machine politicians are ready "to join them if we can't lick them," the question always arises whether it is the part of political wisdom to attempt an uneasy coalition or to fight for an uncompromising victory. The defeat of Merriam, however, by a narrow margin of votes could be ascribed to many causes.

One amusing and embarrassing incident of the campaign was a visit to me shortly before the election of a representative of the brewers who were the practical owners of most of the saloons. The brewers felt that Merriam would probably win and their main fear was that the city official who controlled the licensing of the saloons might attempt to interfere with their vested interests. "The professor" had a reputation, not undeserved, of having a very suspicious nature and they feared any suggestion from them would rouse antagonism. So I was asked to give an assurance, not that any particular man would be appointed but that no man hostile to the brewers would be appointed. If I would promise to see that no hostile official was appointed to that particular place, they assured me that the day before election when the beer wagon drivers made their deliveries to the saloons they would pass along the word to vote for Merriam.

There was no doubt that if they kept their promise this would be a powerful influence. On the other hand, they might be playing both sides against the middle—get my promise, pass the word to vote against Merriam, and then come back on me if Merriam won despite their opposition. The upshot was that I made no promise, but simply urged the brewers' representative to support Merriam, who I believed was going to be elected. And I agreed to do everything I could to persuade the new mayor to deal entirely fairly with the brewers' interests.

I don't know to this day what the brewers really did. Amusingly enough, when I told this story to Merriam after election, he said, "Why didn't you give them your promise?" and I answered, "Because I had no feeling of certainty that I could deliver on it and I'm just such a rotten politician that I haven't acquired the habit of making promises that I doubt whether I can keep."

The next spring the Progressive movement in Chicago was again in full swing, for a time under the separate leaderships of La Follette and Roosevelt, it being uncertain which would carry the banner in the ensuing national campaign. The Progressive group called upon me to make a campaign for the Republican nomination for state's attorney, the very powerful office of county prosecutor for Cook County which embraces, or one may say is overlaid by, the city of Chicago.

This first experience of running for public office provided me with what might be called a grade school education in practical politics. I learned that a candidate was not merely a man who ran around making speeches and issuing public statements. He had to see that funds were raised to pay the necessary and wholly legitimate expenses of a campaign.

Fortunately, as a reform candidate, I had no illegitimate expenses to meet. I received a number of quite innocent requests to contribute to the maintenance of small churches in the colored districts. Some of these requests were in a very naïve form. My campaign manager reported that a certain precinct boss had already promised to deliver to two other candidates, but if I made an appropriate contribution to a worthy cause he would agree to see that I got one-third! My campaign manager assured me that this man had a good reputation for doing just what he promised. But I must admit the prospect of such a "break-even" with two rivals did not appeal to me.

I launched my campaign on a high plane guaranteed to arouse the opposition of all practical politicians. I asserted that the state's attorney should be the watchdog upon all public officers to see that funds were expended honestly and no corrupt bargains were made for protection of criminal elements. Since the great majority of petty public officials sought public office for the purpose of improving their private fortunes, and since one of the best ways to do this was to make bargains with lawbreakers, the prospect of nominating and electing such a state's attorney as I promised to be could have no appeal to the rank and file, or to the top level, of politicians, whose influence was always more effective in primary than in general elections.

While I do not think I really expected to be nominated, I did expect to make a creditable race. My own conviction and vociferousness, combined with the fact that a great many solid citizens openly supported me, created some worry among the professionals. As a result I was approached by the leading Republican candidate, who was subsequently nominated, to withdraw in his favor and then join forces with him in winning the election and subsequently enforcing the law. I must say this candidate was an honorable individual of whose personal morality I had no question. On the other hand, we Progressives were engaged in a crusade against the old guard who we believed were incapable of really good government. So with the customary impertinence and assurance of youth, I strongly urged my powerful rival to support me rather than to attempt to persuade me to support him.

It is curious how professional politicians are often overimpressed with the vigor of a small group of militant reformers. Perhaps I would have polled more votes than I did but for the final strategy of the so-called Deneen Republicans. In the closing days of the campaign they raised the battle cry that if their "pure" candidate was undermined by a lot of high-minded Progressive votes for Richberg, the terribly "impure" Lorimer candidate would be nominated. My voting strength, if I ever had any, disintegrated rapidly. This was in the days when the scandals of Lorimer leadership were as notorious locally and nationally as those of the Pendergast leadership in more recent years. My vote in the primary election was so small that it only barely exceeded that of a notorious criminal lawyer who was running for the office largely for purposes of advertisement!

Before closing this chronicle of Chicago politics prior to the beginning of my involvement in national politics in the Bull Moose campaign of 1912, I should perhaps add a couple of footnotes on my private activities in this period. Prior to 1911 the sense of contrast between my business life and my social life, to which I have referred, along with a sensitiveness to the rising tide of political reform, had led me to put in a great deal of time evenings and Sundays in an effort, dear to everyone with an itch to write, to produce a "novel of significance." I wrote and, by my good fortune and his misfortune, obtained a publisher for *The Shadow Men.*

Strangely enough, I have never been ashamed of this book, although I recognize many of its weaknesses and crudities today. But it was an earnest effort to create some understanding of the devious activities of many so-called captains of industry of that era. From my active practice I had a pretty good idea of facts that I portrayed as fiction. Indeed, more than one man afterward said to me: "There were parts in the book in which I felt as though you had been listening in on many private discussions in which I had participated."

A most enthusiastic letter about the book came from the man in the Department of Justice who was at that time its leading authority on the subject of monopolies. Years later I received a strong letter of commendation from Theodore Roosevelt who had not only read the book but had, as he smilingly informed me later, immediately adapted the title to his own uses. He wrote:

> MY DEAR RICHBERG:
>
> I really like the book. I see the faults of execution of which you speak. . . . But, essentially, the lesson you teach is just, and is one that ought to be taught; indeed which it is imperatively necessary to have taught. The big reward, if society is to remain healthy, must be given for service and not for exploitation of a man's fellows. Of course, unless the man not only gets but insists upon as a rule having a reward commensurate to the service, he will in the long run do no good to anyone; but it must be, emphatically, a reward for *service.*
>
> Faithfully yours,
>
> (*Signed*) THEODORE ROOSEVELT

As a final footnote, I might state that I had written the words and music for a musical comedy which, supplemented by additions of fellow club members, was performed by the University Club of Chicago in the spring of 1912 to large and apparently amused audiences. At that time, when I was running for the office of state's attorney, it was discreetly decided that the announcements of the show should read only, "Words and music by members of this Club," thus leaving the militant candidate for state's attorney free from any advertised implication that he had a fundamentally frivolous nature. This was particularly desirable because, although as a resident of "dry" Hyde Park I was being attacked in the "wet" wards as an "anti-saloon reformer," the same opposition was whispering throughout the "dry" areas of the county that I "drank like a fish" and represented liquor interests! I had enough of such slanders to overcome without being publicly labeled as a "University Club playboy." But my campaign was so unsuccessful that perhaps it might have improved my chances if I had sung my own songs instead of making speeches.

CHAPTER V

Theodore Roosevelt and Armageddon

THE YEARS from 1911 to 1929 were a period of violent changes in living conditions and prevailing political opinions unprecedented in our history. In the first three years we were preoccupied with a nation-wide overwhelming demand for a reformation of political misgovernment. Everywhere in local, state and national politics people seemed to have awakened to the undoubted fact that they were being very poorly governed. There were strong groups in both the Republican and Democratic parties which were staunchly insisting upon maintaining as the most powerful influence in government large business and financial interests. But against this domination the outstanding leaders such as Roosevelt and La Follette, Wilson and Bryan were preaching, each in his own way, a new gospel of "social justice." Any doubt as to the popularity of their views was settled by the 1912 Presidential election, when Wilson was chosen President by a plurality of over 6,000,000 votes, Roosevelt ran second with over 4,000,000 votes and Taft ran third with something less than 3,500,000 votes.

There can be no doubt that this election marked the beginning of the end of control of government in the United States by the economic power of what may be called organized money. Wilsonian legislation from 1912 to 1916, and then Wilsonian controls of the entire economy during World War I, were followed by a terrific reaction at the end of the war, which apparently placed and kept big business in the saddle for the next twelve years. But this was only a surface appearance. The scandals of the Harding administration, combined with the brief depression of 1921–22, might have restored a progressive Democracy to power, except for the party split between Smith and McAdoo factions and the progressive Republican candidacy of La Follette which gave Coolidge the election of 1924. Luck was with Coolidge and seemed to be with Hoover until the 1929 depression overcame him.

In reality the power of organized money to control politics was diminishing all during this so-called "reactionary" period. This power had been rising steadily for decades after the Civil War. The tremendous expansion of industry which transformed the United States from a primarily agricultural nation into the most powerful industrial nation in the world necessarily brought with it a vast increase in the political power of business and finance. Those enterprisers who were mainly responsible for the growth of great cities, the employment of millions of manual workers and the spread of material comforts and innumerable opportunities for self-advancement, were naturally accepted as civic leaders apparently competent to guide the people in the process of self-government. Furthermore, their ruthless use of money not only enabled them to control both venal politicians and the minds of the electorate but also made opposition difficult and discredited militant reform.

But the obvious and well-advertised disparity between the wealth and extravagant waste of the unduly rich and the mean, precarious existence of masses of poverty-ridden workers was certain to give increasing power to those politicians who knew that discontent could be organized to register the power of numbers in the ballot boxes and place "champions of the people" in public office. Furthermore, intelligent and well-informed men and women provided a rising moral support in at least the second generation of the beneficiaries of successful commerce.

The typical cry of the times was in the slogan of the Progressive Convention, "Pass prosperity around." The exact method of doing this was not well defined, but in general there came a demand for the curtailment of "special privileges," a demand for new laws that would limit the ability of men of money to buy political offices and political favoritism and, probably most significant of all, a demand for the encouragement and legal support of labor organizations.

My close association with Theodore Roosevelt began in 1913 when I moved to New York to spend a year trying to advance the uncertain fortunes of the original Progressive Party. It was popularly known as the "Bull Moose Party" because T.R., on being asked one time in Chicago by a reporter how he felt, cried lustily: "I feel like a bull moose!" In view of the fact that the La Follette Progressive Party in 1924 was a wholly separate adventure and the Wallace Progressive Party in 1948 was an utterly different affair, it is fortunate for the Progressives of 1912 that they have an alternative appellation.

Although I had not met Theodore Roosevelt prior to 1912, I had studied him much at long range and, with the brashness of youth, had described him in a book published in 1911 as "the apostle of the obvious." It is significant of the later intimacy that I dared offer this book to him to read and received from him a cordial reviewing letter from which I have quoted.

In 1912 I heard him speak for the first time as he stood up in his automobile on arriving at a Chicago hotel and was more surprised by his Eastern accent than by what he said. Still critical, I heard him a day or so later speaking to a huge audience in the Auditorium and finishing his speech: "We stand at Armageddon and we battle for the Lord." At that time I was politically but not religiously enthusiastic and I complained to a sympathetic friend: "It's too bad he can't leave the Bible and the Lord out of this row." But within a few weeks I was helping to swell the convention chorus of "Onward Christian Soldiers" and quite agreed with the hard-boiled New York reporter who wired his editor: "I can't make fun of this convention. This is a religion."

In fact, many years later I wrote what I still believe: "The Progressive movement of 1912 was religious; a revolt of youth against age, of idealism against materialism. My generation was spoiling for a fight with the ancient enemies of progress—the self-satisfied. It was sick and tired of potbellied politicians; tired of bankers and business men preaching a one-day-in-seven version of the Golden Rule. It wanted to get religion, but not in churches patronized by thieves. So when T.R. located Armageddon and the band played marching hymns, we put on shining armor and went out to battle for the Lord."

It was a fact that I became a Progressive not because of Roosevelt, but at the outset almost in spite of Roosevelt. My liberal friends were much impressed by the leadership of La Follette in nearby Wisconsin, which had become a national leadership. We were also impressed by the fight of Woodrow Wilson in New Jersey. To a certain extent, Bryan's leadership in the Democratic Party since 1896 had been based on a similar demand for "social justice."

But it began to be evident in 1912 that a liberal must make a choice between national leaders whose programs were not entirely in harmony and whose personalities were antagonistic to one another. Wilson in the Democratic Party had expressed the pious hope that something could be done to "knock Bryan into a cocked hat." I have a personal letter from Roosevelt, written in 1917, describing Senator La Follette as "one of the very few men who is distinctly worse than President Wilson." Obviously no one could follow all four leaders without being regarded, to say the least, as a suspicious character. My own appraisal of the four, which I wrote in 1928, I still adhere to:

> It happens that I worked intimately for years with Roosevelt and La Follette, that I had a long acquaintance and many associations with Bryan, and very close contacts with President Wilson's administration. . . . Upon this unprejudiced basis for appraising the public services of all these men, I know they were all truly "progressive"—in that their common goal was to lift up the level of the average well-being. Unfortunately they were so different in temperament, in personal habits and interests which inevitably shaped conduct, that not one could effectively cooperate with or appreciate the other. Yet, in his autobiography La Follette wrote: "Roosevelt is the keenest and ablest living interpreter of what I would call the superficial sentiment of a given time, and is spontaneous in his response to it." In cruder but quite forceful language, Medill McCormick, in a conference over platform writing, once said: "Fellows, we must remember that T.R. is great because he understands the psychology of the mutt."

In a vague way I felt in 1912 that Roosevelt expressed more accurately the mass sentiment and yearnings of my generation than the evangelic Bryan, the uncompromising La Follette or the erudite

Wilson. Now, looking backward, I can see that one thing which influenced me, and which I think was a good influence, was that the progressivism of 1912 did not question the fundamentals of the existing order, that is, the "new order of things" promised on the Great Seal of the United States and born in the American Revolution. But one limit of that progressivism was that its proposed changes in law were largely for the purpose of compelling men to be good instead of bad, to compel public officials to be honest and forward-looking, to compel employers to treat their employees well, to compel big business to render a good public service and not be greedily selfish. In forty years since 1912, I have lost a good deal of early faith that men can be compelled to do good. At the same time, I have gained some faith in trying to establish conditions in which encouragements for good living are even stronger than preventives of evil living.

From August to November 1912 was one of the toughest periods of night and day work that I can remember. Because of the illness which had partly incapacitated my father since 1909, I had a very heavy burden of carrying on the law business in which he and I were partners. In addition to this, I undertook to devote a large part of each day to the handling of litigation for our Progressive Party. This was a heavy chore because the election machinery locally and throughout the state was in the hands of regular Republicans and Democrats.

The Democrats were willing to see the Progressives make trouble for the Republicans. But the professional politicians had a keen desire not to make it easy for revolters within a party to throw monkey wrenches into political machines. Hence we had to fight desperately to ge our candidates on he ballot for local, state and national offices, even wherc Democratic politicians controlled the election machinery. And we certainly had a tough time where Republicans were in control.

Our task was not so difficult where we merely sought by petition to put new names on the ballot. But there were many instances in which we sought to nominate as our candidate the same man who had been nominated by the Republican Party, for there were many acceptable progressive Republicans whom we did not wish to defeat and who naturally desired to have the combination of Republican and Progressive votes in their favor. The inevitable weakening of the Republican ticket by such dual nomination was fought bitterly by Republican politicians. Of course no one could vote twice for a candidate, but if he were in the Progressive column and the Republican column, he would benefit by any straight ticket vote for either party.

It seemed to us that the law was quite clear and the constitutional right to nominate a candidate by petition and to have the candidate's name on the ballot was not qualified by any requirement that a name could not appear twice on the ballot. We carried a partisan ruling against us all the way to the Illinois Supreme Court, confident that our right to have the names of our candidates printed on the ballot in our party column would be sustained. The opposing argument was so weak that we made great fun of it in private. Yet, that argument was sustained by the Supreme Court of Illinois, which made the extraordinary holding that it was not necessary to print the name of a candidate on the official ballot under the party designation because the voter would learn who were the candidates of his party from other sources!

A startling event occurred the night before our argument in the Supreme Court. Edward B. Burling (later of the notable firm of Covington and Burling in Washington, D.C.) and I were to make the argument. While holding an advance discussion in our hotel room, we heard the shouting of an extra on the streets. We hurried downstairs and learned that Theodore Roosevelt had just been shot in Milwaukee by a would-be assassin; that, although carrying a bullet in his chest, he had insisted on going forward with his speech. We discussed this event more than our case during the rest of the evening. I well remember Burling's comment: "If he lives this might elect him. For the first time maybe there is really a chance."

Many years after the Milwaukee episode I asked Colonel Roosevelt what he had ever done with the bullet which had been fired into his chest, assuming that it had long ago been removed. He grinned and said: "Oh, it's still there. We never bothered to have it taken out." Following this inquiry, I sent him some verses which I had written at the time of the attempted assassination, which he subsequently assured me amused both him and Mrs. Roosevelt. They were:

THEODORE ROOSEVELT

October 14, 1912

There's no doubt that he's crazy
And foolish and queer!
His notions are hazy
And rightly cause fear.
The man doesn't worry
When shot in the chest
Nor get in a flurry—
He quiets the rest!
Insists upon speaking
An hour and more;
What's a little blood leaking,
A wound that is sore?
There's no doubt that he's crazy,
Doesn't understand fear,
All his notions are hazy,
How can people cheer?

There's no doubt he's a liar.
Men asked: "Are you shot?"
But he answered with fire
And said he was not!
Then he said he was thinking
But little of death
When others were shrinking
And holding their breath.
So he lied to them vainly,
He lied at his best,
When he tried to speak plainly
With lead on his chest.
There's no doubt he's a liar,
Unhuman and grand,
Heart of oak, brain of fire
And all through him—sand!

As Burling's remark indicated, level-headed amateurs as well as old politicians did not have much hope for Roosevelt's election in 1912, especially after the nomination of Wilson. This had made it certain that forward-looking Democrats, as well as old-liners, would vote their party ticket. They were practically assured that with the Republican Party divided they could remain Democrats, support a liberal candidate, and have the unusual and comforting experience of winning a national election. It should be recalled that not since Cleveland's second term, which ended in 1897, had the Democrats won a national election. Furthermore, Cleveland was the only Democrat who had occupied the White House since the Civil War.

In view of the comparatively modest expectations of the politically wise Progressives, the enormous vote for Theodore Roosevelt, over 4,200,000, compared with the Taft vote of about 3,480,000 and the Wilson vote of 6,280,000, was a tremendous victory for Progressivism. Over a thousand workers gathered in a "victory dinner" in Chicago on November 14 on which occasion I wrote some verses which can be regarded as a fair expression of the opinion of those present and their political companions throughout the country. This poetic effort read in part as follows:

"I am not dead," the Elephant rolled up one bloodshot eye;
"I may lie prostrate on the ground but yet how well I lie!
"My eyes are blurred; I cannot hear men shouting in my ears;
"But what of that! I have been blind and deaf for many years.
"When I have eased my broken bones I shall stand up again;
"And legs that now are scrambled will be legs unscrambled then."
The Elephant half rose and cried again: "I am not dead!
"I shall arise and then progress—as soon as I am fed."
"We do not wish you to progress"; thus coldly spoke E. Root;
"Stay here and listen to the steam calliope toot! toot!"
He rang a bell and whispered to Jim Watson: "Do your worst."
The steamer tooted: "Darling, I am growing old"—and burst!
Loud shrieked the tortured Elephant: "Bring on the funeral wreath!
"My tusks have been extracted and made into Teddy teeth.
"Oh, where, where are the doctor men who tied me up last June,
"When I had fits and tried to dance to that Progressive tune?
"Before the cyclone hit us they were with me standing pat."
"We're with you now," a thin voice gasped—"beneath you lying flat."

The Bull Moosers were sure that a new day of idealized and refined politics had dawned and that a new method of waging political campaigns was called for. The professional politicians began urging an intensive organization from the lowly precinct upward. But the more romantic and spiritually elated Progressives urged a new type of political organization which would seek a mass education of voters through instruction in the objectives and merits of the party program. They would plan such a program not on the simple materialistic basis of proposing reforms which would appeal to the self-interest of large groups of voters, but on a more complex and subtle appeal of political and social advances.

To carry out this ambitious and novel program state services were coordinated with a national service which would devote their educational efforts to uniting the voters behind political programs. These would then be espoused in state legislatures and in the Congress under the leadership of a limited number of party Progressives, with the hope of cooperation from liberals in the older parties. From the outset the project of the Progressive services was regarded with skepticism and considerable disapproval by trained politicians. They saw that a great deal of money and energy would be devoted to work which they felt, in the end, would be far less productive of votes than precinct meetings and doorbell ringing. However, the enthusiasm of the amateurs had to be fostered; and as a practical matter they were able to raise a good deal of money which it would have been hard to raise for purely political action.

Already, there were overtures everywhere from old-line Republicans to the erring brothers and sisters to return to the party of their fathers and to work for a restoration of Republican national rule in 1916. An activity such as the Progressive Service, which enlisted both former Republicans and former Democrats, was certain to continue and widen the breach in the Republican Party. The new Progressive partisans, having tasted the blood of a victory over old-liners, were more interested in widening than in narrowing this breach.

So the Illinois Progressive Service Board was organized, of which I was made chairman, and, in addition to a group of distinguished men, its membership included such outstanding women as Miss Jane Addams, Mrs. Joseph T. Bowen, Miss Mary McDowell, Mrs. Medill McCormick (subsequently Republican National Committeewoman) and Mrs. Kellogg Fairbank (subsequently Democratic National Committeewoman). Before we had properly organized this Illinois Service I was asked to join the National Progressive Service and become director of its National Legislative Reference Bureau, which was intended to draft bills for introduction into Congress and to assist the Progressive block of twenty members of the House of Representatives. Of the many men in this block who left considerable impress in their local and national activities, the three most widely remembered would be Victor Murdock, the Kansas editor, our leader in the House and later a member of the Federal Trade Commission, Charles M. Thomson, a previous reform alderman and later a distinguished judge in Illinois, and C. A. Lindbergh of Minnesota, best known to fame as the father of General Charles Lindbergh.

The National Legislative Reference Bureau was controlled by a national committee of such extraordinary ability and achievement in the law and in national affairs that I felt exceedingly proud of the association offered me. The members included William Draper Lewis, Chairman, Jane Addams, Henry F. Cochems, James R. Garfield, Francis J. Heney, George W. Kirchwey, Ben B. Lindsey, Charles E. Merriam, Gifford Pinchot, Herbert Knox Smith and Walter E. Weyl.

To accept the directorship required me practically to abandon my Chicago practice and to live in New York City. Remembering in later years the enthusiasm with which I sliced down my income and undertook the difficulties of existence on a small salary in New York, I feel sure that my decision resulted from a compound of reforming enthusiasm and vanity. A more practical-minded person than I would perhaps have been moved by the consideration that my association with the members of my committee and the galaxy of notables who had followed the leadership of Theodore Roosevelt might well, in the long run, be profitable to a young, ambitious lawyer. Perhaps my neglect of this factor will be more easily understood in the light of my eventual break of relations with our national chairman, George W. Perkins of J. P. Morgan and Company. Certainly, if I had had an alert eye on the main chance, I would have endeavored to cultivate the favorable opinion which Mr. Perkins for a time had of me.

From April 1913, I worked for a year in the New York headquarters with a zeal that took no regard for the eight-hour day, but rather with a continuing delight in what resembled more an eighteen-hour day. In this year we drafted the "Progressive Congressional Program," which included an Anti-Child Labor Bill, an Anti–Convict Labor Bill, Workmen's Compensation for Federal Employees, a Women's Eight-Hour Law for the District of Columbia, bills for a Commission on Social Insurance, a Commission on Naturalization and a National Rivers Commission (intended to do away with the notorious "pork bill"); an amendment to the United States Constitution to make amendment easier; a bill for a Tariff Commission, and three bills to solve the monopoly problem, including one to create a Federal Trade Commission, a second to empower the Commission to prevent unfair competition, and a third to empower the Commission to suppress monopolies.

When I recall the composition of my committee and the vigor of independent judgment which would be expected from each member, I am amazed that our program was completed and introduced into Congress within a period of one year.

The only adequate explanation which I can offer is the profound learning, ability and character of the chairman, William Draper Lewis, then dean of the University of Pennsylvania Law School. Subsequently, as the director of the American Law Institute, he carried forward the complex, highly important and controversial work of that institution to the end of his extraordinarily useful career of public service. Dean Lewis had the rare faculty of turning over a job to an energetic person, leaving him alone to do as much as he could by himself, and then revising the work with such a gentle, persuasive hand that in the end his co-worker had the happy feeling that the final performance was something for which he himself could take great credit.

With the same sweet reasonableness, Dean Lewis would handle the deliberations and discussions of his committee. He always relieved members of the burden of doing too much work, and at the same time made them feel that they were all helpful participants in a common production.

One particular example of the perspicacity and wisdom of Dean Lewis should be recorded. The Anti–Child Labor Bill had been drafted and introduced into Congress by Representative Copley. Prior to a committee hearing on the bill, Dean Lewis and I had discussed at length and prepared arguments on the important question of constitutionality. The aim of the bill was so commendable and its provisions so reasonable that we anticipated most of the hearing might be devoted purely to discussions of the constitutional question.

At the hearing the purposes and methods of the bill were carefully explained by Dean Lewis. Then came the sixty-four-dollar question: "Dean, do you think this bill is constitutional?" To my surprise and delight, Dean Lewis answered: "Oh, undoubtedly so." No further questions were asked! After the hearing I congratulated him on the forthrightness of his answer, since I had rather anticipated he would launch into an extensive argument to dispose of this vital issue.

Dean Lewis replied in substance: "There is no use expressing any doubts on a constitutional issue. If you think a bill is constitutional, you might as well say so as positively as you can and not even suggest any doubts as to what the Supreme Court may eventually decide." The practical wisdom of this philosophy had been demonstrated that day. But I still admire the courage of a law professor whose colleagues would expect him to produce an extended dissertation not only to fortify his conclusions but also to show that as a scholar he had given consideration to all precedents and learned writing on the subject.

Included in the Progressive Service work of 1913–1914 was the development of the anti-trust bills, which were called the "trust triplets." At the outset it was agreed that George W. Perkins would not be consulted. For his sake and ours, he should have no responsibility for these measures.

It will be recalled that J. P. Morgan and Company were the most notable financiers of this period, responsible for the launching of the United States Steel Corporation and for unnumbered other mergers, consolidations and intercorporate agreements, many, if not all, of which raised questions as to their conformity with the requirements of the Sherman Anti-Trust Act. Any effort to rewrite the anti-trust laws would be charged either as an attack upon certain corporate activities with which Morgan and Company were greatly concerned, or as an effort to legitimatize others which might have been attacked.

I can hardly assume that the "trust triplets" met the approval of

Mr. Perkins. They involved far more government interference with business operations than would have been tolerable to financiers of that era. Nevertheless, I think he was broad-minded enough to realize the need for some improvement of the anti-trust laws, some effort to define what was tolerated and what prohibited, some attempt to eliminate business practices that served only temporary selfish interests and in the long run did harm to our business prosperity. At any rate, when our congressional program was finally completed and published, he did make the flat statement that the work of the Legislative Bureau, in its effort to deal comprehensively with the trust problem, was one job that was certainly worth the entire cost of the bureau. Furthermore, he made the statement that the work of the Legislative Reference Bureau was the only thing in the Progressive Service that had proved of positive value and which ought to be continued. In fact, he proposed to reorganize the entire Progressive Service so as to eliminate largely the so-called "educational" work and to retain primarily the legislative reference work, and to put me at the head of the entire business.

It was evident, however, that Mr. Perkins' idea was to save the legislative reference work as a practical aid to Progressive office holders, and to eliminate all efforts to educate a great mass of voters into an intellectual support of the party program. He took the side of the practical politicians whose idea was that the major purpose of a political party was to get control of public offices and then to manage those offices in such a way as to retain political power.

A friend of mine who had intimate dealings with the Pendergast machine in Kansas City has often told me of his experience sitting next to Jim Pendergast, listening to a debate in the City Council over an ordinance in which my friend had a strong business interest. The arguments of the opposition were so vehement and persuasive that he became more and more anxious as the debate proceeded. Finally he whispered urgently to the big boss that his cohorts ought to shut off the debate. Pendergast turned to him with a broad smile and whispered: "Lave them talk, lave them talk. We have the votes."

It was an understanding of the necessity of spending the major energies and money of the Bull Moosers upon direct activities to get votes from the grass roots that led to the death of the Progressive Service. I had enough sympathy with the practical-minded politicians to feel that the Progressive Service was wasting a good deal of money and energy which could be better spent. The job I had done was a thoroughly practical one which had practical results. But I felt very deeply the necessity to conduct educational campaigns, to appeal to the minds of voters as well as to their immediate interests. I was not willing to continue to give up the freedom of my private practice to become a cog in a political machine which was rapidly losing the idealistic qualities that had attracted so many men to its leadership. Mr. Perkins could not understand my opposition to his program, and my espousal of the cause of some of the radical troublemakers particularly annoyed him.

"If that is your attitude you are not fit to be head of this work," he told me.

"That is what I wanted you to understand," was my answer. Thereafter I wrote to one of my committee, "Perkins approves of me, except when he gets mad. When an office boy or a valet is needed, I am happily *persona non grata.*"

The National Progressive Service was put to sleep quietly and privately buried so that the public would not see in its death too many signs of the impending death of the Progressive Party. I have a file of bitter letters and unpleasant reports that were prepared at the time by various persons for release to the newspapers, but happily were never published. They may, however, some day aid an interested historian to explain some of the reasons why the Progressive Party as a separate party died in infancy. The fact is that despite the testimony of Albert J. Beveridge, the party did not "come from the grass roots." It had a birth somewhat like that of Minerva, born full-armed from the brain of Jovian Roosevelt. But it did not have Minerva's immortality.

My appreciation of the value as well as the complexity of Theodore Roosevelt's activities grew rapidly during my year in New York, when I had many intimate associations with him. Also I had glimpses of the extent of his influence upon millions of Americans as well as upon countless persons of high and low degree throughout the world.

For example, Colonel Roosevelt wrote an article in the *Saturday Evening Post* which referred rather generously to what my bureau was trying to do in explaining the need for certain legislation and drafting laws to accomplish needed reforms. As a result of this rather casual reference, letters of inquiry flooded into my small office. Overnight I devised a printed post card which explained why we would be delayed in answering a letter. We prepared mimeographed copies of various parts of our "Congressional Program" pamphlet which would answer specific inquiries and then organized an emergency force to handle our flood of letters.

It would have been very easy to act as secretary for Colonel Roosevelt if one had an adequate acquaintance with his life, letters and correspondence, because he was an easy taskmaster for whom to ghost-write. On one occasion a congressman wanted a special letter from him endorsing workmen's compensation. T.R. told me to give him a short memo of what I thought he should say. A day or two later he phoned me to see him and then handed me a letter, practically word for word what I had written.

"Is that all right?" he asked, peering at me through his glasses. Then he added with a grin, "If it isn't, you write it over."

"No," I answered, laughing. "It suits me the way it was originally written."

When the "trust triplets" were finished it was arranged that I should meet T.R. at Newport where we were having a Progressive Service meeting at which he was to deliver the principal address. By returning to New York together on the night boat, we would have an opportunity to go over the bills in peaceful solitude. The captain of the boat courteously roped off the forward part of an upper deck so that we could sit comfortably gazing out over the moonlit waters.

We took up the anti-trust bills and I explained them section by section. When I had finished, with very few interruptions, T.R. said: "Now let me see if I understand this." Thereupon he summarized in a few words the legislation which it had taken me at least half an hour to explain, thus giving a remarkable demonstration of his ability to absorb information rapidly and retain the gist of it. We then entered upon a discussion of several matters of detail and in conclusion he said: "That's fine. I approve absolutely. I will endorse them and support them in any way I can. You tell Murdock [the congressman who was going to introduce the bills] that he can count on me."

Shortly after this conversation I wrote down my recollection of exactly what he said immediately following these remarks, which would certainly refute the notion, current particularly among his enemies, that he was a man of extraordinary egotism.

On this occasion Colonel Roosevelt said to me:

> You know it is the way of American politics that some one person must always be standing in the limelight, shouting "I stand for this" and "I stand for that." I used to think about it often when I was in the White House, announcing my position or my policy on this or that subject; and all the time back there in the shadows were those splendid fellows, Pinchot and Newell and Smith, doing all the drudging work. It doesn't seem quite fair, but that's the way it has to be.

When I quoted this some years later to Gifford Pinchot, he commented, "Yes, that's what T.R. would say. But he did a lot of the work himself; and his policies were really his policies." To this I would say Amen. It was as easy to make suggestions to the Colonel as to any man with whom I ever worked, but he accepted an idea only when it had become his idea. He did his own thinking, but was most generous in acknowledging help. I remember once meeting him at a train and before he stepped off the platform of his Pullman he called out: "Did you see my editorial? I took an idea from you." In similar vein was his comment upon an article which I wrote explaining the much-abused and misrepresented doctrine of "recall of decisions" as a demand for easier amendment of the Constitution. He wrote me:

> That's a capital article of yours. I am inclined to think that the expression you used is better than either of those I invented in the groping effort to formulate in a precise and short phrase just what I was after.

It was Colonel Roosevelt's attitude and his participation which made the work of the Progressive Service so enjoyable to me. He always seemed to appreciate any effort to be helpful even though it was clumsy and ill-conceived. He would sharply criticize opponents and foolish friends. But he was extraordinarily tolerant of human frailties. On one occasion, when Albert J. Beveridge, one of the Progressive stars, had been as temperamental as a grand opera star, someone said to T.R. in my presence: "Oh, Beveridge is just a baby."

"Ah, yes, but a very brilliant baby," replied T.R.

The Newport meeting produced an example of the Beveridge temperament. It was a gathering for all New England, with a monster clambake, and there were places for two main speeches. We wanted one by T.R., who would be the great drawing card, and the other by Beveridge, whose eloquence always assured a good crowd. But Beveridge did not like to play second fiddle. He kept insisting that, since we had T.R., we did not need him. We finally prevailed upon him to come, with assurances that he would be specially featured and we were really looking to him to make the great speech of the occasion.

When I arrived in Newport I thought we had overdone our promise to Beveridge. Certainly we had not underplayed him. Every streetcar in town and other prominent locations carried a placard reading: "Monster clambake at Bailey's Beach. ALBERT J. BEVERIDGE and others will speak." I think this is probably the only occasion, at least in the last twenty years of his life, wherein Colonel Roosevelt was billed among "others" to speak!

When I returned to Chicago in the spring of 1914 I was still hopeful that the Progressive Party would grow in strength even though the arm of the Progressive Service was withering away. I had a good deal of satisfaction in the parting testimony that I received from my committee, and from Victor Murdock's letter expressing "appreciation of the great service you have been to the cause, the Progressives here and myself, in putting our constructive program on its feet. You were indispensable."

Despite a note signed "T. Roosevelt," stating that he had never heard any criticism of me and would not "pay any heed to any criticism I may hear," there was a criticism in my own mind to which heed must be given. My first flaring enthusiasm for public service still burned, but it seemed a little silly. Yet I was able to whip up a lot of energy for the Illinois senatorial campaign of 1914.

The nominees of the two old parties were so totally unfit by their records that the need for a Progressive nominee was obvious. Our selection was Raymond Robins. Whatever he lacked in political experience or proven value as a public servant he made up by strength of character and proven ability to be of service to his fellow men.

On the other hand, the Republicans of Illinois offered as their candidate for United States Senator "Larry" Sherman, who had once been carried into the State House on a stretcher to vote for the most scandalous law that crooked utilities and political racketeers ever bought and paid for in Illinois. (And that is something of a record.)

As Sherman's opponent, Roger Sullivan, the Democratic boss, had named himself, who was the almost perfect product of politics for private profit. It seemed to me almost incredible that either man could be elected whose sordid record was printed in the carefully documented "S.S." (Sullivan-Sherman) pamphlet which I prepared and which was sent into nearly every home in the state.

The Republicans compared Sherman to Lincoln because he looked like a very poor copy of the original. The Democrats sobbed that the bereaved Wilson (he had just lost his wife) was waiting for Roger to come to Washington to help him. President Wilson declined to affirm this anxiety.

The Progressive Party dared the "bipartisan alliance of greed and graft to meet them at Armageddon." But there was no such battle. The voters registered their choice, Sherman first, Sullivan second, Robins third. A few days later Raymond Robins wrote me: "I regard your work as the most effective one element in securing the defeat of Mr. Sullivan." But I disagreed with him then and now. We didn't defeat anybody. We took some votes from Republicans who could not stomach Sherman. We took some votes from Democrats who could not stomach Sullivan. As a result, the remaining regular Republican vote defeated the remaining regular Democratic vote in what was then normally a Republican state. Not much of a victory.

CHAPTER VI

The "Bull Moosers"

NO ACCOUNT of the "Bull Moosers" and the subsequent activities of the Roosevelt Progressives could be complete without devoting considerable space to Harold L. Ickes, best known to fame as the Secretary of the Interior appointed by Roosevelt in 1933 and serving longer in that office than any previous occupant. Our paths ran together, crossed and recrossed, from the year 1897 to the date of his death.

He graduated from the University of Chicago in the year in which I entered, 1897. Having supported himself through college, he continued in newspaper work after his graduation and was only able to achieve his ambition to study law when he entered the University of Chicago Law School in 1904, the year of my graduation from Harvard Law School.

Being a young man of great energy and boundless ambitions, he soon became active in Chicago politics. In fact, he managed the unsuccessful campaign of John M. Harlan for Mayor in 1905 and then managed the successful campaign of Charles E. Merriam for the Republican nomination in 1911. But he was unable to accomplish the election owing to the obvious "knifing" by Republican leaders who were far from enthusiastic at the prospect of electing an anti-machine Republican and having to deal with a new Republican boss in the person of the vigorous and often venomous Ickes.

Out of this campaign Merriam and Ickes emerged as the outstanding leaders of Republican progressivism in Chicago. Naturally they played prominent parts in the Roosevelt revolt of 1912 and the subsequent formation of the Progressive Party. In the next year I invited Harold to join my father and myself in a law firm entitled Richberg, Ickes and Richberg. Shortly thereafter I accepted the invitation to go to New York as director of the National Legislative Reference Bureau of the Progressive Party, thus leaving my father and Ickes to a somewhat hazardous association in the practice of law.

As I have previously indicated, my father was a man of strong convictions and irascible temper. He was also a conservative Democratic politician of considerable influence. As is well known, Ickes was a man of somewhat uneven temper, an intense partisan of any cause which he espoused and definitely a reformer of the type far from agreeable to my father's disposition. Yet, strange to say, they managed to get along together, so the firm was still intact when I returned to practice in Chicago in 1914. In the next year a stroke not only incapacitated my father, but made him a helpless invalid confined to his bed for the remaining three years of his life. In this situation we added in succession John S. Lord and then Morgan Davies (a cousin of my subsequent partner, Joseph E. Davies) and expanded into larger and more impressive offices under the firm name of Richberg, Ickes, Davies and Lord. The four of us maintained our association for several years until I left the firm in order to practice alone in 1923.

There were many reasons for this amicable separation, but chief among them was my personal desire to devote myself exclusively to the two major elements in my practice. One was the representation of labor organizations, which was far from agreeable to the conservative business clients Mr. Lord brought into the office in increasing numbers. He was very successful then, as he has been all his life, in building up a large and profitable clientele and, although we used to joke about it, I know that my activities in representing labor unions and in carrying on litigations in behalf of public interests against private utilities were not helpful in attracting substantial business clients.

There was another reason motivating my separation which I never discussed but which had a strong influence. Ickes was engaged in many political activities of a reform nature, in the course of which he drew heavily from time to time on my voluntary services. I had enough political troubles of my own, but found it very difficult to resist being drawn constantly into the controversies developed by my good partner. His activities were not profitable to me in any way, but were merely a heavy drain on my energies. For example, a fee collected for my services in a litigation in one campaign was transferred to the campaign fund by my dear partner (without informing me) when he found I assumed I was acting as an unpaid volunteer.

In another instance Ickes earned a very substantial fee in a case which he acquired as a result of political influence. But I had made what I regarded as a large contribution to the winning of the particular case, having worked out the theory and legal support upon which it was won. When I accepted the small amount of the fee to which my partner felt I was entitled, my mind was finally made up to divorce myself from such activities so far as possible.

There is no purpose in this recital to do anything except to point out the admirable quality which Harold Ickes afterward displayed as Secretary of the Interior in being careful, even to a point which might be called penurious, in spending other people's money. This was characteristic of a tendency never to overrate the value of other people's services. A simple but amusing example of this occurred one day when the four partners were lunching at the Palmer House in Chicago—a very modest luncheon in the days when one could still buy a good lunch for a dollar or less. In customary fashion, we matched to see who would pay the bill, and the lot fell to Morgan Davies. Having paid it, he left fifty-five cents on the table for the waiter, not an extravagant tip even in those days. Ickes said: "That's too big a tip," and, with a gleeful laugh, put five cents in his own pocket. With equal humor, Morgan Davies said: "What do you think of a man who would rob a poor flat-foot waiter of a nickel and then keep it himself!"

From 1923–1933 my acquaintance with Harold continued with, however, much less professional association. In the 1932 campaign, there was a great deal of difficulty in persuading Ickes to join other notable Republicans in support of Franklin D. Roosevelt. After he had been appointed Secretary of the Interior, without any assistance from me, our relations were somewhat strained and perhaps I could have echoed a comment which was reported to have been made by him about me: "I don't know anyone whom I like as much who annoys me as much as he does."

As my relations with the President became more intimate and, willy-nilly, I had a finger in more departmental pies, it became increasingly difficult for me and my old partner to work harmoniously. Particularly in my job as Executive Director of the National Emergency Council, where I was supposed to iron out conflicts of interest or objective that would involve one or more members of the Cabinet.

One of my tasks was to endeavor to get rid of a large number of interdepartmental committees which were either doing nothing useful or actually creating frictions within the administration. I found most of the Cabinet members cooperative, but all too frequently I had to say to the President: "This is a matter involving Ickes and you know I will have to get your help on that." An imposition which he always took good-naturedly, for it was well known that no Cabinet officer threatened so frequently to resign as the Secretary of the Interior. I recall particularly one occasion during a campaign when Ickes had gone off on his own and created a situation quite embarrassing to the President. Subsequently Steve Early informed me that in an indignant discussion of the affair with the President, he had said: "Mr. President, there is one resignation you have promised me heretofore that one day you are going to accept, and I hope when this campaign is over you will keep that promise." According to Steve, the promise had been emphatically reaffirmed, but it was never kept.

There is much to be said in extenuation of the temperamental qualities of Harold Ickes. He had suffered for many years from several varieties of ill health, particularly from a mastoid disease which several operations had failed to relieve. From this and other causes he had persistent insomnia and anyone who has been harassed by sleepless nights will understand the ragged condition of one's nerves in the following days. Indeed, it was always a surprise to me, and evidence of his strength of character, that Ickes remained only a moderate drinker, since the temptation to relieve jangling nerves with soporific doses of alcohol must have always been with him.

His greatest weakness was a soul-eating jealousy and suspicion of anyone who rivaled or crossed his ambitions. This led him into believing and circulating, without any verification, backstairs gossip and personal slanders about opponents to an extent discreditable even to a proverbial fishwife.

I think that history will credit Ickes with extraordinary ability and devotion to public interests as he saw them in his administration of one of the most difficult departments of the government. He was a hard taskmaster and most of his subordinates were conscious of a surveillance indicating a lack of confidence in them which would alienate many sensitive people. Nevertheless, he was able to create real loyalties based, I think, largely on a feeling in most of those who worked under him that he had a strong sense of justice. Probably this is one reason why, after many years of rubbing each other's fur the wrong way, I felt a continuing affection and admiration for the man who not unjustly described himself as "an old curmudgeon."

One of Ickes' close associates in the Bull Moose movement was Raymond Robins, after whom he named the first child of his first marriage, Raymond Ickes. Robins might be described as a preacher turned politician. He was actively a settlement worker and at heart an evangelist, one of the most eloquent and persuasive speakers to whom I ever listened. One of his peculiar qualities was the fact that he could not write a speech, but, having outlined it in his mind and made a few notes literally on his cuff, he could talk anywhere from an hour to two hours with a beautiful flow of vivid language. He was thoroughly well-read and cultured, with a curious habit of interlarding his conversation with vulgarisms such as "It ain't so," apparently with an unconscious intent to appear a simple man of the people.

He had a keen mind, strong political convictions and extraordinary vision as to the future course of national and international politics. A striking example of his prescience came when I was writing the keynote address of the Progressive Convention of 1916, which he was to deliver. He had given me a broad outline of what he wanted to say which, as we were in intellectual and political sympathy, it was not difficult for me to translate.

When I read over my production with him he was very well pleased, but suggested the addition in the conclusion of a paragraph which would prophesy (remember, this was in 1916!) that out of the First World War, in which the European empires were then destroying themselves, there would emerge three great powers: Russia, Japan and the United States. Of course no thought of the Russian Revolution entered into this prophecy and there was no certainty, although a strong possibility, that the United States might be drawn into the war. But the dominant thought of Robins was that the vast resources of Russia would be left unimpaired, that Japan would grow in strength and in ambition to a dominance of the Far East, and that the United States, with its constantly expanding industrial power, would have a financial and economic strength unimpaired by the carnage in Europe. The course of history has shown the intelligence of this analysis.

Among the most brilliant though unstable of the Bull Moosers was Medill McCormick. He had a keen desire to render good public service, along with an underlying cynicism, an ambition for personal power and a willingness to use whatever means seemed best adapted to gain his ends, as well as an interest in the fleshpots which made him an entertaining but quite unreliable associate. When, in the family disagreement over the management of the Chicago *Tribune*, the compromise was reached whereby he was to alternate with his brother Robert every six months in control of the paper, it was obvious such an arrangement could only be temporary. The predestined end was clearly in the shrewd brain of the lawyer who engineered the program. Medill was expected to eliminate himself, which he did. The incredible spectacle of the *Tribune* moving from rock-ribbed conservatism to Roosevelt progressivism every six months did not last long. Medill's exit into the United States Senate permitted the curtain to be rung down on his editorial career with all concerned relieved and happy.

An interesting example of the unreliability of Medill McCormick affected me markedly during the second Wilson administration. As a result of my work of 1913 in drafting the Interstate Trade Commission Bill, friends had kindly suggested my appointment as a member of the Federal Trade Commission. Since the Democratically enacted Federal Trade Commerce Bill had followed important lines of my draft, it did not seem illogical that I should be appointed one of the commissioners. This had a certain appeal to me because it would take me out of the nasty Chicago gas fight which was becoming increasingly obnoxious to me. Apparently I would be elevated to what I futilely imagined would be a higher public service in Washington.

It is entirely possible that some politicians of both parties in Chicago were anxious to get me out of town and quietly supported my appointment. I made no personal effort except in discussion of the matter with a few friends of mine who were close to the President. Finally word was brought to me that President Wilson was ready to make the appointment, but that he was waiting for the formal approval of Senator Medill McCormick of Illinois. The vacancy required a Republican appointment which naturally would be referred to the Republican senator. Then, to my considerable surprise, I learned that McCormick had another candidate. Even though this man was not appointed, McCormick would not give up his stubborn insistence on his own choice and made no effort to see that I was appointed. This was a particularly interesting attitude in view of the following letter, entirely unsolicited, which I had received from him some years before:

> MY DEAR DON:
>
> I know that you have received no due recognition for your services. I wish you were a candidate for some office within the party, within the city or within the state, that I might in the most public fashion possible, demand your recognition for your most unselfish devotion to the cause.
>
> (*Signed*) MEDILL MCCORMICK

A sharp contrast to men like Medill McCormick was to be found in Miss Jane Addams whose saintly presence on the Bull Moose platform showed the vast differences in purpose and expectation with which men and women entered into the Roosevelt revolt. If the Woodrow Wilson star had risen a little earlier and Chicago had not experienced the reformers' uprising of the Merriam campaign in 1911, probably Miss Addams would have moved toward the Democratic standard. Possibly, however, her early life in northwestern Illinois may have imbued her with faith in the Republicanism of the rural districts as opposed to the somewhat odoriferous Democracy of the City of Chicago. Anyhow I know that Miss Addams was far from happy in association with some of the hardboiled, very practical-minded politicians who gathered under the Roosevelt banner.

But in the 1911 campaign there had been a great uprising of young Republicans against the old-line Republican politicians in Chicago. There was no sign of any similar revolt in the Democratic Party. We moved out of the 1911 campaign quite naturally into the nation-wide campaign for Republican progressivism in 1912. Then, after the campaign, the Progressive Service was organized which nationally and locally was a new thing in politics. Here was an organization in which men and women could join, not for the purpose of electing precinct committeemen and county and city officials, who would then parcel out jobs to their deserving supporters, but to draft and work for the passage of laws that would advance "social justice," an organization in state and nation which would seek to end child labor and the exploitation of convict labor, would try to substitute for "pork barrel" projects useful public works, and would try to improve public education. In other words, we sought to make government a servant of the underprivileged and not the means of their exploitation.

Women like Jane Addams, with a deep understanding of how masses of people lived in the submerged areas of great cities, could see clearly the need for this change in political attitude and, whatever their misgivings as to their associates, could play their part in encouraging and spreading the idealistic spirit generated in the early progressive movement. To my mind, it was the attempts of both the Democratic and Republican parties to capture this youth movement that prevented either party from slipping back into the old conservative grooves when Theodore Roosevelt, Woodrow Wilson and Robert M. La Follette had passed away. They had developed powerful minorities in both parties and neither conservative majority could risk losing its minority to the other party.

There were dozens of Bull Moosers who played an interesting part not only in the Theodore Roosevelt Progressive Party, but before and afterwards in our political history. Space permits me to mention only a few with whom I had intimate contacts, omitting others of equal or greater importance with whom my associations were limited.

Gifford Pinchot, another member of my Legislative Reference Committee, was to me primarily an altruistic, wise and lovable associate. During my year in New York, he was still a bachelor and it was common talk around the New York offices that, despite the limited number of his appearances there, all the women of the staff were in love with him. When, therefore, it became rumored that he was showing a special interest in Miss Cornelia Bryce, whom he subsequently married, there were many heart-burnings which came to the ears of my secretary from the confidences of her sister employees. My own wonderment was that such a handsome and charming male had so long escaped the nets which must have been cast in his direction for so many years.

I shall never forget an experience that I had with Gifford at a time when I was having my very serious disagreement with George W. Perkins, chairman of the Progressive Party Committee. I had asserted my independence of thought and activities with a vehemence characteristic of a young man and had finally appealed to my committee to support me.

In this troublous time I met Gifford Pinchot and in the course of a long talk I had expressed my insistence on independence with a vigor which I thought might not appeal to the older man. But when I inquired somewhat fearfully as to whether he thought I was all wrong, he responded very quickly: 'I think that's what we fought for in 1776, wasn't it?"

In future years, when Pinchot was Governor of Pennsylvania, and in the years thereafter, I had intermittent associations with him in which we were not at all times in agreement, but throughout which I always had deep admiration and respect for his transparent sincerity and devotion to very high ideals of public service.

Another member of my Legislative Reference Committee was Herbert Knox Smith, who had been commissioner of corporations. He had then taken an active part in the Progressive Party fight and during my association with him was practicing law in Hartford, Connecticut. My work on the Progressive anti-trust bills involved more extensive discussions with him and with Dean Lewis than with any others.

No man in his time knew more about the dangers of too great freedom exercised by giant corporations than Herbert Knox Smith. At the same time he was keenly aware of the dangers of government supervision and bureaucratic restraints upon the freedom of private enterprise. It was a great satisfaction to me that Smith approved of the anti-trust bills which received the formal approval of the entire committee. There were other able lawyers on that committee, but none of them had Smith's wide experience and none of them except Dean Lewis gave the intimate consideration to the bills in the course of their drafting that he did.

I still remember vividly the many hard-working hours spent in Smith's office in Hartford, high up in a building overlooking the river, and the more relaxed but equally interesting discussions in his home above the beautiful Farmington Valley. He was a man who not only served the public interest faithfully in public office, but who had a keen devotion to the general welfare as a private citizen.

The Western phalanx of the Bull Moosers included such men as Hiram Johnson, Francis J. Heney, Victor Murdock and Judge Ben B. Lindsey. Each one has left a public record which it would be foolish for me to attempt to summarize. Their personalities varied, but I would say they had a common sense of "marching with the crusaders," to use the title of Victor Murdock's lecture, which he delivered throughout the country as a means of supplementing his small salary as a congressman whenever official duties in Washington permitted. He was the leader of the progressive bloc in the House. He introduced the anti-trust bills, the bill for a Permanent Tariff Commission and the bill for a Naturalization Commission. He was an able parliamentarian and helped to make the influence of the Republican progressives in the House much more effective than their small number, twenty, would appear to warrant. However, they were mostly men of considerable force and compelled regard for their views, particularly with respect to the twelve bills which were drafted through my Legislative Reference Bureau.

My acquaintance with Judge Ben B. Lindsey was intermittent rather than intimate, but he was a man of such intense convictions and extraordinary courage that even these associations were bound to leave a strong impress on his younger colleague. I treasure my copy of his own account of his *Dangerous Life* which he inscribed and sent to me in 1931. It should be required reading for all those who wish to understand the way in which a man endangers his reputation by seeking to pioneer in the field of "domestic relations." It is, indeed, unfortunate that Judge Lindsey's imaginative excursion into his project of "companionate marriage" should have created so much misunderstanding and hostility as to have probably obscured for a while the great value of his services in the development of the Juvenile Court. Of course, even in this pioneer work, for which he was later universally acclaimed, he aroused bitter enmities, particularly because as a crusader for clean politics his influence was ruthlessly fought by old-line politicians in the odoriferous field of municipal and state government.

He was probably classified for many years as one of the "lunatic fringe" of the Progressive Party referred to by Colonel Roosevelt in one of his exasperated moments. But I would testify that a few lunatics of his character are essential and most valuable to the development of government in a democracy. Also, I am sure that his sanity will not be questioned when the history of the times in which he lived is eventually written in the impartial hindsight of future generations.

For a few months following the senatorial campaign of 1914 I had an opportunity to devote more time to law practice than to politics. Then in the spring occurred a strange upheaval in Chicago local politics. The regular Republican organization bosses were challenged by a strange, repulsive type of "reform" under the master mind of Fred Lundin, a relict of the discredited Lorimer machine. William Hale Thompson was nominated and then elected mayor, in a campaign in which I am happy to say I had no part since, along with most of the Progressives, I was suspicious of this type of reform. In fact, we made an abortive attempt to nominate a Progressive which ended with the withdrawal of our candidate, Charles Thomson, a genuine reformer who, having sought the Republican nomination, felt that he should honorably support even a dubious winner.

Shortly thereafter, in order to prevent the election of a slate of unfit judges, there came a coalition of regular Republicans and Progressives to nominate judges for the Circuit Court.

As might have been expected, our Thompson allies knifed all but one of the four Progressive nominees. As a gesture of political gratitude, they supported the candidacy of Charles Thomson whose withdrawal aided in Mayor Thompson's election. I was one of the three other Progressives who received the conventional stab in the back. Thus the Court and I were saved from each other.

If Big Bill Thompson could have seen the amount of trouble which I was destined to make for him, he would certainly have done all in his power to immure me on the bench. This was, however, another instance of the good fortune which has followed me throughout my life when I have been saved from my own worst mistakes by the opposition of my enemies. As I once wrote: "There should be a profound lesson in this experience. But I don't know just what it is—unless perhaps it is humility. Tolerant friends, angry enemies and lots of luck are great aids in the scramble up."

Twenty-odd years ago I observed that "my defeat for a judgeship in 1915 marked for me the end of youth." I think this was an accurate statement. I was then thirty-four years old, but in many ways I had been a boy too long. I had been adventuring with life with something approaching a reckless disregard of consequences both for myself and others dependent upon me.

In March of 1915, shortly before the judicial campaign, my father who had been partially crippled by a stroke in 1909 was again stricken and doomed to three years more of almost helpless existence, lying in bed, requiring the services of a nurse night and day. Our practice had suffered during his previous illness and my absence in New York. Our family debts were much greater than our assets. As a result, for many years beginning 1915, no less than six and frequently eight adult persons were dependent on my earnings.

This realization hit me hard at the end of the judicial campaign. I had been required to contribute the regular candidate assessment of $2,500 to the party treasury. Since it was evident that I was not beloved by the regulars, it was necessary for me to raise funds for a separate campaign in the hope of making up for the organization support which would be taken away from me. The fact that I lost the election by only about 5,000 votes, when a total of 190,000 was needed, indicates the wisdom of this independent effort, even though demonstrating its failure.

Out of this campaign I came to a sudden understanding of the hard reality in what I had previously theorized about as a "struggle for existence." My feeling at this time I once expressed in this way:

> There were many days and nights when I knew all too well the fear that besets the man out of a job, the fear of the beaten

man, that puts timid despair or sullen hatred in his eyes. I had my days of walking around with hands in empty pockets, trying to look cheerful—and prosperous. I had my days of struggling with bills payable and receivable that simply couldn't be balanced. It did not require long years of this sort of thing to teach me the feelings of the under dog or to bring understanding of the self-confident exultation of the self-made man who has fought his way up from poverty to plenty. To slip back from comparative comfort to desperate need for a few months was enough.

At the low ebb of my personal fortunes in 1915, a municipal job came to me in a most unexpected fashion. At the end of weeks of political maneuvering, a most unfriendly committee of Chicago aldermen selected me as special counsel for the city, to fight an extensive litigation against the Gas Company. I had only one friend on the committee, Alderman Charles E. Merriam, the reformer from the University district. The committee, named by the new Mayor Thompson to carry out his campaign pledge to fight the gas consumers' battle, had been carefully chosen with an eye to ensuring the selection of an attorney who would not make this fight too unpleasant or costly for the Gas Company, the head of which was Samuel Insull, who had contributed something like $100,000 to the campaign to elect the mayor! Mr. Insull had also made sure that the mayor should appoint a partner of his favorite law firm to the office of corporation counsel.

Under these circumstances, I thought Alderman Merriam's assurance to me that he wanted to get me selected as gas counsel was a friendly gesture that would be without consequence. It was well understood around the City Hall that the only person who would *not* be selected would be anyone acceptable to Charlie Merriam.

Nevertheless, there was a glimmer of hope in the fact that another alderman on the committee did not want to vote against me for fear I would become a candidate against him for re-election from our ward. I had no intention of becoming a candidate, but I did not advertise this fact.

Another alderman on the committee was generally regarded as a semi-Progressive. Thus the committee became deadlocked from its first meeting because out of the six members three, for strangely different reasons, favored my selection. It was assumed that in the end one of the three (but not Merriam) would give in to a prolonged argument that I could not be selected. He would then vote "reluctantly" for some person of sufficiently neutral character to be tolerable to the Insull-Thompson combination.

Glenn E. Plumb, a lawyer previously associated with the Lorimer machine, but personally a respectable man of considerable force of character, was put forward by the other three Thompsonite members of the committee, including its chairman, Alderman Lawley. Plumb (later universally known as the author of the "Plumb Plan" for the socialization of the railroads), whom I had not known before, eventually came to me with the suggestion that he be named counsel with an understanding that he would name me as his assistant. I did not like the idea but left the decision up to Alderman Merriam who made the counter suggestion that I might be made counsel with an understanding that I would appoint Plumb my assistant.

In this situation the appointment was deferred for weeks, with a lot of political jockeying all around. In the end Plumb became agreeable to the program of my appointment. He managed to sell the idea as a compromise to Lawley. Then, to the horror of the Thompson administration, in a secret ballot one day, four votes were cast for my appointment and the chairman, with every evidence of deep sorrow, hastily announced that I had been selected. I promptly fulfilled my part of this peculiar arrangement by announcing that I wished to have Mr. Plumb associated in the work with me.

There was one incident of this political employment which particularly disturbed me. It was understood in my discussions with Plumb that the committee would be agreeable to paying fees of $100 per diem to each of us. It was also made very plain that liberal contributions to the dominant political organization would be expected from those drawing such handsome emoluments from the public treasury. This did not strike me as iniquitous because it was well understood that all office holders were expected to be liberal campaign contributors. Indeed, as I have recounted, each judge in my unsuccessful judicial campaign was openly assessed $2,500 without any assurance of being elected.

Naturally, after election, he would be expected periodically to express his gratitude in a monetary fashion. The "kick back" from official salaries to political sponsors is sometimes forbidden by law, but there is, as a rule, nothing to prevent a voluntary political contribution by an office holder. Office holders who do not make voluntary contributions are not highly regarded by political organizations. Nevertheless, this sort of preliminary "understanding" griped me.

But my embarrassment was relieved by the economical attitude of my chief sponsor. Alderman Merriam, whose particular chosen job was being watchdog of the treasury, objected to the establishment of a fee of $100 a day for a friend whose appointment he had been effective in obtaining. Because of his insistence, the committee only voted a compensation of $50 a day to me and the same amount to my assistant. My alien political sponsors agreed with Plumb that I should be relieved of any obligation to contribute to the Thompson machine. Some time later the committee did increase the fees to $100 a day, but by this time I was in such violent open opposition to the Thompson organization that no one could have possibly expected me to contribute any money to its support, although I have a suspicion that my friend Plumb, who was a direct beneficiary of this political aid, was duly milked for contributions.

Merriam's service as an alderman in the City Council of Chicago demonstrated his ability to deal with practical-minded politicians and earn their respect if not their liking, while making real contributions to the public good. He was an unusual combination of scientist and politician. He was so deeply interested in political science that he made great contributions not only to teaching but to research and writing, which fully warranted his eminence as a scholar, indicated, for example, by his presidency of the American Political Science Association and his headship of the Department of Political Science at the University of Chicago.

Merriam had a deep interest also in practical politics and developed political ambitions which might well have led him to follow in the steps of Woodrow Wilson through governorship to the presidency.

The most hard-boiled spoils politicians in the City Council of Chicago, commonly known as the "grey wolves," came to respect and even to like him. He was always attacking pet projects from which an alderman or some of his constituents were obtaining some form of what the Tammany politicians called "legalized graft." Hence his demands upon the Council floor for more information, his committee investigations and personal searching inquiries, annoyed the "grey wolves" exceedingly. His "Commission on Municipal Expenditures" produced a far-reaching revelation of the manner in which city revenues were wasted and siphoned off for private profit.

One day in the course of a debate, when Merriam was opposing a pet project of political gangsters, he made the situation so uncomfortable for the opposition that Bathhouse John, an alderman from the notorious First Ward of Chicago, whose nickname came from the fact that he had started life as a rubber in a bathhouse, took a hand in the proceedings. The Bathhouse was an extraordinary character who wore vivid clothes, a large black mustache on a florid face, and who tried to make up with his large physique and powerful voice for what he lacked in mental equipment. His colleague was Hinky Dink, a little weazened man who ran a saloon which served the largest glass of beer and the biggest free lunch in Chicago. Hinky Dink was the brains of the combination, but the Bathhouse always got the publicity, particularly because of his ill-founded flair for literary expression. In the course of his career he produced at various times songs, supposedly of his composition, but actually written for him by newspapermen carrying their tongues in their cheeks. The most famous of these was one called "Dear Midnight of Love," one of the literary sensations of Chicago in its day.

On this particular day, the Bathhouse rose finally and interrupted Merriam to shout at the top of his voice: "Aw, let Caesar get what's coming to him." The roar of appreciation for this witty sally ended the debate. As the Council session closed, the Bathhouse, meeting Merriam on the way to the door, flung a friendly arm across his shoulder and said: "Did I get that right, Professor?" Merriam said: "I think the original version was 'Render unto Caesar the things that are Caesar's,' but you certainly got the idea."

Unhappily, Merriam became imbued with a suspicion of both opponents and associates in politics which was so poorly concealed that even those who worked loyally with him were constantly annoyed and discouraged by his attitude. At a time when I was as intimate with him as probably any other man, I expostulated at lunch one day: "You are so infernally suspicious of everybody! Sometimes I think you are even suspicious of me." To which he responded, without even disavowing the implication: "Well, if you'd been through all that I've been through, I think you would be equally suspicious."

It was quite true that he had been the victim of almost every kind of double-dealing and chicanery which could be experienced in politics. His earnest work as a public servant, his faithful search to learn and to expound the truth as a teacher, had all been besmirched and discredited not only by rascals whom he had exposed, but even by highly respectable persons who were pretending to be his admirers. Nevertheless, I felt then, and I still feel, that any man engaged in politics must learn to preserve at least the appearance of putting trust in people when he is doubtful of their worthiness.

This is not a novel idea. Long ago Seneca wrote: "It goes a great way toward making a man faithful to let him understand that you think him so." Over and over again I have had the personal experience of finding that selfish, hypocritical and essentially dishonest people wish to be regarded as high-minded and yearn for a respectability to which they are probably not entitled. As a result, such persons would often respond in a surprising manner to a trust imposed upon them.

Merriam gave long and useful public service to many men in high office, most conspicuously to Franklin Roosevelt. But I always had the feeling that even greater opportunities might have been his if he had not been so early burned by unscrupulous politicians and fair-weather friends, so that he put on heavy asbestos gloves whenever he approached the fire of public controversy.

To resume my political chronicle: the Bull Moose Party was obviously on the decline after the elections of the fall of 1914, when such campaigns as our Illinois senatorial campaign showed all too clearly the intention of masses of those who had voted for Roosevelt either to return to a fight within the Republican Party to liberalize that party, or to go over to the Democratic Party which, under Woodrow Wilson, was giving great encouragement to progressive-minded citizens in all sections of the country. Also, in August 1914 began the First World War in Europe, creating new issues in domestic politics and international issues of a character new to our electorate. The reabsorption of most of the Bull Moosers into the Republican Party, or their transfer to the Democratic Party in the Presidential election of 1916, developed so inevitably from the war in Europe in the years 1914–1915–1916 that political events in the United States can only be discussed and interpreted coincidentally with a narrative of how the United States became more and more involved in the First World War.

CHAPTER VII

The First World War

PERHAPS my personal experience in relation to the start of the First World War will give a good example of the ignorance of international affairs which prevailed in 1914 among those who regarded themselves as fairly well-informed American citizens.

In the spring of 1914 my wife and I became well acquainted, through an intimate friend on the faculty of the University of Chicago, with three officers of the German Army who were making apparently a sightseeing tour of America. My friend was closely connected with the American management of the North German Lloyd and hence was asked to extend hospitalities to these three German visitors. It should be noted that all such international operations as that of the North German Lloyd were intimately associated with the government of Germany.

It did not occur to me and probably not to my friend that there was any significance in the fact that these three German officers had been spending considerable time in the Panama Canal Zone. Long after the war broke out, it did occur to me that they might have been engaged in an official tour of the United States, including an inspection of the Canal Zone, for the purpose of obtaining information useful to a military government in Europe making plans for a war in which the attitude of the United States and the possibility of an open or a closed Panama Canal might have considerable importance. These three officers included a very attractive young man named Busso von Bülow. His father, General von Bülow, commanded the Second Army which was soon to smash through Belgium and drive across France to the Marne. His uncle had been Chancellor of the Empire. His companions were a captain of artillery and a captain of engineers, both of whom would be peculiarly interested in the Panama Canal.

We Americans were quite unaware of the pertinency of great events when we were entertaining these three German officers at dinner on August 1, 1914. Young Busso, limping out to the dining room, testing a leg which had been broken by a fall from horseback in the spring, made a gay remark: "I must get my leg strong for the Kaiser." He explained that they were leaving for Europe as soon as they could get word from the Consul as to how they were to go. They were able in some way to get passage to Greece, and all three eventually returned to Germany to get into the war.

I asked Busso what he thought was going to happen—whether all Europe was going to get into the war and how long it might last. My questions sound silly in retrospect, but at the time the idea of a general European war seemed incredible. We had been reading Norman Angell's *The Great Illusion* and were all convinced that the time of great wars was ended, that wars in our day would be too destructive and too costly for any large nation seriously to contemplate going to war with another.

Bülow answered very carefully: "It all depends upon England. If England does not come in, we are all right. If England comes in, I am afraid it will be very hard for us. Oh, no one knows, but I can't believe England will come in!"

England did go in and the holocaust in Europe had an immediate and profound effect upon America. Even though we were not involved in the actual fighting in the early stages of the war, our whole economy was seriously disturbed. The demand for war supplies by the fighting nations fell heavily upon the largest commercial nation not directly involved. The mental effect on our people was equally pronounced. In the first place, divisions in our foreign-born and second-generation Americans quickly appeared along the lines of the belligerent nations. It may be questioned whether Great Britain would have gone to war, at least immediately, if it had not been for the invasion of Belgium, creating treaty obligations which could not be ignored. The Germans' disregard of "a scrap of paper" aroused antagonism toward the aggressor among not only American descendants of the resisting nations, but quite widely among others whose racial strains might have inclined them toward neutrality.

One inevitable effect of the war was to slow down the program of Wilsonian legislation, particularly since many campaign pledges had already been redeemed in the first two years of Wilson's administration. Even from my somewhat partisan position, I had to pay tribute then and now to the achievements of a Democratic Party which, after sixteen years of "peerless leadership" (under Bryan) and defeat, rallied behind Wilson to carry out a program fundamentally in harmony with that of the Roosevelt Progressives. If an old-guard Democrat had been nominated and elected, such men as Bryan, who became Secretary of State, Secretary of the Treasury McAdoo, Secretary of War Baker, Secretary of the Navy Daniels, Secretary of the Interior Lane, and Justice Brandeis, might have found themselves forced to join hands with the Bull Moosers in establishing a Liberal Party, leaving old-line Republicans and Democrats to the choice of a counter amalgamation or continued minority opposition. In a realistic view of politics, it is difficult to believe that this would have happened, however, particularly because of the distrust with which such outstanding Democrats viewed Theodore Roosevelt. My friend and fraternity brother in Phi Gamma Delta, Newton D. Baker, expressed this distrust in a letter to me dated October 12, 1912:

> I wish I could persuade myself to believe that the Third Party you fellows have formed is a Third Party that either ought to have been formed or to continue. My difficulty with it is in its leader, but we are too far apart to quarrel on that subject. This is certainly true in politics as in religion, that if the thing you are doing ought to succeed it will succeed, and the permanence of the Progressive movement which you have started will demonstrate itself if it is to be permanent very shortly.

Prior to our entry into the war, the Bull Moosers, high and low, suffered three years of exasperation and frustration. First, we had to watch the Democrats create a Tariff Commission, a Federal Reserve System and a Federal Trade Commission, and write laws to promote the welfare of wage earners, to protect seamen and to prohibit child labor, in all of which we were compelled to join in the applause without the pleasure of receiving any bouquets. It was a part of the policy of the administration to ignore the Progressives as a third political organization. Instead of encouraging the Bull Moosers with patronage and other political favors, it appeared to be the Wilsonian strategy to maintain a two-party government, to establish the Democratic Party as the liberal party, and to force the Republicans to accept a conservative role and thereby drive Progressive Republicans into the Democratic camp.

This strategy, exasperating to us at the time, appears in retrospect to have been one of political wisdom, since Wilson's minority victory of 1912 became almost a majority victory in 1916 when his popular vote rose from 42 per cent to more than 49 per cent. In this trying period, however, the Bull Moosers felt first, that Wilson was playing poor politics, and second, that our only opportunity to advance our cause permanently was to reunite with the Republicans under a Progressive Republican banner. It was the prevailing Progressive theory that the Democratic party would not be permanently progressive because of what we regarded as the ultraconservatism of the South; that the Republican Party could make its appeal to the industrial workers of the North and the perennially distressed farmers of the Midwest and should be established eventually as a truly liberal party.

The Wilson strategy proceeded, I am sure, from Wilson's deep-seated belief in the values of party government. He was an academic believer in partisanship, as shown in his early writings; and he proved in office to be a more stubborn partisan than even practical politicians who were quite accustomed to trade favors with each other and to help each other against any revolting movements which were literally "revolting" to practical politicians.

The greatest weakness of Wilson's career developed out of this intensity of partisanship. His deep-seated conviction in favor of party government boiled up to the surface in his speech of October 24, 1918, wherein he called for an election of a Democratic Congress, conceding that the Republicans were not "anti-war" but claiming that they were "anti-administration." This was political partisanship of a most offensive character, particularly since only a year before he had announced that "politics is adjourned," calling for a nonpartisan prosecution of the war. The Republicans had responded cordially, since it is a matter of record that he had more votes from a Republican minority for many war measures than he obtained from his own Democratic majority.

The reaction of the electorate to this partisan appeal was impressive. Republicans won both houses of Congress in 1918, which would have meant in a European country the resignation of the Chief Executive. That should have served warning upon Wilson to draw to himself a Republican support in the Peace Conference, which he did not even attempt to obtain. The ultimate result was the defeat of Wilson's great effort to establish the League of Nations with the United States' participation. Republican support, with proper encouragement, should not have been difficult to obtain, since such a league was first proposed by Theodore Roosevelt. But by the time Wilson returned from the Peace Conference, Roosevelt had died, and that strong liberal voice was no longer heard in Republican councils.

The dominance of Wilson in the Democratic Party was an amazing phenomenon. He did not possess a rabble-rousing personality and his speeches, although of surpassing eloquence and high intelligence, were not those of great crowd appeal. Some of his slogans had far-reaching effect, such as "To make the world safe for democracy." Some created confusion and misunderstanding, such as "Peace without Victory." But there is no doubt that his sheer intellectual ability made it easy for him to dominate in such political conferences as meetings with Congressional leaders. Behind this intellectual ability there was a sort of cold ruthlessness which terrified weak opponents and convinced his supporters that he was going to have his way.

Bryan, whom he "knocked into a cocked hat" in the State Department, found he had to go along or quit, and in 1915, opposing a truculent attitude toward Germany, Bryan quit. Garrison, a strong conservative in the War Department, found, on the other hand, he could not move his chief rapidly enough toward a preparedness which he regarded as an inevitable concomitant of belligerent words toward Germany. So he quit. In hundreds of minor incidents, friends and foes of the administration were early convinced that that somewhat chilly gentleman in the White House was going to have his way and that they either could go along with him or be brushed aside.

I remember with amusement the attitude of a Progressive national leader who had been specially commissioned in the course of the 1912 campaign to investigate what was called a "scandalous affair," in order to ascertain whether, in the moral and political judgment of the opposition, attacks should be made upon the personal morality of the Democratic candidate. Few Presidential candidates have been free from personal attacks. It may be recalled that Cleveland was accused of an immoral relationship and he met the charge by frankly avowing it. It will be a never-answered question as to whether this gained or lost votes for him.

The charge against Wilson may have been as unfounded as charges which were made against other Presidential candidates, such as against Theodore Roosevelt (of insanity), against Harding (of tar-brush ancestry), against Hoover (of business chicanery). So it was not exceptional that charges were whispered against Wilson and, as always, the question arose, first, as to whether the charges were justified, and second, if justified, whether they should be exploited in a campaign. The investigation of Wilson's conduct produced evidence convincing to some and scorned by others. It had the effect of intensifying T.R.'s dislike for Wilson, but he took the position that privately scandalous charges should not be exploited in the Presidential campaign, a decision which I think was both morally sound and politically wise.

But the politician who had been commissioned to investigate the entire matter had collected a lot of data which he felt should at least be preserved. Some time after Wilson's election he talked to me about this, exhibiting in his attitude that positive fear of the President which seemed to affect everyone who faced the possibility of rousing his violent opposition. This man told me in great detail the results of his sleuthing and then whispered, as though fearful that a Secret Service man might be concealed behind the curtains in the Club living room: "I have all the documents in a safety deposit box in New York. I think the President knows that I have them. Honest, I am afraid to go to Washington. Can't tell what might happen."

This man's mental state, exaggerated though it may seem to be, is some indication of the respect, intensified by fear, which Wilson inspired in his opponents. Frequently during the years of his first administration I heard the complaint made that congressmen had gone to the White House all steamed up for a big fight and then had left, saying, "Yes, Mr. President. You are quite right, Mr. President."

This brief and seemingly critical estimate of Woodrow Wilson is necessary for an understanding of the kind of deep antagonism which arose in a man like Theodore Roosevelt, who was himself a hard fighter, but much less of a ruthless intellectual machine, which was the image of Wilson in the minds of many of his opponents. On the other hand, it should be stated that Wilson inspired extraordinary admiration in the minds of many of his close associates. The secretary of the Democratic Committee said to me one day with utmost sincerity: "I think he is the greatest man since Christ." Another close associate and appointee of the President said to me one day: "Ye gods! But he is radical. If our friends in Wall Street knew the things he thinks—and sometimes even says—they wouldn't be sleeping peacefully tonight."

Fortunately for their slumbers, many people in Wall Street forgot or did not believe that he meant what he said in 1912: "We have come to be one of the worst ruled, one of the most completely controlled and dominated governments in the civilized world—no longer a government by conviction and vote of the majority, but a government by the opinion and duress of small groups of dominant men."

In the light of these statements one can easily understand why Wilson distrusted and opposed the Roosevelt campaign for preparedness in 1915. Apparently President Wilson privately felt that this preparedness campaign was another example of the propaganda of those business interests unpleasantly and frequently referred to as "merchants of death." It was popular at the time and for many years thereafter to assume that the big companies who would be called upon to produce the machineries of war (the makers of steel, explosives, chemicals and other agencies of destruction) always encouraged preparations for and engagements in war. Whether this charge was ever justified, we in the United States have at least sufficiently matured in recent years to be sure that no one except the most hopelessly shortsighted and ruthlessly selfish business man now regards a war as a profitable enterprise.

But the Roosevelt campaign in 1915 could easily be attacked as a warmongering procedure and not so easily defended then as it can be now in the light of history. Since I was frequently attacked for many years as a pacifist, it may be understood that when I wrote Colonel Roosevelt in 1915, praising his campaign for preparedness, I was motivated by no desire to see the United States engaged in war. Also, considering the fact that I had the hostility of most big business men who knew anything about my existence, I was not motivated by any desire to increase the business of the steel companies, or the Du Ponts. The answering letter which I received from T.R. dated September 4, 1915, shows his attitude at the time and clearly indicates his hostility toward President Wilson, as shown in the following extract:

> I think you are exactly right. I believe that I have helped wake the people up. I believe also that in doing it I have increased the animosity to me personally; and I am sorry to say it is possible Wilson will profit by what I have done, because . . . [he] . . . will now bow enough to the inevitable to make some recommendations for half-preparedness; and the American people will then credit it to him for righteousness. You really please me when you say that you do not believe that I care for the political cost to myself. My dear Richberg, I think I can conscientiously say that I have always been willing to sacrifice my own political chances for a national object which I consider of sufficient weight. But in addition I feel at present that there isn't any sacrifice about it. It is utter folly for any man to think of my holding political position again; and there is the great compensating advantage that this enables me to speak with entire freedom without feeling that thereby I am damaging faithful followers with whose fortunes my fortunes are tangled.

In answer to this letter I wrote him at some length "wishing to take issue with you somewhat regarding your own estimate of your political strength." In this letter I said in part:

> The Atlantic seaboard may persist in its devotion to the soft and parasitic life, but west of Pittsburgh I firmly believe there is a strong sentiment for a robust, full-blooded nation, not seeking a quarrel, but not avoiding hard issues because too proud to fight. I don't believe these people are afraid of you. I don't think they are reconciled to a stand-pat candidate as the alternative

to Wilson. I don't say there is a determined sentiment for you as yet of the impressive proportions that there should be, but I do think that more and more people every day are becoming reconciled to the thought that even swallowing the worst interpretations which they have been fed of your actions and attitude, they are nearer to what they think our president's should be than those of anyone else in sight.

The reason for this letter was that I wished to help in a small way to counteract the defeatist strategy which was prevalent in the Progressive Party leadership. Our politicians were generally moving in the direction of seeking to rejoin the Republicans in the nomination and election of a Presidential candidate in 1916. This would, of course, not be Roosevelt, but some fairly liberal Republican such as, for example, Justice Hughes, then sitting on the Supreme Court. At the time of my writing, the enthusiasm for T.R. was steadily rising everywhere and in late December I went to Oyster Bay to urge him particularly not to play a part in the coalition movement, but to hold himself available at least for a while longer as a Progressive Party nominee. At this time I insisted that public sentiment was swinging rapidly in his favor. He smiled at my enthusiasm and with a friendly slap on the shoulder ended the discussion by saying: "That would be very interesting if more than half of one per cent of the American people felt the way you do."

Nevertheless, some weeks later we met at a private luncheon in Chicago and, as I came into the room, he walked abruptly across to me and said: "You remember our conversation last winter? It is coming that way, isn't it?" He was greatly pleased with the tremendous change in public opinion which was then obvious. Unhappily, his earlier doubts had eliminated him from the Presidential race. Being convinced of his own unpopularity and determined at any cost to defeat Wilson for reelection, he had made it clear to many politicians that if the Republicans nominated such a man as Hughes, he would not run as a Progressive and would support the Republican nominee.

As a result, the nomination of Hughes became a practical certainty and the death of the Progressive Party inevitable.

The conventions of the Republican and Progressive parties were called for the same day in June in the same city of Chicago. As a columnist wrote, the Progressive Party advertised that it would be on a certain corner at a certain time, wearing a red carnation, and that its intentions were matrimonial.

Up to the day of the conventions, the hope of the Bull Moosers persisted that the Republicans would not feel it necessary to nominate Hughes or that Hughes might decline. He had been sitting in a monastic isolation in the Supreme Court and declined to indicate that he would accept a nomination if one were offered. Men like Frank Hitchcock had gone around the country collecting delegates for Hughes and beating down all questions as to whether their candidate would run by giving their personal assurance (on what basis was never revealed) that he would accept a nomination. Some diehard Progressives wanted to nominate a candidate even if Hughes were nominated and Roosevelt announced his support. Others felt that the Progressive Convention should nominate Roosevelt prior to the nomination of Hughes and thereby be in the political position, first, of having forced Hughes's nomination, and second, having given Roosevelt the powerful position of openly rejecting a nomination and being, therefore, primarily responsible for an anticipated victory by Hughes.

Our Progressive Convention was a *mélange* of well-conceived and hastily modified procedures. We had, for one thing, the problem of making sure that we nominated Roosevelt there in the Auditorium before the Republican Convention in the Coliseum a few blocks away actually nominated Hughes. The Republicans were going to go through the motions of nominating a lot of candidates and taking ballots before the well-organized machinery decided to start a stampede for Hughes. We had to drag our feet so as not to nominate Roosevelt too soon, but be alert not to nominate him too late. As a part of this strategy, I was provided with a desirable seat in the gallery at the Republican Convention so that when I decided that the stampede for Hughes was actually on I could notify the Progressive leaders. This might have been a very delicate piece of political judgment. But, as a matter of fact, when I hastily deserted my post and phoned the Auditorium excitedly: "The stampede for Hughes is on!" the reply came: "We are already nominating Roosevelt." In a word, our convention had gone through the formality of nominating and seconding speeches and was approving the nomination by acclamation, as I recall it.

Then ensued a period of great distress and uncertainty. Roosevelt promptly declined the nomination and suggested, to the horror of our leadership, the nomination of Senator Henry Cabot Lodge, who was regarded as an ultraconservative and particularly as an opponent of child labor legislation by the mass of Progressives. The intensity of feeling regarding what was called Roosevelt's desertion of his party ran very high for many days. Personally, it seems to me he took the right course, for he had refused the previous year to encourage the Bull Moosers in the idea that he would run again, except in the possible event of the nomination of a reactionary candidate by the Republicans.

The campaign of Hughes was, however, a great disappointment to the Bull Moosers and particularly to Colonel Roosevelt. Two episodes in which I had a major part will explain why Justice Hughes did not become President Hughes in 1916.

An intensive speaking tour was arranged for Hughes, in which he passed through Chicago on his way to Minnesota, the Northwest and California. His campaign chairman, William R. Willcox of New York, was unfortunately a man of limited political experience. He had early adopted a policy of putting the management of the campaign, including the Hughes speeches, in control of the state Republican organization. At first this had seemed a smart move, but it turned out to be disastrous. The old-guard Republicans had engineered it to make sure that they retained control of the party organization and could thus prevent any of the returning Progressives from exerting enough influence to be able to claim large credit for an anticipated election of Hughes. In some states, however, the old guard were led with sufficient intelligence to realize that they could not possibly win except by a transfer of a large part of the Roosevelt vote and that it would be disastrous if they kicked the Progressive leaders in the shins.

The situation in California was particularly bad for this Willcox policy. Hiram Johnson, who had run with Roosevelt as vice presidential candidate, was still governor of the state and had such popularity that he was elected United States Senator in 1917. The old-guard Republican survivors of what Johnson had denounced as the Southern Pacific machine, had taken over the Republican machinery when Johnson became a Progressive. It was quite apparent that they intended to prevent any cordial relations between candidate Hughes and Governor Johnson if they could. They were planning the state campaign and the Hughes campaign accordingly. My partner, Harold Ickes, was very close to Johnson (and indeed managed his campaign for the Presidential nomination in 1920). So, naturally, our office was thoroughly informed of the California situation. By the time the Hughes campaign squadron arrived in Chicago, I had received urgent messages, including a long, revealing telegram from Governor Johnson, as to the peril of the Republican ticket which was daily increasing through the management of the campaign by the Crocker (old-guard) machine.

Armed with these imperative documents and adequate credentials, I had a long talk with Chairman Willcox in his hotel suite. He walked up and down the room debating the situation. "What can I do?" he kept saying. He explained how his hands were tied by his own policy and how he could not afford to break the policy in California without both offending the Republican management there, and bringing down upon him a lot of demands from Progressives in other states. I tried to emphasize the peculiar importance of California and the special danger in alienating not only Johnson but all his followers. Johnson might not say anything openly, but the resentment against his exclusion from even meeting the candidate, to say nothing of presiding at a big meeting, would be violently expressed.

As historical records show, nothing was done in California to save the situation. Indeed, the deepest kind of offense was given when Governor Johnson and candidate Hughes were in the same hotel the same day and did not even meet. Hughes was almost elected President. Indeed, he went to bed before midnight confident of his election. In the early hours of the morning it became evident that California was going against him and with the fairly well-defined returns it appeared he was not going to win. A reporter sought to disturb him, but an attendant assured him pompously, "The President cannot be disturbed." Whereupon the brash reporter said: "Well, you had better disturb him and tell him he is not going to be President."

I participated in another example of very bad campaign management. Theodore Roosevelt had carried on an extensive speech-making campaign in favor of Hughes in which he had been assailing the "hyphenates" with his usual vigor. The "hyphenates" were those foreign-born or second-generation Americans who called themselves German-Americans or Polish-Americans and were taking sides strongly in the European war, while the nation was seeking to maintain a wobbly neutrality. For many years I had been a director in and attorney for a group of German newspapers and, therefore, was well acquainted with the professional foreign-language politicians who had increased their verbosity and trouble-making greatly since the outbreak of the war.

When Colonel Roosevelt was on his way to Chicago it became known that he intended to deliver a special attack on "hyphenate" Americans in Chicago and a group of German "hyphenates" protested to the Hughes campaign committee against such a speech. The campaign politicians were wise enough to refrain from trying to persuade T.R. not to make a particular speech in a particular place for a reason which would arouse all his opposition. Hence they developed a cute strategy of pulling wires so that he was induced to agree to make a great labor speech in Chicago on the theory that this was a great industrial city. Both Roosevelt's friends and his political enemies learned about this trick. A Democratic newspaper in Chicago prepared to follow up the Chicago speech with a great exposé in which they would attempt to demonstrate that the Republican organization, with Roosevelt's approval, was deliberately trying to carry on a pro-German campaign to elect Hughes in order to reverse the alleged pro-Allies policy of Wilson. Anyone who lived through those years knows that if the issue between Hughes and Wilson had been clearly drawn between "pro-German" and "pro-Allies," Wilson would have been easily elected. The Republican management was guilty not only of bad faith with Roosevelt, but of stupidity because of the injury that would have been done to Hughes.

When full information came into the hands of the Chicago Progressives, the time was too short for anything except direct action. I was commandeered to carry the story to Roosevelt. I met him at Denver and took the same train with him to Chicago. There we had long sessions in his private car regarding the Chicago speech. As soon as the situation was unfolded to him, his anger and resentment reached staggering proportions. He dictated lengthy telegrams which were sent off and answers received at practically every stop. He explained that he would go through with the program, filling his fixed engagements, and then retire to Oyster Bay. He would not say anything in public to injure the campaign. If Hughes was going to beat himself, the defeat was not going to be charged to Roosevelt.

In the course of this telegraphic correspondence, the Colonel explained quite thoroughly to his addressees, and even more in detail to me, what he thought of the campaign—its blunders, hypocrisies, double-dealing and treachery toward the Progressives. As we neared the Mississippi River, the evasive answers turned apologetic and then beseeching. The campaign management finally realized something of the folly of their program. In the end T.R. made his most vigorous anti-"hyphenate" speech in Chicago. So the Democratic exposé never came off. But we may be sure that President Wilson knew that it was the pro-German element which had tried its hardest to beat him, and had obtained undue comfort from the Republican organization. The sequel was not inevitable, but it was a fact that Wilson was re-elected and a month after his inauguration we went to war.

A month after the election I had a meeting with Colonel Roosevelt at a Chicago railroad station. As we were riding over to the Club where a private luncheon had been arranged, he suddenly turned and slapped me on the knee and cried with obvious relief: "Well, we did all we could, but we have the satisfaction now—we were not responsible for Mr. Wilson and we were not responsible for Mr. Hughes!" He knew very well that if he had made another Progressive Party fight in 1916, he would probably have been responsible for the reelection of Wilson. His antipathy to Wilson was thoroughly sincere, although I thought on some grounds it was unjustified. As he wrote me in 1916: "Of course I feel much more strongly about Wilson than you do." It might be said that he had no more faith in Wilson's loftiness of spirit than Wilson had in his; and that both men were wrong. Both men had lofty concepts of public service, but both were such high opportunists that their methods could be easily criticized and their achievements belittled by partisan opponents.

With our entry into the World War, a tough personal problem was presented to me. I had not only my immediate family dependent on me, but also a paralyzed father, a mother in her late sixties and, intermittently but all too frequently, three sisters and a brother. Also, I had a public job to stick to instead of running after some military commission which would give me only the appearance of rendering a more patriotic service. So I did not seek even a stay-at-home commission as an "officer of the armed services." I mention this because many years later a reporter for the Chicago *Tribune,* John Boettiger (who subsequently married Anna Roosevelt), came into my office in Washington when I was general counsel of NRA and said abruptly: "I've got another dirty assignment, to get the war records of the prominent New Dealers." I explained briefly that my record was staying at home, taking care of my family and representing the consumers of the city of Chicago in a fight to keep down gas rates. Boettiger later reported to me with a grin that the best combat record he found was that of Mordecai Ezekiel, one of Henry Wallace's aides, who was regarded as a particularly annoying radical by his newspaper.

One thing I did not mention to the *Tribune*—and have not yet reported in these memoirs—is that I was also a judicial officer from 1916–1919, a Master in Chancery of the Circuit Court of Cook County. This position of an assistant judge was awarded me as a sort of consolation prize by one of the judges whom I had helped to nominate and who had been elected when I was defeated in 1915.

Of course I volunteered during wartime as a four-minute speaker, absorbed all the propaganda put out from Washington, some of which was reliable and some mere fiction; and then expounded it in churches, circus tents, theaters and school rooms, wherever a crowd of people could be gathered for indoctrination.

One old Swedish clergyman summed up my labors with what I suspect was conscious humor. My plea to buy Liberty Bonds had been substituted for his sermon, and in the small suburban church I thought I had been quite eloquent. When I finished, the minister quietly announced that the services would now be concluded by the singing of "our favorite hymn, 'Revive us again.'" The congregation sang every verse and chorus while my accompanying colleagues in the rear of the church hugged themselves and choked down their laughter.

Now and then I engaged in some voluntary effort to aid in maintaining the home front, particularly in avoiding conflicts between management and labor. There was very little coddling of labor in the First World War. The government machinery operated quite well to straighten out a good many difficult situations. But the attitude of the country as a whole was very strongly of the opinion that when millions of men were being drafted and sent to fight overseas, anyone permitted simply to work hard at home and earn a modest living in safety should not complain. Under cover of such a sentiment a great deal of injustice to hard-working men and women went uncorrected.

For example, the Chicago stockyards were feeding the world. I went to J. Ogden Armour, head of one of the big packing houses, to protest against the Armour Company's labor conditions, which were sure to bring a strike and disorganize food supplies for our fighting forces. My theme was: "How can I talk about democracy when you make a mockery of the word in the yards?" Mr. Armour was feebly and vaguely distressed at the charge, which he was sure was not justified. But I knew whereof I spoke. Individual employees in numbers had told me of facts which public investigators had confirmed: men called in the middle of the night for a little work, waiting hours for more work, wasting fifteen hours for four hours' pay. Working conditions were cold, damp, filthy, ruinous to health, and wages were utterly inadequate to meet the mounting cost of living.

The employer wanted names and assured me he would see that wrongs were righted. I could not violate confidences and expose men to possible discharge. I kept insisting that individual wrongs were not the issue; that they needed a labor organization. I assured him the men were going to be organized and it would be far better if they organized with his help. The employer assured me there would be no strike, that they had "arrangements with the government." But within a short time a great strike was under way in the packing plants. The government had to intervene and wages were raised by government order. After that, the Armour Company decided to organize its employees in a well-controlled company union, which I may add was not a very successful job, and as a result of which they eventually found themselves dealing with a very militant independent union. I had not been advocating a company-controlled union, but a union organized with the company's blessing; one with which the company could deal as with a friend, not as with an enemy.

Shortly before my visit to Mr. Armour I had written an article entitled "Democratization of Industry," a copy of which I left with him, not to convert him, but with a feeling that it might restore his equanimity. It would make him realize that I was just a theorist whose advice could properly be disregarded by a practical business man!

My article was highly speculative, pointing out that in the democratization of our political and social life, big business had remained a conspicuous remnant of the autocracy with which for centuries the political, social and working life of masses of people had been governed. My suggestion was that if labor were adequately organized so that it had a voice in the councils of industry, and the workers themselves came to play the part substantially of stockholders who had an interest in the success of the business while at the same time they had the power to prevent their own exploitation, we would gradually attain a democratization of industry able and willing to give strong support to a democratic government.

I could rewrite this article today to make it a little more realistic and practical and a little less visionary, but I think that the philosophy I expressed then is still reasonably sound.

My article may have had some more far-reaching influences than I can actually trace. The phrase which I thought I had originated —"democratization of industry"—appeared subsequently in a Presidential message by Woodrow Wilson, December 2, 1919. The article itself was quoted extensively in a later book, *Industry and Humanity,* by the Prime Minister of Canada, Mackenzie King. In a letter from Colonel Roosevelt, after deploring my writing for "that pestilential *New Republic,*" he went on to say:

> Now as to your article. Not only do I agree with it, of course, but curiously enough in something I wrote a couple of months ago I used the same idea. If the *Metropolitan* ever publishes it I hope you will see it.

My program of "democratization of industry," which I had believed original, furnishes an example of something which constantly happens. It occasions many heart-burnings and every now and then a lawsuit. Men and women who are unknown to each other will write substantially the same thing at the same time, and accusations may result as to who took an idea from whom. I have always believed in the free trade of ideas (with due respect for rights of copyright) and have spent little time worrying whether I got my ideas from someone else or someone got his from me. In my case, seeds of the idea of democratizing industry were undoubtedly germinating in thousands of minds in these years. Probably some of them had been kept in the deep freeze for centuries and only found a soil and climate in which they might sprout in the years preceding or during the First World War.

Long before our entry into the war I had attempted to express my reaction to its suicidal insanity, and a vision of what the outcome might be, in verses which may be entitled to a high mark as a direct prophecy of the Russian Revolution—a higher mark than they may receive as poetry. They were in part:

The world is mad—
And hate has flung fagots aflame
Into a million homes—
The will to live
Fear driven, terror shamed before
The master will to kill—
The iron strength
Of saviours, for the work of death
Wrath hardened into steel.

* * *

The world is mad—
While tortured lips and writhing tongues
Shriek truth across the seas,
Yet still the chants
Of unfrocked priests of broken creeds
Fill all the air with lies;
And we are told
Millions of backs must bend and ache
And puzzled brows must sweat,
To sow and reap
For master men and thus fulfill

God's meanly ordered way;
And we are told
That when the world's hard work is done
They who have built and borne
Shall waste and slay—
Hurl havoc up from hell—to prove
Where God and right prevail!

The world is mad—
Yet when that madness pass—perhaps,
Bitter and bleeding left,
It may be sane;
And 'neath the soldier's bandage, eyes
Long blinded may begin to see;
And battle scars
May blush with pride where once the whip
Left welts dead white with shame.
They learn to die,
Nations of men, who had not learned
They had the right to live.
The world is mad—
But shattered chains may find them sane
Whom madness hath set free.

My exclusion from activity in the war was a trifling regret compared with the really tragic grief of Colonel Roosevelt. As he wrote me in August of 1917:

> Remember, however, that the instant the war began I put myself unreservedly at the disposal of the administration. I heartily backed it for having gone to war and I have backed every one of its actions I possibly could. The administration took every means directly and indirectly not merely to refuse my aid, but to injure me personally because I had offered aid; and so far as it was safe, it made it evident it would do the direct reverse of anything I suggested.

Colonel Roosevelt laid the refusal to use his services to a personal dislike of him and a petty political attitude on the part of Wilson. It was easy for him to feel this way because he disliked

Wilson so intensely himself. Also, because of Wilson's partisan attitude, even toward the conduct of the war, which I have previously explained, it was easy to understand how T.R. could write this bitter accusation in a letter to me: "Apparently Wilson is concerned solely with his own political fortunes. He will do anything either to help or to hurt the country precisely as doing so does or does not help or hurt him politically." This, I would say, was the unjust anger of a justly embittered man.

There seems no question in retrospect that Roosevelt, a courageous and most widely popular leader of his time, could have been used in some high service in the war. But he said to me during one of his passages through Chicago: "This is a very exclusive war and I have been blackballed by the committee on admissions." He grinned as he spoke, but there was real pain in the eyes of an old warrior who felt he was denied his rightful place in the most terrible conflict in which his country had ever engaged. In the correspondence between Colonel Roosevelt and Secretary Baker, the reasons given for the rejection of Roosevelt for any military service have always seemed to me incomplete. They do not include any hint of what Secretary Baker wrote to me in 1912, namely, that his objection to the Progressive Party was principally to its leader. I am sure neither Wilson nor Baker had any difficulty convincing themselves that Roosevelt's leadership during the war would not benefit the country. Nor can I blame President Wilson for not seeking comradeship with a man whose opinion of him Wilson must have sensed, even if he had not seen it bluntly expressed in a letter which T.R. wrote me on May 18, 1917, a few weeks after we entered the war: "No man can honestly praise Mr. Wilson's message of April 3rd to Congress without unstintingly blaming him for all his previous two and a half years of insincere and double-dealing conduct and hypocritical speech making, which did more to lower the tone of the American people than anything that has happened since the days of Buchanan."

It should be quite plain that these two men simply could not understand each other.

Conversations with T.R. nearly always led to interesting developments. Shortly after one Chicago talk I received from him a copy of his book *American Ideals,* in which he had written all over the flyleaf as follows:

Sagamore Hill
May 12, 1917

Dear Richberg,

Glance at "True Americanism" and the "Forgotten Maxim." They make pretty good doctrine in essence now; except that 20 years ago neither I nor any other human being foresaw the need of universal obligatory military training and service—at least I was later on the first to advocate it!

Always yours,
Theodore Roosevelt

Side by side with this book in my library is his biography of Thomas H. Benton. This has a peculiar interest to me because the chair in which I have been sitting writing my autobiography is the same one in which Senator Benton sat and wrote his *Thirty Years in the United States Senate.*

The last year of the war rises in my memory as a year of death. In February 1918, my father died. Then kind words long withheld from a man who made enemies more easily than friends came in personal letters and formal resolutions. He had been a midshipman in the Navy in the Civil War, a member and then president of the Board of Education for Chicago, commissioner and president of the Illinois Commission for Uniform Laws. When Knox College, from which he ran away to war, conferred its honorary degree of LL.D. upon him, the president was justified in speaking of long years of uncompensated service to city, state and nation.

Shortly after this began the deaths in Europe, of friends and relatives of friends. Roosevelt's son Quentin died, and, on the enemy's side, Busso von Bülow, whom I could only think of as a charming young man. A Home Guard patriot stopped me in the suburban station and said, "I think ——— is disloyal, don't you? Think of demanding to know what we are fighting for!" "He must be disloyal," was my curt answer. "His only son was killed in battle the other day." But it really was not a time to ask what we were fighting for. It was too disturbing to ask questions. We must feel sure that it was something noble and splendid or we would all go mad. Looking back, I can feel today that we were fighting for a noble cause. Whether we were making the most effective fight, whether going to war as we did and when we did was the greatest service we could render to a noble cause, may be debated a thousand years. But there is a certain defeatism in stopping in the middle of any fight to say, "What are we fighting for?" This is not likely to strengthen a fighting arm or to inspire a fighting spirit.

Regarding the end of the war, I wrote a few years later something which well expresses my feeling today:

> Then came the Armistice (preceded by the false dawn) and immediately thereafter could be heard on every side the brittle rustling of falling leaves. It was as though a hard frost overnight had killed the rank growth of war emotions and ideals. The murmur of private interests rose into a great wind that swept across the land, stripping the trees of public service bare. The hopes of youth were thick as they fell; and there came back to me many times the prophecy of Jane Addams when the European war began in 1914: "This will set back progress for a generation." It certainly stalled progress for my generation. We had our long night of bestial intoxication. Then came the dreadful headache in the cold gray dawn; and before us lay the long day when we should struggle dizzily to put the house of carnival again in order. We would be haggard and weary in the afternoon and ready for our beds early in the evening!
>
> Something of this sense of frustration gripped me as I lay in bed recovering from influenza, shortly after New Year 1919. There was one hope of a fight for something worth while still left. Wilson had been defeated in the fall elections of 1918. In the swing back to the Republicans, there was only one first-class leader in sight. The old guard must swallow its animosities and turn to him. In fact I knew of certain recent overtures that were quite significant. . . . The telephone rang. A reporter for an afternoon paper was on the wire: Did I know that Roosevelt had died in his sleep the night before? . . . I was weak with fever. I could only press my face into the pillow and cry like a child. There were many others who wept that day.

There was a huge memorial meeting held in the Auditorium Theatre in Chicago soon after Roosevelt's death and the task was assigned to me to draft resolutions to be presented there for adoption. I was very happy that those in charge of the meeting accepted my draft without any revisions. The resolutions were read to the assemblage by one of the leaders of the Chicago Bar and of course adopted without discussion. Rereading them, after all these years, I still feel that they summarize the impress of Theodore Roosevelt upon his time and epitomize his character sufficiently well so that I would like to leave them as my permanent tribute to his memory.

Resolutions

Let it be written down that Theodore Roosevelt—a great man—is gone. We have assembled to testify to his worth and to do reverence to his memory. We would join in America's tribute to her true son, in the world's memorial to a valiant leader of mankind.

He loved and served his fellow men.

He lived generously, with natural friendliness, living close to life and finding it good. He served joyously, with insatiable vigor, ever attacking the immediate and palpable wrong with the instant remedy.

Thus he labored upon his generation. With word and action, clean, simple and direct, he harrowed and fertilized contemporary thought, sowed common purposes, uprooted weedy notions and made his day fruitful with healthy growth.

His time shall be his monument.

Let us therefore declare that which Theodore Roosevelt wrought in us:

His courage—quenchless as immortal fire—kindled our hearts.

His faith—steadfast as starlight—upheld our aspirations.

His energy—radiant and unfailing—whipped away our lethargies.

His conscience—audible and dynamic—thundered, and kept our souls awake.

His omnivorous interest, his versatile faculties, his surpassing vigor of mind and body, humanized by homely habits and simple virtues, endeared him to men and women of every walk of life, inspired them with wholesome ambitions and refreshed their daily lives.

Student, soldier and statesman, of righteousness—his strenuous life is done; the quickening voice is still; the ministering hand is at rest. It is for us, who cherish his memory, to raise our voices in his words and lift our hands to carry on his work.

Let us then resolve to preserve and to transmit our heritage from Theodore Roosevelt. Let us perpetuate the tradition of his character—exemplar of pure purposes, plain speech and fearless action. Then let us weave into the manhood of the future the clean, strong fibre of his soul.

CHAPTER VIII

A Legal Battle for "The People"

FROM the year 1915 to the end of my government service I regarded myself, not unconsciously, as a lawyer for "the people." The early years of my service as special gas counsel for the city of Chicago put me in the position of trying to serve the interests of the gas consumers, that is to say the people, of the city of Chicago. Out of this work, which absorbed my major energies for a few years, developed services for organized labor, masses of people scattered throughout the country whose interests I naturally came to regard as fundamentally those of all the people.

From these services to several million people rendered in opposition to the formidable power, first, of the Insull public utilities and then of the managers of the privately owned railroads of the country, I graduated into the officialdom of the national government, wherein I could, and certainly did, feel that I was trying to represent "the people."

Nevertheless I must insist, if only as a matter of definitions, that I never had the sense of serving a class interest such as the interests of "the proletariat." To me the people whom I was serving were not only industrial workers but farm owners, small and even big business men, educators, doctors, lawyers, engineers and ministers of the gospel. In a word, to me "the people" I was seeking to serve were all the people of the United States. This may seem a grandiose concept, but it was one which gave me an enthusiasm which I have never been able to feel in a purely partisan advocacy of any special interest.

I have made this point strongly because I have had to play the part of an aggressive partisan in so many bitter conflicts that my subsequent toleration of opposing views or my advocacy of contentions offensive to former clients has been often misconstrued. I hope, although it may not be true, that I am right in feeling there has been a consistency in my espousal of many causes and many interests sometimes in conflict. I have had the feeling that above all things the preservation of individual freedom is the most important function of government and that when a lawyer is working in that cause, regardless of who his clients may be, he is engaged in the highest type of professional work. The oppressed of today may be the oppressor of tomorrow. For my part, I would like to feel that the major part of my life work has been fighting against oppression, whether by rich or poor, whether by an autocrat or a mob.

The manner in which I had to fight in my years of warfare with the Peoples Gas Light and Coke Company in Chicago provided me with a liberal education in the law and politics. Some may regard this as the story of a legal battle of long ago which would not be duplicated today. I hope that the tactics of members of the Bar and of public utilities have improved. But I have had some experiences in fairly recent years which indicate that contests between public officials and public utilities have not yet reached that refined level in which all the facts can be printed and shed luster on all concerned.

Before I could start my case I had to fight an injunction which had been issued several years before by a judge who was notoriously friendly to the Gas Company and who persisted in retaining control of the case. In all fairness to him, it should be stated that at the time of my entrance into the case he had also become notoriously senile, which was made clear by the rambling discourse with which he greeted my first appearance and refused to take an action which I clearly had the right to demand.

Faced with the impossibility of accomplishing anything before such a judge, I took a completely unprecedented course of action. First, I moved respectfully that he transfer the case to another judge. This he promptly declined to do. Then I filed a petition with the entire court, consisting of twenty judges, alleging his incompetence to hear the case and demanding that the court as a whole assign the case to another judge.

There followed a terrific battle inside the court. But "virtue triumphed," and by a narrow margin, because of the obstinacy of one high-minded judge, the court acted as a whole and transferred the case. Thereupon the Gas Company appealed to the Supreme Court on the ground that each judge was a law unto himself and the entire court could not act as a body. To my great joy, and I think to the surprise of the company, the Supreme Court sustained the lower Circuit Court. So I got my case started before an impartial judge.

This judge was a very conscientious, hard-working man, sufficiently distrustful of his own ability so that he was willing to have lawyers argue practically forever before him before he made a decision. The Gas Company brought in the outstanding lawyer of Chicago, John S. Miller, to argue the fundamental legal points upon which the gas consumers might or might not recover some $10,000,000 which we alleged had been overcharged them.

Mr. Miller and I argued our legal problems before Judge Torrison for many weeks. Finally Mr. Miller came to me and explained that he had accepted a substantial fee (something like $25,000) to make a brief argument and that his large law practice was being completely disorganized by the necessity of being in court day after day for such a long time. I explained I would stop arguing whenever he did. So he finally stopped and let me have the last word.

The judge took the case under advisement and, after we had waited about a year, I went in with a courteous motion for a decision. The judge looked at us sadly and said that when I had made my motion he had endeavored to look up the extensive notes he had taken of our argument. They had been misplaced. He could not find them. He would have to ask us to argue again. To shorten the story, I will explain that the judge finally decided the case in my favor with a very long, well-written opinion which if affirmed on appeal would have meant the refund of something over $10,000,000 to the gas consumers of Chicago. That was quite a tidy sum in those days. However, the Gas Company appealed the case and by a narrow margin the State Supreme Court reversed the lower court and ended this refund litigation.

Shortly before my engagement by the city, Samuel Insull, who was head of the Electric Light Company, had been asked to take over the chairmanship of the Gas Company. Because of his acknowledged executive ability it was hoped that he would straighten out the affairs of the Gas Company, which had been more or less of a scandal throughout its history.

Mr. Insull had a strong sense of good public relations. He was a poor politician and a dangerous financier, but he was a very good operator. After the company lawyers had been defeated in their various efforts to block the trial of the refund case and to block adequate investigation into the company records and properties, by which it could be determined what gas rates could reasonably be charged, Mr. Insull suddenly called me on the telephone one day and said he wanted to talk peace. He said: "I am not for peace at any price, but I am willing to discuss a program for peace on a reasonable basis." He tried to lay down the condition that my chief engineering and accounting adviser, Edward W. Bemis, should not participate in the peace negotiations. Bemis was very much disliked by all utility operators and particularly by Mr. Insull because he was a very meticulous critic of public utilities and a constant thorn in their sides.

I explained that I could not start peace negotiations on the basis of dispensing with Dr. Bemis' services. Otherwise I would be under immediate suspicion of having sold out and no agreement we would reach would have any chance of public acceptance. So Bemis and I; together with Mr. Insull; William G. Woolfolk, who was personal engineering adviser to Samuel Insull; and Woolfolk's assistant, Christopher T. Chenery, sat down to negotiating. Our problem was in some way to get "70 cent gas" for the city of Chicago. That had been the slogan of so many political campaigns that it was one of those difficult things that seemed impossible to the Gas Company and essential to any agreement.

We finally did work out a rate which would enable the average consumer to buy gas at 70 cents per 1,000 cubic feet. To do this with fairness to the Gas Company, we had to raise the rates for the smallest consumer—as difficult politically as to raise income tax rates for the little man. Mr. Woolfolk has always given me credit for devising a "readiness to serve" charge through which we surmounted this difficulty. This was a small and reasonable charge on every consumer for having facilities for service. If he used no gas or little gas, he paid for the privilege of being able to have gas. If he did take gas then he began to pay regular rates after the first 500 cubic feet.

In the course of it, when we were working out an agreement on pending rates with the City Council, the Gas Company had offered to pay back to the consumers one-third of the refund. I advised acceptance of this offer. Unhappily the aldermen, who had heretofore been very flabby and critical in their support of my case, were inspired to reason that if the company would offer to pay over $3,000,000, it was worth while to fight for over $10,000,000. I was reminded of a charming lady client for whom I once obtained a very good offer for a piece of property she was anxious to sell. She promptly refused it on the ground that the purchaser would not have offered that much if it had not been worth more.

The proof that they were utterly wrong came within one year when Insull found the agreement so onerous (with his increased costs which resulted from our entry into the war) that he broke the agreement and went to the newly organized Illinois Utilities Commission, insisting that they alone could fix gas rates and that our agreed ordinance had no validity. As his lawyers put it, "it was not worth the paper it was written on."

This was an example of Mr. Insull's bad politics, because if he had come to me and explained his situation, I would have readily opened negotiations to work out the increased costs to the company and tried to revise the ordinance to meet them. I was never foolish enough to wish to throw a public utility into bankruptcy as a method of improving public service. But Mr. Insull was so annoyed by the situation in which he found himself and so pressed for time and, incidentally, so little fond of me, that he smashed into the Commission office without even a day of warning and demanded the Commission act to save him from his mistakes.

Of course I raised a terrible clamor and I had Mr. Insull in a very tender spot. He was English born, but chairman of the Illinois State Council of Defense. The Allied world was shouting against Germany for having disregarded its treaty with Belgium as a "scrap of paper." Here was the chairman of the State Council of Defense repudiating his own signature to a treaty of peace with the City of Chicago and letting his lawyers denounce his own work as a valueless scrap of paper. Not even a politically minded State Commission could swallow the insult to its integrity. After violent argument the Commission ruled that the rates must remain in effect for a year and then they would consider changing them.

In the course of these bitter arguments Mr. Insull sufficiently lost his temper so that in the presence of two newspaper men he denounced Dr. Bemis and myself as "crooks." He afterward claimed he said we had crooked minds, but the newspaper headline was "crooks." I had sense enough not to respond immediately to this attack. I waited a week until I filed my printed brief with the Commission, at the end of which I asked the Commission to view the matter without emotional bias and to pay no attention to the ravings of the "gold-plated anarchist" who was chairman of the Gas Company. I may say that "gold-plated anarchist" not only filled the front-page headlines that day, but remained for many years a popular designation of Mr. Insull. So I think I had the better of the exchange.

The accuracy of my observation regarding Mr. Insull arose from the fact that, like all too many of the big business men of his time, he had a feeling that he and all his activities should be somehow above the law applying to small men and little affairs. It will be recalled that these years were not far distant from those in which Commodore Vanderbilt of the New York Central was responsible for the famous assertion, "The public be damned." It was not long after the time, also, when Mr. Baer, the coal magnate, had asserted that the coal mines should be and would be operated by the men into whose control God had placed them!

The regulation of public utilities in any effective way was still in its infancy, particularly in Illinois where a state regulatory commission first began functioning in 1914. Prior to this time, it had been the custom for public interests to be protected by city councils, and private utility interests to be protected by buying control of city councils! Mr. Insull should not be greatly blamed for his attitude of irritation with all forms of public regulation of a business which to his credit, it must be admitted, he was trying to conduct efficiently. He had made a great success promoting and increasing electrical service and he earnestly desired to make a success of a gas service that had always been a stench in the spiritual as well as the physical nostrils of the city.

Mr. Insull's idea of avoiding vexatious political controls was a simple one. It was explained to me succinctly by a friend who subsequently became the head of the strongest bank in Chicago. He said: "Insull has developed a new technique of corruption. He does not buy public officials, which is always a dangerous business. He simply buys the bosses." All the political bosses in Chicago were the victims of Mr. Insull's generosity. His principal adviser was Roger Sullivan, the Democratic boss of whom I have previously spoken.

In the course of my litigations with the Gas Company I had to file an affidavit in court concerning the early activities of Roger Sullivan in the state capital where he engineered the passage of certain laws affecting the Gas Company to the considerable profit of himself and associates. Sullivan came roaring into my office one morning threatening me with various forms of annihilation because he said I had falsely accused him. I met him with a grin and asked him to explain what was false in my charges. Thereupon he sat down and told me the whole story of the ancient scandal and confirmed not only my charges but also many rumors that I had heard. Having relieved his soul, he became very friendly and departed, saying: "Now that's the true story. But if you ever tell what I told you I'll say you are a damn liar."

Threats of the character uttered by Sullivan were a commonplace during the early years of my fight against the Gas Company. Spies employed by the company were following me everywhere. Anonymous telephone calls sometimes brought threats of harm and sometimes offered secret information if I would meet the speaker, who might be male or female, at some dubious rendezvous. I had just enough intelligence to make no such appointments.

Long after these occurrences a city policeman told me of his assignment to follow me constantly and, incidentally, the private detectives employed in the same business. He told me that in police circles it was confidently expected that I would be "rubbed out," a pleasant name in Chicago for fatal accidents which happened to annoying people. He also explained to me that the reason it was assumed that I was never assaulted was because of the prominent people, locally and nationally, with whom I was fortunately acquainted. Some of them might be expected to make searching inquiries if anything violent happened to me. This policeman said: "It was your friends like Roosevelt that had them buffaloed."

According to this same police officer, there was great excitement in December 1915 when I left my office suddenly and literally ran through the streets to catch the Century for New York. Just behind me hurried detective number one. Farther back another detective scuttled along the sidewalks. In the rear followed a friendly city policeman. My undesired companions learned too late that I was going to New York. They could not get authority and money to travel with me, so arrangements were made to have me met at the train and followed around New York. But somehow they lost the trail at my hotel.

I went to Oyster Bay unattended and spent some hours there with Roosevelt and an editor going over a series of articles which the Colonel had written and which he wished me to criticize. Then the editor and I drove back to New York in his car. I found a yard-long list of fictitious telephone calls in my hotel letter box, showing the persistent efforts made by detectives to re-establish contact with me. I have this list preserved among my souvenirs and I often think what a pity it was that the human bloodhounds lost the trail. How they would have enjoyed reporting on my visit to Oyster Bay, together with some wise guesses as to what I was doing there!

These threats finally reached a climax which I found beyond quiet endurance. In February 1918 Insull walked into the office of Harold Ickes, who was at that time serving with Insull on the State Council of Defense, and announced that if I did not stop attacking him he would publicly denounce me and my father, without specifying the crimes of which we would be accused. My father had died only a few days before, which Mr. Insull knew, so the making of such an unconscionable threat just when my father was no longer able to defend himself stirred me into a blood-bursting rage.

For some days thereafter I had enough sense to struggle with myself to regain self-control before taking any action.

After careful consideration I made an appointment with a former law schoolmate who was one of Insull's lawyers. I told him I would stand for no more of this sort of spying and threatening. I told him, as was true, that I had statements signed by detectives who had followed me and evidence that they were reporting to Insull's lawyer and to the corporation counsel in the City Hall.

I had various forms of corroborative evidence of admitted blackmail and bribery. I was prepared to launch a very unpleasant attack on the men who were fighting me and I said, as I recorded at the time:

> In the end they will probably ruin me. That I recognize. But if I go down there are plenty of big names that will go down with me. I want you to go back and tell Mr. Insull that I am not interested in disclaimers of personal responsibility; that I will not stand any more and that if this campaign of terrorism does not stop I will expose the whole dirty business.

Quoting further from my records:

> Two hours later, as I sat in a committee meeting in the City Hall, denouncing the Corporation Counsel as a betrayer of the city, another Insull lawyer stepped up to me and whispered: "The chief told me to tell you there would be no personal attack unless you started it." From that time on the opposition flattened out. Newspapermen who had been tipped off to the terrible things that were about to happen to me waited in vain for the promised stories. Within a month the City Council had passed an ordinance by a two-thirds' vote over the Mayor's veto, creating the office of "Special Counsel for Gas Matters" as an official position superior in its special duties to the Corporation Counsel and had named me in the ordinance itself as this Special Counsel. This position I held until I resigned in 1927; and after 1918 my authority was never questioned.

In my unique position as an official of the city government, subject to no control except by the City Council itself, I was able to wage a long, and I should call it a successful, fight to get for the first time a valuation of the Gas Company's properties as the basis for the fixing of rates, which then had to be reasonable since the Commission was obligated to allow the company to make a profit over expenditures only equal to a fair return upon the value of its properties.

After years of hearings and arguments the State Commission fixed a valuation of the company's properties at $85,000,000. Since the company had claimed $140,000,000, but indicated that about

$120,000,000 would be acceptable, this reduction of at least $35,-000,000 in property valuation meant a reduction in charges to gas consumers of 6 per cent of $35,000,000, or over $2,000,000 a year.

If it should be assumed that this tremendous victory brought forth a roar of citywide applause, I hasten to explain that this did not happen in Chicago. On the contrary, whenever the gas question became an issue in the newspapers, the Mayor, whose campaign fund had received $100,000 from Insull, and the City Lawyer, whose old law firm continued to receive at least $14,000 a year from Insull, issued public statements declaring that the gas case had cost the city $400,000 and produced no results.

The advantage of the big lie in politics is shown by the fact that even my personal friends usually refrained from praising my work as gas counsel; and at the time I resigned a political columnist, without mentioning that anything had been achieved, observed that I held the long-distance record for holding a municipal job.

One might assume that this experience in public service would not create in me any overwhelming desire to hold public office. The assumption would be correct. Indeed, by the time Franklin D. Roosevelt came into national power and offered me, as I shall relate, several public positions, one of which I finally accepted, I had no enthusiasm and no illusions about the rewards of public service. But in the meantime I had been carrying on another public-utility battle of much greater significance and ultimate importance than the one that was carried on for twelve years in the city of Chicago.

CHAPTER IX

Legal Battles for Labor

BEGINNING with the year 1920, I was engaged for many years in a combination of work for the railway labor organizations and for the National Conference on Valuation of Railroads which these organizations supported. (Meanwhile my gas litigations in Chicago continued.) The work of this conference was sufficiently successful so that it was eventually described by impartial reporters as having saved the shippers and travelers on the American railroads several billion dollars in increases of freight and passenger rates which were prevented. In recent years I have had a clear view of the other side of the picture as an attorney for various railroads (but not in rate-making proceedings); and I am not sure that the public would not be benefited by paying more generous rates for the services it receives. On the other hand, forcing the railroad operators to accept small margins between income and expense has had the effect of forcing them to an extraordinary economy and efficiency of operation and to a progressive improvement of their properties which may have played a part in giving the United States the best railroad service in the world.

However, when I began in 1920 my battle for a fair valuation of railroad properties, there was such an arrogant unfairness animating many of the great railroad managements that I feel my labors were of a necessary constructive character although regarded as wholly destructive by railroad managements. The way in which my employment in this job came about was most peculiar.

My employment as a lawyer for labor organizations began about 1920 in a curiously indirect way.

In private practice we had had no labor union clients nor any contests with labor unions. While I had had some rather remote contacts in political campaigning with labor leaders whom I did not wish to offend, none had had more than a mild interest in my campaigns. My fights with Mr. Insull and my futile efforts to help improve the condition of the wage earners during World War I may have attracted some sympathetic support from labor organizers, but I certainly had no standing as a labor lawyer.

With the end of the war a serious question arose as to what should be done with the railroads which had been taken over and operated by the government during the war. Labor had fared very well under William G. McAdoo's management as director general. He had removed all barriers to labor organization, thereby strengthening not only the old brotherhoods, which had been strong for years, but opening the way to a great increase in the numbers of union men among the shop craft workers and other crafts. As a natural result, the labor organizations were opposed to a return of the railroads to private ownership, which was widely demanded at the end of the war and had the sympathetic consideration of President Wilson.

An amusing instance of the popular clamor for a return to private ownership was the annoyance expressed by Senator Cummins, the powerful chairman of the Senate Interstate Commerce Committee, who had always inclined toward public ownership. On returning from a railway journey he announced that he no longer favored it. While many things must have contributed to the changing of his opinion, he cited one absurd incident as having been the decisive factor. Under wartime regulation, only one cube of sugar was allowed with each cup of coffee. Cummins who liked two, was sitting across the dining table from a fellow traveler who said to the waiter: "I don't care for sugar." Cummins promptly said: "Then let me have your piece." The waiter interposed and said emphatically: "No, sah! Only one piece of sugar with each cup of coffee. That's regulations."

It was obvious that Wilson was not going to continue complete government control of the railroads. Glenn Plumb, my associate in the gas case, devised a scheme for a sort of compromise management intended to eliminate the evils of pure government management and at the same time to meet complaints against the alleged greed and definite anti-unionism of private management. The "Plumb Plan," which was a notorious issue for some time after the war, proposed a tripartite management, one-third chosen by private owners, one-third by the government and one-third by the railway workers. He convinced railway labor organizations of the possibilities and advantages of this plan and they launched a tremendous campaign under his promotion to gain support in Congress and of the public.

Plumb was a natural promoter, a sort of economic evangelist. As an aggressive champion of their interests he persuaded the railway labor organizations also to support Senator La Follette's program for a complete valuation of all railway properties by the Interstate Commerce Commission. The theory of this campaign was that if the railroads were held down to a modest return upon capital invested they could pay better wages out of charges which could be reasonably imposed on shippers and travelers.

Plumb became so absorbed with speech making, writing and organizing that he could not carry on the heavy legal work of representing the railway labor organizations before the Interstate Commerce Commission in the valuation proceedings. At his suggestion, the organizations invited me to take over this work.

Ultimately I found myself in a conference in Washington with the executives of the labor organizations and Senator La Follette to plan ways and means of carrying on the rail valuation fight. Although up to that time I had not met Senator La Follette, he knew something of my work. So it gave me a glow of pleasure when Warren Stone, Grand Chief Engineer, introduced me to him, saying: "We have had a lot of experience with lawyers and here's one we think we can trust." And Senator La Follette replied: "Oh, I am so glad you are here; I have been told by so many people that you are the man for this job."

Later I understood also that close friends of Wilson had recommended me for this work. Hence I can say that I had the blessing of Theodore Roosevelt, as described earlier, Wilson, La Follette and Bryan, as will hereafter appear, in one of the major battles for a fair valuation of public utilities. Out of this meeting grew eventually the National Conference on Valuation of Railroads, which cannot be properly understood without some knowledge of the shopmen's strike of 1922 and its origins.

When Woodrow Wilson returned the railroads to private ownership, a bitter controversy immediately developed between the railroad executives and the labor unions. The unions had a just cause to demand increased wages which had been denied to them while costs of living had mounted steadily during the war, but most of the railroads, led by General Atterbury, President of the Pennsylvania, rallied to his slogan: "Make no contracts with the labor organizations."

In the Transportation Act of 1920 under which the railroads were returned to private ownership, provision was made for a Railroad Labor Board consisting of three members designated by the government, three by railroad management and three by the labor organizations. This may have been regarded as a slight concession to the Plumb Plan demand for "tripartite" management. However, the board was given power only to hear and decide issues between management and labor. It had no power to enforce its decision.

In its early stages the board was fairly popular with labor because it ruled in favor of long-delayed wage increases which the railroads put into effect. Soon thereafter came the depression of 1921 and then the board issued a wage-reduction order which was naturally unpopular with labor. Unhappily, the depression conditions lingered and new demands came from the railroads for further reductions of wages. In the face of threats of militant opposition from the strong transportation brotherhoods (engineers, firemen, conductors, trainmen and switchmen) the Labor Board diplomatically made no decision. Instead, it ordered a reduction of wages for the shop craft group, whose organizations were in a strategically weak position. They had never been thoroughly organized on the railroads prior to the war, and while they had grown enormously in membership under McAdoo's benign regime, they were not powerful, seasoned organizations. The veteran officers of these shop craft unions were highly indignant that the strong transportation brotherhoods had been left alone while they had been made the victims of management's demand for reduced wages.

By this time I had been accepted as a common lawyer for these organizations, which were knit together in the "Railway Employees Department of the A.F. of L." under the exceptionally efficient, sound and intelligent leadership of Bert M. Jewell, one of the outstanding labor leaders of his time.

I met frequently with the Executive Council of the Department and it became apparent, as was expressed to me, that "we are going to be forced to strike. Any union official who tries to oppose the strike is going to be overridden by the rank and file. He is going to lose his job."

The wisdom of this judgment was demonstrated later when the president of the Maintenance of Way Men did take it upon himself, for honorable reasons, to oppose the strike. He not only lost his job, but permanently lost his position in the labor movement.

The shopmen's strike was declared, the first and one of the very few national strikes of railway employees. It was not difficult for me to persuade the organizations, whose treasuries were too weak to stand any heavy strain, that they must not endeavor to defend all the injunction suits which would certainly be launched against them. They issued public and private statements opposing all forms of violence and backing this up with the firm assertion that the national organizations would not help in any way to defend lawsuits brought against men charged with violence.

As we anticipated, there was a good deal of violence which developed a mass of lawsuits against local and national organizations. At one time there were three hundred injunctions outstanding from courts all over the country. The national officers of the labor unions were deeply concerned to prevent violence, for they realized that this would be fatal to their cause. On the other hand, they viewed eruptions of anger and brutality with the tolerant eyes of men who knew how deeply it hurt workers to feel that they were sacrificing their earnings for a common cause while other workers were helping their opponents. As one president said to me: "There's no use shutting your eyes, Don. A strike ain't no pink tea."

The shopmen's strike dragged along through weary weeks toward ultimate defeat. When this defeat became evident, a few wise railroad presidents, headed by Daniel Willard of the B. & O., opened their doors to negotiating a settlement. Jewell and his colleagues agreed to enter these negotiations.

As a sample of the unfairness of publicity in a strike, a story was widely circulated that Jewell went to meet Willard in the president's "well-stocked private car," implying that there was something improper in the negotiations. I happen to have been with Jewell when he purchased his upper berth in a train to go to this meeting. It was certainly not a "well-stocked private car," although I would not have criticized Jewell if he had carried a small flask with him! It was a trying time and a depressing journey.

A settlement with some thirteen of the railroads had been practically assured when, like the fabled "bolt from the blue," came the filing of a government injunction suit and the issue without notice of an outrageous restraining order by Judge Wilkerson in Chicago. The effect of this was intended to paralyze all the operations of the organizations, to deny them the use of their funds and to prohibit necessary communications and conferences between their representatives. This was not an injunction against a strike; it was an injunction to prevent the settlement of a strike. There is no doubt in my mind whatever that it was engineered by those railroads which were determined to crush the labor unions once and for all and who were certainly out of sympathy with President Willard and his associates in their effort to arrive at a peace treaty.

Because the injunction was obtained at the very time when negotiations were on the verge of success, it was necessary for me to act practically without communication with my clients so as to keep their activities free from injunctive restraint long enough for them to go ahead with their efforts to end the strike. In this we were successful, despite the flagrant abuse of the power of the government.

There was a dramatic hearing in the court room in Chicago a few days later when the government moved for a further "temporary injunction." In behalf of the organizations, I moved to dismiss the government's bill. My motion took precedence over the government's and thus, contrary to the government plans, enabled us for the first time to go to the country with our demonstration of the unfairness and outrage of the government procedure.

Thereafter weeks and months were consumed taking testimony throughout the country in support of the government's demand for a final and permanent injunction. My Chicago work would not permit me to travel with the government attorneys, but my most able associate, Frank Mulholland of Toledo, traveled through state after state taking testimony.

He and I spent weeks digesting the results and finally came to the conclusion that it would be impossible to defend successfully against the weight of evidence that there had been a great deal of violence. Some of it had been exaggerated. Some of the published reports were pure fabrication, such as reports that "trains had been abandoned in the desert." One particular instance of alleged tar and feathering, supported by horrifying pictures of the victim, turned out to be pure fakery. The alleged victim had been supposedly transported over a long railroad journey to be photographed before his sufferings were relieved!

On the whole, however, the evidence was conclusive and supported the permanent injunction sought by the government. I told my clients there was no use fighting the case further before Judge Wilkerson unless we were going to fight all the way to the Supreme Court. The strike was ended and we would be fighting only for an historical verdict. Furthermore, we would lose all the way and end up with a condemnatory opinion spread on the records of the Supreme Court. It would cost at least fifty thousand dollars in expenses and legal fees to see the case through and they would gain nothing in the end.

I then proposed to resign and, with all the other counsel, to withdraw from the case, simply stating that we would not put our clients to the expense of carrying the defense any further. They agreed that this was a good idea. So far as I know, it was the only time in legal annals when counsel had recommended and been permitted to withdraw from a case of such importance without having the dubious pleasure, or at least the financial gain, of carrying it to the last court of appeal. Anyhow, it was a great shock to the government and the judge when we respectfully withdrew and left the government to win its victory over unprotesting defendants.

The final satisfaction that I had in this case came when I had to present my bill for services to the Executive Council. I thought I had made the bill very reasonable, but I had found from experience that what seemed a reasonable fee to a lawyer often seemed like a large fee to labor union officials who in those days received no high salaries themselves. To my amazement, one of the veteran presidents, known as definitely "tightfisted," rose from his chair, walked around the table, grasped my hand and said: "I want to shake hands with a gentleman." All in all, I must admit I got a good deal of satisfaction out of the so-called Daugherty injunction case.

Because of my role in this case, the railway labor organizations, including the transportation brotherhoods who had not been actively engaged in the shopmen's strike, trusted me as an attorney who would do his best for his clients' interests and not overcharge them. This, I am sure, is one of the reasons why railway labor thought it worth while to support my continued representation of them before the Interstate Commerce Commission.

It was felt, however, that this representation should be broader than merely that of railway labor. Consumers of railway service of every variety should be interested in holding rates down to a reasonable return upon the fair value of the property employed. So it was decided to organize a National Conference on Valuation of Railroads and a meeting for this purpose was called in the city of Chicago, May 23, 1923.

The conference was impressively sponsored by a progressive group of senators and representatives in Congress cooperating with a group of governors, and in it were associated the railway unions and other labor organizations, big shippers, commercial travelers associations, farm organizations, mayors of cities and many individuals of notable public spirit.

Senator La Follette was there and William Jennings Bryan; Carl Vrooman, Assistant Secretary of Agriculture under Wilson; William Kent, former Chicago alderman, congressman and tariff commissioner, who gave Muir Woods to the nation and who for many years had battled the gray wolves in the Chicago City Council. Mayor Dever of Chicago presided and welcomed Mayor Hylan of New York. Among others present, I remember Senator Shipstead of Minnesota and, of course, Warren Stone and other presidents of the railway labor organizations.

The "Wisconsin idea"—that public utility rates should be fixed on the basis of reasonable valuations of the property used—was a doctrine which Senator La Follette took into the Senate and sought to apply to the Interstate Commerce regulation of railroad rates. Today when it is so universally applied it seems amusing to recall a time when this doctrine was not accepted. During La Follette's speech on railroad regulation a large number of Republican senators left the Chamber as a silent rebuke to this new radical member. And then La Follette made his famous prophecy: "Unless this important subject is rightly settled seats temporarily vacant may be permanently vacated by those who have the right to occupy them now."

Senator La Follette introduced his Railway Valuation Bill in every session of Congress and it was approved by Taft in his annual message of 1910. The La Follette bill finally became a law on March 1, 1913, just prior to the inauguration of President Wilson.

The major idea behind La Follette's bill was to find out the *original cost* of the railroads, that is the amount of private investment which had been honestly made in them. This is what Justice Brandeis made famous as the "prudent investment" theory. But by 1923 La Follette's dream of fair value had become a nightmare to its supporters. The Interstate Commerce Commission had been reporting in practically every valuation issued that it was "unable to ascertain the original cost of the property," although this was the principal object of its investigation. At the same time the Commission had been reporting estimates of what was called "reproduction cost," that is, the cost of reproducing the railroads under present conditions, which of course had not existed when they were built. Anyone can imagine the difference between the theoretical cost of building a railroad through Chicago today compared with the actual cost when Chicago was a small town in the midst of a prairie!

When the Valuation Act was being debated, railroad witnesses had estimated that the value of all the roads was about fourteen billion dollars. Ten years later, although investments of less than five billion dollars had been added, the railroads claimed their value had increased as "roughly estimated" to about thirty-five billion dollars.

Even in the year 1920 railroad operators had asked Congress to pass a law that would fix the total value of the railroads at about twenty billion dollars. Yet in 1923, when prices were lower than in 1920, the railroads were claiming a value of fifteen billion dollars higher than they were willing to accept three years before.

It may be observed that this ballooning of value some twenty billion dollars would authorize the roads to charge, at six per cent, over one billion dollars more than they would otherwise be entitled to. From the standpoint of labor, we could assert that one billion dollars more for wages would mean an average of $500 to a man for two million workers.

The National Conference on Valuation of Railroads, therefore, was organized to fight for a big stake. In those days it seemed important to prevent an unjustified increase in public utility rates that would cost either the consumers or the workers one billion dollars a year. As a magazine writer said at the time, I was engaged to handle "the greatest lawsuit in history."

After the organization meeting in the Council Room a small group sat down to dinner at the invitation of former Senator Owen. The contrast between Senator La Follette, with his lined and anxious face, and the rather bland, assured confidence of Bryan, interested me particularly. For all of his zeal and intensity of conviction, La Follette was essentially a more tolerant man. He was very fond of his friends as well as fond of humanity. Bryan seemed to me a much colder, self-centered person. Most of the boyish charm which I had found in him when I first met him twenty-three years before had evaporated. You could see in his face the stubborn certainties that the Bible should be believed "from cover to cover"; that alcohol was utterly evil. He would not yield to any blandishments of Satan or the demon rum, yet that very day he had shown an undue willingness to compromise on an economic issue because there he was without conviction.

In contrast, La Follette was uncompromising on economic and political issues where he had strong convictions, but on social and religious issues he accepted life as an experiment in which it was hard to arrive at certainties.

On the organization of the National Conference I was made general counsel and assured of a continuing support, largely through the labor organizations, in the battles before the Interstate Commerce Commission. This battling came to a climax in a case subsequently famous as the O'Fallon case. This case involved the valuation of one small railroad wherein the issue was plainly made between the advocates of an *original* cost valuation and a *reproduction* cost valuation. Prior to the selection of this as a test case there were years of hearings and arguments before the Commission.

It was the particular purpose of counsel for the railroads to impress the Commission with the idea that they must take into consideration all kinds of evidence, including incomplete records and estimates of original cost, but they should lay the main emphasis on the complete estimates of reproduction cost. This would, of course, enormously increase the value placed on the railroad properties. These railroad lawyers insisted that the Supreme Court had practically decided the question and the Commission must follow the Supreme Court. They adopted a positively reverential attitude in speaking of the Supreme Court which led the able and clever John E. Benton, representing the Association of State Public Utilities Commissioners, to describe one very solemn railroad lawyer as "frowning down upon us like the messenger of one vested with power to destroy all our works . . . not exactly like one preaching a new gospel, but rather as one who speaking with authority condescends to expound to the blind and unregenerate the justice and reasonableness of the decrees of the everlasting God."

I had urged the Commission that while it should seek light from judicial opinions, it should not listen reverently to every casual opinion of a judge on matters of public policy; that the courts themselves agreed that public policy should be decided by the legislative and not by the judicial branch of the government.

Judge Brantley, one of the leading counsel for the railroads, stated that his only reply would be to tell the Commission about an old doorkeeper in the Capitol who was trying to keep a visitor out of the crowded Supreme Court room. The man insisted that as a citizen he had a right to enter even though there was not a seat vacant. The old colored doorkeeper then stepped aside with a gesture of great dignity and said: "Very well, sah, but you'd better remember this: If you gets in contempt of this court you ain't got nowhere to appeal except to God."

At the end of extensive arguments the railroads suffered a narrow defeat in a six-to-five vote by the Commission. The railroads appealed this test case to the Supreme Court.

It was the view of some of the Interstate Commerce commissioners that I should be selected as special counsel for the Commission to argue the case, since my theories had been sustained by a majority. It was the view of others, which was not unreasonable, that the Commission should not be represented by a victorious advocate.

On the other hand, the regular counsel for the Commission wished to remain impartial in the face of such a strong division in the Commission. So the decision was made to select as the Commission's lawyer Walter L. Fisher of Chicago, an eminent attorney who had been Secretary of Interior in Taft's cabinet. Possibly the fact that Taft was then Chief Justice had an influence in the decision. The railroads countered with engaging George W. Wickersham, who had been Attorney General in Taft's Cabinet! Of course the Solicitor General, William D. Mitchell, who became Attorney General, was also in the case.

As attorney for the National Conference, which had played such a strong part in the Commission hearings, I sought an opportunity to file a brief and be heard in the Supreme Court arguments. But the railroads refused their consent, which meant that the Court might receive a brief, but would not permit me to participate in the arguments. This greatly disturbed the senators who were supporting the Conference, which included Senator Norris of Nebraska as chairman and other militant persons such as Senators La Follette, Wheeler and Shipstead.

At a conference called by Senator Norris, there was considerable indignation expressed regarding my exclusion from this case which we had been fighting for several years. Finally Senator Wheeler suggested the Senate pass a resolution asking the Court to hear me. I was embarrassed by the suggestion, because the idea of a lawyer forcing himself on the Supreme Court was not wholly pleasant to a young man of thirty-eight who had already gained something of a reputation as a radical. But the following day the resolution was introduced and after a hot debate it was adopted by a vote of 46 to 31. This debate gave me some fine testimonials, not only from my supporters but from the opposition, headed by Senator Reed of Pennsylvania, himself an eminent lawyer, which adopted the strategy of not opposing me personally, but insisting that the Supreme Court, without any urging, would certainly permit a lawyer of my recognized standing in valuation proceedings to participate in this tremendously important case.

I filed my petition and to my great relief the Court granted it, allowing me the same time for my argument that was allowed the other exponents of the Commission decision. Thus I had the great opportunity of participating in this historic argument and sharing in the defeat. However, in compensation it should be pointed out that the dissenting opinion of Justice Brandeis in that case became eventually an expression of the majority opinion of the Supreme Court and the original cost or "prudent investment theory" of the valuation of public utility properties became a part of the law of the land.

Justice Brandeis had done pioneering work in public utilities long before I began my practical education in 1915, so it would be an unwarranted assumption that my brief in the O'Fallon case had any influence upon the shaping of his opinion. My brief was, however, highly praised by lawyers of authority in this field. I venture this boast because I feel impelled in some way to justify my injection into the case by virtue of an unprecedented Senate resolution. Some time afterward I spoke to the veteran deputy clerk of the Court, Reginald Dilli, and somewhat shamefacedly expressed the hope that the Court was not offended by the passage of the Senate resolution which I had acquiesced in but had not instigated. He grinned and said that he didn't think the Court was particularly pleased, but that apparently the resolution had been effective. "However," he added, "I wouldn't do it again if I were you."

My work for the railway organizations after the 1922 strike had been settled included the hangover of a contempt case which resulted in a landmark decision by the Supreme Court. A federal law provided that a man accused of violating an injunction by a criminal act committed outside the presence of the court was entitled to demand a trial by jury. That is, the judge who had granted the injunction could not try him alone and thus determine his guilt and his sentence.

There was a great deal of hostility to this law among conservative lawyers who felt that it was an effort by the legislature to take over the inherent power of the judiciary to protect its orders from violation. When, therefore, a man named Michaelson, accused of criminally violating an injunction, demanded a trial by jury, the court refused to grant it. He was tried and convicted by the judge alone. I agreed with the labor organizations that this case was worthy of an appeal to the Supreme Court. Organized labor could not afford to have a federal law providing for jury trial held unconstitutional by any tribunal short of the Supreme Court.

In presenting my arguments I was able to prove that in England (from which came our common law) it was the exception to have such contempt cases tried by a judge. Normally they were tried by a jury. Also, I made the point that a "court," although constitutionally authorized, could be made by statute to consist of either a judge alone or of a judge and jury.

In the course of the argument an amusing incident occurred when Justice McReynolds interrupted me to say: "You don't mean to claim that a court could be made up entirely of laymen." While I was hesitating to make the simple answer, "Of course it could," Justice Holmes leaned forward from the other side of the Bench and snorted: "Why not? Why not? I think all or a large part of the highest court of New Jersey is composed of laymen. Why not?"

I was thus saved from the awkward situation of trying to instruct the Court on such a simple question, although I was almost equally embarrassed by another question from the Bench. One of the justices asked me to explain the difference between civil contempt, which I admitted could be punished by the judge, and criminal contempt, which I contended required a trial by jury. It was like going back to law school to make the answer that a civil contempt was remedial, that is, an action to bring about compliance with an order of the court, whereas a criminal contempt was, although partially remedial, essentially the punishment for a violation of law. This distinction may not seem clear either to laymen or to all lawyers. But the distinction was made by the Supreme Court and in a unanimous opinion the Court sustained the federal law which has assured a trial by jury in all such essentially criminal cases since that time.

The most constructive result of the shopmen's strike was in the impetus it gave to the railway labor organizations to have a law written by the Congress which would provide for the peaceful and just solution of railway labor disputes.

All the labor organizations joined hands to work out a bill for the enactment of a law which would provide for the unions' rights of organization and negotiation, with the certainty of government mediation in unsettled disputes and the possibility of arbitration where both sides were agreeable. With only a skeleton outline of the ideas of my clients, I entered a long period of intensive labor. The result was the draft of the major provisions of the Railway Labor Act which became a law in 1926. In this work of draftsmanship I had the infinitely valuable assistance of a young man who had graduated from Harvard Law School in 1923 and was recommended to me very strongly by Professor Felix Frankfurter.

On leaving my old law firm for the pleasures of single practice in 1923, I had intended to keep my organization down to my secretary and one assistant attorney, both of whom came with me from the old office. But Frankfurter was insistent on my talking with David E. Lilienthal. He impressed me as having such exceptional intellectual power, energy and integrity that I changed my mind and took him, which was fortunate for me.

Lilienthal was so successful in attracting a personal clientele that I could not retain him in my small office for many years. He undertook the editorship of reference books on public utilities and became soon such an authority on public utility regulation that his services were widely sought. As a result, his income increased rapidly and he was able to buy a substantial North Shore home and to acquire offices appropriate to his expanding practice.

At this time Phil La Follette had become governor of Wisconsin and had conceived the unconventional idea of appointing me, a Chicago lawyer, chairman of the Wisconsin Public Service Commission. It was impossible, however, for me to accept this appointment (or a later suggested appointment as Dean of the University of Wisconsin Law School) for my private financial obligations demanded the making of an income far beyond the modest salaries available in Wisconsin. In excusing myself for not taking advantage of a great opportunity for an interesting public service, I ventured to suggest that Dave Lilienthal would make a magnificent member of the Commission, full of mature knowledge and youthful energy. I told Phil I did not see how Dave could make the sacrifice, but that I knew he had such a flair for public service that he might undertake it. The Governor explained that he did not dare to attempt to make such a young man chairman of the Commission, but he would offer him membership. To my amazement, Lilienthal accepted the invitation, gave up his very profitable law practice, sold his home and moved, with his wife and two children, to Madison, Wisconsin, where he rendered a fine public service for a very small salary. He made such an impression there that when his reappointment came up, conservative newspapers that had been violently opposed to him endorsed his continuance in office.

When Franklin Roosevelt was organizing his administration, he was strongly urged by many to appoint Lilienthal to the Federal Power Commission. By a peculiar series of events his once-scheduled appointment failed, but when the TVA legislation was passed the President promptly named Lilienthal as one of the three commissioners. After eventually becoming chairman of the TVA and carrying the load of that tremendous enterprise for many years, he then assumed the extraordinary and delicate functions of chairman of the Atomic Energy Commission. Regardless of agreement or disagreement with his policies, I have never heard anyone suggest that Lilienthal was not a devoted public servant who gave the best years of his life to a tremendous straining effort to render the best of public service he could in three public positions of constantly increasing importance. It is worth adding that he had difficulties to contend with which never had public recognition or appreciation. In the first place, having no independent means, he and his wife always had to live with great economy in order to take care of his family responsibilities and meet the demands of his public offices. In the second place, he had a long period of ill health involving a most dangerous and harassing undulant fever.

Through the many years of my increasing disillusionment with socialistic programs and Dave's absorption in some of them, our ideologies may have drifted considerably apart. But I suspect that the extremists of the Truman administration and the subsequent return of Lilienthal to private life may have again brought us nearer together mentally. I may say that emotionally I have always been proud and happy to have been associated with so fine a character.

In 1923, when I took Lilienthal into my office, I put him to work particularly on the problem of drafting a voluntary arbitration provision for the Railway Labor Act. Since I can give Lilienthal credit for the results, I may say that I think these provisions laid the foundations for a great improvement in arbitration technique and provided a model for many later enactments.

After more than a year's work, when the bill had been drafted to the satisfaction of my clients, we took the embryo law to Senator La Follette. Acting on his advice, I was able to persuade Senator Robert Howell of Nebraska and Congressman Alben Barkley of Kentucky to introduce the bill in their respective houses in 1924.

When I came into Senator Howell's office one morning, I found in his private office a huge blackboard covering practically one wall. On it was a simplified diagram of the law. He had translated twenty-five printed pages into a few sentences set off in squares connected and related to each other by heavy lines and arrows.

"What do you think of that?" he said. "I am going to take that into the committee room and then onto the floor of the Senate. The hardest thing to do is to get these men to think. I must make them see it without thinking. Most of them won't read the bill and those who do won't study it enough to know what it is all about."

A beautiful example of this was given by the action of Nicholas Longworth, the Republican floor leader in the House, who was opposing the bill. He misstated its main provision so absurdly that a roar of protest drove him red-faced from the floor. Only a week before I had given him a condensed summary of the bill and offered to explain the whole document at length.

"No," he said to me. "We have decided to oppose the bill, so there is no use talking about it." Nor could I find any other member of the Steering Committee who had made a careful study of the bill. Yet the entire Republican organization from the White House down opposed it in the first session when it was before the Congress. Then, after a limited revision between sessions, the same organization supported and passed the bill in the next session!

The reason for this change of heart was important to the future success of the act. In the session in 1925, Senator Howell had managed, with the great aid of Senator La Follette, who rose from a sickbed to vote, to get the bill reported favorably by the Senate Interstate Commerce Committee, despite the opposition of the railroads. In the same session Congressman Barkley was able to get the bill before the House, without a report from a hostile committee, by the device of getting a petition signed by a majority of the members of the House requiring consideration of the bill.

Then ensued a remarkable session in which, despite the forcing of twenty-four roll calls by the opposition, Barkley was able to keep the bill before the House, registering one defeat after another of its opponents, until 11:00 P.M. Then he called me into conference, suggesting it would be wise to adjourn because, although we might not be able to get the bill again considered, it would be dangerous to risk a defeat from a very tired and long-suffering House. I agreed, and Barkley went back to the floor where he moved an adjournment after telling a typical Barkley story in which he said he insisted on having the last word because he was like the wife of a man who died and whose son, on being asked, "What were your father's last words?" answered, "He didn't have any. Mother was with him to the end."

In the interval between the two sessions of Congress, Barkley and Howell and I had various discussions with Colonel Thom, the general counsel for the railroads, who was their very shrewd and most effective lobbyist for many years. Thom had become convinced that, with the favorable temper of Congress shown in both houses, it would be practically impossible to defeat the Howell-Barkley bill at the next session. As a result, he was able to persuade most of the railroad executives that it would be to their interest to see if the bill could not be modified so that management and labor could go to Congress unitedly in favor of a bill which they felt would keep peace in the railroads.

It is a tribute to the good sense of the railroad managements that they agreed with this argument. In the end the two parties agreed to have a committee of railway presidents and union presidents sit down together—"without any lawyers"—and try to reach an agreement. Of course Colonel Thom and I were invisibly present, but I think it gave the clients on both sides a curious sense of satisfaction to feel that they finally did the job themselves.

Then came an act of political injustice which was accepted in rare spirit by the victims. In order to ease its passage through both houses, it was decided that the bill should be introduced by the respective chairmen of the two Interstate Commerce Committees, Senator Watson in the Senate and Congressman Parker in the

House—both of whom had, of course, been opposed to the bill the previous session. Senator Howell and Congressman Barkley accepted this demotion with good grace, although some of our labor executives were outraged.

This official sponsorship of the bill was of great value. It assured an almost solid Republican support, including that of a somewhat reluctant President; it assured the railroads that the potentially powerful mediation board to be appointed under the bill would be a conservative Republican one; and finally, it was far better that an administration favorable to management should be anxious for the success of a bill wherein the position and bargaining power of the railway unions were definitely improved.

However, the enactment of this beneficent law was not without difficulty. There was a small body of powerful railroads who had never agreed with the majority who joined us in proposing and supporting the bill. This minority was not strong enough to beat us, but able to make a good deal of trouble. The great factor on the side of the majority was that General Atterbury, of the Pennsylvania, who had been the leader of the anti-union crusade of 1920, had seen the light in the events of the intervening years. He not only decided to support the law, but he testified in its favor. When he testified before the Senate Committee on January 14, 1926, he said with obvious pleasure, "[this] is an epoch-making occasion. Never before have I been before a committee of the Senate or of the House that I have not been in opposition on any labor question with those of our employees with whom I have had to live. Today we come to you with an agreed-upon program."

Against the passage of the law were arraigned not only a small group of strong railroads, but also the always powerful National Association of Manufacturers. Their opposition was guided, as it was for many years, by their clever attorney, James Emery, and it took the form of proposing a series of amendments, some of which seemed comparatively harmless, but all of which were merely preparing the way for further and more harmful amendments.

This opposition worried President Coolidge. Colonel Thom and I therefore met with the President one afternoon after lunch in his study. I was highly entertained when the President produced a large box of long Havana cigars, which he and I smoked with equal relish, for I had only recently read an article about the President in which his frugal nature was "proved" by the alleged fact that he smoked Pittsburgh stogies.

This was my first intimate meeting with Calvin Coolidge, in whom I had had a special interest because we were members of the same college fraternity, Phi Gamma Delta. It was traditional that he was recommended to the chapter at Amherst by a friend who had written, speaking well of him, "although," he added, "he looks like a singed cat."

Shortly after he became President, all the elite of the fraternity waited upon him to congratulate "our first President." (I might say we had specialized in Vice Presidents, since the fraternity members had included Vice President Fairbanks, Vice President Marshall and, finally, Vice President Coolidge.) The brethren gathered in a standing semicircle around the President's desk. He fumbled with some slips of paper, but evidently did not find the proper memorandum explaining the purpose of the gathering, so he finally looked up and said, "Well, gentlemen, what can I do for you?"

Because I had heard so often of the President's taciturnity, I was quite surprised at the loquacity with which he explained what was bothering him about the Railway Labor Act. He did not see why we could not accept the amendments proposed by the National Association of Manufacturers. I pointed out that we had an agreement with the railroad executives that both sides would carry out the law without opposition and in good faith if it were not amended. The amendments might not seem important, but they would make it easy for some railroad to oppose full cooperation with the organizations on the ground that this was not the law they had agreed to.

The President seized upon my concession and said in substance: "If these amendments don't mean anything, why don't you consent to their addition? If you do that, then when these people come to me and want me to veto the bill I can point out that I got these amendments for them and they should be satisfied."

This was certainly a frank argument, if not one based on high principle. I was considerably taken aback because Colonel Thom was entirely willing to have the amendments accepted. But I had to stick to my guns and I explained to the President that our only safety lay in insisting that the bill should be passed as written because it was an agreed-upon program which in effect enabled Congress to say to management and labor: "You have made a contract to preserve the peace and now it is up to you to make good on your contract." The President was not greatly impressed by my argument and I think my apparently stubborn and undiplomatic refusal to make any concession accounted for the halfheartedness with which he supported and finally approved the bill, which was one of the few constructive pieces of legislation enacted in his administration.

Some time after this I had another experience regarding the same bill. On emerging from the White House one day, Senator Smoot of Utah told reporters what he understood the President "thought" about the legislation, indicating a lack of any confidence in it by the President.

We were very much disturbed at the effect of Senator Smoot's attempt to line the President up against the bill, since this was bound to have a bad influence on the Hill. I therefore got an appointment with the President to suggest some counter statement or action on his part since he was, as a matter of fact, assuring the majority leaders on the Hill that he was not opposed to the bill. Here I had another example that "silent Cal" could be a very talkative person. No sooner had I said that I was disturbed by Senator Smoot's remarks than he burst forth in an extensive tirade against people who were always sounding forth as to what the President thought or intended. "What business is it of theirs as to what the President thinks? What right have they to say what the President thinks? The President can speak for himself and will speak for himself when he wants to. What business have other people trying to put words in his mouth and thoughts in his mind and misrepresenting him?" He went on in this vein for several minutes. All of a sudden he seemed to realize the impression he was making. His mouth snapped shut and he said: "Well, there's no use my talking about this. What was it you came to say?" Whereupon I made my suggestions, to which he made monosyllabic comments, and the interview ended with the supposedly reticent President once more in his accustomed role.

Mrs. Coolidge was notably a fast talker, but after this brief experience I had the idea that in case of any family discussion Calvin Coolidge would be fully able to hold up his end.

With the reluctant approval of the President, the Railway Labor

Act became a law, and there began for me several years of arbitrations and negotiations for the peaceful settlement of controversies between management and labor, years of the most notable industrial peace in any major industry of the United States. But before reviewing these, it is necessary to retrace our steps briefly to cover the campaign of 1924, which had more profound effects upon American history than could be evident at the time.

CHAPTER X

What Was Called "Normalcy"

IT WAS inevitable that a national government headed first by Warren G. Harding and then by Calvin Coolidge could be satisfactory only to persons completely satisfied with maintaining the status quo. This, at any time, in any place in world history, is sure to be a minority in any community, unless for scientific accuracy we except the lotus eaters in a few communities, so backward that they cannot go back and so lethargic that they have no impulse to go forward. I may have been a bit cruel, but I do not think unjust, when I wrote of President Harding, viewing the Alaskan glaciers, as follows:

The world moves on
And leaves him standing there
Quite satisfied,
Completely unaware.

Proudly—with face
Turned toward the crimson west—
He cries: "The dawn!"
And adds: "Old ways are best."

O, head of oak!
No wonder that you sigh
At youthful haste
As glaciers pass you by.

As to my dear brother in Phi Gamma Delta, President Coolidge, he was an appropriate instrument of the time in which a President could do no great harm and might even do some good, by avoiding anything which would upset anything in the status quo. It was not surprising that after the tremendous sacrifices and waste of the First World War, through which the American people apparently gained nothing except new troubles, there should be a tremendous reaction to self-service, a great desire for more of the fleshpots and a great impatience with any demands for reform.

I believe that my acid comment many years ago on what happened after the World War, while exaggerated, was pretty well justified:

> When the war ended the people looked around for new leaders since the process of making peace had destroyed those who had been too busy making war to have developed acceptable ideas about making peace. And the new leadership of peace promptly adopted the successful technique of war leadership—Usurpation and Command, supported by camouflage and propaganda.
>
> The prohibitionists were sure that alcohol was a social evil. They commanded it to go and the politicians bowed to the Command. They had learned during the war to bow or be broken. Their heads were bloody and much bowed.
>
> The communists of Russia were sure that a Marxian State would be a social good. They commanded it to come and it came.
>
> Mussolini was sure that he was good for Italy. Fascism became the voice of the Command and Mussolini produced from what was "left" of labor the divine "right" of capital.
>
> Intelligent women were sure that short hair and shorter skirts would be more comfortable. So the Command went forth, cleverly propagandized from the fashion centers of Paris and New York, and behold the tyranny of centuries of Tabu was overthrown in a season!
>
> But this flouting of old authority—of Church and State and Mrs. Grundy—could not be confined to the intelligent. They had led the mob againt the Law and the mob would go on. The Sermon on the Mount, good government, hard work, in-

> dependence, wives, children and paradise on earth—all the objectives of intelligence in the pre-war period had been attacked by the intelligent and the herd had followed them. Prosperity alone remained a common desire; and the common means was: Go get it! The hard flapper, the soft sheik, the bootlegger, the automobile bandit, the real estate boomer, the race track gambler, the bathing beauty, the star athlete, the political crook and the political briber, all found the way to prosperity—to the hotel in Palm Beach, or the jail in Atlanta.

In such a time a reformer in the White House might have been regarded as a common nuisance. Certainly Calvin Coolidge was generally regarded as a gift of the gods to Americans who wanted to be let alone. There was no real militancy in the Democratic preparations to oppose him. What was left of Wilsonian reform in the Democratic Party was prepared to support McAdoo for the Presidency. The essentially conservative group which also recognized the need for some Wilsonian reform, but wanted it to be a businesslike process, supported Al Smith, who had undoubtedly been a good and progressive governor. Al Smith was nominated as "The Happy Warrior" by that gallant figure, Franklin D. Roosevelt, who was only metaphorically on his feet again after the cruel onslaught of polio. The railway unions were strong supporters of McAdoo and when he and Smith fought to an impossible deadlock and the Democratic Party nominated John W. Davis, a "Wall Street lawyer," for President, the railway groups, along with other disappointed liberals who had followed Smith or McAdoo, were rarin' to go somewhere else. Senator La Follette, who was aging more rapidly than he himself would acknowledge, was also rarin' to go for one last try at the Presidency. Once again a third party appeared in American politics. It was, as nearly as it could be identified, an honest successor but not a lineal descendant of the Bull Moose Party. It was organized by the "Conference for Progressive Political Action," largely a railway labor creation, and it proceeded to nominate Senator La Follette as candidate for President and, to show its bipartisanship, Senator Wheeler, Democrat from Montana, as candidate for Vice President.

To understand the reason for Senator La Follette's Presidential campaign one must recall the frustrations of the Progressives in both parties which developed out of the return to "normalcy" under Harding, followed by the "keep cool with Coolidge" era, and also realize the waning strength of Senator La Follette, who was sixty-nine years old in 1924. He was a man who combined personal ambition with an intense desire to feel that he had made his life a great public service. Persons who did not know him intimately, or had heard about him through disparaging reporters, would not understand what an intense idealist and lovable individual he was. He had a keen sense of theatrics, but he always used his dramatic ability to impress a lesson in economics or politics upon his audience. I remember one time when he spoke in Orchestra Hall, beginning quietly, as most trained orators do, but raising his voice in response to some cries of "Louder!" Then, after a moment or two, he waved his hand toward listeners in the top gallery and said: "Can you hear me way up there? If you can't, just let me know and I'll send it across to you."

In private discussions he was the most persuasive politician whom I had met up to that time. He had an obvious sincerity and devotion to whatever cause he was espousing that made it seem impossible for anyone to refuse an opportunity which he offered for the acceptance of some sacrificial task. He didn't attempt to fool you with hopes of great sudden victories. He was more likely to emphasize the prospect of a glorious defeat. One day he called me into his office in the Capitol and offered me "a great opportunity." Groups were organized and ready. Reasonable campaign funds were assured. All I had to do was to agree to become a candidate for the United States Senate from Illinois. He didn't pretend I could win, but pointed out that through my campaign we could organize the Progressive voters in Illinois in this fight and thereafter in the fall of 1924 we would have a strong organization for service in the Presidential campaign. In some remote day we might even win the state.

He pointed out that North and South Dakota, Minnesota, Wisconsin, Iowa, Illinois and Michigan were all good battle grounds for Progressivism. Illinois, a highly important unit in this group of hopeful states, was a tough problem, but we must tackle it, and I was the logical person to be an immediate sacrifice for this great cause.

I could not have resisted La Follette's persuasion if I had had only my own feelings and economic problems to consider. How could one answer a man who said with a happy smile on his face: "It is a bitter, discouraging struggle—many defeats for a few victories, but it brings inner satisfactions that are lasting and repay for all the pain." Deep down inside me I knew that I would rather feel the happiness that shone from the old warrior's eyes at the end of life than have the vanities and comforts that might be obtained from other forms of "success." But I also knew that I was not for him the "man of the hour" and I explained certain private embarrassments that I write about elsewhere in this book, which would destroy my apparent availability as a candidate.

I think I understood the Senator's reasons for his final decision to launch an independent Presidential campaign. I am sure he had no real hope of winning, but that he felt the campaign must be made for the education and organization of people for future campaigns which he could only lead in spirit. Although he had all the appearance of extraordinary energy, he must have known something of the hidden weaknesses which brought about his death the following year. This was his last chance, not to win the Presidency, as his detractors would have assumed, but his last chance to lead a great battle for the ideas and ideals to which he had given his life. After the nominations of Republican Coolidge and Democrat Davis the situation was ripe for the independent campaign which La Follette had been considering and he called me to Washington to help in laying down the lines of that campaign.

At his request I prepared a speech to the convention, but it was never delivered because, while I was traveling from Washington to Cleveland with "young Bob," the convention leaders had named me chairman of the resolutions committee—enough of a job and enough speech making for one delegate! In the ensuing campaign I had once more the main responsibility of the complex and difficult job of placing the names of independent candidates on the ballot in forty-eight states.

This Progressive Convention held in Cleveland in 1924 was largely organized and dominated by the railway labor organizations. But many other labor organizations took part and eventually the American Federation of Labor, for the first time in its history, officially endorsed a Presidential candidate. It regarded the choice between Calvin Coolidge and John W. Davis as an impossible one to present to the wage earners and therefore advised the casting of their votes for Senator La Follette, although I am sure that those shrewd and comparatively conservative labor executives were not possessed with any illusion that La Follette had a chance to win. Nevertheless, his vote of over 4,800,000 contrasted favorably with that of Davis of approximately 8,400,000, although Coolidge won by more than 15,700,000.

However, I did feel that the La Follette campaign served a definite purpose and had a great value in demonstrating again to both the old-line parties that there was a tremendous Progressive vote in the country which could not be safely disregarded. The effects of this lesson were certainly evident in the 1928 campaign when the choice of the voters was not between any ultra-conservatives (such as Harding and Coolidge) but between men who might be designated: the liberal conservative, Herbert Hoover, and the conservative liberal, Al Smith.

My part in the 1924 campaign gave me the feeling that as an official expounder of the Progressivism of 1912, 1916 and 1924, I could properly serve thereafter as a critic as well as a friend of that Progressivism. As such a critic, I would venture now to say that throughout this period the Progressive forces in American political life had only a vague idea of where they were going. If their leadership had been successful in acquiring the power of a national administration, it would not have been a radical leadership in any real sense. It would not have been a leadership of enthusiasts trying to "make the world over," such as thronged into the administration of Franklin D. Roosevelt. It would have been a leadership of men seeking largely to improve government by making it more honest and more responsive to popular needs. It would certainly not have been a leadership into the paths of socialism. Its government would not have been a government undertaking to take over and direct the operations of the economic system. It would have been a leadership more of the kind exerted by Franklin Roosevelt in his campaign for the Presidency and in the early months of his administration. Then he was seeking to save a system of private enterprise by correcting and preventing abuses of private power. Our national leadership was not then attempting, as in the later years of Roosevelt and all through the administration of Truman, to socialize the economy of the nation.

The Roosevelt–La Follette–Bryan–Wilson leadership was seeking, to use Wilson's phrase, "a new freedom" for the individual by curtailing the power of large monopolistic organizations to dominate the industries of the nation and incidentally its politics.

CHAPTER XI

Prosperity and Then the Deluge

FOLLOWING the enactment of the Railway Labor Act in 1926, I was engulfed for several years in arbitrations, lawsuits and negotiations seeking to advance the interests of railway labor. The machinery of the new law went into effect in whirring mechanisms operating throughout the steam transportation system. Individual organizations and groups of organizations made requests for revisions of contracts. Conferences were held as required by law and when these failed government mediation endeavored to bring about agreement.

As the months went by the law seemed to be working admirably according to the intent of its sponsors. But there were quite a number of railroads clearly reluctant to comply with the law, particularly with the requirements of recognizing the authority of labor representatives where the men were not strongly organized. There were many of the organizations which became exasperated with delays, extended conferences and negotiations and other impediments to quick action. These organizations would have made more trouble except for the fact that we had created an organization representing all the railway labor groups whose main purpose and object were to try to make the law a success. This acted as a restraining influence against hot-headed local and individual union action.

This organization was the Railway Labor Executives Association, for the creation of which I can take some credit. The railway brotherhoods and unions, like all national labor organizations, cherished their autonomy—it is commonly misunderstood that the American Federation of Labor has a power over its constituent unions which it does not possess. These railway unions were not willing to give over their self-government to any central body. But they recognized the need of a cooperative organization and they finally arrived at an intelligent compromise by which they organized an association of the presidents of all the separate brotherhoods and unions, with duties only of consultation and joint action where unanimously acceptable.

I was appointed general counsel of this organization, but I did not seek or obtain any retainer. I made the arrangement that I would render services when called upon at $100 per day plus expenses. However, I would accept no obligation nor would the association be under any obligation to me for a continuance of services beyond the time when they were mutually agreeable. In brakemen's language, the compact was, "We can tell you to go to hell any time we want to and you can tell us the same."

In the three years immediately following the enactment of the Railway Labor Act and preceding the depression, which began in the fall of 1929, I engaged in a great many arbitrations for individual organizations or for groups, such as the shop crafts, sometimes with a single railroad, but usually with a group of railroads such as the Southeastern or the Western railroads. These were very arduous undertakings, but the results on the whole were successful because, in a time of prosperity, with costs of living rising, it was nearly always possible to gain some sort of favorable award out of an arbitration.

The most vital legal battle over the Railway Labor Act arose out of a case in Texas wherein one of the subsidiaries of the Southern Pacific, the T. & N.O. Railroad Company, having been enjoined against violations of the act, challenged its constitutionality. This was the test case for which I had been waiting.

It had been my conviction that we should not risk a test of the constitutionality of the law until it had been in successful operation long enough to create a strong public sentiment in its favor, and until a case arose in which we had clear proof of the violation of a vital provision of the law.

The details of the lawsuit need no tiresome recital. In substance, the management of the railroad had refused to recognize the authority of officers of the clerks' organization to represent their members in collective bargaining. An injunction suit was brought in Texas for the purpose of compelling this recognition. Happily the evidence in the case was so clear that we had no fear of either losing or winning the case on a minor point. The railroad was indeed forced to make its major argument on its contention that the law was unconstitutional.

It should be realized that up to this time the federal government had passed no law compelling employers to deal with a labor organization of their employees. In favor of the employer's position were the earlier decisions of the Supreme Court in the famous Adair and Coppage cases in which the Court had sustained the constitutional right of employers to refuse to employ or to discharge men because of membership in a labor organization.

In addition to this fundamental defense of an employer's liberty of contract, the railroad also made the point that the regulation of interstate commerce which was authorized in Congress by the Constitution could not be extended to the control of labor relations between the railroad management and employees. The defense of the constitutionality of the Railway Labor Act, therefore, rested on two difficult propositions. The Court must either overrule or distinguish the Adair and Coppage cases, and the Court must extend interstate commerce power to cover labor relations in or affecting interstate commerce. Until the decision of the T. & N.O. case there was a strong basis for the contentions of a railroad management that discrimination against union members could not be forbidden by law, and that labor relations in interstate commerce were beyond the Congressional power of regulation.

There were two events preceding our argument in the Supreme Court which gave us considerable assistance. In the first place, a most persuasive opinion of the lower court sustaining the injunction had been written by Judge Joseph C. Hutcheson, Jr., a judge of great ability and forceful power of expression.

In the second place, former Justice Hughes had been appointed Chief Justice by President Hoover. In the course of a struggle before the Senate Judiciary Committee over his confirmation, he had been both attacked and defended as to the liberality of his views particularly on the subject of labor. There was a particular opposition to his confirmation from labor organizations on the ground that he had been representing big business for many years and had a conservative predilection which unfitted him for impartial service as Chief Justice. In the light of his subsequent record, the opposition appears to have been ill founded. However, after Hughes was confirmed we went before the Supreme Court with a certain comforting assurance that, in view of the criticisms of his confirmation, he was not likely to demonstrate any reactionary partisanship for business management. We felt that he would be anxious to demonstrate his impartiality, and we felt our case was so strong that an impartial judge would sustain our position. Our expectations were borne out when the Court handed down a unanimous opinion written by Chief Justice Hughes sustaining the constitutionality of the law.

About the time this case was decided in the Supreme Court, another case affecting railway labor was on its way to that august tribunal.

A suit in Arizona was brought jointly by the Southern Pacific and the Santa Fe railroads in which they sought to enjoin the Attorney General from enforcing the state train limit law. The state law limited the length of freight trains to seventy cars and passenger trains to fourteen. The railway labor organizations had fought for such laws in various states on the ground that longer trains were dangerous to life and limb of the employees, as well as to the safety of passengers and the security of livestock.

The employees had assembled a mass of evidence to show injuries resulting from long train operations. On the other hand, the railroads contended that the train limit laws were just "make work" laws, to require more trains to be run and more workers to be employed. Since the evidence was bound to be extensive, the Federal Court in Arizona referred the case to a commissioner to take testimony.

As a result, beginning in 1929, I spent a large part of three years in Arizona acting as special assistant attorney general, although my compensation was paid by the labor organizations. This offered a rare opportunity to a practicing lawyer to spend his winters in the salubrious climate of Arizona at the expense of his clients.

The summons to participate in this case came in the middle of August 1929, when the prospect of going to Arizona, where a temperaure of 110° was regarded as comfortable, did not appeal to me. In fact, I so dreaded the trip across the hot plains of Kansas and Nebraska that I made a special effort to go by airplane. It is amusing to recall now how difficult this was in 1929. First, I took a night train from Chicago to Kansas City. There I boarded a plane which dropped me in northern Arizona in the afternoon. In the evening I boarded the sleeper from Williams, Arizona, to Phoenix. Thus I saved an entire day in the railroad trip, and I was able to boast that I was only thirty-six hours away from Chicago, which I think was a record trip at that time!

There were many amusing incidents of my early experience in Phoenix. I installed a thermometer in the hotel room, which was air-conditioned, and found it often registered as low as 98°! I got another thermometer and placed it in the back of the Ford coupé I had rented. Throughout my stay it never registered below 110° in the daytime. The first day I was there I went to a doctor to find out what I should eat and drink in the unaccustomed heat. When I said tentatively, "I suppose I should not drink any alcohol," he replied: "On the contrary, it would probably be a good idea for you to take a couple of highballs in the evening." "Fine and dandy," I said. "Can you give me a prescription?" (This was during Prohibition.) "Well," he said, "we are not allowed to prescribe whisky, but you ask any bellboy in the hotel and he will be glad to get it for you."

Certainly the transportation and sale of illegal liquor was well organized in Arizona. All that was necessary was to call a number furnished by a friend and within a reasonable time a man would drive up to your house with a tin of bathtub gin or corn liquor reposing under the hood of the car. From then on the illegality was all yours.

I remember a conversation I had one day in Phoenix with the clerk of the Federal Court. I mentioned that the previous day, in sentencing a couple of bootleggers for transporting liquor from El Paso, the judge had facetiously remarked: "I am not going to permit such competition with our Arizona bootleggers." The clerk replied seriously: "Oh, that's no joke. I wish the Judge hadn't said that because the federal men get most of their tips from the Arizona bootleggers who don't like that competition."

As to the final outcome of the Arizona train limit case, after many months (I might almost say years) vast volumes of testimony were taken and the commissioner made his findings in favor of the railroads. Then, since this was a suit to enjoin the operation of a state law, the case went to a three-judge court which convened in San Francisco. It was presided over by Circuit Judge Wilbur (brother of Secretary of the Interior Wilbur) and included the Arizona district judge, Jacobs, and another San Francisco district judge, St. Sure.

Before the case could be argued, however, an election had taken place. The Attorney General whom I represented had run for governor and had been defeated and a new Attorney General had been elected. The railroads moved to substitute the name of the new Attorney General. When we were brought before the three-judge court I had to oppose this substitution on the ground that the suit was a personal one against the Attorney General who had insisted on enforcing the train limit law.

The new Attorney General had taken the official position that he would have to study the case to determine whether or not he would enforce the law. He declined to be substituted voluntarily, and under the law I contended he could not be substituted compulsorily. Although the law was clearly in my favor, the judges announced, without any opinion, that the substitution was granted and the motion to dismiss the case was denied.

Thereupon, to the extreme surprise of the railroad attorneys and also the Court, Assistant Attorney General Strouss and I picked up our briefcases and I informed the Court that, since we had no client to represent in the argument, we would have to withdraw from the case. My position was that no judgment could be entered against the former Attorney General, because he was no longer concerned, and the new Attorney General could not be made a party against his will.

The case was argued by the railroads and it was quite obvious the Court would decide in their favor. I immediately went East and filed a petition for mandamus in the Supreme Court to order the judges to expunge their illegal order. The petition was granted and after argument the Court held that under the statute the new Attorney General could not be compulsorily substituted for the old one, so the case must be dismissed. This was the peculiar triumphant end of three years of litigation.

During the time of the Arizona and Texas cases, the country was moving from an inflated prosperity into the worst depression of our national experience. Its effect on me personally can be briefly described. I had cautiously invested such savings as I could make out of a very active but not exceptionally profitable practice almost entirely in bonds, particularly municipal bonds. The percentage of these bonds which were defaulted was a sad lesson to a man who had sought to disprove the common saying that lawyers take great care of everybody's money but their own. To my sorrow, I found that the stock advice of investing in real estate and bonds in a time of deflation had not saved me from heavy losses. I sold my house when I moved to Washington, for about one-third of the money I put into it.

From the standpoint of earning power, however, the depression years were times of increasing income, owing to the enormous amount of work which I carried for solvent clients, so I maintained a comfortable private economy until I became a "tax eating bureaucrat" in Washington with an income of about one-third of my previous private income. However, the work for the railway labor organizations changed rapidly from aggressive campaigns for increased wages and improved working conditions to a defensive campaign to prevent wage reductions and to hold onto diminishing jobs for the workers. I took part in a great many legislative activities in Washington, in which various efforts were made to transform the government from a mere protector of private enterprise into a fostering angel. As I look back upon these efforts, most of them appear to have been poorly designed, but they helped to develop a national psychology which condemned the Hoover administration for its failure to achieve the impossible and hurled into the White House Franklin D. Roosevelt with his optimistic and courageous cry for action.

There was one really constructive action in the depression period for which railway labor and management deserve great credit That was the negotiation between all the railroads and all the labor organizations which resulted on February 1, 1932, in an agreed temporary reduction of wage rates by 10 per cent. This was described by Daniel Willard as the greatest reduction in wages (about $300,000,000) ever voluntarily agreed to by organized labor. This statesmanlike procedure contrasted favorably with such nonsensical proposals as to relieve unemployment and a nation-wide depression by reducing the length of the work day and maintaining the same daily wage—thus increasing the cost of goods and services that couldn't be sold at prevailing prices!

I take particular pride in this railway labor-management agreement because in the final stages I had to take the responsibility and hazard of openly fighting for, and winning the support of, some twelve hundred labor representatives against the opposition of some of the chief labor executives who were my nominal clients. Naturally there was much satisfaction and relief to me in the gradual restoration of the original wage rates which was completed in April 1935.

CHAPTER XII

From Hoover to Roosevelt

MY ACQUAINTANCE with Herbert Hoover, which began in the course of his campaign in 1928 for the Republican nomination, was due to the bipartisan activity of the railway labor unions for whose cooperative organization (the Railway Labor Executives Association) I was general counsel after the passage of the Railway Labor Act in 1926 until I accepted the position of general counsel for the NRA in 1933.

These unions were generally favorable to William G. McAdoo for the Democratic nomination in 1928 since he had been their great friend when he was director general in control of all the railroads, which were taken over by the government in World War I. But they were properly fearful of another Republican victory and were most anxious that someone like Herbert Hoover (who had made a valiant effort to settle the shopmen's strike during the Harding administration) rather than such a conservative as Charles G. Dawes should receive the Republican nomination.

My old friend in political and newspaper enterprises, Walter S. Rogers, who had been cable censor in World War I, had worked closely with Mr. Hoover, and through him I felt I knew a great deal about this man. However, I must confess I was deeply worried in my early meetings with him, and often later, by his persistent habit of not looking at one squarely when in conversation, and of doodling steadily the while. It gave one the impression that he was not much interested in what was being said and did not want anyone to know what he was thinking. But, as the result of many more contacts in later years I have come to the conclusion that the unhappy impression which he made on comparative strangers was due to an essential shyness on his part, and perhaps also a desire not to hurt other people's feelings. Always a man of intellectual strength and strong convictions, I am sure he must have had to school himself not to reveal to many with whom he talked his poor opinion of their views or suggestions.

One friend of mine who knew Mr. Hoover very well and who went to him with a rather complicated solution of a pressing current problem, told me that he talked steadily for twenty minutes while Mr. Hoover shuffled papers and doodled designs on blank sheets. When he ran out of words, Mr. Hoover looked up suddenly and uttered one violent expletive. My friend said he judged Mr. Hoover didn't think much of his idea, so he pursued the matter no further.

Although Mr. Hoover and I had many serious disagreements over the years, and particularly when I was an aggressive member of the Franklin Roosevelt administration and he was an outstanding critic, I have had genial associations with him, especially in recent years. I learned to admire profoundly his intellectual integrity, the strength of his convictions and his deep devotion to principles of government, economics and morality in which he consistently believed and for which he persistently fought and for many years under most discouraging conditions.

Also, I know from private conversations that the humor which he injects occasionally in his public utterances is genuine and not a product of any literary aides.

The impatience of my early political attitudes may be indicated by the fact that, after playing a trifling part in aid of Hoover's nomination, I became so annoyed at what seemed to me his undue conservatism during the campaign that I transferred my allegiance to Al Smith, the Democratic candidate, and presided at the last campaign meeting addressed by Governor Smith in Chicago. Nevertheless, when Mr. Hoover was duly elected I did endeavor, from time to time, to render some small services to him, although these were usually in support of some interest of my labor union clients. For many years, however, I was either in opposition to him or trying to get him to do something he did not want to do. I have a cartoon hanging in my house which represents a football practice of New Dealers against the opposition in which I was represented as assailing a large tackling dummy marked "Hoover Article," and Ickes was attacking the "Liberty League." We were being backed up by Hopkins and Wallace, with the "Quarterback F.D.R." shouting: "Hit 'em hard and low, boys. We'll be ready for 'em in November!" Since this cartoon is dated 1934, it is quite evident that Mr. Hoover and I were on opposite sides in that campaign.

Years later, in 1940, at a summer encampment, I joined with the chairman of the program committee in an effort to induce Mr. Hoover to make one of the informal speeches which were called "lakeside talks." We were a particularly inept committee of two since the committee chairman was a member of the Stanford Faculty who had always been outspoken in his opposition to Mr. Hoover's policies. Obviously I had not endeared myself to the ex-President. Our pleas were definitely unsuccessful, but others eventually persuaded Mr. Hoover to talk, although he had assured me that "nobody is interested in what I have to say." I assured him quite honestly that everyone was interested, even those who disagreed with him.

One enigma about Mr. Hoover's public life constantly bothered me: how could a public man of such exceptional intellectual power be completely lacking in popular appeal? If he had been as dour and misanthropic as he was frequently represented, he could never have inspired the strong personal loyalty that was characteristic of his intimate associates. If he had been lacking in real devotion to public service, he would never have gone through the long years of public misunderstanding in which he gallantly and persistently espoused unpopular public policies. He would have retired to a pleasant obscurity, either satisfied with his own righteousness or embittered by reverses, instead of fulfilling the part of a great public servant long after the time when there was any possibility that he would again attain the great powers of high office.

My personal conclusion has been that Mr. Hoover had more intellectual power and a more intelligent understanding of what was good for the American people than any President of my lifetime. By that I do not mean that he was the greatest President. Rather, he stands out as an example of the fact that pure intelligence and a high idealism of public service are not the primary qualities for the Presidency. The basic requirement is the ability to sell one's self to the public and to gain the confidence of the masses that one is a fearless leader who will lead them where they want to go.

I still believe that if Mr. Hoover had met the problems of the depression with a really huge program of public works, and adequate measures for emergency relief of distressed farmers and unemployed industrial workers, he might have hastened the end of the depression, perhaps even in time to permit of his re-election.

Although the tremendous expenditures and supports for agriculture and industrial labor that were projected in the Roosevelt administration did not end a huge unemployment problem, they did raise new hopes and inspire new activities among the American people which turned them away for a time at least from even more radical political programs. It was only preparations for and participation in World War II that finally made possible the utilization of all the manpower and natural resources of the United States. But the fact that we could incur an enormous national debt for the prosecution of a war with its inevitable waste of human lives and of natural and accumulated wealth did demonstrate that we could have mortgaged our future in 1931 for a few billion dollars in order to get back on our feet, just as sometimes a business enterprise which goes into a slump can well afford to go in debt for constructive improvements which will eventually pay off its debt and permanently improve its income.

It seems to me that if Mr. Hoover's intense conviction that a government should be operated as conservatively as a large business enterprise had been moderated temporarily by emergency demands, and if he had been for a time inspired by a Rooseveltian boldness in risking huge expenditures and debt to relieve immediately widespread distress, the welfare of the United States might have been better served by a continuation of his administration.

On the other hand, I can see, as I have heretofore pointed out, that the times were ripe, and rotten ripe, for a change. If Mr. Hoover had been able to preserve the dominant influence of big business organizations over the economy of the nation, he himself had too keen an understanding of the abuses of economic and financial power that had played their part in producing the depression to have regarded the increasing concentration of such power with equanimity. It was the more liberal and progressive elements in the Republican Party which made possible Mr. Hoover's nomination and election. It was the humanitarians and intellectuals who supported him against the inflexible conservatives and time-serving politicians who had brought about the nomination of Senator Harding, and who later transferred their allegiance to Calvin Coolidge as a "safe" man who would not move forward one step so long as it was possible to stand still.

When Democratic orators and Left-Wing Republicans lump together the Harding-Coolidge-Hoover administrations as examples of the ruinous effect of big business controls over the government of the United States, they do Mr. Hoover a great injustice. He was always a staunch believer in private enterprise. While he saw "creeping socialism" in many government activities that seemed to those who espoused them only necessary expansions of public services, he was no reactionary, no lead-footed or wooden-headed opponent of all change. He was a wise man, skeptical of whether every change or alleged reform was necessarily progress.

The failure of President Hoover's efforts to lift the country out of the depths of the depression produced an overwhelming demand for a change of administration. The difficulty of opposition to President Hoover's natural desire for renomination, combined with a Republican sense of defeatism, made any change through the Republican Party appear impossible.

The stage was obviously set for the entry of such a candidate as Franklin D. Roosevelt as the hero of the new drama. He had attained national fame and considerable praise as governor of New York. He was an old opponent of Tammany (and yet Tammany would have to support him), which took away that stigma from a New York Democrat. He was distinctly a Democrat of the progressive Wilson tradition and yet a man of personal wealth and associations which should allay the fears of the owners and managers of large properties.

The bravery with which he had overcome his physical limitations would counteract any such brutal criticism as an opposition newspaper man had made to me when he asked, "Why did the Democrats have to nominate a cripple?" As a matter of fact, he bore his infirmities with such apparent disregard that even those who became intimate with him, as I did, were never conscious of the fact that he actually had no use of his legs and could not stand or walk without support. I remember well the surprise expressed by a sympathetic newspaper woman who spoke to me of her shock on seeing him carried up to the platform at the Convention to accept the Democratic nomination. A year or more later, when I used to swim with him in the White House pool, I was always more impressed by his magnificent torso than by the fact that he could not use what he called his "bad legs."

The railway labor unions early made up their minds that he was their choice for President, although some of the chiefs and their constituents, particularly in the older, higher-paid brotherhoods, were ordinarily more inclined to the Republican than the Democratic Party. As general counsel for the unions I made arrangements for a meeting of the labor executives with Roosevelt, who was still governor, in Albany. I was personally strongly inclined toward his candidacy because practically all my progressive friends in the Congress and throughout the country favored him. Indeed, Senator Norris, nominally a Republican, had aroused great enthusiasm at a gathering of Progressives in Washington in the fall of 1931, by asserting stoutly that "what the country needs is another Roosevelt in the White House." Many unsympathetic newspaper men, supposedly familiar with the Governor's administration in New York, persisted in asserting that he was inclined to be weak and compromising and would not make a strong President. But others just as stoutly asserted that he had unusual force of character and that he would at least do something; it might not be wise but it would be something.

When my labor clients gathered in Albany I made a careful list of their names and organizations and had a preliminary interview with Governor Roosevelt, explaining the personality of each executive and identifying him with the type of employees he represented. He was surprised and delighted to find that all the organizations were represented; and pleased by this preliminary briefing. He at once decided that the crowd was too large for his small study where he had expected to receive them. He had them seated instead in a much larger room, which required him to hobble in to the gathering, giving me an early example of his lack of self-consciousness in exhibiting his crippled condition to strangers on whom he desired to make a favorable impression.

The meeting was a very pleasant and fruitful one and my part in arranging it evidently pleased the Governor, for, in referring to me shortly thereafter to one of his associates, he said: "There's a man I want to have near me in Washington." I quote this as an interesting example of the quickness if not of the wisdom of his judgments.

After F.D.R. had been nominated I had an appointment to see him in New York City. A suggestion had been made to me that I might be of some assistance in the ensuing campaign. On the way to New York from Chicago I stopped in Washington and dropped in on Speaker Garner who was the Vice Presidential candidate. I told him that I was going to see Roosevelt and I would be glad to have any suggestions for the campaign that he cared to have me transmit.

The Speaker mentioned the fact that he had not seen his running mate since the nomination, but he would like me to take one message to him. This message, which I quote with only slight necessary revisions, was in substance: "Tell the Governor that he is the boss and we will all follow him to hell if we have to, but if he goes too far with some of these wild-eyed ideas we are going to have the stuffing kicked out of us." I felt a little embarrassed to deliver this message from the Vice Presidential candidate to the Presidential candidate but promised to do so. My embarrassment was increased when I finally met Governor Roosevelt in his library in the company of Mrs. Roosevelt and Louis Howe. However, I carried my message to Garcia, which tickled F.D.R. immensely.

As a result of my offer to help if I could in the preparation of campaign speeches, particularly on the subject of the railroads about which I was fairly well informed, he said: "Go to Columbia University and see Ray Moley, Rex Tugwell and Adolph Berle. They are working up some material for me on all sorts of questions." Thus came about my introduction to the "brain trust" in which for a period of some years I had at times an active, and at times what might be called an associate, membership.

These were three brilliant men, but of very different personalities and abilities.

Adolph Berle, an infant prodigy, maintained to maturity the intellect of a worldly chess player. He might get fantastic ideas, as when he once suggested to me that it was time to issue a "manifesto" of the "Roosevelt Revolution." But usually he kept his feet on the ground even when his mind was soaring.

Rex Tugwell was always so considerate in manner that one could ignore, or might even fail to note, the slight condescension with which he would try to explain what was what to the unenlightened who ventured to disagree with him.

Raymond Moley was the all-around political scientist. He had the combination of vision and shrewd energy that equipped him ideally to serve F.D.R.'s needs. His elimination from the inner circle (largely by intrigues of the palace guard) did more harm to Roosevelt than to Moley, whose life must have been lengthened by escape from the tortures of living in a goldfish bowl.

My contributions to the campaign speeches in 1932 were largely confined to those dealing with the problems of the steam transportation industry and labor relations. My most helpful work, however, in that campaign consisted in the organization of the National Progressive League, of which Senator Norris was honorary chairman and I was the executive chairman. The purpose of this league was to bring into open support of the Democratic candidate those progressive Republicans who could be regarded as inheritors of Theodore Roosevelt's progressivism. Notable among those brought into this organization was Henry A. Wallace. One of those who caused me most anxious hours was Senator Hiram Johnson of California. He was definitely in favor of Roosevelt, but he leaned at that time considerably on the advice of Harold L. Ickes who had managed one of his campaigns for the Presidential nomination and who had been a partner in my law firm for ten years beginning in 1913. In 1923 I had left my firm, not on account of any disagreements but because I desired to devote myself almost exclusively to my local and national engagements in public utility valuation and regulation proceedings, and to my work for the railway labor organizations. Both these activities ran contrary to many of the interests of large corporate clients of the office and it seemed to all of us that we would be better off if we separated our offices.

In retrospect I may say that this separation from the old firm, which had originated when my father began to practice law in 1868, proved to be highly advantageous to all concerned. My former law firm went ahead to build up an enormous practice which has made it in recent years one of the largest and most successful in Chicago. I was freed from the burdens of a miscellaneous practice and the adjustment of the many problems of a growing law partnership, and could specialize in those branches of law in which I was particularly interested and which provided me with a very satisfactory income.

It has been necessary to make this digression from the campaign of 1932 to explain one reason why I now found it very difficult to induce Harold Ickes and, through him, Senator Johnson to join in the work of the National Progressive League. Ickes had many good qualities which, along with some peculiarities, have been well advertised in the last twenty years. One of his peculiarities, which may have been a source of strength, was his desire to run any job in which he participated and a distinct disinclination to take a subordinate position. He quite naturally did not care to play second fiddle to his former partner who was not only a younger man but had had much less experience in practical politics than he had had. Messages came to me from the East inquiring why I could not bring Harold Ickes and Senator Johnson into the campaign. I did not want to explain that in a somewhat peevish moment Ickes had indicated that he was not sure he wanted to support Roosevelt, because I felt sure that in the end he would do so. Eventually a scheme was worked out whereby Ickes was specifically authorized to organize his own pro-Roosevelt committee and to accept the responsibility and honor of having induced Senator Johnson to join in the parade.

When the campaign was over and Roosevelt had been triumphantly elected I had to spend considerable time in Washington on legal work prior to the inauguration and was so wearied with capital gossip, politics and crowds that, instead of staying for the inauguration, I took a train for Chicago and listened over the radio to Roosevelt's great inaugural address. There I felt part of the thrill which went through the nation at his resolute demand for action. Immediately thereafter I received a telegram from Senator La Follette (the son of the old Senator) which read in substance: "Come at once to Washington. Great things are under way."

On my return I found the Progressives among both Democrats and Republicans seething with excitement and anticipation. The time apparently had come when, under the leadership of an aggressive, courageous President great experiments could be undertaken to bring about temporary relief from distress, and to devise permanent remedies for avoiding any repetition of the economic disasters that had followed the collapse of 1929.

Harold Ickes had been named Secretary of the Interior, which I was happy to see, although I did not foresee the outstanding record he was to make as an administrator. I do not mean to indicate that I was in accord with all his ideas or projects, but I think even his bitterest enemies concluded that he showed great executive ability and a most unusual capacity for supervising the expenditure of enormous public funds without any of the accompanying scandals for which few high public officials are directly chargeable but for which they will often be held indirectly responsible.

At the time of Ickes' appointment, I incurred his deep and probably justified displeasure by refusing to recommend it to the President. As he himself has explained in his autobiography, he needed someone to place his name before the President-elect. It was finally done at the eleventh hour by Mr. Mullen of Nebraska, who had been disappointed in his ambition to be named Attorney General and wanted at least the satisfaction of being responsible for the naming of another Cabinet officer. But for a long time Harold was deeply embarrassed because progressive senators like Johnson, Cutting, La Follette and Costigan, although willing to endorse him, were not willing to request the President to name him. This was reasonable on their part because the position had been offered to both Senator Johnson and Senator Cutting and none of the senators wanted to be in the position of having asked for and received payment of a political debt by the naming at their request of a member of the Cabinet.

My own reasons were similar. I had no wish to appear to be exploiting my chairmanship of the National Progressive League by seeking to have a high appointment made at my request. I was not a candidate for any office myself, although I knew that one or more senators had suggested my name to the President as a possible appointee for Attorney General, which I was sure was not even a remote possibility. Furthermore, I had an idea, which I have since learned was naïve, that a President would only wish to appoint persons whom he knew very well and whom he personally desired to serve in such a close relationship.

The notable "first hundred days" of the Roosevelt administration were momentous ones for me. I made more decisions and took more actions profoundly affecting my own future than at any other time in my life. Rumors constantly floated in to me that I was about to be appointed to some office and from these rumors emerged a few interesting incidents.

One day Professor Felix Frankfurter of Harvard Law School telephoned me to arrange a meeting on a nearby park bench. When we met, he said to me very bluntly, "You don't want to be named Solicitor General, do you?" and indicated his disapprobation of the idea. I told him the office had not been offered to me. But it was apparent from his talk that I could have it if I wanted it. I explained that as a lawyer I would rather be Solicitor General of the United States than occupy any other public position except possibly a place on the Supreme Court; but that I had very heavy financial demands upon me which could only be met out of the substantial income from my private law practice. Therefore, much as I would really like to be appointed Solicitor General, I could not accept the position if it were offered me.

Felix was obviously relieved although I never did understand his objections to me. Apparently he had no other candidate and I am sure he had no part in the naming of the amiable Crawford Biggs whom Roosevelt appointed his first Solicitor General. Frankfurter was certainly not unfriendly to me, because years later when the possibility of a Supreme Court appointment developed he assured me that I was his favorite choice, although subsequently, when I deviated from policies and programs which he espoused, he became definitely opposed to my appointment to the high bench.

The next rumor arose from a suggestion made, I believe by Ray Moley, that the President would like to appoint me as counsel for the Bureau of Internal Revenue. I was able to brush this aside very quickly by explaining that, if I were unable to consider the post of Solicitor General I certainly could not consider this appointment. The reason why the President allegedly wanted me as counsel was amusing. He was uncertain as to whether the man he was appointing Commissioner of Internal Revenue was a good choice. With his well-known caution, therefore, he sought to counteract a possible mistake by appointing as counsel another man in whom he had confidence and who would be in a position to exercise both a helpful influence and a restraining hand on the Commissioner.

Just when I thought the rumors were subsiding Joseph B. Eastman, Commissioner of Interstate Commerce and a close friend of mine, said to me quizzically one day when we were resting after squash racquets: "Have you heard about the latest job for which you are being considered?" I had heard a rumor which I could hardly believe, but, knowing that Joe's sources of information would be much more reliable than a whisper from an elevator operator, I answered: "What have you heard?" He said: "I understand it is Comptroller of the Currency." "Well," I said, "at least there is precedent for appointing a lawyer who knows nothing about finance. Cleveland appointed James H. Eckels to that job. He was only a Chicago lawyer, but on the basis of his governmental experience, subsequently became head of one of our largest banks." However, in spite of the dazzling picture of a future free of economic worries that might result from this appointment, my own feeling of utter incapacity for the job fortified my previous objection on the ground of my existing economic responsibilities.

Many times I had wondered how seriously these possible appointments had been considered by the President. But my doubts were somewhat settled when I had a talk with him one day about some pending legislation. When I was leaving, he looked up at me with a grin and said: "I'll get you in this administration yet." I believe that at that time one of the chief reasons for the President's interest in me lay in the fact that, in our many conferences and discussions during this period, I never hesitated to say exactly what I thought and to disagree amiably with the President when I felt I must. In those days he enjoyed the frankness and lack of deference with which the original "brain trusters" and I discussed problems without that yes-yessing with which so many men, either because of their own lack of convictions or from pure sycophancy, defer to men in high office and particularly to the President of the United States. Typical of our discussions was one in which I had taken part when a delegation was opposing one phase of a program on which the President had embarked. I lingered for a moment after the delegation had left the room and said to him very earnestly: "I think, Mr. President, we can be most helpful to you by opposing you in this matter." He looked up at Secretary McIntyre who was standing beside him, and with an entirely genial laugh said: "That's a new one, Mac, isn't it?"

CHAPTER XIII

Franklin D. Roosevelt—My First Boss

A LAWYER in general practice has no single boss. He may be required to conform to a considerable extent to the wishes of his clients, but unless he accepts exclusive employment by one client he does not have a boss to whose policies and programs he must either conform or resign his job. In my own experience prior to 1933 I had a few large clients, such as the railway unions or the city of Chicago, and quite a number of smaller clients. But I had no sense of subservience to anyone.

Although I had served as general counsel for the Railway Labor Executives Association for about seven years, I had by my own desire no fixed retainer, salary or employment. I had made an arrangement whereby I agreed to serve as general counsel at a fixed per diem plus expenses with the understanding that if at any time we disagreed, I could quit or they could end my services.

When, however, I accepted a position in the Roosevelt administration, it became evident to me that for the time being I had acquired a boss, although a very easy one. A public official chosen by the President accepts a definite responsibility to support the policies and programs of the Chief Executive. He cannot criticize them publicly or decline to carry them out, without a definite disloyalty. If his disagreement is deep enough to impair his cooperation or to trouble his conscience, he should resign. In my case, although I was general counsel of the NRA, nominally selected by General Hugh Johnson, the administrator, he was not actually my boss. I only accepted the position at the direct request of President Roosevelt as an opportunity to serve him and his administration.

From the very beginning of his administration one of the President's major problems had been to determine what the government should do to bring about an industrial recovery that would put millions of unemployed workers back to work. There were a hundred schemes laid before the President, varying from highly radical controls of business by government to comparatively mild programs of expanding the work of the Reconstruction Finance Corporation or the inauguration of great public works which would directly and indirectly insure vastly increased industrial employment. I had participated particularly in projects for public works expansion. In collaboration with Senators La Follette, Costigan and Cutting, I had drafted in 1932 a bill providing for a huge program of public works financed directly by the federal government. The theory of this was that by "priming the pump" with a large government expenditure for worthwhile construction, there would be an immediate increase in industrial employment which, like a nuclear reaction, would start a chain of industrial activities.

At this same time the American Federation of Labor was backing a program embodied in the bill introduced by Senator Hugo Black to provide for a thirty-hour week, thus spreading employment. This theory was regarded by many as merely sharing the poverty, and fundamentally unsound. I agreed with this school of thought. What we needed was more production, more employment and more purchasing power and not merely a somewhat arbitrary effort to pay more men more for doing less work, since of course the labor organizations did not propose to allow the earning power of employees diminished. But, as support for the Black bill began to increase, it was obvious that the administration could not long delay the initiation of some industrial program that would appeal not only to the labor unions but to millions of unemployed workers and to the industrial managers whose initiative and energy would be essential to industrial recovery.

Raymond Moley had been commissioned by the President to serve as a sort of clearing house for industrial recovery plans. At the suggestion of Bernard Baruch, Moley enlisted the services of General Hugh S. Johnson to work out a comparatively short and simple program in the form of an industrial recovery bill. General Johnson was not particularly familiar with the labor phase of this problem and had been advised by Moley to get my cooperation in drafting the bill with a view to inducing the support of organized labor. After he and I had been working on this project for some time a conference was called by the President at which the sponsors of several fairly definite programs were invited to present their views.

The trend of the discussions at this conference led to two major programs, one along the lines of General Johnson's industrial recovery bill and the other embracing the best features of several programs for heavy expenditures for public works. After the arguments of these two schools of thought had been thoroughly advanced, but without reconciliation, the President asked me for an opinion, since I had been silent while various senators and other conferees had been expressing themselves volubly. As I had worked on the drafting of a public works bill and also on the drafting of General Johnson's bill, I was in a good position to say that I thought there was nothing irreconcilable in the two major contentions.

This appealed to the President who very shortly ended the discussion with the statement that he was going to appoint a committee which was to be locked up in a room and instructed to bring out a brief but comprehensive bill which he hoped might merit the support of all those present who were striving toward the same objective. With his customary diplomacy he did not name the committee until after the conferees had departed. Then he designated Secretary Perkins of Labor, Assistant Secretary Tugwell of Agriculture, Assistant Secretary Dickinson of Commerce, Director of the Budget Douglas, Senator Wagner, General Johnson and myself. After a few sessions, the three officials of Labor, Agriculture and Commerce ceased active participation in the work, all of them being loaded down with administrative duties in their departments. This probably accounts for the confused and rather inaccurate explanation of the drafting of the Recovery Act included in Miss Perkins' book *The Roosevelt I Knew*. Douglas, Wagner,

Johnson and I worked almost continuously for several days in the office of the director of the budget who kept in close touch with the President until we four had finally completed the bill which eventually became, with a few revisions, the National Industrial Recovery Act.

As soon as the bill was introduced in both houses, coincident with a strong message from the President, it became rumored that General Johnson would be named administrator. The General himself had recommended the appointment of Bernard Baruch in view of his highly successful service in a similar capacity for President Wilson in the First World War. It is interesting that, as Miss Perkins later wrote, Baruch himself thought that Johnson was a good "number three" or "number two" man (as in his service to Baruch) but too unstable to be made a "number one" man.

However, when the newspapers generally began to discuss General Johnson as the oncoming administrator of the National Industrial Recovery Act the possibility of Baruch's appointment receded rapidly. I always had my suspicions that Johnson himself was responsible for the leak to the press. It was also my impression that the President did not want to name Baruch. He may have felt that to appoint a man of great wealth and large industrial interests would be regarded as turning the administration over to a notable representative of big business. Or possibly the President wanted personally to control the administration of the new law and preferred not to have as strong-minded an individual as Baruch in a position to run the show according to his own ideas.

Whatever the reason, the President definitely decided to name General Johnson who promptly informed me that he wanted me to serve as general counsel, fortifying this invitation with the suggestion that the President also wanted me.

For the many reasons which had previously deterred me from either seeking or accepting any public office, I was not anxious to become general counsel. I was, however, vitally interested in seeing whether the program which we had devised would work. I finally asked the President whether he really wanted me to take over the job of general counsel, and if so, why. His answer shed a definite light upon a notable characteristic of his administration.

It was no reflection on General Johnson that the President did not feel sure of how effective an administrator he would make. It was, indeed, quite characteristic of President Roosevelt that, through caution or a desire to keep all the reins of government either in his hands or within close reach, he repeatedly divided authority in such a manner that he could always balance the recommendations of one administrator against the opinions of perhaps a subordinate or someone of equal and confusing co-authority.

The difficulties which arose between Secretary Hull and Assistant Secretary Moley are a matter of history. But the frequently divergent views of Secretary Hull and Under Secretary Welles, which for a long time were not so apparent, were of more lasting consequence. In my own later experiences in the administration I found it frequently difficult to determine whether the President was relying on one of two or three persons of overlapping or interlocking authority, or whether he really was not relying on anyone's judgment except his own.

So at the outset of my public service I found myself in the somewhat difficult position of being not only an adviser to General Johnson but also an adviser to the President, a lawyer who was expected to present his own views and to follow his own policies, if they met with the approval of the President, without subordinating them to any different views or policies of his technical superior. General Johnson himself thoroughly understood the situation. Although he resented and opposed any direct relationship between the President and his own deputy administrators, he accepted without criticism my increasingly intimate relationship with the President, even when it had reached the somewhat tragic situation where the President was anxious to relieve General Johnson of his single-handed authority and to reorganize the command of the NRA under a board.

Another difficulty in my appointment was caused by my insistence that my salary should be large enough to relieve me of some of the financial strain that was going to be inevitable. The salary was finally set at $14,000 which was as much as was attainable, without serious objection from Cabinet officers who were paid $15,000. This was at a time, however, when all federal salaries, which could be reduced, were made subject to the 15 per cent reduction that was imposed as a gesture to carry out the "economy" promises of the Presidential campaign. It is probably generally forgotten that the Roosevelt administration started out as an economy administration.

Thus, despite the 15 per cent deduction, I had the dubious honor of being acclaimed the highest-paid government official short of the Cabinet. This was never referred to in the press as a creditable matter but rather as an indication that I was a greedy tax eater, which was particularly annoying inasmuch as I had to exhaust all my cash resources in the course of the two years' service in public office. The difficulty of maintaining a position of increasing responsibility in Washington made the problem of household economies one of continual distress both to me and to my wife.

The beginning of my service as general counsel was marked by the sudden imposition of extraordinary responsibilities which set the pattern for the next two long years. I was unable to take on the work during the first few days when General Johnson was establishing headquarters in the Department of Commerce building because I had to settle up some pending problems affecting the railway labor unions before I could properly resign my work with them. When I finally arrived at the bare and largely unfurnished office of the NRA I found we were on the eve of the first public hearing of the first proposed code—the textile code—with no program for the conduct of the hearings. William Allen, the deputy administrator, although a very competent business man, was completely unprepared for the job of conducting an unprecedented taking of evidence on which to establish a code for an entire industry.

I found a vacant desk with one chair which I offered to a very competent young lady, a Miss Elliott who, as a result of this sudden introduction, became my secretary. I sat on the edge of the desk and dictated a single page of items of procedure for the public hearing on a code. Having had long experience in protracted arbitrations and confused committee hearings up on the Hill, I had definite ideas as to what we ought to avoid. As a result, in this one-page outline I laid down rules that shocked most lawyers and politicians.

All witnesses would be examined by the presiding administrator;

no direct or cross examination by lawyers would be permitted; witnesses would testify as to facts and not make arguments; any arguments which lawyers wished to make, or any legal issues which they wished to raise, would be submitted in the form of written briefs filed with the administrator. By this means I proposed to eliminate the interminable wrangling in direct examinations and cross examinations which makes an exasperating farce of most hearings before administrative tribunals.

We could do this, of course, in the NRA because we were not engaged in determining anyone's rights or duties, or imposing decisions upon anyone. Our hearings were for the purpose of obtaining advice as to industrial problems which might be solved by drawing up a code of fair competition which would then be accepted by the industry as the rules of fair play under which they would try to operate. The representatives of the industry gathered together would themselves select a code authority. The whole scheme was one of what we called "self-government of industry."

The rules of procedure for public hearings which were dictated that first day remained substantially unchanged throughout the life of the NRA. They served the purpose of making public hearings comparatively brief and actually informative. I have always felt quite proud of that first day's work.

Deputy Administrator Allen insisted that I preside with him over the first hearing. This established an unfortunate precedent for me because all deputies thereafter felt they must have either the general counsel or one of his staff at their elbow, not only for public hearings but most of the time. As a result, instead of the modest staff of a few lawyers and a small clerical force that I had envisaged, it was necessary to develop a legal division of several hundred persons before the end of the NRA.

My dream of escaping from being the executive head of a large law office, which I had realized in 1923, became a nightmare in 1933–1935, when I found myself the head of an enormous government law office which spread throughout the United States and into the Island Possessions. Happily, one of my first discoveries was an exceptionally able young lawyer with a great talent for the organization and management of a large law office. Very soon I made Blackwell Smith assistant general counsel and turned over to him with a great sigh of relief all the oppressing details of managing a large law office.

Thus I was enabled to give my major attention to the job of being an assistant administrator of NRA on whom the President was relying for advice as to how the project was working internally, and how cooperation or resistances were developing in the industrial world which we were trying to reform by multiple experimentations.

CHAPTER XIV

Learning To Be a Bureaucrat

EXCEPT for the distortions of gossip columns the public outside of Washington gets little understanding of the living conditions under which a government official strives to do his job. If he happens to be blessed with independent means he may establish himself in a comfortable home, and if his wife is not socially ambitious he may be able to relax and recuperate during some evenings. If he is in a position of any prominence he is certain to have more invitations to cocktail parties and dinners than his digestive system and his nervous system can bear. These open up a social life quite different from that previously enjoyed in his home town, be it a small or a large city.

The social life of Washington is much broader and more varied than that of New York City or Des Moines, Iowa. The legations, representing practically all the nations of the world, are interested in a personal acquaintance with government officials of any prominence. The ruling officials in departments and agencies are interested in obtaining personal relationships with their political colleagues. Senators, congressmen and governors, representing all sections of the country, are likewise concerned with establishing intimate contacts with those influential in the executive department of the national government. Business men and politicians throughout the nation and many coming from abroad have a similar flattering interest in anyone close to the White House.

Any man projected into this scene without previous experience is sure to be overwhelmed with the amount of attention he will receive not only during his business hours but practically all around the clock. Particularly exciting and bewildering will be the attention received from the press. The Washington correspondents of leading newspapers and wire services are among the ablest newspaper men, and the success of their work depends to a large extent upon establishing a wide and fairly intimate acquaintance with possible sources of important news among government officials.

It is a startling experience for one whose previous activities have merited only limited national interest, even if he has had some local prominence, to find that his casual or inadvertent observations may be given much more publicity than his deliberate efforts to make clear what he is trying to do and how he is trying to do it. I remember, for example, a speech I once prepared with great care hoping to create a better understanding of just what we were seeking to accomplish in the NRA. Following my formal address there was a brief question period in which someone in the audience cried out: "How about inflation?" I had not prepared myself particularly to deal with that subject, but offhand I answered with considerable misplaced conviction: "If I understand what you mean by inflation, I think I can assure you that as long as Franklin D. Roosevelt is President there will be no inflation." The next day there were headlines all over the country, "Richberg Says No Inflation."

Both my wife and I found the social life into which we were thrust more burdensome than really enjoyable. It was, of course, amusing and often exciting to be entertained at private and public functions, to meet and exchange ideas with persons influential in shaping the destinies of our own and many other nations. Fortunately for us, although my position in the administration was relatively high, our official rank according to protocol, which is very important in Washington, was quite low. Not one of the various offices which I held was a statutory office in the sense of one created by act of Congress. Even the head of a minor commission or agency outranked me, so that at dinners, for example at the White House, we were placed below all officialdom and usually found as our companions newspaper men or private professional and business men—an interesting and constantly changing association.

In contrast to this happy situation, members of the Cabinet, justices of the Supreme Court and other high officials had to be seated in strict order of official precedence. Many of these complained humorously to us that time after time they were seated at dinners next to the same persons with whom they had had to carry on conversations so frequently that they became progressively bored and envied our remote but more amusing companionships. For this reason we early came into very friendly association with the most perennially and assuredly interesting group in Washington—the very well informed and entertaining newspaper men and their wives. High officials come and go but today, about twenty years after the beginning of my government service, there are still in Washington a large number of the newspaper correspondents who became personal friends so long ago.

There is a curious feature of Washington life which is worthy of mention because of the contrast between what might be regarded as luxurious entertainment and the financial resources of a great many who participate. Dinners and parties of an expensive character are an almost daily occurrence, paid for by the large expense accounts of the embassies, business organizations and wealthy individuals who find Washington an attractive playground. To some extent government funds are also available for quite a number of lavish entertainments because obviously many public officials are required to entertain those with whom social relationships are officially important. It is quite impossible for most members of Congress, executive officials and other residents dependent on moderate salaries to return such hospitalities, and so they are not expected to do so although a certain amount of moderate entertainment must be offered.

Members of the Gridiron Club for many years gave two imposing dinners, to which invitations were coveted and which imposed a heavy financial burden on those newspaper men who had no entertainment allowance. In this way the newspaper men met a great many of their social obligations. But to a salaried official such as myself, with no expense account for private entertainment, the effort to maintain even a minimum of one's social obligations forced an annual expenditure far beyond annual earnings. The result of this was that in a very few months my wife and I saw our modest surplus diminishing with worrisome rapidity. It was my expectation which I frankly expressed when I accepted appointment as general counsel of NRA that I would spend six months doing what I could to get the work established and then retire. At the end of the first six months it was quite apparent that I could not decently resign. In the rapid growth of a huge new organization it was inevitable that a disorderly house of government had to be better ordered before one could properly ask another to take his place.

In addition to this, an unhappy situation developed in the NRA, so that by April 1934 it had become apparent that the entire National Recovery Administration needed a drastic reorganization. With the dynamic personality of General Johnson at the head it was too much of a "one man show" to continue indefinitely. One of the interesting qualities of General Johnson was the combination of his intense desire to create an organization similar in its division of functions and regularity of authority to the Army, and on the other hand his maintenance and exercise of such an overriding authority in himself that no subordinate was ever sure of the extent or limits of his own authority.

Revised rules, regulations, charts and delegations of authority flowed out of the Administration office with confusing frequency. One Monday morning a wholesale reorganization was announced. When I asked why, the General told me that he had spent the week-end working over the problem and decided, as he picturesquely said, that the whole organization "needed a dose of salts."

On another occasion when a sweeping order was issued which would have disorganized my entire legal department, he, knowing my reaction, sent me a note explaining privately that it was not to be applied to my department.

No man ever overworked himself and overstrained his energies in a government job more than General Johnson. Also I doubt if any man in our political history rose with such speed from practical obscurity to a commanding influence in national affairs. All through the NRA people were afflicted with a certain megalomania because of the extraordinary powers that they were apparently exercising and because of the amazing acclaim which the rise and flight of the Blue Eagle across the land called forth. President

Roosevelt had called for action in his inaugural address and of all the new projects launched in the first year of his administration the NRA seemed productive of more action than any other.

The administrator of the NRA was far better known to masses of people than any member of the cabinet. The NRA had access to an appropriation of $3,300,000,000. Most of this was to be devoted to public works, but from such a vast reservoir the siphoning off of a few millions at a time into the NRA was an all too easy process. No hearings before Congressional committees, no debates in Congress would retard the flow of funds. The President could simply allocate them. We in the NRA were freed from that sense of responsibility in the expenditure of public funds which the ordinary processes of appropriation imposed on all other government departments and agencies. Indeed, the NRA established a most unhealthy precedent, that of a blanket appropriation subject to dispensation by Presidential order.

By the spring of 1934 General Johnson and I were at the time almost co-administrators although there was no question as to his superior authority. But next to him the general counsel obviously was most important in such a legally organized but somewhat lawless administration. Will Rogers came into town one day and at lunch with the General and myself he raised in his humorous way some questions as to the legality of our procedures. I responded jokingly, "Oh, we must keep a little law in it. That we try to do." As he left us and was getting into his taxicab he turned to me and said, "Don't forget that. You must keep a little law in it." He was highly amused, but my joke had had more than a little truth in it and I was frankly worried.

In our discussions of the future of the NRA General Johnson was very frank. He would say, "I think we ought to both resign so the President could go ahead with a new management." Then he would add reflectively, "But I don't see how I can resign just yet." The implication was clear that he could tolerate the thought of *my* retirement.

My own situation was becoming increasingly delicate and difficult. In long talks with the President he made me clearly understand that he thought General Johnson should retire. He also wanted me to continue in the service to aid in the reorganization, but he agreed with me that I should not be appointed to succeed the General. That would place me in an impossible position in an organization largely created by General Johnson. Furthermore, the President and I were in agreement that a board should be created in substitution for a single administrator, so we would be rid of the embarrassment of a ponderous one-man authority which encouraged all opponents of the NRA to denounce it as "fascist."

President Roosevelt had a deep appreciation of the service that General Johnson had rendered. He did not want to force him out and I think that politically he felt that any forced resignation of such a man, who was as widely popular as he was unpopular, would be unwise.

F.D.R. devised various means of easing the General out, one of which was the creation of a commission of notable industrialists, economists, etc., headed by the General, to go abroad and study for some months what every European country was doing to meet problems of depressed business and unemployment.

He put this proposition to General Johnson one night in his study in the White House in the presence of Secretary Perkins and myself. He outlined his plan to appoint this notable commission, and explained that he would also appoint a committee to be temporarily in control of the National Recovery Administration while the commission was out of the country. The implied assumption was that General Johnson would return to his old position, but in view of many current rumors and much newspaper gossip about the General's retirement, the underlying purpose of the President's proposal was all too obvious.

The General hardly waited for the President to complete his suggestion. He rose abruptly and said, "I understand perfectly well. You wish me to resign." I said, "General, I don't think you understand." He said, "I understand all too well," and walked out of the room. He went back to his office and dictated a long sorrowful letter which he sent to the President that evening, whereupon F.D.R. sat down and replied in a longhand letter explaining how much he appreciated Johnson's services and assuring him that he did not wish him to leave the administration.[1]

A short time later, General Johnson had a conference with the

[1] See letter of August 20, 1934, in *F.D.R.: His Personal Letters,* Vol. I, Duell, Sloan & Pearce, Inc., New York, 1947, pp. 412–413.

President and came out of it announcing that he had been told to stay with his feet nailed to the floor. The curious part of this entire episode is that immediately thereafter F.D.R. enlisted the aid of General Johnson's former employer and close friend, Bernard M. Baruch, to prevail upon him to retire. Since I was present at conferences between the President and Baruch, I do speak from first-hand knowledge. Eventually, General Johnson had agreed to take a sixty-day vacation with the understanding that he was to have nothing to do with the NRA during that period. Unhappily, the General did not devote the period solely to rest and relaxation. He actively interfered with the Administration's efforts to meet a most difficult strike situation, as I shall later recount.

CHAPTER XV

On Being "Assistant President"

During lengthy discussions with the President in the spring of 1934 regarding reorganization of the NRA and many other matters, he developed the idea of relieving me from my active duties as general counsel and creating some sort of position in which I could be of assistance in a variety of ways. He was becoming particularly concerned with the overlapping of the work of many departments and agencies and was seeking to find some machinery for coordinating their activities.

In July 1933 the President had created an Executive Council consisting of members of the Cabinet and heads of important agencies. Then, as the number of commissions and agencies continued to expand, he had created in November 1933 a National Emergency Council. This was a very ambitious effort to eliminate duplications and inconsistent policies and to create a better understanding of the purposes and programs of the Administration among its principal executives. The council included not only the President, all members of the Cabinet and the chairmen of various statutory commissions, but also the heads of the various administrations and boards which had come into existence since Roosevelt's inauguration. This was, however, too large a body for anything much beyond exchange of information, discussion of major policies and small conferences and committees which might be created to deal with special problems. The President had become more and more concerned with the need of having a small committee to make recommendations and to help carry out programs which involved related problems of relief, public works, labor disputes and industrial recovery.

In one of our discussions he told me he was considering creating a special office of Assistant to the President. He would appoint me to this post so that I could work under his direction and take some of the load off him. I had an immediate premonition of trouble which I did not express to him but promptly explained to his very efficient and shrewd secretary, Marvin McIntyre. There was neither statutory authority nor precedent for creating the position suggested by F.D.R. and, since I had by that time come to understand the jealousy of statutory officials when someone like myself was put in position of even comparable prestige, and given a sort of extralegal authority, I was quite sure that "an assistant to the President" would be quickly termed "Assistant President," arousing hostilities that would make it doubly difficult to do any good work.

From a political standpoint I thought it would be generally resented, and I begged Mac to indicate to the President the folly of such a course. I heard no more about the creation of the office of "Assistant." It will be noted, however, that long after this the President met his constantly growing need of such aides by arranging for the creation of six assistants "with a passion for anonymity." Thus, of course, no one could be designated in the press as an "Assistant President" because there were six of them.

When I was catapulted into my NRA responsibilities with a great deal of national publicity, it was inevitable that I should be called upon to make a great many speeches designed to interpret what the President was seeking to accomplish in many different directions. After the first months of widespread acclaim the inevitable reaction had set in and there was much adverse publicity which it was important to combat.

I made a great many tiring engagements in the next six months and found myself plagued with intermittent attacks of my old enemy arthritis as a result. I did break away from Washington for a brief vacation in the Berkshires visiting friends in July 1934.

A general strike was in progress in San Francisco which the Administration was seeking to solve through the efforts of the Secretary of Labor. General Johnson arrived in San Francisco on July 15, where he made a speech and injected himself into the situation in such a way as to set everyone in Washington on edge. I don't know whether the story is true that people in San Francisco insisted on General Johnson leaving town abruptly. I do know that General Johnson in his book *The Blue Eagle from Egg to Earth* said he called the White House, talked to Marvin McIntyre and to the Secretary of Labor, and that he had been authorized to speak for the President's Special Board which was sitting in San Francisco.

According to the General he took command of the entire situation and between condemning them and persuading them induced the labor leaders to call off the "general strike," which he denounced as subversive and intolerable.

According to Miss Perkins in her book *The Roosevelt I Knew* there was no "general strike"—although she admits that Secretary Hull (acting President in the absence of Roosevelt on a trip to Hawaii) and Attorney General Cummings thought there was one.

The stories of General Johnson and Miss Perkins are irreconcilable about what was happening in San Francisco and Washington. Johnson, exercising his great gift of relating self-laudatory fiction as fact, has told about how he moved courageously into this desperate situation, obtained authority from Washington to be Pooh-Bah and High Cracker-Down, and smashed the strike.

Miss Perkins, with her ever-flowing bias for any organized labor project or personality, has told how she, by negating mistaken efforts of Hull, Cummings and Johnson, gave "sensible labor leaders" an opportunity to get their men back to work. Harry Bridges, the villain of General Johnson's drama, is only a pathetic, misunderstood "mandolin player" in Miss Perkins' scenario. She refused as Secretary of Labor to deport him and she apparently is proud of her continuing defense of the lonesome mandolin player whom stupid capitalists have regarded as a subversive menace just because he is a specialist in conducting costly and unnecessary strikes.

As to the San Francisco strike, all I can do is to add a few simple facts to the melodramatic fiction which has already been published:

Secretary McIntyre called me up in the Berkshires, explaining that he and the Secretary of Labor were deeply disturbed by the

San Francisco situation, and I asked him if it would do any good for me to come back to Washington. McIntyre not only jumped at my suggestion, but said he would send an Army plane at once to pick me up and take me to Washington. As a result, a few hours later two Army planes circled above the small town of Great Barrington and caused much local excitement by managing to land in the rather small airfield. During the day I spent in Washington, the San Francisco situation took a turn for the better, so I was promptly flown back to resume my interrupted vacation.

What I learned in Washington was not a complete, reliable story of what had been happening; but, piecing together information obtained that day with more that I learned later in San Francisco and Washington, I would summarize the situation as follows:

There was a longshoremen's strike in San Francisco led by Bridges, in which a labor board appointed by Miss Perkins and including Assistant Secretary of Labor Edward F. McGrady was mediating. Then developed a sympathetic strike of labor unions which Miss Perkins did not regard as a "general strike," although most everyone else thought it was—particularly San Franciscans who had to suffer it.

General Johnson arrived in San Francisco to make a speech and receive an honorary Phi Beta Kappa key. His assumption of government authority was resented by persons representing government, employers and strikers, and there were strong efforts to stop him from speaking. Johnson claimed the protesters were afraid of violence against him. San Franciscans claimed that they were afraid he would make a bad situation worse. He made a very "rugged" speech demanding prompt settlement of the strike to stop a "civil war."

General Johnson then left San Francisco and men there have always claimed that his exit was forcibly demanded. Before he returned the labor leaders had acted and the "general strike" was ended. Anyone who wishes to do so can give General Johnson some credit for this. The government people in Washington credited him with harmful interference. My own part in the controversy was simply that of one called in to give advice which so far as I know contributed nothing to the solution. All the glory I got out of it was an Army escort and air transportation to and from Washington.

This flight in July 1934 was comparatively uneventful, but it recalls to my mind another emergency flight which bid fair for some hours to end my activities altogether. This was the 29th of September, 1933, when a coal strike was harassing Pennsylvania and disturbing the rest of the country which had not yet become accustomed to sweeping stoppages in coal production. The President was at Hyde Park and being called upon continually for aid by Governor Pinchot. I was in Washington endeavoring to work out an agreement with the steel companies and John L. Lewis through NRA which would end the strike.

Late in the afternoon I informed the President by phone that the agreement had just been reached. He told me to fly at once to Hyde Park by Army plane so that he could approve and announce it that evening. At the field I found I was to fly in an open tandem-seated plane, and since I was wearing a very light-weight summer suit I was furnished with an overall zipper suit—the Army pilot wore a heavy sheepskin-lined coat. As I settled myself in the plane I asked the pilot if he knew Little Hackensack, the tiny airfield nearest to Hyde Park, which was called a "handkerchief field," on which no big planes wanted to land. He said "Yes" in a rather grim way.

General Johnson, who had flown to Hyde Park some time before, had told me that his plane had to land so abruptly that it bounced ten feet in the air when they hit.

After we had been in the air a few minutes, the pilot turned and motioned to me to put the stick in the duplicate steering gear, since the plane was arranged for flying from either seat. I was puzzled but I obeyed. Then he began dipping from side to side, apparently to show me how the plane could be controlled by the stick. I was not amused.

We took off about six o'clock and were supposed to arrive at Hyde Park about eight o'clock. I recognized Baltimore and Philadelphia as we passed, but somehow we did not seem to be hitting New York. Suddenly I saw the moon shining on what appeared to be a large expanse of water. Something like a large hook of land lay below me. I tapped the pilot on the shoulder and motioned for his map. For some strange reason we were flying over Sandy Hook, but happily our course abruptly altered and the next thing I knew we were flying over New York City. My recognition of

42nd and Broadway gave me no pleasure, however, for it seemed to me that the pilot's intention was to drop into one of the hotels for dinner.

Eventually we hit the Hudson River north of New York City and I breathed a sigh of relief. But we went on and on with no sign of Little Hackensack Field. Some time after nine o'clock we sighted a large airfield. To my amazement we leveled off far away from the administration building and well-lighted runways, skimmed over the treetops and landed in a plowed field. The pilot attempted to taxi in but could make no headway. I followed him out of the plane and asked him where we were. "I don't know," he said. "Somewhere between Troy and Syracuse, I think." Then, as I stood there half frozen in my thin clothes, he shook himself in his big thick jacket and observed, "Gee, it's cold!"

I plodded across the large plowed area and the runways into the administration building of the North Albany field, which was where we had actually landed.

As I was explaining to the clerk that I was very anxious to telephone to Hyde Park, a man standing by turned to me and said, "Do you want to get to Hyde Park?" I said, "Yes, I have an appointment with the President." He said, "I was here to meet a man, but I can arrange to have him taken care of and I'll take you to Hyde Park. I have a car." He was evidently friendly to the Administration.

I never thought of making any further effort to phone Hyde Park because I supposed the pilot would report in. Later I learned that he did not report in until after ten-thirty. Unhappily we got lost going through Albany, but we arrived at Hyde Park shortly before midnight, somewhat to the disappointment of the newspaper men who had been diligently writing my obituary. When my plane did not appear and the hours went by with no report, there was apparently only one answer—we must have crashed. Although I had many friends in the Army Air Force and later became very well acquainted with the man who was in command of Bolling Field at that time, I was never able to get the slightest explanation of that mad flight from Washington to North Albany.

The President showed such relief at my arrival that I was deeply touched by his affectionate interest. Years later when a newspaper woman asked the President what had been some of the most try-

John C. Richberg, the author's father, in 1894

Dr. Eloise O. Richberg, the author's mother, in 1900

Donald Richberg as a proud violinist of thirteen, with his brother Windsor and sister Leda, 1894

Track athlete (mile walker) at the University of Chicago, 1900

General Counsel of the NRA, 1933

President Roosevelt, General Hugh S. Johnson and Mr. Richberg—speakers at the NRA Convention, 1934

Washington Times Photo

The "Assistant President" in his Washington home, 1934

Courtesy of Wide World Ph

otball practice" of F.D.R.'s team, 1934

Courtesy of the Washington Star

Friendly quarreling with Clarence Darrow over NRA, 1934

Courtesy of Wide World Photos

.bor conference at the White House, 1935. *Left to right:* Donald R. Richberg,
lney Hillman, William Green, John L. Lewis.

Courtesy of Wide World Photos

Placating labor opposition to the remade NRA, 1935

Courtesy of the Washington S

The Supreme Court shoots down the Blue Eagle, 1935

Courtesy of the Washington Star

Last meeting of the NRA Board, 1935. *Standing:* Charles Edison, Philip Murray, Leon C. Marshall. *Sitting:* W. P. Witherow, Donald R. Richberg, Sidney Hillman. *Absent:* Walton Hamilton.

ening conference on oil seizure, in Mexican Palace, 1939. *Left to right:* Donald Richberg, President Cárdenas, Ambassador Castillo Nájera.

The author, his wife and daughter, on vacation in Montana, 1940

Mr. and Mrs. Richberg at a meeting of the Virginia Bar Association

Mr. Richberg and his long-time law partner, former Ambassador Joseph E. Davies, on the terrace at Tregaron, the Washington home of Mr. Davies.

Photo by Murillo

ing times in his administration, he said, "The worst time I can remember is that night in September 1933, when at seven o'clock we received word that Governor Lehman had been operated on for appendicitis and died (which we learned an hour or so later was false). And that same time Richberg's plane never arrived and only hours later we heard that it had landed up at Albany—that was one of the most trying evenings I can remember."

As the difficulties with regard to the reorganization of the NRA increased and it became desirable for me to retire from active control of the legal division (thus making it easier for General Johnson to retire) the President finally devised a new idea, which was somewhat startling to me. On June 30, 1934, he created "The Industrial Emergency Committee," composed of the Secretary of the Interior, the Secretary of Labor, the administrator of federal emergency relief, the administrator for industrial recovery and the director appointed by the President. He appointed me director and gave me leave of absence as general counsel of NRA. Also, in the same order he appointed me to serve as executive secretary of the Executive Council and as executive director of the National Emergency Council, taking the place of Frank Walker, who had been seeking to be relieved of his duties in these offices.

This consolidation of functions of apparently far-reaching importance in one person was naturally a matter of great interest to the press and it was necessary for me to hold promptly a press conference. To my profound embarrassment almost the first question shouted at me was, "How does it feel to be Assistant President?" I begged my newspaper friends not to tag me with that title, but it was too good a label for them to resist and I suffered from it for the rest of my public service.

CHAPTER XVI

Last Days of the NRA

Reorganization of the NRA under direction of the board headed by Clay Williams was more of a success internally than externally. The machinery for handling the revision of, and compliance with, the codes of fair competition was definitely improved. Benefits and detriments to private and public interests were subjected to an orderly analysis and there was a constant effort to clarify policies and programs of the Administration and to lay down lines of future action. But externally the NRA was suffering from an accumulation of private discontents and political opposition which naturally received much more attention from the press than unsensational progress in handling public business efficiently and fairly.

In the first year of the NRA, General Johnson had provided a continual succession of exciting and amusing stories for the newspapers. He had a genius for phrasing his statements, and particularly his attacks on opponents, in vivid language that made easy headlines. With his flair for spectacular methods and his ambition for getting immediate results, he had devised and gained the approval of the President for a wholesale drive to increase employment and at the same time to extend codes of fair competition through what was called the President's Re-employment Agreement. The Blue Eagle emblem was created so as to identify all business establishments that were cooperating in this program. Thereafter, the NRA had a flag under which its expanding army could march. Huge parades and mass meetings helped develop almost hysterical enthusiasm for what appeared to be a great cause.

The President's Re-employment Agreement was in part created to meet an increasing and difficult problem caused by the adoption of a few codes of competition in a comparatively few industries.

It was to remain in effect until an industry or trade was codified, when the provisions of the approved code would be substituted for the blanket provisions of the Re-employment Agreement. This would offer a strong inducement to employers in all trades and industries to get together and adopt codes of fair competition, in order that the employer's risk of shortening hours and increasing wages would be lightened by the elimination of unfair business practices.

According to General Johnson's report in his book, the PRA was to bring 96 per cent of employers under the NRA, to put 2,785,000 workers back on the pay rolls, and to increase annual purchasing power by $3,000,000,000; also to abolish child labor, to establish 40 hours as a maximum work week and $12.00 as the minimum weekly pay for the lowest paid common labor. Yet, there was so much opposition in the Cabinet that, except for the stubborn courage of General Johnson and of the President who backed him, the PRA and the Blue Eagle would never have been created.

There is certainly no doubt that the PRA and the Blue Eagle aroused universal interest and widespread hopes of industrial recovery under the inspiration and encouragement of the Recovery Administration. Unhappily, the almost universal codification of American industry and the coincident strengthening of unionism aroused also many deep-seated oppositions and countless minor antagonisms. As a result, the reorganized NRA had no longer the benefit of the national acclaim which aided General Johnson as Administrator. Members of Congress now began receiving far more complaints than praise of the Recovery Administration.

Because of our own appreciation of constitutional and other weaknesses in the National Industrial Recovery Act, we began working in the fall of 1934 upon the draft of amendments. These we planned to submit to Congress when we asked for an act extending the life of the NRA which would otherwise expire, under the original act, on June 16, 1935.

The presentation of executive proposals for legislation had

become more difficult than in the early days of the Roosevelt administration. There was a rising opposition to the presentation of a law to be "rubber stamped" by the Congress. We therefore faced a variety of oppositions in seeking to provide for the continuance and improvement of the National Recovery Administration. The extremists of the radical Left and of the conservative Right were all against us. In addition, organized labor, which had been enormously benefited, exhibited its customary annoyance at the failure of the Recovery Administration to give 100 per cent support to its proposals.

President William Green and John L. Lewis, then the strongest influence in AFL councils (there was no CIO in 1935), became very bitter in their opposition to me and to any legislative proposition that I would advance.

Sidney Hillman, labor representative on the NRA Board, was feuding, quite unreasonably, with Clay Williams, the chairman. Since Clay Williams was also the president of Reynolds Tobacco Company and Sidney Hillman president of the Amalgamated Clothing Workers, this made for unhappy anti-business publicity.

In this most confusing and disheartening situation I was faced with the problem, delegated to me by the President, of arranging for a second reorganization of the NRA, including a new chairman and a new board. Clay Williams had only agreed to take the chairmanship for some sixty days and he had been persistently demanding that he should be relieved of his onerous and increasingly unpleasant duties.

There were two men available for the chairmanship: Arthur D. Whiteside, President of Dun & Bradstreet, who as a deputy administrator had rendered invaluable service to the NRA from its inception; and Averell Harriman, who had had almost as long experience in the NRA and who had been serving as chief executive officer under the Williams board. For my part, I would have been willing to recommend either one, although for various reasons I thought Mr. Whiteside would probably be more effective internally and externally. Mr. Harriman was less widely known, had much less experience with Congress, and was a younger man.

There was a strong demand from the labor organizations for equal representation on the board with employers, so it was early decided that the new board should have seven members—two labor men, two employers and two or three public men. I would not say that either Mr. Whiteside or Mr. Harriman engaged in any wire pulling, but there was so much activity on the part of some aggressive supporters of each that the President hesitated to make a choice for fear of creating a discordant new board.

There was no expectation or desire on my part to be made chairman. I had been trying to persuade the President for some weeks to let me retire entirely from the Administration. My surplus funds were exhausted and my private financial problems becoming more and more difficult. Furthermore, when even the possibility of my appointment was rumored there was such outspoken public opposition from Green and Lewis that such an appointment would have been clearly undesirable. Nevertheless, the time for further consideration was running out rapidly and the President was becoming impatient of further delay. We had a lengthy discussion at lunch one day regarding my desire to resign. We went into such detail, discussing not only my finances but the financial difficulties of so many men in public office (including some of his own which had never occurred to me!), that the luncheon hour, which had begun at one, extended to 3:00 P.M., to the intense annoyance of his faithful staff.

On either this or some similar occasion we finally came to an understanding that I would remain in the Administration, presumably as executive director of the National Emergency Council, until the middle of June 1935. By that time the work of extending the life of the NRA would be ended and I could retire with my part in that task at least finished, happily or unhappily.

At a meeting in the President's office shortly thereafter, we reached a practical agreement upon the membership of the new board except for the uncertainty as to the chairman. But while we were talking he penciled a memorandum which I still possess as having extraordinary interest to me and perhaps to many others. He explained the memorandum by saying, "We'll ask Whiteside to remain for a time as a member of the board and Harriman to continue as executive officer. We'll put on Witherow, Phil Murray, Sidney Hillman, Walton Hamilton and Leon Marshall, and then [he looked up with a grin] you will be chairman until June 16."

"What will Green and Lewis say?" I asked.

"Oh, they will be all right," he said confidently. The reason for his confidence subsequently became clear because he explained to them before my appointment was announced that it was only temporary, that I was going to resign in the middle of June. So they had the satisfaction of announcing publicly that they had helped push me out of the Administration.

As a consequence of my assumption of the chairmanship of the NRA Board it became necessary for me to testify and argue on the Hill for many weeks vainly seeking the enactment of the amendments to the National Industrial Recovery Act which we had been working out in conferences and discussions of several months.

A lawsuit in which I had no active participation was moving toward the Supreme Court. My anticipation, shared apprehensively by many of my associates (and gleefully by many of our opponents), was that the Court might well hold that the NRA involved an unconstitutional delegation of undefined authority to the President.

Unfortunately, the politicians in fundamental opposition to the President and to the NRA did not want to see any curative amendments enacted. Many others were either personally unenthusiastic about NRA or were worried by complaints of their constituents. Thus a sort of informal coalition against amending the Recovery Act developed which delayed Congressional action until eventually a beautiful excuse for further delay developed. In Congress it was argued that cautious legislators should wait until the Supreme Court had passed on the Schechter case so that they could act in the light of its high guidance.

So we of the doomed Administration waited in a state of suspended animation for the decision of May 27, 1935, in which the Supreme Court unanimously held the code-making features of the law to be unconstitutional.

CHAPTER XVII

The "Sick Chicken" Case

THE STORY of the Schechter case, popularly known as the "Sick Chicken" case, in which the Supreme Court practically ended the existence of the NRA, has been written from many angles. For my part, I reviewed the development and results of this case in my book *The Rainbow* written shortly after the historic decision; and in speeches and articles in the ensuing years, as well as in lectures on constitutional law, I have discussed the case as a political and legal landmark. Now, perhaps, it would be useful for me to review it as a personal experience.

Among the multitude of NRA codes of fair competition was one covering the handling and marketing of live poultry, a business in which it was claimed there were many unfair competitive practices injurious alike to poultry dealers and to their customers. The Schechter Poultry Corporation, operating in New York City, was found guilty of violations of the live poultry code and the defendants appealed to the United States Circuit Court of Appeals for the Second Circuit (New York), which unanimously sustained these convictions and unanimously upheld the constitutionality of the Recovery Act and its administration in this case. This court has been generally ranked among lawyers as the one of highest authority next to the Supreme Court. Furthermore, in the Schechter case the opinion came from three of the ablest judges of the court.

The defendants had the right to petition for a review by the Supreme Court of the United States. The decision, therefore, to have the constitutionality of the NRA tested in the Supreme Court did not lie in the hands of the government. Admittedly we did not have an ideal case because dealing in live poultry in New York City was not clearly engaging in interstate commerce. Hence the question could be raised as to whether the federal government had power to enact and enforce a law regulating the conduct of this business. Live poultry were shipped in to a New York dealer, the chickens were killed and then sold largely locally. This operation might or might not be regarded as one in the so-called "stream" of interstate commerce, although it was closely akin to the operations of the great stockyards, such as in Chicago, where cattle were brought in from other states, slaughtered, and the meat sold locally and nationally. Such a business had been held over and over again by the Supreme Court to be a part of interstate commerce subject to federal regulation.

But there was also an additional factor favorable to the government in that only one year before live poultry dealers in New York had been held guilty of a conspiracy in restraint of interstate commerce. This conviction had been upheld by the U.S. Supreme Court.

Of course, I had hoped that the debatable issues of constitutional law arising out of the language and provisions of the Recovery Act might be eliminated by amendment to the law prior to a review by the Supreme Court.

However, since the Congress had evaded improvement of the statute, we had to hope for the best in the Supreme Court review. It was my own opinion that in view of a fairly recent decision in the Panama Refining Company case, the Court might merely hold that too much power had been delegated to the President without defining its limits. Thus the Court might hold the Recovery Act to be unconstitutional on this ground, but the Congress could, by amendment, make provisions for executive action more precise and thus perpetuate the NRA.

All things considered, I looked forward to the Supreme Court's decision with modest hopes and lively fears. Nothing in my NRA experience irked me quite as much as public criticisms subsequent to the decision attacking my bad judgment in taking a weak case to the Supreme Court and my supposed pre-decision confidence that we would win the case. The frequently inaccurate and to me often malicious column of Drew Pearson, then in association with

Robert Allen, falsely quoted me as boasting to William Green that I was highly confident we would win the case. In the first place, Green and I were barely on speaking terms at the time; in the second place, I had made it clear by repeated public statements that I thought the law should be amended so as to avoid a probable unfavorable decision by the Supreme Court. In the third place, although avoiding any public expressions of doubt, I had expressed my grave doubts of our success to everyone with whom the case had been privately discussed.

As an example of such private discussions, I recall a talk I had after a private dinner with Judge Learned Hand, one of the three members of the Court of Appeals which had sustained the conviction of the Schechter Corporation. This talk occurred after the arguments of the case in the Supreme Court and before its decision was handed down. I remember vividly standing with Judge Hand in front of the fireplace in Dean Acheson's house when he asked me what I thought of the prospects for a favorable decision. I replied: "I start with the possibility of one vote in our favor, although of course I hope there will be more." Whether I named this one justice I do not recall, but I do remember saying, "It is not Mr. Justice Brandeis." But I was thinking of Mr. Justice Cardozo, and, in the light of later opinions written by him, sustaining sweeping exercises of the federal interstate commerce power, it should be understood why I did not anticipate his joining in any opinion that would restrict the federal power over interstate commerce. But I had good reason to fear that he might be against us on the other, less harmful issue of an excessive delegation of power to the President, which we could easily correct by amending the act.

Despite the fact that Justices Brandeis and Holmes had long been noted for their willingness to permit extensions of legislative power to meet changing conditions, I was well aware that Justice Brandeis was highly critical of the NRA experiment in trying to establish codes of fair competition. He was one of a considerable group of liberals who were fearful that codes of competition provided stepping stones toward the cartelization of industry (similar to European monopolies) whereby big business could exercise an overriding influence to the injury of small business and lead to the exploitation of consumers.

I am not going to duplicate the "blazing indiscretion" of General

Johnson who once deeply embarrassed Justice Brandeis by making a public statement to the effect that he had been in constant consultation with the Justice regarding the operations of the NRA. The implication that Justice Brandeis was engaged in political activities inconsistent with judicial impartiality was particularly offensive to all of us who knew him well.

In recent years some members of the Supreme Court have engaged in such efforts to spread their political views that it may not be realized today how very carefully former members of the Supreme Court avoided not only any public expression of their private views but even private expressions which might imply any prejudgment of issues to come before the Court. I recall a conversation authentically reported that took place when the issue of public utility valuation was being hotly debated and frequently a subject of Supreme Court action. At a private party, a pompous and indiscreet gentleman said to Justice Stone in the hearing of others, "I hope, Mr. Justice, when this issue comes for final decision before the Supreme Court that the Court will sustain the constitutional rights of property." To which Justice Stone replied, "I think you may be sure of that, but the question is, what are the rights of property?"

As a friend of Justice Brandeis for many years and long prior to his appointment to the Supreme Court, I had the privilege of many conversations with him. He always discussed public questions with utmost freedom in general terms, but not with specific application to issues pending before the Supreme Court. I was well aware of his attitude toward big business concentrations, of his intense interest in preserving a genuine competition and in protecting small businesses which are essential to such competition. During the development of the NRA he studied and discussed the advantages and disadvantages of NRA operations to competitive business, to labor organizations and to consumers. He never discussed the constitutionality of the law or the legality of NRA operations, but only the economic and social factors. From all of this I felt sure that he was so dubious as to the value of our experiment that any doubts as to its constitutionality would loom much larger in his mind than in the mind of a judge who enthusiastically approved of what we were trying to do.

To anyone like myself who has spent a large part of a long practice of law in studying and arguing issues of constitutionality, it is plain beyond all quibbling that close issues are usually resolved by the political or economic predilections of the judges who must pass on them. The entire course of constitutional law in our history fortifies this conclusion. A conservative-minded court is a court of strict construction, a liberal-minded court, a court of loose construction. Judges who fear abuses of legislative power will erect constitutional bulwarks against legislative advances. A liberal court will find fewer barriers and tear down some that have been previously erected.

On clear issues you may expect conscientious judges to approve laws they personally dislike, or to disapprove laws which they wish could be enacted. But doubtful issues of constitutional law are frequent because a constitution must be written in broad language. "Free speech" and a "free exercise of religion," for example, are not simple questions when freedom of speech may be the means of inflicting grave injuries on the public, and a free exercise of religion may seem to be only a cloak for disregard of the welfare or opinions of others.

The opinion of the Supreme Court in the Schechter case may have been shaped to some extent by the weakness or strength of the arguments advanced in the case, but in last analysis I think the arguments had little effect except to leave the judges convinced that they could properly follow their political and economic predilections.

For example, in my oral argument I was endeavoring to discount the widely held opinion that we were engaged in a price-fixing operation. That question was not really involved in the Schechter case, but I felt it necessary to point out that our major effort and purpose was to prevent unfair competition which was a legally established purpose of the Federal Trade Commission. We were not seeking positively to control how business should be operated but negatively to prevent unfair practices. The argument for the government had been divided between the Solicitor General, Stanley Reed (later appointed to the Supreme Court), and myself, acting as a special assistant to the Attorney General, Homer Cummings.

It is amusing to recall that my appointment, although I welcomed it, was not of my seeking. The Attorney General, although a personal friend of mine, was opposed to the NRA operation and I think that, not only in fairness but with perhaps a touch of gentle malice, he suggested that I should participate in the argument of the case. Solicitor General Reed, a very good lawyer and also a personal friend, had never participated in the NRA, and I felt he might not be able to represent the real intentions and purposes of the Administration with the same accuracy and conviction which I might give. My misgivings were justified when one of the justices asked Mr. Reed whether he claimed that "fair competition" was the antithesis of "unfair competition," and Mr. Reed replied that he did not. That claim was, in fact, a major basis of my argument in support of the NRA.

When it came my time to argue I had to go to great lengths to explain that although we called them "codes of fair competition" their purpose was simply to prevent unfair competition, not to establish new standards of fairness.

A very good example of the difference between these two theories lay in the realm of price fixing. A code, according to our ideas, could properly prohibit anyone from selling goods at a loss (the so-called "loss leader"), in order to attract trade, because it would be unfair to a competitor who had to make money on everything he sold. But we did not propose to fix the price at which goods should be sold.

During this discussion one of the justices asked me whether we did not in effect have price fixing in some of the codes, citing one which had been frequently denounced as a price fixing code. I replied that while a few codes could be subjected to the criticism of price fixing, we thought they were mistakes and were seeking to eliminate all price fixing from the codes. Then I added wryly, "Of course that is not the matter involved in this case because there is no price fixing clause in the code before the Court and I can hardly review all NRA codes in the instant case." The Justice smilingly acknowledged that the issue was not involved, but it was quite apparent the issue was in the minds of some of the justices.

An amusing example of how a false impression may be given in oral argument without deliberate intent to deceive arose when Justice McReynolds asked the Schechter Corporation's lawyer what "selective killing" meant. As a rule live poultry were bought and sold by the crate so that the dealer could figure his profit on the transaction. However, some dealers would permit certain favored customers to select the best-looking chickens from among several crates, and then have those killed for them, thus getting an exceptionally good crate for the price of an ordinary one. This practice of giving special favors to certain customers, which prevailed in many industries, was almost universally regarded as unfair competition. The prohibition of "selective killing" in the poultry code, therefore, was the prohibition of unfair practices common to many other codes.

However, when Justice McReynolds asked his question, the rather excitable lawyer for the Schechters went into a voluble and quite misleading explanation of "selective killing." In substance he answered:

"You want to know what is selective killing? I'll tell you. You come into my place and look over my chickens and you say, 'I want that one, I want this one, I want that one.' You pick out the chickens you want and they are killed for you. What's wrong with that, Judge?"

This sounded as though to forbid "selective killing" was like preventing a customer from picking out a sack of good apples in a self-service market. Certainly the answer did not improve the standing of the NRA. We were pictured as an arbitrary bureaucracy, trying to enforce a trade regulation which prevented a dealer from selling to his customers what they wanted to buy.

As previously observed, I do not believe that the briefs and arguments in the Schechter case had much to do with the opinion except in providing the basis on which the Court could rule against a government experiment which ran contrary to the political and economic predilections of the justices. This is indeed evident to any lawyer who reads the opinion in the Schechter case which held the Recovery Act unconstitutional because it extended the federal power to regulate interstate commerce into the realm of manufacturing, mining, building and agriculture, which the Court held to be local business beyond the regulatory power of the federal government.

Yet, within two years after the decision in the Schechter case, the Court began a long line of decisions in which it has been held that the federal power to regulate interstate commerce can be extended to regulate labor relations, production and prices in these very realms of manufacturing, mining, building and agriculture. For my part, I think the opinion in regard to federal regulation of interstate commerce in the Schechter case was entirely too narrow in the light of a long line of precedents and that the opinions in recent years have been far too broad and have extended the federal power not only far beyond that which was denied in the Schechter case, and beyond that which had been justified in many previous cases, but far beyond any extension of federal power which is authorized by even a liberal construction of the Constitution.

Perhaps I may be permitted with due immodesty to make one answer to many personal criticisms of my own handling of the case. Because I have said that I thought the briefs and arguments had little to do with the final outcome, I do not want to leave the impression that I think my own presentation was inadequate. I was not wholly happy about it, but I would like to record the fact that one of the men in the packed audiences in the court room when the Schechter case was argued was Congressman James M. Beck, an eminent constitutional lawyer who had been himself Solicitor General. I knew him, but not intimately. I knew him also as a notable outstanding opponent of the Roosevelt administration, highly critical of all such experimentations as the NRA. I was deeply surprised and gratified to receive a note passed over to me when I was sitting in the court room after my argument, which read as follows:

Supreme Court Room
May 3, 1935

MY DEAR RICHBERG:

My congratulations on a well reasoned, finely balanced and forceful argument. While I may not concur in all its reasoning and am unable to accept its conclusions, yet I have seldom listened to an argument in the Supreme Court with greater interest and admiration. It was worthy of a notable cause.

Sincerely yours,
(*Signed*) JAMES M. BECK

CHAPTER XVIII

Return to Private Life

MAY 27, 1935, was a memorable day in the annals of the Supreme Court. In the opinions read from the Bench the learned justices ruled unanimously three times against the New Deal Administration, nullifying Farm Debt Relief legislation, denying the President's power to remove an appointee from office, and holding the NRA attempts to establish codes of fair competition to be unconstitutional. As these blows fell, one by one, those members of the Administration like myself who were sitting in the court room tried to assume an air of cheerful disappointment. My own efforts in this regard were somewhat thwarted by the unfortunate fact that an alert photographer snapped a picture of me, accompanied by my wife, descending a narrow steep stairway from the old Supreme Court Room in the Capitol building. Since I was looking down anxiously to avoid stepping on my wife's dress or stumbling, the picture, taken from below, gave me a most doleful appearance which was duly exploited in the press. Of course I was disappointed, but hardly to the point of incipient tears indicated by the photograph.

The next few days were full of contention and harassment. It was my duty to recommend whether amendments of the law should be suggested to Congress by the President in order to carry on the fundamental purposes of the NRA under such limitations as the Supreme Court opinion and decision required. There was no danger that the President would be unduly influenced by any advice of mine since he was promptly deluged with public and private advice ranging all the way from complete abandonment of his program to demands for constitutional amendments either to enlarge the powers of the Congress or to reduce the powers of the Supreme Court.

At a conference with the President and Attorney General Cummings, the latter pointed out with no evident sorrow that the opinion of Chief Justice Hughes would certainly prevent the NRA from functioning effectively except in a comparatively limited field of industry and trade. I have always suspected the Attorney General's construction of the opinion and its consequences inspired the President to criticize strongly in the subsequent press conference what he regarded as a return to the legal doctrines of the "horse and buggy days."

In the next few days I had a most unhappy time. If the NRA was to come to an end on June 16, it was clearly necessary to release a host of pay-roll employees and volunteer workers from any obligation to remain on a sinking ship. On the other hand, if we were to try to have the Congress enact an amended law extending the life of the NRA, it was most important to retain as many of our trained personnel as possible until Congress determined our future. My own future was also hanging in the balance. I had intended to resign in the middle of June, but I could not do so until the issue was decided, and if the President should seek to continue a reorganized NRA I might be obligated to remain in office for at least a brief period.

In an afternoon conference with the President, he gave me to understand that he had decided to seek an amendment of the law under which the NRA would be continued. This decision he specifically authorized me to make public.

The next day a large conference was held in the President's office attended by Congressional leaders and others, at which the President read a long mimeographed statement which seemed to be received with general satisfaction, but which rather stunned me. The tenor of the statement, as I heard it, appeared to be that, bowing to the decision of the Supreme Court, the work of the NRA would be gradually brought to a conclusion. The Congressional leaders, who had been fearing that they would have to make a fight up on the Hill, were obviously relieved to learn that the President wished only a limited extension of the act in order to permit the existing activities to be closed up in an orderly fashion.

When the conference broke up I waited until I could speak to the President alone. I expressed my surprise at his decision, in view of our conference of the previous day. He in turn expressed his surprise, insisting that his statement had contained a clear proposal for an extension of the Recovery Act and hence a "continuance of the NRA." "But," I replied, "you spoke of a skeleton NRA." He again expressed surprise, and when I pointed out that the words had been used at least twice in his statement, he brushed it aside as something of little importance. But I left quite convinced that some time between his meeting with me and his Congressional meeting, the President had become convinced that the only "continuance of the NRA" which he thought desirable resembled the continuance of the life of a patient after the doctors had discovered in an exploratory operation that death was inevitable and all that remained to be done was to arrange for a comfortable demise.

One thing which I learned in my governmental service was that the final decision always lay with the man of final responsibility. The President had the right, and indeed the duty, to make his decision according to his own lights, unmoved by any considerations of its personal effects on those who were endeavoring to support his leadership. So I may say that the President's decision in this instance, although exceedingly discomforting to me, was not in any way embittering. Perhaps my lack of any deep chagrin lay in the fact that I was very weary, physically and mentally, and looked with longing on the prospect of returning to private law practice.

My retirement from public office was duly recorded in a mimeographed news release issued by the White House which I take the immodesty of quoting in full.

IMMEDIATE RELEASE June 7, 1935

FOR THE PRESS

Donald R. Richberg, Chairman of the National Industrial Recovery Board has tendered his resignation "to take effect upon the expiration of the present National Industrial Recovery Act on June 16, 1935."

The President today accepted the resignation with "great regret, both personal and official." In his letter to Mr. Richberg, however, the President expressed the hope that the retiring Chairman of the National Industrial Recovery Board would "be willing to stay in Washington for a short period after June sixteenth, in order to transfer, as effectively as possible, your duties as Chairman to the succeeding administration."

Mr. Richberg's letter to the President, dated June 5, 1935, follows:

"Dear Mr. President:

"In line with several conversations which we have had upon the subject in recent months, I am herewith tendering my resignation as Chairman of the National Industrial Recovery Board (and as General Counsel, NRA) to take effect upon the expiration of the present National Industrial Recovery Act on June 16, 1935.

"I appreciate deeply the opportunities to serve in your Administration and the evidences of confidence which you have generously given me. May I take the liberty of adding to an expression of faith in the extraordinary value of your public service, a reference to the affectionate regard which you inspire in those who have the privilege of working with you? I shall have a continuing regret in the loss of that association.

"Most sincerely yours,
"DONALD R. RICHBERG"

The President's letter of acceptance, dated June 7, 1935, follows:

"My dear Donald:

"I scarcely need to tell you of my great regret, both personal and official, that I must at last, with great reluctance, accept your resignation. You have given unselfishly of your time and energy during this critical period in our history and, because I know of the personal considerations which make it necessary for you to return to private life, I can no longer ask you to stay in Washington.

"You carry with you my affectionate regard, and, as I have

told you, I know that I can count on your service and help in the future.

"I hope that the Senate Resolution in amended form will have passed before June sixteenth. I shall want to talk to you in regard to the administrative set-up after that date and I hope that you will be willing to stay in Washington for a short period after June sixteenth, in order to transfer, as effectively as possible, your duties as Chairman to the succeeding administration.

"Very sincerely yours,

"FRANKLIN D. ROOSEVELT"

I was particularly gratified by the note which Steve Early, the President's press secretary, wrote across the top of the mimeograph which he sent to me:

> D.R. Never gave out a story with less heart or more reluctance.
>
> S.E.

Now I faced the difficult problem of any lawyer returning to private practice after an extended government service. I had given up my Chicago office, stored or transferred my files, and had to decide where I would start all over again. Furthermore, in my public service I had lost the affections of many, although not all, of my labor clients. At the same time, I had not won any encomiums from large business organizations since most business executives regarded me as a devoted servant of the Roosevelt Administration, to which they were hostile, as well as one of the planners and administrators of the NRA, to which they were largely opposed.

If I returned to the practice of law in Chicago I could undoubtedly build up a certain clientele among former clients and in time substantially increase it. The recollection of how my father had done this after his disastrous business venture encouraged me in the belief that I could do likewise. Nevertheless, as one who had suffered the rigors of the Chicago climate for about fifty years and found more comfort in the much more criticized one of Washington, I was not happy in the thought of returning to my old home. Furthermore, my wife, our young daughter and I had all formed a surprising number of close friendships in Washington. We had enjoyed the living conditions there, despite the constant strain of living beyond our current income.

Opportunities were presented to me to form professional associations in New York or in Washington. But for many reasons of personal taste and comfort I did not want to live in New York. Indeed, if I practiced there it was inevitable that because of my familiarity with men and affairs in Washington I would be expected to spend a great deal of time there. On the whole, I leaned toward remaining in Washington, but I did not care to accept one of several invitations to join a Washington law firm, principally because I recalled with keen pleasure that period of my Chicago practice when I had been completely independent of partnership obligations.

Recognizing that I should take a rest before making any final decision, we went to Rehoboth Beach, Delaware, for the summer and I spent the next sixty days half in relaxation and half in writing a book reviewing the NRA adventure. By the end of the summer I had practically completed the book published in 1936 by Doubleday Doran and Company, with what I considered the unfortunate title of *The Rainbow*. I would have preferred the less enigmatic *The Rainbow of the NRA*. Unhappily, the publishers felt that the NRA, as a discredited moribund institution, should not be overemphasized in the title.

On returning to Washington in the fall of 1935, I established a small law office at 726 Jackson Place and hopefully sat down to wait for clients, only one of whom had up to that time shown any particular interest in my services. I was immediately importuned by a number of persons who had cases which they had not been able to persuade any lawyer to accept, or which were of such a speculative nature that it was evident they wanted either a lawyer who could achieve miracles or one who could exercise influence in government circles. Consequently I spent much more time in my first few months of private practice examining hopeless cases and turning down undesirable clients than in carrying on a profitable business.

However, one of the many so-called "Indian claims" which was brought to my attention seemed to me soundly based. This case, however, required the institution of a suit by the government which the Department of Justice had seemed loath to undertake.

I pleaded with the Department of Justice for action with such persuasiveness that, to my surprise and considerable embarrassment it was suggested that, if I would accept an appointment as a special assistant to the Attorney General, I would be given the opportunity to prosecute this case myself. The success of this case would enrich my clients, but as a government lawyer I would receive only a fixed compensation and could not have any contingent interest in the outcome which might have produced a very substantial fee from the private client. It seemed to me, however, that I had entrapped myself in a situation in which, in justice to the claimants, I must accept the opportunity to carry forward their suit. This I undertook to do until, in December 1936, I found it desirable to join the old established Washington law firm in which I am still a partner. This made it impossible for me to continue in my government appointment. On my retirement, prosecution of this case was undertaken by Assistant Attorney General Harry Blair who carried it on after his retirement from that office.

Since I was relieved of the pressure of any large number of valuable clients, I had plenty of time in 1936 to devote myself to volunteer services for the President. It was a Presidential election year, and a major concern of the White House lay in the Democratic platform, the nomination and the subsequent campaign.

The renomination of Roosevelt was assured in view of his great popularity and the decisive control which a President in office can exercise over his party convention. But there was one plank in the platform which was worrying the White House particularly. How should the platform deal with the Supreme Court problem? It was obvious that, after the judicial nullification of New Deal legislation and Roosevelt's outspoken criticisms of the Court, he must offer some constructive solution of this conflict between the legislative (and executive) power and the judicial power. Should the Supreme Court be reformed by a change of its membership or by limitations upon its power to declare laws unconstitutional? Could this be done by acts of Congress or could it only be accomplished by a Constitutional amendment?

Proposals for legislation had been made which would provide for an increase in the membership of the Court, permitting the President to appoint additional judges more sympathetic with his political views. Proposals had been made to compel the retirement of judges at a certain age which, in view of the average advanced age of the sitting justices, would permit the President to replace several with more favorable appointees. Other proposals provided for requiring a large majority, such as two-thirds of the justices, in order to declare a law unconstitutional.

If legislation by Congress to reform the judiciary could not be enacted because of popular opposition or because such legislation itself could be invalidated by the Court, the question arose as to a Constitutional amendment. An amendment which would reform the Court itself would be open to all the objections of "Court packing." An amendment definitely enlarging the powers of the Congress would seem to be the most forthright and least objectionable attack upon the problem. Such an amendment, however, would be difficult to draw without centralizing too much authority in Washington, overriding the powers of local self-government in the states and thus arousing sufficient opposition to make the ratification exceedingly difficult.

The Democratic Party platform had to seek in some way a remedy for what President Roosevelt had strongly criticized as an intolerable conflict between the judiciary and the executive and legislative branches of the government. The question of "judicial supremacy" had caused bitter controversy from the very foundation of the government. Now it was again the question of the hour.

In my volunteer efforts to be helpful I had drafted a proposed plank for the Democratic platform and sent it to the President some time before the convention. But no solution had been reached up to the time when the platform committee under the chairmanship of Senator Wagner was meeting in Philadelphia. Then one evening I received a call from the White House asking me to see the President after breakfast the following morning. I had an intuition of what was in the wind and went to the White House with a carbon of my proposed plank in my pocket.

At that meeting the President informed me that they were troubled about the judiciary plank and Senator Wagner was calling for help. I pulled out my proposal and handed it to him. He read it, and whistled softly, and then remarked, "I think this is it." The others to whom he read it aloud were in agreement. As a result, the plank finally adopted in Philadelphia followed very closely my draft which I still think was very useful inasmuch as it did not commit the party to a specific course of action but definitely asserted the intention to do something about this thorny problem.

This incident is important because it foreshadowed the determination of the President as soon as possible after his re-election to deal with the Supreme Court issue. Although I was not the author of the subsequent "Court packing" plan, this was one of the reasons why I happened to be one of the very few people who participated in White House discussions of the plan before it was made public.

In the campaign following the President's renomination I rendered such services as I could, particularly in the matter of speech writing, up to the day of the election. My last effort along this line came under unusual circumstances. For a long time my physician, Dr. Roy Sexton, had been advising me that I ought to have my appendix removed.

As the result of repeated admonitions I finally agreed to enter a hospital on October 20, 1936, because I was sure that by that time the campaign would be practically over. This is a common belief among those who have participated in many Presidential campaigns and I think it is ordinarily a sound opinion. I was operated on by a very competent surgeon, Dr. Orr, and apparently made a good recovery, although Dr. Sexton later told me he was fearful at one time that I would pass away shortly after the operation. However, at the time I was happily relieved, as are most patients, of all the fears of my medical advisers.

A few days later while still in bed I received a telephone call from the President who had just returned from a campaign trip in New England. He told me that if the crowds which had greeted him in New England meant anything, there was not much to worry about in the election. It will be recalled that Roosevelt carried all the electoral votes except those of Vermont and Maine in that election. Evidently the New England crowds meant what they seemed to mean.

Then the President told me he was sending over some drafts of one of his final speeches which he wanted me to look over. I was delighted to have the opportunity to do something and I informed him that he would be amused to know that Mrs. Richberg was sitting by my bedside and we were marking our absentee ballots for our votes in Illinois. He could make his own guess as to how we were marking them. He evidently mentioned the matter to someone in the White House because almost immediately I had a call from photographers who made Mrs. Richberg and me pose all over again marking our ballots. This is the only time I have had a newspaper picture taken in bed and, strange to say, although it was duly published, I have never seen a copy of it.

For the next day or two messengers went back and forth between my hospital room and the White House carrying a lot of suggestions for F.D.R.'s speech which I wrote out in longhand on a tablet, some of which were utilized and most of which, as might have been expected, were discarded. Finally, I had a call from Tommy Corcoran saying, "That speech is finished and I think you are going to like it." The day the speech was delivered I was taken home in an ambulance and deposited on a couch in the living room, where I tuned in on the radio. I enjoyed the speech except for two sentences of which I had no forewarning and which frankly horrified me. "I should like," the President said, "to have it said of my first administration that in it the forces of selfishness and of lust for power met their match. I should like to have it said of my second administration that in it these forces met their master." Both my wife and I exclaimed when we heard it delivered and accurately assumed that it would annoy a multitude of people as it annoyed us. It did not seem in character with F.D.R., who, even if at times he felt arrogant, usually managed to repress any evidence of such an attitude.

My only reason for recalling this episode is that I think it demonstrates a weakness inherent in human nature which is likely to develop when any human being gains the eminence of extraordinary power. Then those around him, if they do not help him to retain a sense of humility, can do him great harm by encouraging in him an undue confidence to rule the lives of others.

It is not surprising that President Roosevelt, who reached an eminence of influence and power in the world rarely attained by any human being, should have come to feel an arrogant certitude as to his own wisdom and capacity. Such an attitude is a frightful error since the problems which the President must seek to solve are utterly beyond the physical and mental capacity of one human being. The President must not only have trusted advisers in large numbers, but he must be able and willing to repose confidence in some of his subordinates who will often know much more about the particular affairs entrusted to them than the President can possibly know.

CHAPTER XIX

An Unheroic Husband

I HAVE no liking for those intimate revelations which some autobiographers seem to feel necessary. There is, however, a certain unfairness to my descendants in not giving a brief account of my matrimonial adventures, for unless I do, anyone interested in these matters could only gather a misleading history from fragmentary records and the gossip of a few surviving persons acquainted more or less inaccurately with stray events. Furthermore, I would prefer to attempt a candid statement rather than to leave a blank in my memoir which could be filled in by either a too kind friend or a too unkind enemy.

When I was an undergraduate at the University of Chicago, the small group of charter members of the Chicago chapter of Phi Gamma Delta made a boyish compact providing that the one first married should give a dinner to the others. The one last married was to give a dinner to the surviving members, their wives and children, if any. As things turned out, I was not only the first but also, many years later, the last one married. It was practically impossible for me to give a dinner for my brethren in the years following my first marriage because they were "scattered far and wide," but eventually, after all the surviving members were married and I was married for the last time, I did have the pleasure of paying my debt.

In the course of studying law for three years in Cambridge, Massachusetts, I became acquainted with a young woman of interesting quality and strong ambitions. Elizabeth Herrick was a member of a distinguished New England family. Her ancestral names of Emery and Peabody, as well as her own, indicated her consanguinity with what she often referred to as "cold roast beef Boston." I first met her during my first year in law school when she blew into a neighbor's house one snowy evening where I was paying a call on her friends to whom I had a letter of introduction. She flung aside her coat with the remark: "Gee whiz! It's chillsome! Who brought in all that snow?" It was clear that she was referring to the tracks which my overshoes had left in the hall. I was immediately impressed with her outspoken manner as well as her good looks and proceeded to make sure that I should see her again.

In my second year she entered a dramatic school in Boston. With two fellow students in the same school she took up residence in a Boston apartment, which became a frequent rendezvous for Harvard men. Since I had been offered a position in the public speaking department at the University of Chicago and regarded myself as the proper coach for an aspiring young actress, I undertook to assist her in preparing for her work in the dramatic school. Very soon I reached the opinion that she had no native ability as an actress. On the contrary, her inherited reserve would make it impossible for her to get her personality across the footlights. At the end of the year when she left the dramatic school to try her luck at newspaper work in New York City, I was much relieved.

However, Bess's move to New York City during my senior year had a nearly disastrous effect upon my legal education. It seemed imperative that I spend every week-end, at least, in New York. This was made financially possible by offers which came to me to do bits of work in New York for the New York *Journal*, on which Bess was employed.

But the lady's stage ambitions had not been satisfied. Her brother, Robert Herrick, the author, was a friend of Clyde Fitch, at that time a most popular playwright. Through his aid she obtained a small part in Fitch's play *Glad of It* which began rehearsals in the fall of 1903. It proved to be one of Clyde Fitch's few failures and closed after a brief run. By this time I had assumed somewhat the position of a young Lochinvar come out of the West, who must rescue the object of his affections from the miserable life of either a newspaper writer or an actress, for she seemed likely to succeed in neither of these occupations.

I took advantage of the collapse of the theatrical adventure to propose that we get married, with the intention of keeping our marriage a secret until I had graduated and could really offer the bride a home. But the secret marriage, before a kindly minister in a New York suburb, became a subject of increasing embarrassment. Early in the New Year, therefore, we agreed to inform our respective families and to live in Brookline, a short distance from Cambridge.

The dream of my father's life had been that I should go through Harvard Law School and join him in the practice of law in Chicago. I was not particularly attracted by this prospect. To me it seemed a dull career compared with the creative work of writing fiction, plays and poetry, all of which I had been attempting for several years without any evidences of ultimate success. The choice before me, as I now put it to my indulgent parent, was either to go forward in a profession of which I was not enamored, as the speediest way to provide a good living for my wife and myself (a somewhat prosaic prospect) or to launch the adventure of trying to make a living by doing work in which I was keenly interested. I had, in fact, been offered a regular job as a newspaper reporter in New York. This, combined with my wife's small salary, and mine, we thought optimistically, would be sufficient to start us on the long and uncertain road to success in the writing field. Although I wasn't sure of my father's reaction to the need for a larger allowance in the remaining months of my law studies, I did feel that if he proved unwilling to carry this additional load I could then happily say good-by to the law.

Here again, as on many future occasions, I made only part of the decision that shaped my afterlife. The final decision came in the paternal blessing upon a marriage in which my parents could take only the small satisfaction that I was marrying a girl of good family. At least I had not run off with a chorus girl.

My wife's family also took a philosophical view of our marriage, particularly after they had discovered from her brother, who was a professor in the University of Chicago, that I had apparently a creditable record in the University and that there was nothing wrong with my family.

Despite the restrictions of married life, I did manage to graduate from the Law School in June and pass the bar examinations in Chicago immediately thereafter. I then went into partnership with my father.

In the ensuing years Bess and I lived in the neighborhood of the University of Chicago, in a congenial circle of friends composed mostly of professors and their wives. Apparently we were making a fair success of our married life. What gradually drew us apart was a fundamental difference in our daily and ultimate objectives. We both loved a good time, but I had a driving ambition to achieve something beyond earning a living and enjoying an unending round of parties.

If Bess had continued her newspaper career she might have had a similar urge for personal achievement, but, having abandoned it and being rather averse to raising a family, it was natural that she sought an outlet for her amazing energies in amusements which gave her only transient satisfaction. Typical of her desire to enjoy life while she was young was her statement one day that she was not interested in what happened to her after she was thirty years old.

To avoid misunderstanding, I should explain that she was keenly interested in literature, and took a lively part in discussions of books and plays. Dinners at home or with friends were never dull occasions. There was practically no resort to cards to while away the time. But there was an insatiable demand to go somewhere and do something, to ride horseback, to dance, or go to the theater. We had what might be called a gay life in Chicago, and also in New York during the year when I went there in the service of the Progressive Party.

By the year 1910, however, I had become surfeited with too much play, and was hankering to use my spare time in pursuit of my old passion for writing. That year I began to write my first book, a pretty poor novel, *The Shadow Men,* which was published in 1911. Since I had only evenings and holidays to devote to writing, I began to avoid a lot of parties and to suggest that Bess enjoy them in the companionship of others who got more fun out of them than I did. In this manner, according to the stock phrase, we drifted apart.

In later years, when I have associated more with couples apparently well satisfied with each other, I have come to see that my early married years in Chicago were lived in what was really an unhealthy atmosphere. The men and women with whom we associated, being mostly University people, were not superficial in their professional interests. But their social life was, on the whole, a superficial sort of existence. The unintelligence of it was concealed by the fact that the men were all engaged in intellectual work; their wives were well-educated and well-informed; conversations were not on simply trivial subjects. Indeed, most of the men were making steady progress toward a high rank in a profession which they enjoyed. Perhaps the trouble was that I did not feel that I was making any progress in my profession, so that, after the relaxation of a hilarious evening, I went back to a dusty office full of dusty problems in which I had little interest beyond a natural desire to do a good job and earn a decent fee.

In reviewing my first marriage, I wish I could make clear the extent of my responsibility for its failure. I was not a great playboy, a great spender or a great lover. Had I been any one of the three, I might have held the affection of my wife. I was not content to sacrifice time and energy and money in giving my wife the good times which she should have had in my company; and at the same time I was often annoyed by being a sit-by-the-fire when she was enjoying herself with other people. This also entailed counter hospitality which put an excess burden upon a lawyer with a very modest income who, as time went on, had to devote a substantial part of that income to supporting other dependents.

The final break came from my insistence that if my wife did not change her way of living I would be forced to leave her and live by myself. The exact reasons to justify this insistence are not so important as the fact that I had become unwilling to struggle any longer to maintain a marriage relationship which seemed to me to have lost all reality.

After two years' separation my wife filed a bill for divorce and obtained it on the obvious ground of "desertion," with no contest and certainly no counter charges on my part.

In fairness to her I should add a final note that although I paid her alimony for many years, there came a time when she wrote that it was no longer necessary to continue the payments.

I did not particularly enjoy living alone for three years, 1915–

18, although it did give me a much greater opportunity to devote myself to those things which seemed to me of major importance. I had become involved in the fight in behalf of gas consumers with the Gas Company, had been able to work literally night and day on the job and had learned the rewards obtained in the practice of law from working harder and longer hours than anyone ought to work. In this case Kipling was right: "He travels the fastest who travels alone." But in 1918 I married again. This time both my new wife and I made a vital mistake in the choice of a mate. She had been married twice, the first time when she was very young, to a much older, tyrannical husband, from whom she had finally been separated justifiably, at least according to her story. She had then married a very handsome, attractive man who, again according to her story, looked like but had failed to be a great lover. She had ardent, romantic ideas which were deeply disappointed in what turned out to be a prosaic marriage. I could not testify that her various complaints against her husband were warranted, but from my own knowledge of her I would say that she was a person of great ambition and strong social sense who wanted to be attached to someone who was going to make a great name in the world, and who, either mentally or physically, would transform her life from the normal humdrum of middle-class housekeeping.

Whatever the causes, she had divorced her second husband and was looking for a third. I too was looking for a new mate, and it was inevitable that with both of us intensely anxious to make a successful marriage, we should have been readily attracted to each other. I made no effort to conceal my ambitions, and being at the time a conspicuous public figure, my prospects seemed good. She made no effort to conceal her intense desire to be the wife of a man she could "adore" and for whose success she could give her all. When you add to all these elements a strong physical attraction, it should be evident why we were married.

It is a strange phenomenon that after an unsuccessful marriage a man or a woman is likely to bounce back into precisely the same kind of marriage. This, Lynette and I learned very soon. She was a perpetual party-giver and party-goer. We took a more expensive apartment than I had ever lived in and filled it with more expensive furnishings than I had ever known. The gay life began all over again and at this time I was so deeply involved in enormous litigations that I had to burn the candle at both ends to keep up with my business and my wife. My principal respites came when I had to spend time on business in Washington and other cities. In addition to this difficulty, my wife insisted on retaining old associations which aroused continuing annoyance and jealousies. The climax came when she insisted on going to Florida with a gay woman friend to spend a pleasant winter vacation surrounded by detached or semi-detached males while I was left alone to carry on my exacting work in Chicago.

This vacation was cut short when Lynette was bragging one day about her husband who, *in absentia,* was always a wonderful person. A worldly woman, who was present, remarked: "And you have gone off and left that man alone for three months? I think you're a fool." Shortly afterward she returned to Chicago. But the harm had been done. And while I did not suggest our immediate separation, I did make it very clear to her that for me she had lost her glamour.

The lady had always taken great pride in getting her way. Now, unable to recapture a lost affection, she proceeded to work herself into an hysteria which in the beginning I felt she was feigning. Ultimately, however, she had a severe nervous breakdown. The situation distressed me deeply because I felt that the rigidity of my attitude might really have been responsible for her breakdown. Daily threats of suicide, which made it almost impossible for me to concentrate on work when away from her, finally made it necessary to place her in a sanatorium. That effort proved a failure, as did my own clumsy efforts to calm her down when she returned home. A long visit to relatives was equally ineffective.

I do not believe I was the cause of her condition, but that would be a natural unfriendly interpretation of the situation. We consulted one outstanding neurologist after another. The final despairing verdict, given to both my wife and me by the physician whom I regarded as the top-notch man in Chicago, was that I should no longer try to live with her; that it would wreck my life and not save hers. We therefore arranged for her to return to her home town to live with her sister and niece who would take care of her so long as I provided the means.

Months passed with no break in the situation. Then, without a word of warning, she suddenly reappeared in Chicago, dressed with her former extreme interest in good clothes (after two years of letting herself look like a hag) and informed me that the only answer to our problem was for her to get a divorce, if we could agree upon a substantial alimony. I advised her promptly to go to a very competent lawyer. Since Clarence Darrow acted for her, I think it can be safely said that her interests were well protected. At least I thought so. The most amusing and typical part of the alimony agreement was her insistence that she should have an additional $100 a month for the first year because, she said gaily, "That will enable me to dress better and do more things and get a husband quicker, which will all be for your benefit."

Thus ended my second matrimonial misadventure. Despite her conceded abilities and careful planning, Lynette did not get a new husband. In 1929 she became engaged to a prosperous man who lost his fortune in the depression and took his life. This, reasonably enough, caused another nervous breakdown, and although I was at that time married again, I had once more to carry the mental and financial load of a sanatorium patient. Happily there was another recovery and Lynette lived (and the alimony payments continued) until the year 1952.

If it would not sound ungallant, I would say that Florence Weed, who made my life perennially worth while by marrying me on Christmas Eve, 1924, was primarily responsible for our marriage. Although I pursued her with appropriate ardor, it was her confidence rather than mine and the obvious integrity of her character that gave me courage to urge my suit. And it was her willingness to marry me that settled the doubts I had of my capacity to make a good husband for any woman. The advice of mutual friends was far from flattering to me. As one man put it: "That girl bats one thousand per cent and if you don't make a success of this marriage it's going to be all your fault." I quite agreed with this judgment, but it should be a little terrifying to any man to be told that he must live up to the exalted standards set by his wife. Here again the lady's disposition lightened what might have been a heavy obligation.

There is many a clinging vine who holds her husband by the constant appeal to his strength. On the other hand, many a woman of strong character, capable of standing and walking alone, creates a sense of competition often exasperating to the self-confident male.

It was my happy fortune to marry at long last a woman who had a mind of her own and ample ability to take care of herself, but who regarded it as her main business to encourage her husband in his ambitions and not allow him to feel that her own ambitions required any particular consideration or sacrifice on his part.

Any person of my strong ambitions and convictions is certain to be rather selfish in the planning of the objectives and the manner of his living. But he also must be blind if he does not realize the extent to which a devoted wife is making daily sacrifices of her special interests to which in decency he ought to give, from time to time, as much unselfish consideration as is possible to a normally selfish male.

As a result of implementing our theories, Florence has always been able to foster the illusion that I generally have my way in all momentous and in most trivial decisions. At the same time I have had the comforting sense that her course of living was on the whole more satisfactory to her than any other which she could have experienced. Sometimes, lying awake at night, indulging in the sort of introspection where one is dubious of all his virtues and acutely conscious of all his vices, I have wondered whether my feeling that both of us have found complete satisfaction in our marriage was only an illusion. But in the morning sunlight, watching my wife's face across the breakfast table, such doubts always happily disappear.

Immediately after our marriage we decided that we did not want to live inside the city limits of Chicago. We wanted a home of our own rather than an apartment. But we did not want the ordinary suburban life. So we drove around the southwest unfashionable countryside and finally located a small house in two and a half acres of wooded hillside in Palos Park, adjacent to the great forest preserves that ring Chicago. It had few modern conveniences. The water supply was a primitive gem, consisting of huge cisterns in which rain water was gathered and then pumped by hand to a tank in the attic. For drinking purposes it had to be filtered; and for all household purposes it was beautifully inadequate.

We promptly had a well drilled which went down 210 feet before reaching a bedrock water supply. I can still hear the clink-clank of the drill as it pounded hour after hour at what we called a nickel a stroke. The pure water finally tapped was so hard that only one company ventured to assure us that its softener would make it usable for washing. But Florence and I had been taking turns at the pump in the basement. It required 80 strokes to fill the tank in the attic, which would then be emptied with surprising speed. Hence, when the well was finished, a gasoline pump installed, the water softener set up, and hard and softened water flowing through the new plumbing system, we felt the glow of an achievement which no city dweller who just turns on a faucet will ever know.

Our home had so many other inconveniences that within two years we came to the fateful decision that we must rebuild it. We were unable to go ahead with our plans, however, until our daughter, who arrived in August of 1926, had reached an age to make it feasible to move into a temporary home.

The rebuilding of our home in the summer of 1927 probably remains as one of the most trying episodes of my wife's life. Fortunately for me, I was engaged at the time in extensive litigations which kept me away from home most of the time, living in comfortable hotels. Meanwhile, the family had been moved to the artistic but quite uncomfortable residence built by the noted sculptor Lorado Taft in the Palos woods. He had had the wisdom not to spend many of his days there! Florence had to carry on the task of caring for a year-old child and traveling back and forth between her rather gloomy abode and our home, which was first reduced practically to a skeleton of walls, and then rebuilt into a reasonably modern residence.

The effect of this summer on my wife was a firm determination never again to live in a house in the woods. It sounded romantic, but it was hardly ideal for a woman with a baby, particularly one whose husband appeared only at rare intervals and then departed to the comfort of a metropolitan hotel.

Our rebuilt home proved very satisfactory until we moved to Washington in 1933. It was in Palos that Florence began her favorite hobby of gardening. We built a small ornamental pool, a playhouse for the child, and in my comfortable study I was able to spend a great deal of time, which would normally be spent in an office, working over records and briefs in the labor and public utility cases that occupied most of my time.

One of our near neighbors was David E. Lilienthal, who had come into my office on his graduation from Harvard in 1923. As the Lilienthals' family interests, like ours, were largely in children and gardening, we had many things in common. There were a dozen or more other congenial families in our small community, so we had all the local society we needed in addition to constant visiting back and forth with friends in Chicago. The worst feature of our married life at this time was my long and frequent absences from home.

My absences were perplexing to our small daughter. One night she was saying her prayers, a ceremony on which she herself insisted, always making it a very intimate conversation with "our Father who art in heaven." This time she was calling on the Lord to bless her mother, her grandmother, her dog "Billy," and our maid of all work, Carrie, when she suddenly stopped and asked: "Mummy, where is Daddy?"

"Oh, Daddy is working downtown. He's staying at the Palmer House."

Whereupon Eloise resumed: "And dear Lord, please bless my Daddy. He is staying at the Palmer House. I think you had better bless him twice."

I cannot resist one more "fond parent" story. Florence early explained the simplest facts of life to Eloise, who listened quietly and asked very few questions. But apparently she thought the matter over carefully, for one day she said suddenly, "Mummy, I understand I came from you. Is that right?"

"Yes."

"And you came from your mother?"

"Yes."

"And she came from her mother?"

"Yes."

"Well, Mummy, how did all this thing start?"

No answer.

As the years went on and our daughter Eloise grew older, it often became possible to move the entire family to the location of my work. Thus we spent three winters in Arizona when I was working on a particularly long litigation. We also had occasional visits to San Francisco and Washington, D.C.

The years of the depression impressed us only with the trials and sorrows of others, because my law practice was steadily increasing and the federal income tax had not yet reached the level where a successful lawyer would find himself earning more money for the government than for his family.

When we first moved to Washington in 1933, we did not entirely abandon our Palos home. We simply moved most of our furnishings and turned the house over to friends. In 1935, when we finally decided to take up permanent residence in Washington, we faced a difficult problem. The Palos house could not command a rental that would much more than cover taxes and repairs. It could not be sold for anything like its value, during a period when there was a surplus of housing almost everywhere. Years later we finally managed to dispose of it for about one-third of what we had put into it.

Any account of our life in Washington would be a twice-told tale. It was for two years similar to that of hundreds of public officials who lived in rented homes and tried to meet the cost of living on a government salary. Later, with the improved income of private practice, our economic problems diminished until we were finally able to buy a beautiful home on a hill in Spring Valley. There, between days of gardening and evenings filled with a great variety of entertainments, Florence had a busy, interesting and at times exciting life which we were happily able to share, since my days of long absences on business were over.

That the complications of my early years of matrimony had a deterrent effect upon any budding ambitions for public office, can be understood with little further explanation. Even though a happy and tranquil married life finally provided the background against which I might be able to render effective public service, the earlier unhappy years provided a poor stage setting for a public career. Indeed, I was much relieved that so little of my private life became the subject of publicity during the two years when my public life received flattering and embarrassing attention. But, appointees to public office are seldom subjected to the amount of gossip that is inevitable when a man runs for an elective office. It would have been folly for me, in the years between 1915–1924, to have sought a popular election. It was easy, therefore, for me to reject suggestions, of which there were quite a few, that I should seek to run for this or that position. Indeed, my candidacy for a judgeship in 1915 was the last effort in that direction which I could have wisely made.

As a result of the prominence that I achieved in the first two years of the Roosevelt administration there were many other suggestions, mostly from self-interested persons, that I should aspire to some high office. This account of my adventures as "an unheroic husband" may indicate some of the reasons that made it easy for me to lay aside any youthful ambitions for political fame and to find a real contentment in the comparative and comforting obscurity of private life.

CHAPTER XX

The "Court Packing" Misadventure

THE OVERWHELMING victory of President Roosevelt in 1936 had the effect of assuring F.D.R. that the mass of the people would support his program for extending the federal power to plan and direct an improvement of the economic system, regardless of constitutional barriers raised by the Supreme Court. The immediate problem of his administration seemed to be to overcome the opposition of the "nine old men" in that Court.

Understanding Roosevelt's desire for an immediate attack on this problem, I attempted to work out a solution by an act of Congress which would neither increase the membership of the Court nor impose any legislative limitations upon its procedure. I ultimately drafted an act to provide for the compulsory retirement of all justices from the *active* Court at the age of seventy. This would permit the President to make appointments to complete a membership of the *active* Court of nine justices, all under the age of seventy. This would permit any justice on reaching the age of seventy either to resign and thus make himself free to engage in any other activity, or merely to retire to a non-active status. This would leave him still a member of the Court, subject to an assignment to special duties by the chief justice, or to recall in a particular case to serve in the event of the disqualification of an active member.

It seemed to me that such a law would not reflect upon the value of the public services of any member of the Court, but would at the same time provide an automatic basis for retirement (at full pay) from active service of those members who, according to the law of averages, might be regarded as less capable than younger members of the bar.

With an obstinacy of opinion that may not be approved, I still believe that this program would have provided the best solution for the problem confronting the President. Unfortunately, Attorney General Cummings advised the President that my proposed law would be unconstitutional, apparently as a modification of the constitutional provision that the justices of the Supreme Court should be appointed for life. I contended, and still believe, that a provision to retire justices from active service but to retain them as members of the Court would comply with all constitutional requirements.

I heard nothing further about the matter until, late in January 1937, I received a summons to attend a conference in the evening at the White House. When I arrived I found the President attended only by the Attorney General and Solicitor General Reed. The President informed me that they had worked out a program on which they would like opinion. The program consisted of an outline of the Attorney General's proposal for legislation, the draft of a bill for the enactment of the law by Congress and a message from the President to the Congress transmitting these two documents with his favorable recommendation.

Under the circumstances, rather than argue in favor of my original proposition, I felt it was wiser to accept the program which had apparently been approved and to suggest only such modifications in its presentation as might help to induce its acceptance by the Congress.

It seemed to me that the President should urge his program upon the Congress, not on the somewhat deceptive basis that the Supreme Court was overloaded with work and provision should be made for its relief, but on the more candid basis that he thought that a younger and more vigorous Court would have more modern ideas of the Court's functions and a more liberal construction of constitutional limitations. I particularly urged there should be no appearance of deceptiveness in the President's purposes in proposing such legislation.

Somewhat to my surprise, Solicitor General Reed strongly supported me. Evidently from his extensive experience in handling government litigation he was dubious that a good case could be made for reforming the Court merely on the basis that it was overworked and that justice delayed was, in the old phrase, justice denied. Subsequent developments in the legislative battle showed that the Solicitor General had a sound basis for his attitude.

As a result of several days of discussion, there was some modification in the proposed message to Congress. On the date of the President's birthday celebration, January 30, 1937, Judge Rosenman, a long-trusted and intimate adviser of the President, was called in and informed of the program. So far as I know, no one else knew what was in the wind before the day when the program was made public, first in a conference of Congressional leaders followed immediately by the transmission of the President's message to Congress.

An interesting question, however, had arisen earlier as to the timing of the message. Since the customary White House judiciary dinner was scheduled for early in February, should the President send the message to Congress before or after the dinner? The President, inspired by his ever-ready and somewhat impish sense of humor, had suggested that his choice should be whether to take only one cocktail before dinner and have it a very amiable affair, or to have a mimeographed copy of the program laid beside the plate of each justice and then take three cocktails to fortify himself against their reactions.

The final decision was to hold the judiciary dinner in an atmosphere of comparative harmony, although some rumors of the President's impending action must have created a certain tension among the distinguished guests of honor. One embarrassing incident of this dinner stands out particularly in my memory. On the day of the dinner I was working with the President so late in the afternoon that I had very little time in which to go home to don my "white tie and tails." As a result, I arrived at the White House a little late, which is an almost unforgivable offense. I rushed into the cloak room, and as I peeled off my overcoat, the three studs of my formal shirt popped out. A colored attendant hastened to my rescue, but in inserting the studs he left enlarged thumbprints on the immaculate surface of my shirt. Decidedly flustered, my wife and I hurried upstairs, to be greeted by anxious aides who escorted us into the East Room, where we had no sooner taken our places than the President, whom we had kept waiting, was immediately announced. Of course I apologized for my unseemly tardiness to the President and Mrs. Roosevelt, who accepted it graciously without appearing to notice my even more unseemly shirt front.

After dinner, coffee was served at the main table and at small tables placed in the center of the horseshoe. I found myself at a table including Senator Borah and Justices Butler and Roberts. Justice Roberts opened the conversation with a pleasant reference to the fact that I had spoken recently before the Judiciature Society in Philadelphia and had there criticized his opinion in the case of the United States v. Butler, in which the AAA Act had been held unconstitutional. Justice Roberts who was a personal friend did not hesitate to rag me, observing that he was a member of the Philadelphia organization and wished that he had been present. It reminded him, he said, of a story of the first meeting of the High Court in Pennsylvania after an election. One of the judges said to his neighboring colleague: "Who is that sour-faced man sitting down there at the left of the lawyers' table? His face is familiar, but I can't recall his name." His colleague responded: "Oh, that is the blankety-blank who ran against me in the last election—not that I have any prejudice against him!"

Shortly after the judiciary dinner the President's "Court packing" plan was sent to the Congress and then the storm broke. In the ensuing legislative battle I took no active part, although I did work intensively with the President in various conferences and in the preparation of various speeches. In fact, I had a good deal to do with the preparation of the President's Jackson Day address in March 1937.

Of the various suggestions that naturally came to me, for transmission to the President, from those either supporting or opposed to the program, one was peculiarly interesting. A prominent member of the House of Representatives told me of a conversation he had had with Justice Stone in which the Justice had said that he wished the President would be more patient and trust to the passage of time to solve his problem. This might have been regarded as a hint that some of the older members of the Court were in a mood to resign if they were not compelled to do so under fire; and that, with new appointments, the President might be able to achieve his ends. The message seemed of sufficient significance to transmit to the President, and I accordingly delivered it one afternoon when we were swimming together in the White House pool. He received it with interest although he expressed some perplexity as to why Justice Stone had taken that particular avenue of transmitting his opinion.

There was much uncertainty as to the outcome of the controversy in the Senate where it was most acute. It was generally assumed that a vote in the House would support the President, but the issue in the Senate was very doubtful. There the Administration forces were led by Senator Joseph Robinson of Arkansas, who was almost surely unsympathetic privately with the President's program, but who manfully maintained his responsibilities as the Administration leader.

That the President appreciated Robinson's support was made clear in a conversation which I once had with the President on Supreme Court appointments. My name had been bruited in the press from time to time as a possible appointee and though I had never solicited such an appointment, the President appeared to want me to feel assured that I was high on the list of his possibilities. He referred to the fact that in the event of the retirement of Justice Brandeis, he would anticipate appointing Felix Frankfurter to that vacancy. But he indicated that in the first vacancy that might occur he felt a deep obligation to Senator Robinson. As he explained, Joe had carried on a continuing faithful support of the Administration, although he recognized that many programs were difficult for the Senator to support. He knew that Senator Robinson would regard an appointment to the Supreme Court as a final crown of his public service and he felt that he deserved it.

Although I recognized the fine service that the Senator had rendered, I foresaw with ironic amusement how the public would react if the first appointment which the President made to increase the progressive quality of the Supreme Court's membership should be a staunch conservative like Senator Robinson.

Late in the spring of 1937, when the Court fight was still the main subject of political discussion, Assistant Attorney General Harry Blair had a buffet supper at which both Senator Robinson and Attorney General Cummings, among a large number of Administration supporters, were present. When I asked the Attorney General what he thought of the prospects, he said that Senator Robinson thought he had enough votes in the Senate to put the bill across, but that he, the Attorney General, was a bit doubtful.

At the same party I had a talk with Senator Robinson in the course of which I offered him one of my very mild denicotinized cigars. He enjoyed it so much that I suggested I would send him a box of them. It was rumored that he had a heart weakness and I thought that the smoking of heavy cigars was a habit which could well be modified. I sent the cigars in due course, but I never received an acknowledgment, and if they might have been helpful I am afraid they arrived too late. Shortly after this party my wife and I left for a house party given by the Thomas Blodgetts in Great Barrington. My host and I were returning from a morning of golf when Florence greeted me with the sad news that Senator Robinson had died of a heart attack.

His death signaled the collapse of the Court packing plan. With Senator Robinson gone, the anti-Administration members of the Senate took command and the Administration was compelled to accept a defeat of the President's program. With the passage of the years it is now generally agreed that this was a fortunate outcome.

The plan was really defeated by the shift of opinion in the Supreme Court whereby, during the pendency of the President's bill in Congress, the Court substantially reversed certain previous ultra-conservative opinions. Under the leadership of Chief Justice Hughes, supported by Justice Roberts whose views had undergone an apparent modification, there came into being a five-to-four majority sustaining Administration legislation which would certainly have been overruled two years previously by a vote of at least five to four. In the face of this new majority the older justices resigned one by one as the procession of decisions showed they had become merely dissenters and were no longer controllers of the decisions of the Court. The resignation of Justice Vandeventer, followed by the appointment of Senator Black to the vacancy, marked the beginning of the end of conservative domination of the Court. As President Roosevelt said to me: "We lost the battle, but we won the war." Whether that was a victory for the American people or not is a question which can only be answered by the ultimate judgment of history.

I had an acute interest in the first appointment made by F.D.R. for many reasons. In the first place he had discussed his possible appointments with me in such a manner as to indicate clearly that I would be under serious consideration. Then, after the first vacancy occurred, I was talking one day with Attorney General Cummings when a friendly newspaper man asked him for some help in forecasting an appointment. "I suppose I can start with the two of you," the reporter said. Cummings quickly replied: "No, only one of us. I am too old." He was then sixty-five and the President had voiced publicly his objection to appointing anyone over sixty. Privately, Homer told me that I was high on his list—and the Attorney General's recommendation has always had great weight in judicial appointments.

To be quite candid, I was apprehensively hopeful. Of course I would have accepted one of the highest honors and greatest opportunities for public service that can come to a lawyer. At the same time I was fearful of the financial consequences. I was just beginning to make some surplus income to protect the future of the family trio. At that time there would have been no pension even for myself in case of disability and no financial protection for my wife and daughter in case of my death.

Furthermore, Florence had strong doubts, which I shared mildly, as to whether I would be altogether happy with the confining work of the Court and the necessary restrictions on other public activities. I was only fifty-six, in good health, except for annoying arthritis, and enjoyed sports and social life. It was probable that the sedentary life of a justice (from which a younger man such as Justice Douglas quite obviously seeks frequently to escape) would prove eventually unpleasant to me.

While I could not deny my ambitious interest in an appointment there was actually considerable relief in speculating that opposition to my confirmation in the Senate, which was sure to come from some radicals and probably from some conservatives, would be likely to deter Roosevelt from appointing me. In any event, I did not lift a finger to advance my chances. The day after the appointment of Senator Black was announced, Secretary McIntyre telephoned me to say that the President had directed him to tell me that I was the last person eliminated from consideration before he finally made the appointment. When I repeated this to Florence, she asked with wifely candor: "Was that a compliment?"

CHAPTER XXI

Prelude to the Second World War

An important change took place in my method of practicing law in December 1936. Out of a clear sky I had a call from my old friend Joseph E. Davies, whose cousin Morgan Davies had been one of my partners in Chicago. It developed that Joe was about to be appointed ambassador to Russia, with the prospect that after a couple of years there he might be moved to Great Britain, to the Court of St. James. This meant that, for apparently at least four years, he would be out of the active practice of law. He had built up a very successful law firm in the previous eighteen years since his retirement from office as chairman of the Federal Trade Commission. He felt that to maintain the standing of the firm he should bring in another older lawyer of at least a conspicuous reputation. (I might add immodestly that he wanted to add a man who had a better reputation as a lawyer than as a politician.)

The other members of the firm, all able lawyers, agreed with Joe as to the desirability of such an addition, although I cannot say that they were sure that I would fit the bill. My personal acquaintance with them was limited to a slight acquaintance with Seth Richardson, a former Assistant Attorney General under President Hoover, with whom I had once engaged in a debate before a legal forum on the merits and constitutionality of the New Deal program. When we came to discuss financial arrangements I think it must have been a little shock to Joe and his partners to learn that my first year of practice in Washington had not produced as much income as I had been making in Chicago prior to accepting public office. However, they concealed any disappointment courteously and made a very generous arrangement for the partnership division.

It had been borne in upon me more and more in my year of private practice that it would be difficult for me to handle any large clientele except as a member of a fair-sized law firm. On the other hand, if I were limited to a few substantial clients I would become particularly dependent upon them, a prospect which I did not relish. I had always enjoyed a sense of independence, having had a considerable variety of clients even when they were mostly labor organizations or public bodies.

The shift of my practice into the firm of Davies, Richberg, Beebe, Busick and Richardson (which in 1951 became Davies, Richberg, Tydings, Beebe and Landa), did not produce any particularly interesting results, except some additional clients, until the year 1938. Then more spectacular cases began to develop.

In the spring of 1938, a most interesting and exciting case was offered to me when I was asked to represent the oil companies whose properties had been expropriated by the Mexican government. But, before beginning work on this case, we were to take an unexpected trip to Europe where we saw at close range the gathering storm that preceded the hurricane of the Second World War.

Our decision to go to Europe was made most abruptly. We were taking a vacation at Rehoboth Beach when I received a cablegram from Joe Davies, who had been recently made ambassador to Belgium, suggesting that my family join his in Antwerp and enjoy a cruise on their huge yacht, the *Sea Cloud.*

The war clouds were gathering over Europe. Hitler was threatening to let loose the dogs of war, and this year appeared to be the last time when my wife and I and our young daughter might see a bit of Europe before it was once more devastated and probably permanently transformed by another holocaust. So we took passage on the *City of Paris,* hurried to Paris and thence to Antwerp, where we were met by Joe and Marjorie Davies and ensconced in the luxurious accommodations of the *Sea Cloud,* a 357-foot, four-masted yacht, equipped with auxiliary power, one of the few surviving evidences of the days when the owners of great fortunes could afford to maintain such an expensive toy.

It appeared that Joe had not as yet fulfilled all the requirements for official presentation of credentials, but he was in such a de facto position that he was able to give a very interesting dinner on the *Sea Cloud* to the members of the Belgian Cabinet, which provided a most delightful launching of our visit. After the dinner there was a movie presented on one of the spacious sheltered decks which, strange to say, was an American film recounting the adventures of Tom Sawyer and Huckleberry Finn. I had the impression that it was all very mysterious to the honored guests although enjoyed by the small American contingent.

There was one amusing incident which still gives me a chuckle. Our daughter and Mrs. Davies' daughter Dienie were of the gum-chewing age. This was in the period when bubble gum had just been developed to entertain children and annoy their elders. A steward had been directed after dinner to pass a plate of numerous varieties of gum to the youngsters and, presumably to the distress of our hostess, brought in a large platter which was offered to the assembled guests who, with more curiosity or courtesy than discretion, all took a piece. The lights went out for the movie as the chomping of the gum proceeded throughout the distinguished company, but when much later the lights were turned on again, all signs of gum chewing had disappeared and, as we ascertained thereafter, there were no discarded cuds on the bottom of deck chairs! I am still wondering about the feelings of the Belgian officials and their wives who must have found it necessary to swallow or somewhere conceal their inedible confection.

The next morning we moved out of Antwerp harbor into the North Sea—a beautiful sunny day, with the exhilaration of a spanking breeze, so it was possible to have the crew sent aloft to unfurl the sails of the four tall masts, and we flew north under such a cloud of canvas as is seldom seen in the world today.

Our last night with the Davies' was spent in Brussels, where we were housed for the night in the half-opened Embassy. It so happened that on this day President Roosevelt went into Maryland on a campaign trip to defeat the renomination of Senator Tydings in favor of Representative David Lewis. It will be recalled that this was a part of the famous and unsuccessful "purge" of 1938, and the President was speaking that day in Denton, Maryland, at half past two in the afternoon, which was half past eight in the evening in Brussels.

This speech was of peculiar interest to our company because Senator Tydings was Mr. Davies' son-in-law. For this reason Joe had made extraordinary efforts to get an adequate radio set up in the Embassy. However, there was a great deal of difficulty about tuning in and finally, when dinner was announced, everyone else went into the dining room, leaving Joe fiddling with the radio. I waited with him in faint hopes of establishing our contact. Then, just as he was about to give up, that easily recognized voice came in. It was quite a speech, not unduly offensive, but not one which a man would enjoy hearing in opposition to a son-in-law candidate. At the end of it I looked at Joe, wondering what he would say. He took a long breath and then said: "He is a great man. It was a great speech." We then went in to dinner.

The next day my wife and daughter and I returned to Paris and proceeded with a most enjoyable trip through Switzerland and then back to Paris and over to England. We had a happy time that summer of 1938 except for constant reminders that Europe was teetering along a precipitous road to war.

In London I had a talk with Ambassador Kennedy, another good friend, as to the question of the imminent outbreak of war and the advisability of any change of plans under the circumstances. He advised me to go ahead with our proposed automobile trip in England and telephone him from Southampton, when he might possibly give me a more definite idea as to prospects.

While in London I sent a letter of introduction from a mutual friend to Mr. David Lloyd George and in response received an invitation to drive to his home in Surrey for luncheon.

Knowing that Mr. Lloyd George was then seventy-five years old, I was amazed at the effervescent vigor with which he greeted me, and hurried me into a room where I met Mrs. Lloyd George and an Oxford professor and his wife and daughter, who made up the entire company. Our host perched himself on top of a window seat and proceeded with a rapid fire of questions and comments which lasted throughout the subsequent luncheon and the entire three hours of my stay. Very soon he raised the subject of Roosevelt's running for a third term, a matter in which I was deeply interested. He assured me that as "an old Prime Minister" he had followed Roosevelt's career very closely, read all his major utterances, and regarded him as "the authentic voice of democracy in the world today." He could see no reason why there should be any question that he should wish and ought to succeed himself in the Presidency at the end of his second term.

Against a great volume of protests and counter arguments I tried to explain American historic objections to a third term and our historic fears of executive power too long concentrated in one man. Particularly I stressed the tremendous power of patronage through which a President could dictate his own renomination and steadily increase the number of persons in positions of power who were beholden to him or would, for other reasons, follow his leadership. Lloyd George was somewhat impatient of these objections. He insisted that the Prime Minister of Great Britain had as great a power of patronage. He said: "Why, I even made bishops, didn't I, my dear?"—referring the question to his wife. She agreed that he had indeed made bishops.

We covered many interesting topics of discussion, exchanging ideas about such men as Theodore Roosevelt and Woodrow Wilson. In regard to the latter, he asked an interesting question. He said he was writing his memoirs and was at the moment working on a vignette of Woodrow Wilson. He asked me quite bluntly: "Do you think Wilson was really a great man?" I said, "That is hard for me to answer for many reasons, but I may say, yes, I think he had elements of greatness." He repeated this after me and said, "Now, that's just the phrase I wanted." But I have never learned whether or not he used it.

Just before I left, Mr. Lloyd George asked me to sign his Visitors' Register which, of course, I was delighted to do. He said, "I think the last signature on there is your John W. Davis. You have no objection to signing next, have you?" I said, Oh, no, I thought very highly of Mr. Davis. But when he opened the book and took a look, he said, "Oh, I was mistaken. The last signature is that of Maisky, the Soviet ambassador to Great Britain. I think we will start another page."

After my return to London we took a motor trip of several days, ending up in Southampton, where I telephoned Ambassador Kennedy and received in answer to my inquiry as to how things were, the enigmatic reply: "I think it is all right for you to go on home." I did not know whether this meant that he thought nothing would happen in a few days and the voyage would be a safe one, or whether he meant trouble might break out at any time and it was well to be on the way to the United States! The fact was that the Munich meeting took place while we were on the ocean and by the time we reached America the world knew that Chamberlain had achieved what has been since regarded as either an unfortunate appeasement of Hitler or a much-desired breathing space for Great Britain in which to prepare for the eventual march of the German Armies.

CHAPTER XXII

The New Dealers in Peace and War

FROM the fall of 1938 to the death of Roosevelt in the spring of 1945 the Roosevelt administration became more and more engrossed in international problems. The characters and opinions of the New Dealers became a matter of profound concern to all the world. Although I had been surprised to learn in 1934 that I had become an international figure in whom many people in Europe had a certain curiosity, I had lived in what was obscurity compared with the lives of the New Dealers whose official activities carried on through the war era.

There was a book published in 1934 by Simon and Schuster entitled *The New Dealers* which was anonymously authored by "Unofficial Observer." It has been my understanding that behind this anonymity was the penmanship of Jay Franklin. As a journalistic review of the current outstanding personalities in the Roosevelt administration, it had many merits. It was sufficiently lively to attract a large audience and it was sufficiently inaccurate in snap judgments to provide the basis for several volumes of historical correction. However, the book contained a host of acute observations which recommend it to anyone wishing to understand the first year of the New Deal. Most of the fifty-odd persons discussed played sufficiently important parts in the development of a new progressivism under the second President Roosevelt to make this early appraisal of them of real historical value.

The shrewd Observer separated the radicals, the moderate progressives and the conservatives in the administration with surprising accuracy in most instances. His analysis of the part I was trying to play gave me both amusement and satisfaction, although I would hardly agree with several of his conclusions. The following quotation from *The New Dealers* provided me then and now with a definite aid to self-analysis:

> At one time Richberg's friends were boosting him for the United States Supreme Court, but some of them began to wonder whether his real ambitions were not for a partnership in J. P. Morgan and Company. Perhaps their fears were unjustified, but Big Business had swallowed Newton D. Baker who in his salad days was as liberal as Richberg. The latter may be of sterner stuff, but in general he illustrates the almost inevitable tendency of the aging radical, when entrusted with responsibility and power, to go conservative. If he should opt for the flesh pots after a life with the crack pots, liberalism need not mourn him as a lost soul. He has done as much as any one man to advance the principles of liberalism in his day and age. His contribution to the movement which produced the New Deal and to its initial application has been invaluable. After all, he is over fifty years of age and if any man has earned a vacation from progressivism he has. Perhaps, in the ideal commonwealth which may arise from Richberg's New Deal there will be a constitutional provision by which a man is permitted to change his political opinions and social philosophy, without obloquy, after passing the age of forty-five.

In passing I may say that I never had an ambition for a profitable participation in the operations of high finance. It is true, however, that I did consider it my obligation as a public official to conserve and promote the legitimate interests of business men and financiers as well as those of the wage earners. To me the fundamental need in the preservation of free enterprise has always been the protection of property rights as well as what are called human rights, because one of the most important of human rights is the right of a man to accumulate property and to protect his future by investments in free enterprise.

Some years after I was out of government, I asked John L.

Lewis over a friendly luncheon why he and some of his associates in organized labor had turned against me so bitterly because of some of my official actions. I mentioned that I thought it was the obligation of any man in public office to be as impartial as he could in decisions involving conflicting economic interests. His eyes twinkled with that good humor which those having only a newspaper acquaintance with him would not expect, and he answered: "Well, Don, it seemed to us that when the other fellow got his friends in public office they always expected him to give them a little better of it, and we thought our friends ought to do the same."

That was a simple explanation of what is probably a prevailing view in American politics. It is taken for granted that appointments to public office and profitable contracts should be parceled out among those whose work and contributions have placed the administration in power. Of course a judge is commonly regarded as exempt from this obligation although it was made evident during the Roosevelt administration that judges also are expected to lean in the direction of their friends, not to the point of absolute favoritism but at least to the extent of inclining to their arguments in matters of close decision.

Legislators and executives are assumed to have been placed in power to serve public interests, but, wherever there is no clear conflict with a well-defined public interest, they are expected to use their powers to advance the special interests of their friends. My own conduct in NRA often showed a naïve disregard for this prevailing psychology. Indeed, for a considerable period I rashly disregarded even the A B C of political use of the power of appointment. We were free from any civil service requirements and we failed repeatedly even to consult the appropriate politicians so that they might get credit for an appointment, even if they did not make it. I can remember the somewhat pathetic appeals of Jim Farley for notification at least of our intention to appoint someone so that he might clear it with the appropriate politician who would like to get the credit even for an appointment to which he was personally opposed.

One day in the locker room of a country club after I had learned a little about my political responsibilities, I mentioned to Senator Wagner that I was about to appoint several lawyers from the state of New York and I would arrange to let him know in advance so that he would get credit for having recommended them. Wagner was always a comforting and genial associate. Although he had been brought up in the Tammany school of New York politics, he could say as he did to me one day: "I have been trained as a politician, but I am trying to be a statesman." So on this occasion he chuckled a little ruefully and said: "Well, that's fine. You make the appointments, but at least you're nice enough to give me a chance to get a little credit from them!"

As a result of an equally naïve attitude, I failed repeatedly to take the time and trouble to convince friends in the labor movement, when I was about to take an action disagreeable to them, either that I was either compelled to do so by some commanding legal precedent, or merely carrying out the directions of some superior authority. This latter method of passing the buck is one commonly employed by inferior officers of government. That is one reason why the President frequently gets blamed for some unpopular action by a subordinate who, as a matter of fact, has been left entirely free to make his own decisions. It is much easier for the subordinate to suggest, or actually assert, that the decision is not really his, but proceeds from a policy or directive from on high. The subordinate knows that in most instances there will be no appeal to the upper stratum. If there is one, it is very likely that his overworked chief will merely promise to investigate and then say to his subordinate: "You will have to do what you think is right."

The author of *The New Dealers* was very kind to me because he wrote among other things the following:

> Next to Johnson, Richberg was the strong man of the NRA. He and his associates had a really gargantuan task in eliminating legal jokers from proposed codes, as most of the codes submitted for the big industries were craftily drawn by the highest paid corporation lawyers in the country. On the whole Richberg did splendidly in showing up and eliminating this legal sabotage, but he was not always successful.

Far be it from me to file any dissent to the foregoing.

In his analysis of the conservative members of the Roosevelt administration the Observer listed Lewis W. Douglas as one of the ablest and most valuable, which judgment the later years have certainly confirmed. Other "conservatives" included Cabinet officers like Postmaster General Farley, Secretary of Commerce Roper, Attorney General Cummings, Secretary of State Hull, Secretary of War Dern, Secretary of the Navy Swanson and of course Vice President Garner. Time has brought no change in these judgments.

Averell Harriman he described as "essentially very conservative." But he added: "He is not yet a liberal, but if exposed sufficiently long to the Roosevelt influence he may become a pretty enlightened conservative." The Observer did not realize, as did few others in 1934, that the Roosevelt influence would transform Harriman into a thoroughgoing New Dealer, who was finally to become a thoroughgoing Fair Dealer in the administration of President Truman.

Among the "Utopians," he listed Secretary of Labor Perkins, Secretary of the Interior Ickes and Harry L. Hopkins, who came into the administration as director of Federal Emergency Relief. In my own opinion Miss Perkins was always too practical-minded and shrewd to be classified as a Utopian. But as a progressive, growing up in the era of Theodore Roosevelt progressivism and moving far beyond those early concepts, she proceeded into the vanguard of the liberals in F.D.R.'s administration. She was never fearful of the dangers of increasing federal control and socialization of industry—at least not as fearful as I—in the years when "creeping socialism" began to appear as a real menace to the constitutional liberties originally protected by the founding fathers.

I have said enough about Harold Ickes so that I need add little here. His inherent ambition for power, coupled with his confidence in the integrity and wisdom of his own administration, would naturally blind him to the evils that might come from a centralized all-powerful government. His intense partisanship made him the anointed "hatchet man" of the Administration. He could be relied upon to attack any opposition with a vehemence which would insure bruised, battered and angry opponents wherever he swung his war club. Yet one of the strangest contradictions of his administration was the fact that he got along very well with the oil industry over which he exercised a paternal control from the days of the petroleum code to the petroleum administration in the Second World War. How this miracle was achieved and maintained I do not know, except that I think a great deal of credit must go to his chief aide, Ralph K. Davies. Probably the fact that Davies as an officer of Standard Oil of California had a serious falling out with his original corporate associates endeared him to Ickes and assured the latter that his deputy would not play favorites with the captains of an industry in which he had been treated rather roughly.

Harry L. Hopkins was the most interesting combination of apparently inconsistent qualities in the entire Roosevelt administration. He came to Washington as a social worker imbued with a profound sympathy for the underprivileged and a deep zeal to help them. At the same time he had interests of a fleshly and convivial character not commonly associated with welfare work. He loved to go to the races, to gamble and to drink hard liquor, but not to excess. He had an amazing ability to organize and direct a huge enterprise. He had a vigor of language almost comparable to that of General Johnson. In fact, any discussion between these two was likely to be a joy to all who listened. He had no interest whatsoever in making money, but a great delight in spending it for the benefit of other people. He had a reckless idealism which would permit him to take terrific chances with the good faith of other people. Probably history will demonstrate that his faith in the integrity of men like Stalin, and his encouragement of Roosevelt in the same faith, was one of the most tragic errors of American statecraft.

When Harry first appeared on the Washington scene his willingness to assume large responsibilities and to express himself very freely regarding what was going on and who was doing it, earned him considerable hostility from men who regarded themselves as much older in the councils of the Administration and much more experienced in national politics. Such men as McIntyre and Early, presidential secretaries, and old friends of F.D.R., particularly resented the brashness of this newcomer. However, Harry's ability, his winning personality and, above all, his steadily increasing intimacy with the President gradually overcame these early hostilities. His devotion to F.D.R. was not surprising in view of the exceptional confidence given him by the President, and the constantly enlarging opportunities for public service which, despite the handicap of increasing ill health, he profoundly enjoyed. An interesting example of the extent of this devotion occurred when, during the 1940 campaign, Steve Early became involved in a distressing incident in New York City, which was given wide publicity at the time. Some of the members of the Presidential party were seeking to return to the Presidential train parked in the Pennsylvania Station when their access was barred by some muddled policing. After others had been barred and the time for departure was near at hand, Early arrived. But, despite his obvious identification, he found his way barred too. The officiousness of the policemen roused his ever-ready temper, and he announced his intention of going through the police line. His way was blocked by a policeman who moved forward so aggressively that in checking his surge Early's knee came up and struck the policeman forcibly.

The imminent fracas was avoided by the arrival of a superior officer. But it developed that the policeman who had been struck by the Early knee was recently out of a hospital after an appendectomy. Immediately there developed a vast political hullabaloo particularly because the policeman was a Negro and Early, being notably a Southerner, was promptly accused of having deliberately kneed the officer. It is astonishing to look back and see how this little incident was magnified into something very discreditable to the President and his campaign. Champion Joe Louis was brought in to visit the policeman in the hospital to which he had been hastily transported; and there was a great effort made to rouse anger particularly in Harlem where the President, it will be recalled, was unusually strong for a Democrat. The possibility of swinging enough Negro votes back to the Republican Party to affect the result in the critical state of New York was clearly in the minds of the opposition. The question was seriously debated as to whether Early would be forced to resign and thus be publicly repudiated by the President.

Steve called on me as an old friend to represent his interests in a very solemn conference convened in the White House to discuss what should be done. As I recall it, Lowell Mellett, Judge Rosenman and Harry Hopkins were present, and in the course of lengthy discussions Harry Hopkins made his position perfectly clear. He said to me: "Don, you are here as a friend of Steve. Steve and I are good friends also, but I have only one interest in this matter and that is, what is going to help or hurt F.D.R." In stating his position thus simply Harry expressed the attitude that governed all his activities and judgments.

There are many people who will question whether in his frequent representation of the President during the Second World War, Hopkins did more to help or to hurt F.D.R., but anyone who knew him would at least be sure that his ultimate judgment would always be conditioned by his fixed purpose to help his great friend to whom he showed a gratitude and loyalty exceptionally high in the domain of politics.

The original basis for Roosevelt's reliance upon Hopkins was undoubtedly his admiration for Hopkins' ability to get things done. Next came F.D.R.'s comfort in working with a man who might argue freely as to what should be done and how to do it, but who, when a decision was once made, would work with might and main to carry out the President's program in the way in which he wanted it carried out. When the great decision was finally made as to whether Ickes or Hopkins should be placed in charge of the Civil Works program Roosevelt explained his decision to me in a very few words: "Ickes," he said, "is a good administrator, but often too slow. Harry gets things done. I am going to give this job to Harry."

It was probably Hopkins' love of gambling which led him to take great chances in administrative decisions that risked violent opposition and great failures. This also permitted him in matters of vast international consequence to take the responsibility for a judgment which might as easily lead to ruin as to success. More cautious politicians, even when possessed of great courage, would be inclined to convene conferences of advisers and, through debate and discussion, seek either to fortify their own judgment or to have the responsibility shared by others. Such cautious operators are less liable to make outrageous mistakes, but they are also likely to delay and confuse action at times when only the quick judgment of a general in command of a battlefield can bring a victory.

Franklin D. Roosevelt would discuss and confer and delay action repeatedly when unable to make up his mind on a course of action. But when his mind was finally made up he would move with great speed and become intolerant of further discussion. It seemed that in this regard he and Harry Hopkins understood each other and could work happily together even when geographically apart.

Harry had another characteristic in common with F.D.R., which was an appearance of great frankness combined with great care not to let other people know what he had in the back of his mind. I recall Harry's explanation to me of his surprise at being appointed Secretary of Commerce. He told me that he was sitting reading in the President's study one evening while F.D.R. was working on his stamp collection when the President suddenly looked up and said: "Harry, I am going to make you Secretary of Commerce." This was probably an accurate report of an incident that actually happened. But many years later when I read Sherwood's account of the long period of time during which this appointment had been under discussion, I felt that Harry's explanation to me was somewhat lacking in candor.

There is no doubt that, with all his devotion to the President, Hopkins shared at times the uneasy feeling of all the President's intimates, that perhaps he was getting too much biased information and that it might be wise to confer with several good friends who had no axes to grind and who might give him some counteracting ideas. As he explained it to me, his idea was to form a sort of private conference group of several persons, all undoubtedly friendly to the President, but having various points of view ranging from pretty conservative to pretty radical. If these men could sit down fairly regularly at dinner and spend the evening discussing vital problems of the Administration they might develop sufficient agreement on at least some of them to enable them individually or in concert to express their opinions to the President. Thus they might counteract the influence of someone who had the President's ear but whose personal interest or ideological bias made him a dangerous adviser.

This project was quite fascinating to me and it might have been very useful to the President, but it was never carried out. I suspect that it had seemed more important to him at a time when he was worried about the influence of others than later when his own influence became so much greater than that of any other individual.

Presumably, in the terrific rush and complexity of problems arising out of our entry into the Second World War, Hopkins, like the President himself, became more and more unwilling to take time to confer with anyone whose cooperation was not essential or who had no official connection with policies or programs. It is a paradox of public life that as problems multiply and the need for objective consideration is increased, it becomes more and more difficult for a public official to find the time for discussion with anyone except those with whom he must consult because their cooperation is required by law or otherwise made essential.

My own experience in a minor public office made this difficulty plain to me. The work of the legal division of NRA expanded so rapidly that the problem of clearing my desk of matters that had to be disposed of before sundown presented an intolerable burden. Staff conferences, which are important and should be frequent in any sizable organization, had to be postponed until they became absolutely necessary to preserve the morale of my associates. When the day is so filled with imperative appointments that one must either work half the night or go to the office in the early morning hours in order to read and dispose of important mail, the desire to sit down and quietly discuss the fundamentals of accumulating problems finally disappears in the greater desire to dig out from under a suffocating and ever-increasing volume of work.

It is a beautiful theory that a chief executive should delegate all detailed handling of business to carefully chosen subordinates and leave himself free to work out broad policies. But in conflict with this theory is the overwhelming fact that a chief executive has so much detailed work to do that it often seems more practical to delegate the formulation of broad policies to some subordinate happily relieved of other functions.

Probably the New Dealer who aroused more controversy and hostility than any other except Harry Hopkins was Henry Wallace. It is interesting to look back and see how highly many critics such as the Observer appraised the abilities of Henry Wallace in the early years of the Roosevelt administration. The Observer wrote:

> There are more brains and more real ability per pound of human flesh in the agricultural wing of the New Deal than anywhere else. [And later, describing Wallace himself] He is as earthy as the black loam of the corn belt, as gaunt and grim as a pioneer. Together with that he has an insatiable curiosity and one of the keenest minds in Washington, well disciplined and

> subtle, with a range of interests and accomplishments which range from agrarian genetics to astronomy.

In view of Wallace's later excursion into the candidacy of the very leftist Progressive Party, it is also interesting to quote from the Observer:

> He is no bolshevist or collectivist, knowing exactly how individualistic a creature the American farmer is.

And the Observer prophesied:

> If the young men and women of this country look to the West for a liberal candidate for the presidency—as they may in 1940—they will not be able to overlook Henry Wallace.

This germ of prophecy blossomed into that strange candidacy of Henry Wallace for President in 1948.

I have quoted from this early appraisal by an experienced newspaper man not to show that his judgment was in error, but to show how differently Henry Wallace appeared as a public official in the first year of the first Roosevelt administration. The difficulty in popular understanding of Wallace has arisen from the fact that although seeming to be a simple, rugged character, he has always been a complex, pliable personality. By "pliable" I do not mean a man easily influenced, but a man with such a flexible mind that he could move from one mental attitude to another as the force of events and circumstances impressed themselves upon him.

Anyone who knew Henry might disagree with him violently as to policies and programs, but must become very fond of him as a human being and respectful of him as one having the highest ideals of public service. As events proved, his judgment as to men and measures was often faulty, but, unlike Harold Ickes, his weakness would lie in trusting too much to the goodness of human nature, and in not being sufficiently skeptical or suspicious of the good intentions or intelligence of other people.

Over and over again I found myself asking questions or arguing with Henry Wallace over some matter in which his sources of information and experience would have justified him in brushing aside my ideas. But instead, he would patiently explain his view of the situation and the wisdom or folly, as he saw it, of a particular course of action. He was the most cooperative of all Cabinet members in considering and acting upon any suggestion to improve interdepartmental operations. He had less pride of opinion than any man meeting heavy responsibilities with whom I had any dealings, and certainly no pride of position.

His interests were varied and so lively that his companionship was always stimulating. I remember driving back with him from some party out in the country and referring to his currently advertised interest in boomerangs. Whereupon he stopped the car, produced a couple of boomerangs and we went out into the Ellipse, which was fortunately not well populated at that time of year, and had an immediate demonstration of boomerang throwing.

When Henry Wallace sent me a copy of his book which he had inscribed, "To Don, who knows how to add things up to make sense," I was very much pleased. In later years I thought that both of us had been mistaken sometimes when we added things up. Certainly no one was more innately and staunchly a believer in individual liberty and what is called the American way of life than Henry Wallace. Yet his attitude toward Russia and his "Progressive Party" adventure were dreadful examples of misjudgment and misplaced trust in men and measures. Underneath his exterior of what might be regarded as rustic simplicity he had a mystic view of life which would lead him to explore the unknown to an extent which might easily blind him to the practical importance of sticking pretty close to the known and visible in dealing with political problems.

Henry Wallace is perhaps best known popularly and may go down in history as the man "who plowed under little pigs." But in one of his books, instead of elaborating upon the apparent necessity for temporarily doing what seemed fundamentally wrong, he merely casually observed that such measures were of course crazy but appeared to be necessary in an insane situation. It would be my conclusion that Wallace was not fitted by nature to fulfill the responsibilities of high political office because he was unfitted to be a politician. As an agriculturist, a student, inventor, philosopher and human being, he was a useful citizen deserving of high appreciation, respect and affection. In public office he made many valuable contributions to public service, but he was out of his element as a political leader because he was no politician.

Before I end my gossip about some of the New Dealers perhaps there should be a word of warning as to the accuracy of their published memoirs—including my own. Anyone's recollection of interesting and important events in which he or she played a small or large part is sure to be affected by the bias of personal opinions regarding men and measures. It should be noted that even a contemporaneous diary, supposedly reliable, will have been written obviously with an eye on history and will surely reflect a partisanship that might be modified on later reconsideration. Also, the remembrance of a conversation may well be colored by affection for or hostility to the speaker.

Most disturbing to any future historian must be the irreconcilable differences in the narration of events and episodes of much consequence by the various participants. President Roosevelt in an irritated mood once asked me to review carefully a book by one of his former intimates and list and refute all the misstatements of fact which seemed obvious to him and he thought would be discernible by me. Not feeling quite equal to the task, I never undertook it. One basis of inaccuracies is the lack of records of many significant discussions and conferences. But frequently obvious errors indicate that the writer simply failed to check all his observations against available records. Judge Rosenman and I once spent considerable time trying to resolve a difference in our recollections as to a series of most important conferences. I should add that his book, *Working With Roosevelt,* seemed to me exceptionally accurate and fair-minded. I am sure he spent a great deal of time checking his memory against various records.

When I read Miss Frances Perkins' book, *The Roosevelt I Knew,* I was deeply interested and enlightened by her admittedly "biased" analyses of F.D.R.'s mental processes and activities. But I found myself exasperated by her accounts of events with which I was quite familiar, such as the genesis of the NRA. As one of only four persons who jointly wrote every word of the bill as it was introduced in Congress, I knew just how it was written. Yet, from her account, she apparently had forgotten this participation of mine and did not consult my previously published book which would have prevented many unintentional misrepresentations. It was particularly annoying to read her account of the apparent intransigeant opposition of Lew Douglas to a Public Works program, with no recognition of the fact that he joined with Senator Wagner, General Johnson and myself in writing the Public Works program into Title II of the National Industrial Recovery Act. Title II was simply a rewrite of a bill I had previously prepared for certain senators.

Likewise I read with keenest interest Sherwood's *Roosevelt and Hopkins,* which was so carefully documented and based on such an intimate association with Hopkins that I felt it to be one of the most reliable narratives. Nevertheless, in one or two instances, where I had positive first-hand knowledge of a subject revealed at second or third hand to Sherwood, I was sorely tempted to find some way to "correct the record."

Because of reading the books of other memoirists I have striven hard in this book to limit any statements of fact or quotations of the opinions of others to matters wherein I had either reliable supporting records or where my own recollection was so strong that I would be willing to back it against any contradictory statement. Stored away are voluminous records, correspondence, reports and memoranda which after months of solid reading would provide the basis for another volume or two. But it has seemed to me that I should confine myself to those matters which made upon me such a lasting impression that they might have more significance than other material which would have to be dredged up from the mass of "old, unhappy far-off things." So I make my apologies and hope for the gratitude of many former associates whose activities and characteristics I have failed to chronicle.

CHAPTER XXIII

The Mexican Oil Negotiations

WALTER TEAGLE, with whom I had many close relations in the NRA, was chairman of the board of Standard Oil of New Jersey, and came to me one day in the spring of 1938 with the proposition that I represent his company, and Standard Oil of California, the Sinclair Company and the Dutch Shell Company in their joint efforts to have their expropriated properties in Mexico restored to their ownership and control. My law firm had been for some years Washington counsel for Standard Oil of California, so there was no conflict of interest and obviously this joint representation was one which any lawyer would be glad to undertake. I felt it desirable to explain to the President that I was undertaking to represent these companies for I wanted to establish at once a consortium with our government which was officially supporting the American companies in their opposition to expropriation particularly without payment of due compensation.

It was plain from the first that the Mexican government had no intention of paying what would be regarded as due compensation under American law because the Mexicans took the position that the subsoil rights to the great oil deposits were the property of the Mexican people; hence they were subject to recapture by the government without payment of any compensation. The companies obviously would not be satisfied with even a fair compensation for merely their machinery and other properties above the surface since the major values of their properties lay in the vast oil deposits which they had discovered and developed.

Our State Department was doing its best to support the claims of our companies without destroying the friendly relations which generally speaking had existed between the two governments, at least in recent years. But because of the earlier history of bad relations between Mexico and the United States, including the Mexican War and then in later times the Naval expedition to Vera Cruz and the Army expedition in pursuit of Villa in 1916, hostility to the United States was politically popular in Mexico. There was no doubt that the expropriation of the oil properties, although economically harmful, was a political maneuver which enhanced the prestige and popularity of President Cárdenas of Mexico.

Under these circumstances, any solution of this controversy would require some heavy concessions on both sides and a good deal of face saving in order to make it clear to the partisans of each side that they had won a great victory.

After many conferences with my clients and with the State Department, it appeared evident, at least to me, that the Mexican government could not reverse itself and simply return the properties to the oil companies. On the other hand, Mexico would not and probably could not pay adequate compensation for the subsoil rights, the vast oil deposits.

As for our government, it was equally evident that, although we might apply all possible economic and political pressure on Mexico to induce a fair settlement, we would not and probably could not (as a practical matter) do very much in the way of force. We certainly could not use military force to compel a return of the properties. Indeed it was evident that the diplomatic pressure of our State Department would be exerted principally in favor of obtaining as large an amount of compensation from the Mexican government as it might reasonably be expected to pay.

There was, however, another possibility which particularly appealed to me because I saw in it the face-saving elements which might offer a comparatively easy way out of a bad situation. If the Mexican government could be induced to return the properties to the management of the companies for a period of years with a satisfactory arrangement for sharing the revenue, the conflict over ownership of the subsoil might be deferred and in time operation by highly skilled American management would be so productive that it would be continued indefinitely.

In discussing this idea with the management of the companies I found a violent opposition based on two stubbornly held opinions. One argued that the expropriation was wholly illegal and as a matter of principle should never be accepted as an "accomplished fact" (which is how I regarded it). The other maintained that no arrangements short of absolute control of the properties by the companies would be practical because in any semi-partnership they would be in constant disagreement. The Mexican government would never keep its promises, because even if one administration attempted to do so it would be overthrown by radical opposition. By midsummer of 1938 I had lost hope of any early accomplishment. I made my trip to Europe believing that the best thing to do was to let the situation simmer while the companies were going forward with legalistic efforts to have their position sustained by the Mexican courts. These legal proceedings, in view of the way in which those courts operated, seemed to me quite hopeless, as they subsequently proved to be.

During the fall of 1938 I moved back and forth between Washington and New York, seeking to work out some program for developing negotiations with the Mexican government for a settlement that might be acceptable to the oil companies and receive support from our government. Secretary Hull and Under Secretary Welles were willing to back any reasonable project, but I had a great deal of difficulty in dealing with what I might call legalistic stubbornness in the counsels of my clients. Their representatives in Mexico and the home office, men experienced and responsible in a large degree for their policies in dealing with Mexico, were so outraged that they were convinced that any solution, short of complete backdown by the Mexican government, would be a violation of what seemed to them eternal principles. They believed that if Mexico got away with this ruthless expropriation, there would be no future comfort or security in any foreign operations in Mexico. They wanted our State Department to refuse to encourage any idea in Mexico that a negotiated settlement was possible.

There was plenty of support in Mexican law and international law for such an uncompromising position. There was no question that Mexico was not only unwilling but unable to pay just compensation for the properties expropriated. At that time Mexico was in default on over $1,000,000,000 of foreign debts and at least $400,-

000,000 of internal debts. Obviously, Mexico was unable to pay an adequate compensation for the oil properties whether valued at a minimum of $262,000,000 or a maximum of $500,000,000. But both Mexican and international law were in accord on the doctrine that properties could not be legally expropriated except upon adequate payment of compensation.

The trial on the issue of legality in the Mexican courts was a tragicomedy. Not only was the Mexican Supreme Court pressured with speeches, parades and continual publicity denouncing the oil companies while the case was pending, but leading parts in this "trial by public opinion" were played by Toledano, head of the radical labor organization which was the backbone of the Cárdenas government, by President Cárdenas himself, and even by one of the justices of the Supreme Court.

Just before the decision of the Supreme Court sustaining the political attack upon the companies which had preceded the seizure of their properties, Justice Icaza rose and delivered a passionate denunciation of the companies, to an audience carrying banners and shouting imprecations, and then withdrew from the case, saying that this was "not a conflict of a legal character but of a political character." Immediately thereafter the remainder of the justices announced their unanimous decision against the companies. It was obvious that an appeal to that court against the validity of the expropriation would fall on deaf ears.

Nevertheless, it seeemed to me that the situation required the companies to do all within their power to facilitate some kind of an adjustment which our government could support. This was no time to allow our relations with Mexico to deteriorate, for in a period of growing international tensions it was to the interest of both countries to cooperate against the threat of the spread of fascist activities in the Western Hemisphere.

All American oil companies were, of course, refusing to take any deliveries of Mexican oil from the Mexican government, on the theory that to do so would make them receivers of stolen property. President Cárdenas was protesting that he must find markets for his oil; Italian purchasers were available and despite his disinclination to aid the Hitler-Mussolini alliance he would be forced to sell to them if he could not sell to the United States. In the meanwhile, little fascist cells located strategically throughout Mexico were, with the aid of German subsidies, underbidding Amcricans in the construction of public works. They were allied in interest with the Communist groups which were controlled by the radical labor leaders. Thus President Cárdenas, even if he were so inclined, could not as a practical matter back down in the expropriation. The American government, on the other hand, could not afford to increase the hostility of Mexican public opinion to the United States. The international situation was steadily growing more difficult and dangerous as Europe was drifting into the Second World War.

The realities of the situation compelled conservative executives of the oil companies to recognize the need for compromise. It had, however, become so difficult for me to keep the State Department assured of the good faith of my efforts despite frequent complaints to the Department by other less reasonable representatives of the oil companies that I finally insisted on being given the opportunity to work something out free from the embarrassment of dissenting associates. Otherwise it seemed to me my efforts should cease. I was eventually given an unsigned typewritten memorandum which I still possess as a legal curiosity. It reads in part as follows:

> We are agreeable to your suggestion that you be allowed a period of three weeks to direct your unaided efforts to persuade our government to seek the return of the properties in Mexico to the management of the rightful owners under an arrangement that will secure to us our substantive rights, backed by a treaty which will afford a guarantee of the permanency of such a solution.

The crucial words in this memorandum are those providing for the return of the oil properties "to the *management* of the rightful owners." In other words, I could be permitted to discuss something more practical than a return of the properties to *ownership.* Also, the phrase "substantive rights" would cover any sort of arrangement for operation of the properties which would ultimately provide something approaching compensation for them.

Armed with this authority I managed to work out a program to be launched by the companies with the support of our government. It had never been my intention to conduct negotiations with the Mexican government. I knew very little about the oil business, had never been to Mexico, spoke no Spanish, and had had no diplomatic experience. If I could open the door to negotiations, I expected that experienced representatives of the oil companies would undertake to negotiate an agreement. However, when the door for negotiations had finally been pried open I was suddenly informed that I would be expected to undertake them since this was my program and I had the confidence of the State Department. These sounded like two good reasons for a bad decision, but I am sure two other reasons played their part. One was that the companies themselves undoubtedly felt that their experienced men were for the most part so strongly prejudiced against Mexican officialdom and so convinced of the uselessness of treating with the Mexican government that they would hardly be ideal negotiators. The other was that some of these men recommended my selection with the grim hope that my failure would prove the correctness of their judgment and thus end any further annoyance from my amateurish activities.

Appalled as I was by the prospect of undertaking these negotiations, I could see no answer to the invitation to make a fool of myself except to accept the job. Knowing that this would be no brief episode, I arranged to have my wife accompany me and we started for Mexico with the determination at least to get some amusement out of what promised to be an unsuccessful adventure. Owing to an unexpected recess in Cathedral School, our daughter Eloise suddenly found herself free and, shortly after we left, proposed to follow us. We regarded the trip alone of a girl of less than thirteen from Washington to Mexico City as almost more hazardous than my mission, but she arrived in good health and wonderful spirits.

That a representative of the oil companies was to negotiate with the President was of course a matter of national excitement in Mexico where the oil controversy was the main topic of political conversation. But I was not prepared for the somewhat terrifying publicity of my mission. At the Hotel Reforma, we found ourselves housed in the "presidential suite," a duplex apartment done in the Hollywood manner, with a curving staircase leading from the living room to the upstairs bedrooms and all furnishings appropriate to a first-class movie. Here I met with the local representatives of the oil companies in one of those conferences in which the visiting plenipotentiary must very quickly size up his associates. Happily I found most of the conferees cooperative. The most helpful of all was the representative of Dutch Shell, Mr. B. Th. Van Hasselt, who in time, after holding various positions, became the managing director of his company in Holland. Without his wise and sympathetic advice my task in Mexico would have been much more difficult than it was.

It had been arranged that Señor Castillo Nájera, the able Mexican ambassador to the United States, with whom I had become fairly well acquainted, would present me to the President and participate in the conferences. I was sure he would be most helpful since he understood the difficulties of both governments. Because I was anxious to avoid any leakage from the discussions, and to minimize any constraint between the President and myself, it occurred to me that it would be better to avoid interpreters. So I asked the Mexican Ambassador to serve as an interpreter, which reduced the conference and the possibility of a news leak to the three of us. I had a feeling that if the President had some protection against even correct quotation (which could be officially denied) he would be more candid and that was what I particularly desired.

When I met President Cárdenas I at once suggested that we confine the conferences to himself, the Ambassador and myself. My proposition was accepted, but with much surprise and I think some suspicion. Indeed, I suspect that my hosts may have exchanged a few remarks calculated to betray my acquaintance with Spanish if I had any. But I am sure after our first couple of meetings the President became convinced that I was as unsophisticated and guileless as I think the Ambassador had assured him I was.

There was one fortunate incident in our first meeting. I had not received an introductory letter from President Roosevelt, although I had discussed my assignment with him, but since he did not offer a personal introduction I did not ask for it. Long afterward I learned that he had sent a letter to President Cárdenas through Ambassador Daniels, commending me to the Mexican President. Unhappily, from my point of view, neither President Roosevelt nor Ambassador Daniels informed me of this! President Cárdenas, however, must have thought I knew of it, since I took it upon myself when we were introduced to say: "Although I am not here as a representative of my government, but simply as a representative of private interests, I would like to bring you the personal greetings of my friend, President Roosevelt." Perhaps it was not protocol to deliver such a message, but under the circumstances it was lucky for me that I did so.

At our first meeting, I explained to President Cárdenas that I represented directly the Standard Oil Company (New Jersey), the Standard Oil Company of California and the Dutch Shell interests. Through the cooperation of their counsel, Mr. Patrick Hurley, I was enabled to speak also for the Sinclair interests. While the British and Dutch interests were being supported by the British government, they wished to act in harmony with the American companies. The Sinclair Company wished to go along with the others as far as they could, but reserved independence to proceed, as the company later did, to make a separate settlement with Mexico.

At the outset of the negotiations I made the limitations of my representation clear. My candid expressions of views were to be regarded as my own because I was seeking to find a path to an agreement rather than to make an agreement. The question I sought to explore was whether an agreement could be worked out for the future operation of the properties in some manner acceptable both to the companies and to the Mexican government. There were certain matters that I proposed to eliminate from our discussions. We faced the fact of an expropriation, the validity of which we need not discuss. Furthermore, the oil companies could not possibly accept the Mexican pretension that they had no subsoil rights, because this would amount to giving up a right to compensation for the major value of the expropriated properties. On the other hand, I assumed that the Mexican government would not consider abandoning its claim that subsoil rights always had been the property of the Mexican people, so that on repossessing themselves of these rights they were not liable to pay any compensation. Obviously, if such matters were not eliminated from our discussions, we could and would spend days and weeks in futile argument.

It was very difficult for me to get our discussions launched on the basis I proposed. The President for some time insisted on pursuing the project of an agreement on the amount of compensation to be paid. But when I persisted in refusing to engage in such discussions and kept driving back to my original suggestion, he finally allowed me to outline my program, which provided that we should seek to work out a long-term contract for the operation by the respective companies of the properties which had been taken. The contract should fix definitely all taxes and other impositions to be paid by the companies. There should be "a reciprocal guarantee for the life of the contract of reasonable and workable labor conditions."

It will be seen that this program opened the possibility of avoiding the double-barreled issue of fixing adequate compensation for the properties taken and accepting or rejecting compensation for the subsoil properties. If the ownership question could be left in abeyance but the properties turned back to the management of their private owners, if the companies could be assured of freedom from unreasonable restrictions or exactions to produce and sell oil for such a period as twenty years, they could count on two favorable results. First, they could gradually amortize their original investments out of profits and at the same time earn enough on their diminishing investment to provide a satisfactory return. Second, after an experience of some years the whole arrangement might prove sufficiently satisfactory to all concerned so that it could be extended indefinitely through at least the life of the oil deposits.

From the Mexican point of view, the program had many attractive aspects if the government were to look at the matter from a long-range view of Mexican interests. Mexico needed foreign capital and the expropriation of the oil properties would certainly frighten off any large capital investments in the future. The Mexican government also needed the technical services of the American operators. Although the Mexicans were very sensitive to any question of their ability as operators, it was quite evident that their difficulties since the expropriation did not arise solely from inability to sell their oil. There were well-substantiated reports that the increased costs of operations were due not only to labor domination, but also to technical inefficiency. There were serious possibilities that good oil wells would be ruined and that the properties would deteriorate rapidly under somewhat incompetent management.

By exercising a great deal of patience and avoiding all acrimonious disagreements, I managed to get to the point where President Cárdenas orally and in writing accepted "in principle a plan of collaboration" between the government and the oil companies. However, before we reached the point where technical experts from the companies could be brought in to draft a contract, I had to get rid of two persistent obstacles raised by President Cárdenas. One was his contention that the expropriated properties should be valued as a basis for fixing some of the terms of the contract.

The other, which was even more troublesome, was the desire of the Mexican government to impose a political management on top of the companies' technical management, which would insure unending controversies in the future.

Although conferences at the palace and with my associates at my hotel were arduous work, I found some relief in a few outside activities. My family and I were shown every courtesy in Mexico City not only by Americans but also by Mexicans in private and public life.

I had heard President Cárdenas described in many uncomplimentary terms, but my discussions with him, although not easy, particularly because of the necessity of constant interpretation, were always on a high level of courtesy and apparent willingness to try to understand an opposing point of view. Far from being brusque and arbitrary, his manner and his language as translated to me were always quiet and indeed conciliatory, as I believe mine were.

During my stay in Mexico City he paid me an unusual honor by giving a luncheon at the Chapultepec Castle, the state palace that was used only for formal occasions. The luncheon, to which Ambassador Daniels and the members of the President's Cabinet, together with our wives, were invited, was elaborate, lengthy and informally good-natured, much like many a similar luncheon at the White House during Franklin D. Roosevelt's regime.

One surprising remark was reported to me afterward by my wife. Mrs. Daniels had informed her that, since their arrival in Mexico in 1933, this was the first time they had ever been entertained at a meal by the President. Let me hasten to say that this was no reflection upon our Ambassador's standing with the President, who regarded him rightly as a most friendly representative of the United States. It was, on the contrary, an indication of the disinclination of President Cárdenas for formal entertainments and a definite preference for convivial gatherings of men only. It also indicates that President Cárdenas went out of his way to give a very public demonstration of his friendly attitude toward me. In view of his frequent outspoken denunciation of the oil companies and their representatives, this was evidently intended to prepare the way for a public understanding that if we did arrive at an agreement it would be made possible only because the representative of the oil companies was a "reasonable man"—and also a friend of President Roosevelt who was held in much higher esteem in Mexico than most officials of the American government had been.

Our other social contacts in Mexico City were largely with American business men, particularly with those representing the oil companies, although we also met a certain number of prominent Mexicans. But the American colony did not seem to have the amount of social intercourse with Mexican families of similar interests that I would have thought important not only to good public relations but also to American business.

Occasionally Florence and I, sometimes with our daughter, were able to get away to such nearby places as Cuernavaca and Taxco. We also entertained a little in our "presidential suite." If we had not had these hours of relaxation, the nervous strain of the negotiations would have been much greater, particularly since I found the high altitude not conducive to easy sleeping.

We had one scare which had a comic ending. Both Florence and I had been vaccinated just before leaving the United States. Her vaccination, modestly imposed on one thigh, "took" with such amazing results that the leg swelled to enormous size. In great alarm we summoned a Mexican doctor, who took one look at the misshapen leg and then, his face aglow with pleasure, sighed. "Beautiful! Beautiful!" This was not a tribute to my wife's Betty Grable quality, but rather the delight of a physician in an effective vaccination.

Sufficient progress had been made in two weeks of conferences so that I felt it desirable for me to return to the United States. I needed to obtain either the support of my clients in future negotiations or their decision that my efforts bore no promise, for the constant trickle of misinformation through newspapers and other sources had created an atmosphere back home in which a definite showdown seemed essential. I also felt that President Cárdenas had now become hopeful and anxious for some settlement along the lines proposed. I feared that if we indicated any discouragement from back home he might be inclined to go back to his original two positions which would make a contract impossible. Happily I had a case pending in the Supreme Court as my excuse for leaving, with a promise to return if developments made it desirable.

As I had anticipated, I found on my return to the United States a good deal of misunderstanding as to the nature and progress of my discussions. Those who were opposed to the entire project had done their best to have it appear that I was making harmful concessions on the one hand and getting nowhere on the other. Also, the oil company managements were firmly opposed to any political supervision of their future management of their properties. In due time, however, it became apparent through inquiries from the Mexican Ambassador that President Cárdenas was anxious to resume discussions. This permitted me to state that further conferences would be fruitless if the Mexican government insisted upon raising the hopeless valuation question or maintaining a political control of the properties after they had been restored to private management. Eventually, on April 12, 1939, I received a formal assurance that negotiations could be hopefully resumed in the form of a message from the Mexican Ambassador:

> The President was informed by me of the telephone conversation we had yesterday. Pursuant to instructions from the President I wish to advise you, first, that the discussion regarding the valuation will be postponed until the end of the negotiation and it will be accepted that no discussion of this point be undertaken provided a satisfactory agreement is reached through other means. Second, that the Mexican government agrees to discuss the proposition that refers to contract with each one of the companies.
>
> I wish to remind you that you mentioned the possibility of making contracts, one with each one of the following groups: Standard Oil (New Jersey), Standard Oil of California, Sinclair; and British interests.
>
> Perhaps by this means of four contracts it is feasible to reach an agreement, making it easier to solve the problem of administration.

This message was not sufficiently reassuring to persuade me to go directly to the Mexican capital. I did, however, agree to explore the situation further with the Mexican Ambassador on April 27, at

San Antonio, Texas, where I was urged to meet with President Cárdenas at Saltillo, Mexico, on the assumption that we should be able to agree upon the bases and principles which would underlie the proposed contracts.

The meeting with President Cárdenas at Saltillo involved me in the strangest of all my Mexican experiences. We were together in conferences on May first, which is almost universally a day of celebration for revolutionary parties. As head of the National Revolutionary Party in Mexico, President Cárdenas was naturally expected to review a May Day parade from the balcony of the government building on the Saltillo main square. I was, to say the least, somewhat embarrassed by the request that I join him, but obviously such a sign of friendliness could not be discouraged, so I had the pleasure for the first and probably the last time in my life of reviewing a May Day parade with a revolutionary president of a Latin American country.

Our discussions over a few crowded days produced a tentative accord on the bases and principles of an agreement, the results of which were embodied in a jointly prepared memorandum.

It had seemed to me advisable to avoid any highly optimistic statements in our joint announcement, but here, to my surprise, I found President Cárdenas particularly anxious to be as optimistic as possible. So we issued a joint statement reading in part as follows:

> The discussions have been fruitful and effective progress has been made toward a mutually satisfactory agreement . . . it is anticipated that in the near future the negotiations will reach a definite conclusion without the need for further oral discussions between President Cárdenas and Mr. Richberg.

Apparently vigorous opposition to the tentative program developed among President Cárdenas' intimate advisers and political supporters as soon as it was revealed to them. The policy inaugurated at Mexico City had been continued at Saltillo and the conferences had been restricted to the President, the Ambassador and myself. Undoubtedly President Cárdenas, like any chief of state, was surrounded by a considerable circle of persons always ready to criticize and oppose any program in which they had not participated. This was particularly true of the radical labor leaders who began a series of violent demonstrations protesting against any return of private management to any control of any part of the oil industry.

More than six weeks elapsed after the final conference at Saltillo on May 3 before I received the long-promised statement of President Cárdenas' position. Then the Mexican Ambassador delivered to me a most discouraging memorandum receding from what had been apparently agreed positions and returning to the pre-negotiation proposals to fix the valuation for the properties and provide for payment of compensation in slow installments out of the percentage of the companies' own oil which would be produced by a corporation controlled by the Mexican government. Apparently all the progress at Mexico City and Saltillo had been discarded and I was asked to return to a negotiation which I had from the beginning refused to undertake.

Our State Department, however, urged a further effort to carry forward negotiations along the lines of the Saltillo program. The Mexican Ambassador himself seemed strongly sympathetic to a further effort, and accordingly he and I went to work on drafting what was entitled "Preliminary agreement as basis for contracts to be negotiated in settlement of the oil question." Neither my clients nor President Cárdenas had even intimated their approval of this agreement, but both the Ambassador and I were willing to present our draft for the approval of our respective principals. I think that each of us felt justified in taking a risk if the other was willing to stick his neck out in such a fashion.

I must say I thought Ambassador Castillo Nájera's act called for more courage than mine. I only risked losing clients, whereas he risked losing a political future.

On July 11, 1939, I received a statement of the position of the Mexican government after consideration had been given to our "preliminary agreement." The plan of collaboration was accepted, but the corporations authorized to operate the properties must be under absolute control of the Mexican government, which would appoint the president and a majority of the board of directors of each corporation. Naturally, I pointed out in a letter to the Ambassador that the entire agreement was destroyed by this qualification which in effect established a government corporation to which private investors were expected to contribute money and property without retaining any such control as would justify such a private investment.

Our State Department then undertook discussions of the situation with the Mexican Ambassador. Out of these came an informal suggestion that to break the impasse over the control of the corporations the directors of the operating corporations should be chosen one-third by the stockholders, one-third by the Mexican government and one-third from a panel of neutral nominees agreed upon by Mexico and the United States.

I will not venture to suggest the exact source of this extraordinary suggestion, but I do not think it proceeded directly from either Secretary Hull or Under Secretary Welles. It was one of those amazing suggestions which under the appearance of "compromise" gave everything to the other side. The history of our relations with the Soviet government carries the unhappy memory of similar "compromises."

There is nothing outrageous in the idea of public representatives or labor representatives on a board of directors, but it is certainly of the essence of a system of private enterprise that those who make the investment should control the use of the investment. Under the State Department's proposal this essential control of private business would be abandoned.

Our only possible answer to this extraordinary suggestion seemed to be in waiting for a rejection of the proposal by the Mexican government, which was practically inevitable. Unhappily, the managements of the oil companies were greatly disturbed by an unauthorized newspaper report ascribing the authorship of this proposition either to President Cárdenas or to the collaboration of Ambassador Castillo Nájera and Mr. Richberg. Unwisely they found it "necessary" to issue a statement to the effect that neither the companies nor their representatives had deviated from the original objectives laid down for the negotiations. This relieved the Mexican government from the necessity of rejecting the proposition. The Mexican Ambassador promptly and truthfully denied that it had been sponsored either by President Cárdenas or himself. But he took this opportunity to assert the fixed determination of the Mexican government to retain control of the oil properties and to denounce the objectives which he admitted had been the basis of the negotiations.

This drew from our government a restatement of its original position, whereupon various Mexican officials made attacks on the United States government and denounced the foreign companies and investors who had poured hundreds of millions of dollars into Mexico. Now the fat was all in the fire again. My mission had achieved its prophesied failure. The Second World War was under way. It was of grave importance to re-establish friendly relations between the governments of the United States and Mexico. How was this to be done? That was the problem before the State Department and as a loyal citizen I naturally hoped my government would find a public solution for the problem which I had sought in vain to solve by private means.

CHAPTER XXIV

Aftermath of Mexican Oil

FOLLOWING the breakdown of my negotiations, the companies I represented, and particularly Standard Oil of New Jersey, wanted to publicize the efforts that had been made to arrive at a negotiated settlement. Being fearful of a lengthy, legalistic document with little appeal to popular understanding, I offered to write my own story which could then be published without detailed company approval. This offer was accepted and a booklet of fifty-six pages was published in January 1940 with the following introductory statement:

> As counsel for companies involved in the Mexican expropriation of foreign-owned oil properties, it should be evident that I would not publish this narrative without the approval of my clients.
>
> However, it should be understood that opinions, or statements of fact as to matters peculiarly within my individual knowledge, are presented on my own authority in an effort to portray events accurately as they have appeared to me.
>
> D.R.R.

It was my purpose in writing this review of "The Mexican Oil Seizure" to furnish to uninformed and inexpert persons a compact story of the expropriation preceded by "the historical background" and a clear statement of "the real reason for the expropriation." Then I explained the progress and failure of "negotiations since the expropriation."

My booklet was printed in large quantities and widely distributed both in paper and cloth editions. I was somewhat appalled when I saw my pamphlet in print with a cover design that would probably offend the Mexicans. It was a drawing of a ragged, disreputable-looking, cigarette-smoking Mexican, which I felt could only have been motivated by a malicious effort to express a distaste and distrust for Mexicans that did not reflect my own feelings.

The immediate result of the publication of my booklet was a temporary rift between the Mexican Ambassador and myself. Through him, President Cárdenas indignantly complained that I had accused him of bad faith in the negotiations. I had not, although I did point out the inconsistency between our joint statement that "discussions have been fruitful and effective progress has been made toward a mutually satisfactory agreement," and his denunciation of the proposals in his message to the Mexican Congress on September 1, 1939:

> I do not believe that any government could have accepted an agreement which from the beginning discussed such infamous proposals.

It became apparent, as weeks and months passed, that it would be difficult to re-establish direct negotiations in behalf of the companies I had represented. As I have explained, the Sinclair Company had been officially represented by Patrick J. Hurley, and only as a sort of secondary representative had I been able to negotiate in Sinclair's behalf. Also, my three direct clients were in constant fear that Sinclair would make a separate settlement as he had done many years before in coming to terms with the Soviet Union when other companies were blockading Russian oil after the expropriations of the Russian Revolution.

Thus it was no great surprise to anyone when Mr. Hurley on May 7, 1940, reached an agreement between the Sinclair Company and Mexico, providing for a payment within three years of an indemnity of $8,500,000 for the surface properties and a long-term contract for the sale of Mexican oil to Sinclair. But even though the Sinclair properties were small compared with the others, the cash settlement was so small compared with full value that it provided a distressing precedent for the other companies.

Since I had been in the position of representing to some extent the Sinclair Company, I had discussed this matter of separate negotiations with Mr. Hurley, with whom I was very well acquainted, and he had assured me that he would notify me before any deal was consummated. Naturally I was somewhat surprised to get my first knowledge that an agreement had been made from the newspapers. In Mr. Hurley's subsequent public explanation he revealed something which, if it had occurred, had certainly been kept secret from me. He began by flattering me, saying that the "other major companies selected a lawyer of recognized ability and integrity, an ex-government official of wide experience" to negotiate with Cárdenas. But, he continued, when he and I were scheduled to leave for Mexico together (which was news to me) the president of one of my client companies had asked him not to accompany me. When, according to Hurley, I became "completely *hors de combat,*" Sinclair had "painfully and reluctantly resumed the negotiations alone." He kept the other companies advised until he learned that when "a high official of Mexico" had asked me why Sinclair's lawyer was not with me in 1939, I had replied that it was thought best not to have the Sinclair representative participate, as that would mean "only one more opinion to reconcile" and that, after all, Sinclair investments were comparatively small and that whatever settlement was reached "would have to be acceptable to the Sinclair Company."

My statement, according to Mr. Hurley, had been "proved beyond all doubt." When it was reported to Sinclair, it had broken the united front. The interesting part of this report is that I never made any such statement; I was never accused of making such a statement and thus given an opportunity to deny it; and since any report, if made, must have come from the two Mexican officials who were the only other persons present in the conference, it was obvious that a mischievous statement reported by an adversary would not prove anything "beyond all doubt" to anyone of ordinary intelligence.

The Sinclair settlement put the remaining companies in a particularly weak position. The United States government was now in a position to point out that if one company could make a settlement, why not the others? Furthermore, the government was in a position to urge the oil companies to submit their claims to arbitration. Europe was already engulfed in the Second World War and we were drifting steadily into the same holocaust. It was urgently necessary to have peaceful relations with Mexico, to fight the development of a hostile nation on our southern border, and to obtain from Mexico oil for which we might have a great need. If the companies did not work out some negotiated settlement, I was convinced that they would be under great pressure to agree to arbitration. Furthermore, if they did not agree, the government would probably assume responsibility for settling their claims and itself arbitrate with Mexico what payments should be made.

I felt a desperate effort must be made to resume negotiations for some such settlement as had been almost reached in the agreed memorandum submitted by the Mexican Ambassador and myself. But I was informed by my clients that I was still *persona non grata* to the Mexican government. I did not believe this and in November 1940 I was able to report to the oil companies that the State Department had informed me that it would be desirable and acceptable to the Mexican government for me to continue to serve as a representative and negotiator for the companies. Yet in December the companies were again informed by one of their representatives that I was not acceptable to the Mexican government as their representative.

When I was informed that, to put it mildly, I had been "stabbed in the back" by representatives of my own clients, I promptly terminated my engagement with Standard Oil of New Jersey, although my firm and I continued to represent Standard Oil of California for many years thereafter.

It may reasonably be charged that I was unduly concerned with the national interests involved in the Mexican oil controversy and as a result not a sufficiently partisan advocate of private interests. But even against this charge I would argue that neither by a voluntary arbitration nor by a negotiated settlement could the companies have lost as many millions of dollars as they did through arbitration imposed by the United States government. Nor could they have lost as much in the battle to maintain a principle of fair dealing as they did through permitting their government to establish a standard of unfair dealing in the protection of American interests abroad.

On November 19, 1941, an agreement was signed between the Secretary of State and the Mexican Ambassador, providing for an arbitration of "just compensation" for the oil properties by representatives of the two governments. On April 17, 1942, the two representatives of the two governments filed their agreement by which the companies were indemnified only for actual investments in the surface properties depreciated, and for oil already captured. In a word, they were denied any compensation for the enormous value of oil deposits to which they had given this value by costs and losses of exploration and for which they had risked their huge investments in the surface properties and other developments of the oil properties. If the hidden resources of distant countries are to be brought into wealth by the courage of American enterprises and the risk of American capital only to be expropriated without any compensation for that developed wealth, there will be little if any incentive for American capital in the future to bring prosperity to distant lands, as it has done time and time again.

CHAPTER XXV

The Second World War

ALL THROUGH the year 1941 the United States was preparing for the possibility of being involved in another world war. If it had not been for this prospect in 1940 there can be little doubt that Roosevelt would have been defeated if he had run for a third term. On the other hand, there is little doubt in my mind that he would not have run.

Not long after I returned from Europe in 1938 I had luncheon with the President at his desk. In the course of a good deal of general conversation I recounted my talk with Lloyd George, in which the President seemed to be much interested. He took up eagerly the question of a third term. "In addition to the arguments you made," he said, "this is what you should have told Lloyd George." He then went into an extended historical review to show me the reasons that had motivated former Presidents in not seeking a third term. He was very emphatic about the matter and left with me a clear impression that he was definitely planning his retirement and would not seek renomination in 1940.

This was particularly convincing to me because of the words which I had put in his mouth in 1936 in my book entitled: *Guilty! The Confession of Franklin D. Roosevelt.* The scheme of the book (obviously a campaign document) was to have the President "confess" all the "sins" charged against him in trying to help the farmer, the industrial worker, the home-owner and small business man, to overcome the evils of the depression. The ultimate purpose of all this sinning was to establish the "dictatorship," not of a self-perpetuating President but of each citizen over his own destiny. Then, in words quoted from F.D.R., "anyone can honestly feel that he is 'the master of his fate' and 'the captain of his soul.' That is the goal of our American civilization, so far as I can see it."

The President ended his "Confession" with these words:

> If I have helped to restore that promise of American life to millions of people who feared it had been forgotten, then I have restored it to my own life; and when I leave here and re-establish myself in the rights of a private citizen, I shall become—as to my own destiny, but not as to the destiny of other men—Dictator, at last!

The flyleaf of this book carried a letter from F.D.R. to me saying: "Don't show me that book before it is published . . . But, I will read it when it comes out." In fact, he did not read the manuscript, but I was careful to read to him the words I had put in his mouth because I could not risk any false note there. Among those words were:

> When that desk in there is cleared for the last time by me, when I say good-by to all the helpers and hinderers, when I resume the delightful freedom of private life . . .

F.D.R. and I knew well that at this time he was looking forward to 1941 to "resume private life." We had talked frequently about the need to complete any legislative program in eight years at the most. In one conversation he observed: "A liberal administration can't count on more than eight years in office. Too many objections and opponents pile up against a constructive program. Conservatives may hold office a long time. If conditions are prosperous, people are content with things as they are. But we are changing conditions and discontent will increase even among those who benefit. We can't count on maintaining a progressive party and a progressive administration more than eight years." With such a philosophy he had every reason to believe personally as well as politically in maintaining the two-term tradition.

Until it became fairly certain in 1939 that Hitler was going to plunge Europe into another great war, I believe that F.D.R. was looking around among his associates to determine who, in his judgment, would be the best man for him to support, always on the assumption that his choice could not only be nominated but that he would have a good chance of election. Inevitably he did not find anyone who was completely satisfactory on both counts. One of several of his intimates might have been acceptable to him, yet not a strong candidate. I know that at one time he was considering very seriously throwing his influence to Secretary Hull, who was not a sufficiently ardent New Dealer to be wholly satisfactory to him, but who would make a good race and would reflect credit on the party even if he might be defeated.

But as the war clouds gathered over Europe, the President became more and more concerned with the necessity of preparing the United States to strengthen its military capacity for defense against fascist aggression, either alone or in support of friendly nations abroad. A hint of this changing attitude came to me when I was preparing an article subsequently published in the *Reader's Digest* which I had originally captioned "Why No Third Term?"

In the spring of 1939 I happened to run into Steve Early at luncheon one day and mentioned the prospective publication of my article under the aforementioned title. Steve looked at me a little quizzically and said: "I think, if I were you, I would entitle the article 'Why Not a Third Term?' " While this would not mean a change in the text of the article, the title was a bit equivocal in implying that I was favoring a third term. But I thought, with this hint from his press secretary, it would be just as well to use an equivocal title, so I adopted Steve's suggestion. From then on I abandoned the idea that the President himself was determined on retirement.

In many ways the President did not believe in the indispensability of any leader. As he had eloquently explained to me, if a political party was not strong enough to go forward regardless of a change of leadership, then the party did not merit continuance in office.

Nevertheless, despite his theoretical objections to the indispensability of any man, F.D.R. could convince himself without much difficulty that no one except himself could gain sufficient popular support to carry forward a program of adequate preparedness for war. Certainly he gave his judgment a thorough test when, in a Presidential year, he put through the Congress, for the first time in

American history, a program of conscription while we were actually at peace and not immediately threatened by aggression. With his usual political sagacity, President Roosevelt managed to convince a majority of the people that the United States was preparing only for armed defense of its territory and not for hurling its forces into a foreign war. In his final campaign speeches he gave assurance "again and again and again" that:

> Your boys are not going to be sent into any foreign wars.
>
> They are going into training to form a force so strong that by its very existence it will keep the threat of war far from our shores.
>
> The purpose of our defense is defense.

Historians will debate for a long time as to whether President Roosevelt, in such measures as his aggressive support to Great Britain in the Lend Lease Act, was really engaged in purely defensive maneuvers or whether he was preparing the American people not only materially but mentally for taking active part in the defeat of the Axis powers.

It will be particularly difficult to arrive at sure conclusions as to whether in the fall of 1941 Roosevelt became convinced that war with Japan was inevitable and sought to appear to do everything possible to avoid such a war, while making sure that an aggressive attack would come from Japan; for in a war of defense there would be no question of the unification of the American people.

For my own part, I have always felt that Roosevelt's motives were not only uncertain to those close to him, but even to some extent to himself. Obviously he knew that no nation rendering such enormous aid to one side in an international war could be regarded as neutral in thought or action. He knew too that the only thing that would deter the offended nations from making war on us would be their cold calculation that it was to their advantage to avoid any action that would bring all the resources of the American people into full support of their opponents.

My personal opinion is that F.D.R. never allowed himself to make a deliberate decision that he would bring about our involvement in the war; that he never allowed himself the discomfort of feeling certain that his course would bring us into the war; that he took the tremendous risk of our involvement because of his conviction that it was morally right; yet with the hope, faint and tenuous though it may have been, that somehow we might escape. I remember a conversation I had once with Miss Perkins when we were both greatly distressed by F.D.R.'s postponement of a decisive action that was necessary to end a most unhappy situation. I expressed my exasperation that since a decision must eventually be made, every day it was postponed was injurious to all concerned. Miss Perkins replied that while she shared my impatience, she had long ago learned that Roosevelt had an intuitive sense which often enabled him to wait with unbelievable patience for something to happen which might make his course of action either unnecessary or at least inevitable. She recalled one incident when he was governor of New York when he delayed so long in taking action against someone that all his friends were completely out of patience. "And then," said Miss Perkins, "the man died!"

I am reminded also of a remark attributed to the President's mother, to whom a friend said one day, when fortune had favored F.D.R. in a difficult situation: "It seems to me sometimes as though the Lord had His arms around Franklin." And his mother replied: "Yes, but it also often seems as though Franklin had his arms around the Lord."

In my own mind I have no doubt that President Roosevelt had great confidence in the star of his destiny and that, when at times it became impossible to see the star in a clouded sky, he would wait with extraordinary patience until, at least in his vision, he could see it shining clear again.

But if the Japanese attack settled one great problem for President Roosevelt, it also raised another equally grave. The incredible attack upon Pearl Harbor so depleted our power in the Pacific that it was a long and costly task to build up our forces to a capacity even to retard the triumphant advances of the Japanese. This forced a decision of grave difficulty and tremendous risk upon the President—the decision to turn our immediate major efforts toward the defeat of the Axis powers in Europe despite the dangers of possibly losing the war in the Pacific. Here, it seems to me, was one of the major decisions of Roosevelt for which history may give him great credit.

The tiny part which I played in the events immediately following Pearl Harbor can be quickly told. I prepared a brief memorandum and sent it to the President immediately, suggesting the prompt organization of an agency to review the activities of all the civilian departments and commissions to determine where these activities could be suspended and money and manpower released or transferred to the direct prosecution of the war. In my year as executive Director of the National Emergency Council it had been my job to investigate and eliminate, wherever possible, overlapping activities and to attempt to coordinate all parts of the Administration into a machinery in which at least duplications and conflicts of authority could be ended. My efforts had not always been successful, but at least I knew something of the situation and had an idea of what might be done now to speed up the transition from a peacetime to a wartime bureaucracy.

Knowing something of F.D.R.'s habits, I sent a brief explanatory memorandum and an accompanying outline of a program for a sort of emergency coordination of all the civilian activities of the government, including a few specific examples of activities that ought to be suspended or substantially reduced. I did not expect an answer for a long time, if ever, and was, therefore, astonished to receive a short memorandum dated December 11, 1941, expressing F.D.R.'s keen interest and suggesting that I take the matter up with "Francis Biddle and Jimmy Byrnes." I knew that Biddle was the Attorney General, but the only Byrnes of my acquaintance was a justice of the Supreme Court. So I called Steve Early to inquire as to whether I was supposed to discuss such a matter with a justice of the Supreme Court. He assured me that I was, so I sent copies of my memorandum to both Biddle and Byrnes, with the suggestion that I would be glad of an opportunity to discuss it.

Nothing came of my approach to Biddle, with whom my relations had not always been entirely happy, but I had a cordial invitation from Byrnes and spent a couple of hours going over the matter with him. His final conclusion was peculiarly interesting in the light of future events. He was emphatic in his opinion that the job ought to be undertaken; but if it were to be successfully carried out the President should give whomever he appointed positive assurance that he would leave him absolutely free from Presidential interference. Only in this way could the man be effective and the President be relieved of wasting a great deal of time reviewing decisions of his deputy which were sure to be opposed by many others in the Administration.

My further activities in this regard were not important nor immediately effective. Indeed, I had little opportunity to render war services, which I would have been glad to perform, for a reason which developed somewhat later.

I was vacationing in the summer of 1942 when I had a call from the White House asking me if I would head up one of four interrelated commissions which were being established to administer the major economic controls essential to the war effort. I told Judge Rosenman, who had telephoned, that I would of course undertake any public service I might be called upon to perform, although I had too much trouble with an intermittent arthritis to feel sure I could carry a straining task over a long period. However, I was relieved to be invited to participate because anyone with governmental experience who is on the sidelines in war time feels a bit useless.

A couple of days later I had another telephone call explaining that, owing to a change in the form of organization, the two divisions of the work, of which I was to head one, had been consolidated under one head; so that my services would not be required. I had a combined sense of relief and disappointment. Long afterward, I was authoritatively informed that the reason for the change of plans was Sidney Hillman's serious objection to my return to the inner circle. I do not know whether the nomination for Vice President in the Democratic Convention of 1944 was "cleared with Sidney," but I do know that my appointment to a much inferior position during the war had to be.

Sidney Hillman and I had had a long and intimate acquaintance. He was a member of the NRA Board, of which I was chairman, and I have a beautiful and flattering testimonial of my public services signed by Hillman and the other members of the board. I only point to this incident as a good example of the extent to which representatives of organized labor require undeviating support of the programs of organized labor as the prerequisite to public service even in wartime.

The testimonial referred to was a silver platter presented to me on retiring in 1935 and inscribed:

DONALD R. RICHBERG

In appreciation of services so unselfishly and effectively contributed to the Nation from his associates of the N.I.R.B.

June 15, 1935

Charles Edison
Walton H. Hamilton
Sidney Hillman
Leon Marshall
Philip Murray
W. P. Witherow

and

W. Averell Harriman

As late as 1943 I was arguing cases in behalf of labor organizations in the Supreme Court of the United States, and since that time I have been asked to represent other labor organizations in various matters. With a few exceptions I have refused to represent employer interests in conflict with labor interests because I still have a profound interest in the welfare of those who do what I call "the hard work of the world." But it may be appropriate here to observe that, in both economic and political activities, far too many labor leaders of recent years have been so concerned with maintaining and increasing their own power and the coercive powers of their unions, without adequate regard for the public welfare or even the welfare of individual workers, that I have felt compelled to oppose in public forums and legislative halls their abuses of power to the full extent of my ability.

During the war years I saw very little of President Roosevelt, although maintaining personal contact with him from time to time particularly through correspondence. In the light of my conversation with Justice Byrnes previously described, I took great interest in his selection by the President to serve, first as director of Economic Stabilization and then as director of War Mobilization. I made the suggeston at the time through Steve Early to the President that Byrnes's place on the Court be left open. Steve informed me that the President had offered to do this, but Justice Byrnes had insisted that the President fill the vacancy, for he felt that the Supreme Court should not be used in this manner.

Another man also suggested that the President should appoint an older lawyer who would not be expected to remain on the Court and who would resign at the end of the war, thus permitting the reappointment of Justice Byrnes. Again the word came back that

Justice Byrnes would not be a party to any such procedure. All of which, it seems to me, is much more to the credit of Justice Byrnes than my suggestion probably was to me! However, I was motivated by a feeling that it was deeply unfair to take a man like Justice Byrnes away from his life work for a war service without providing for his return at the end of the war.

During Justice Byrnes's service as director of War Mobilization, he and Justice Vinson, who was then serving as director of Economic Stabilization, became involved in an unhappy controversy with the unions over a raise of wages for railway employees. A wage increase had been awarded by a Presidential board and agreed to by both the railway managers and the unions. But the agreement had not been made effective because of a countervailing order by Byrnes. I was brought into this situation by an engagement to represent the employees. Fortunately, this did not have to be "cleared with Sidney." The employees were permitted to select their own attorney!

The matter was discussed with considerable heat with both Byrnes and Vinson, and when they appeared obdurate, appeals were made to the President on the very simple ground that under the Railway Labor Act the finding of a Presidential board, agreed to by both carriers and their employees, should be sufficient to settle the legality of the wage thus fixed. But the President replied that Jimmy Byrnes had got his back up and that he, the President, could not attempt to override his judgment because Byrnes had insisted, before taking the job, that he should not be subjected to Presidential interference. My mind went back to my early talk with Justice Byrnes and I acknowledged to myself again the firmness and integrity of his convictions. We were, however, finally able to work out a compromise which was approved by Vinson and Byrnes—one of those curious compromises by which the original award was so altered that the employees received a slightly larger increase than had been originally agreed to!

An interesting sequel to this episode was the amendment of the law making it specific that when the requirements of the Railway Labor Act had been complied with no further government review of the results would be permitted. I participated in the hearings in the Senate which were held by a sub-committee of the Committee on Interstate Commerce, the sub-chairman of which was Harry S.

Truman. I remember with interest his searching questions in the course of the hearing about one matter on which he expressed himself plainly. He said: "I want to know if this is in any way inflationary. If it is, I am against it. If not, I think I'm for it." I only wish in retrospect that the keen interest of Senator Harry S. Truman in preventing inflationary measures during the Second World War had persisted and developed into a thoroughgoing antagonism to inflation, particularly through wage increases, during the years of his administration as President of the United States.

CHAPTER XXVI

Off-Stage Glimpses of F.D.R.

THE PERENNIAL contradictions in the activities and apparently in the mental processes of Franklin D. Roosevelt will furnish a perpetual basis for biographical studies of the future. Historians will portray him in many guises and accredit him with many varying intentions, abilities, and accomplishments. His portrait may emerge as that of a profound, farsighted and sincere idealist; or a political opportunist, moving in devious ways toward objectives only vaguely defined by a mind peculiarly lacking in strong convictions, but determined to make its possessor the hero of the hour and ultimately an outstanding historical figure.

Anyone who worked intimately with F.D.R. and was able to maintain objectivity must have been impressed by the reasonable basis for both the wholehearted enthusiasm of many of his followers and the bitter criticism of many of his opponents. There would be times when he seemed to be a Chevalier Bayard, *sans peur et sans reproche,* and times in which he would seem to be the apotheosis of a prince who had absorbed and practiced all the teachings of Machiavelli. It is, perhaps, fair to say that where he had what he regarded as a great end in view, he could justify to himself the use of almost any means to accomplish it. But, at the same time, he had certain ingrained precepts as to what a decent man, a well-bred gentleman, should not and could not do.

A striking example of this occurred one day when I was talking with him shortly after the exposure of Richard Whitney, an outstanding and powerful leader of high finance, whose dishonorable transactions and conduct had been a great shock to Wall Street and to New York society because it seemed to provide convincing proof of all the wickedness which radicals had charged to the "robber barons" of Wall Street.

In view of Roosevelt's notorious attacks upon economic royalists and the continual war between his administration and the dominant forces of private enterprise, it had somewhat surprised me that he had not taken advantage of the exposure of Whitney's malefactions to make some blistering commentaries. But he gave me offhand an explanation of his unexpected reticence.

"You know," he said, "I have had a most surprising experience. I have received a great many letters and personal communications from friends in New York, complimenting me on the fact that I had not joined in the outcry and made any personal attack upon Whitney. I wonder what sort of man they think I am?"

It was quite clear that he felt it would have been very bad taste for him to have whipped up public hostility against Whitney's associates who had been victims of and not participants in his derelictions. It would have been unfair to have smeared "nice people" with "guilt by association," unsportsmanlike to kick a man when he was down. To many who had felt the lash of Roosevelt's denunciations and who thought that they and all their associates were unfairly charged with the evil doings of a few, this reticence in the Whitney matter seemed inexplicable. Many undoubtedly thought that he was showing surprising generosity and charity; and so they congratulated him. Yet to him a gentleman would not think of doing otherwise.

There were many who regarded F.D.R. not so much as a conscious demagogue, as a man who appealed, perhaps unconsciously, to the emotions rather than to the intelligence of the public. It should have been evident, however, in many speeches, that he made a great effort to appeal to the intelligence of the ordinary man. He tried to simplify complex problems. He could do this often with amazing facility, as in his notable fireside chat at the start of his administration when he explained the banking situation. On the other hand, there were many times when, as a politician, he was well aware that only an emotional appeal would be effective.

I remember a certain speech which had reached its final form after a long period of preparation with many collaborators. Late one evening in his study the President said: "I'm going to read the whole thing through now and see how it sounds." There were present only Tommy Corcoran and myself. When the President came to a certain passage he paused a moment and said: "Now, this I must say in the T.R. manner." He thrust his chin forward and bared his teeth. Tommy interjected: "Oh, but Mr. President, the difference between you and T.R. is that you never fake."

This annoyed me exceedingly. As an old admirer of Theodore Roosevelt, I felt strongly that, in a comparison with F.D.R., T.R. could not be decently characterized as a faker. To my delight, F.D.R. leaned forward and promptly replied: "Oh, but Tommy, at times I do, I do!"

In my judgment F.D.R.'s emotional convictions often led him into obvious demagogueries. But I think that in most instances where he was guilty of a purely emotional and unfair appeal (which is the essence of demagogism), he did it deliberately. When he was careless with his facts, it was because of an inherent impatience with such exactness of statement and careful shading of expression as make the speeches of so many learned professors both tiresome and ineffective in swaying public opinion. A dramatic example of this was his famous sentence: "I see one-third of a nation ill-housed, ill-clad, ill-nourished."

This appears in the second inaugural, an address upon which I worked more intensively with the President than on perhaps any other. In fact, I have in my files copies of several revised drafts carrying a great many notations. Hence the circumstances of its preparation are vivid in my memory.

When this important sentence was interpolated, I protested that there were no statistics which could possibly be marshaled to support such a statement. Housing statistics would be very difficult to analyze. Whether people were well-clad or not depended largely on occupation and environment. A ragged farm hand in the South might be better clad than a well-dressed clerk in a Northern city shivering through the winter in a thin suit and light overcoat which gave him a good appearance. No one could tell what percentage of the people were "ill-nourished," but unquestionably only a small fraction of our population was on starvation rations.

I ventured to suggest that if one were going to pull a figure out of the sky it would at least be safer to say one-fourth rather than one-third. But F.D.R. had a certain feeling for numbers which has been commented on by other observers. He liked the one-third and he wasn't particularly bothered by using a fraction which, even if it could not be supported, could not be disproved. So the statement went into the record and I only hope that in after years Roosevelt came to realize that he had perpetrated an unworthy slander on the conditions prevalent in the United States. This sentence was the climax to half a dozen preceding sentences, all painting what appears to me today to have been a needlessly gloomy picture of conditions in the United States. But we must realize that the address was written at the end of the year 1936 when there were still millions of unemployed, with living conditions very grim in millions of homes.

Roosevelt's second inaugural has been described as his "supreme oratorical masterpiece" because of its "architectural construction, eloquence and rhetorical excellence." Opinions as to which speech was his best may differ widely, but it will probably be agreed that the second inaugural was one of his best. Because I had an active part in its preparation, it will serve as a good example of how so many of F.D.R.'s speeches were written.

Prior to the second inauguration the President must have asked several people to submit suggestions for his speech and he undoubtedly received unsolicited efforts from a great many others. For my part, I wrote a complete draft of an inaugural. I do not recall at the moment exactly who the others were who worked on this inaugural, but I was very proud of the fact that some of my suggestions were incorporated almost bodily. But the variations from the original are indicative of F.D.R.'s revisions of anything he used, so that in the end the entire product was characteristic of his thought and expression.

My own draft had begun with a return to the first inaugural and the conditions of that day. The President's first draft used a similar approach, but with entirely different language. In the beginning of my draft was a paragraph incorporated later in the inaugural. I will quote both versions, as well as a few other sentences, to show exactly how my expressions were improved.

My draft:

> Today we are reconsecrating our country to the maintenance of long cherished ideals in a suddenly changed civilization.

The inaugural:

> Today we reconsecrate our country to long cherished ideals in a suddenly changed civilization.

My draft:

> In every land and in every time there are working against each other the forces that draw men together and the forces that drive them apart. In our material ambitions we are individualists. But in our seeking for economic and political progress as a nation we all go up and down together. We are one people.

The inaugural:

> In every land there are always at work forces that drive men apart and forces that draw men together. In our personal ambitions we are individualists. But in our seeking for economic and political progress as a nation, we all go up or else we all go down, as one people.

My draft:

> Maintaining a democracy of effort requires a vast amount of continuing popular education, a vast amount of tolerance of differing opinions, a vast amount of humility. No one man, no group of men can presume to think for a multitude. Political leadership can only voice common ideals and aid in their realization.

The inaugural:

> To maintain a democracy of effort requires a vast amount of patience in dealing with different methods, a vast amount of humility. But out of the confusion of many voices rises an understanding of dominant public need. Then political leadership can voice common ideals and aid in their realization.

One paragraph in my copy of the "fourth" draft had an interesting history before it emerged in its final form.

> If I know aught of the will of our people they will demand that these conditions of effective government shall be created and maintained.

To this I find added in my own handwriting a sentence reading: "They will demand a nation strong among the nations because uncorrupted by the cancers of injustice." Then I find "strong among the nations" transferred and the sentence finished in F.D.R.'s handwriting so that it reads as in the inaugural: "They will demand a nation uncorrupted by the cancers of injustice and therefore strong among the nations in its example of the will to peace."

Now I come to the concluding sentences of the inaugural:

My draft:

> And so, in again taking the oath of office as President of the United States, I have undertaken the solemn obligation of leading the American people forward along the road over which they have chosen to advance. While this duty rests upon me I shall do my utmost to speak their purposes and to accomplish their will, praying ever for that Divine guidance under which we cannot go astray.

The inaugural reads:

> In taking the oath of office as President of the United States, I assume the solemn obligation of leading the American people forward along the road over which they have chosen to advance.
>
> While this duty rests upon me I shall do my utmost to speak their purposes and to do their will, seeking Divine guidance to help us each and every one to give light to them that sit in darkness and to guide our feet into the ways of peace.

It is interesting to note that the last words are a paraphrase of a quotation which I put in my notes; and for the benefit of those who may find something familiar in the concluding words, I refer them to St. Luke 1:79.

> To give light to them that sit in darkness and in the shadow of death, to guide our feet into the way of peace.

There is one other eloquent quotation in the address which I dug up and which *is* quoted:

Each age is a dream that is dying, or one that is coming to birth.[1]

These excerpts from the various drafts of Roosevelt's second inaugural give an indication of the large amount of patient, plodding work which went into the preparation of any major address. I can recall times when as many as ten or twelve drafts of a speech were prepared. Often the attempt to combine too many ideas and incorporate too many good suggestions in one speech would lead to a poorly organized document which the four or five helpers would struggle with, working perhaps late into the evening in the Cabinet room. Here, seated at the long table, it was possible to spread out sheaves of papers and several men, scribbling intently, would try to condense or rephrase a difficult passage. Then when the usually unsatisfactory result was brought back to the President he would be likely to say: "Let me take a whack at that" and, calling in the ever-ready stenographer, who might be Miss Grace Tully or perhaps "Peggy" Dowd (who subsequently married Tommy Corcoran), he would dictate vigorously and then send his aides back to the Cabinet room to incorporate his effort into another draft. When the document had finally met F.D.R.'s approval, there would be one more session of the crew for a final polishing to check punctuation, spelling and grammar and make sure there were no inconsistencies or duplications which might have been overlooked when the mosaic work was under way.

In order to avoid any misunderstanding of my earlier criticism of Roosevelt's use of an apparent statistic in the famous "one-third of a nation" phrase, I should say that one of the most important jobs in preparing a Presidential speech is to avoid statements or statistics that could be attacked as wilfully or carelessly false. This was, of course, a major concern of F.D.R. since the virulence of his critics insured bitter accusations if he could be charged with a misrepresentation. There is no doubt that F.D.R. would have justly resented any charge that he deliberately falsified anything that he said. He was most insistent that anything incorporated in his speech which could be checked for accuracy should be verified.

On the other hand, apart from speeches and other formal utterances, it was evident that he often regarded the use of a deceptive

[1] From the poem "The Music-Makers" by Arthur O'Shaughnessy.

statement as justified, particularly in discussions with someone who was trying to get him to commit himself to a position he did not wish to take.

Often too, if he were planning a project that might be injured by undue publicity, he felt fully justified in creating the impression that he had no such thing in mind. Considering the persistent inquisitiveness of the press, it is hard to see how a President could protect himelf except by a course of frequent deceptiveness.

It is often necessary to practice the same sort of deception with respect to the continual demands and intrigues of politicians. So long as the President can encourage the hope that a request may eventually be granted, he can maintain a host of friendly supporters. These may easily be turned into a host of enemies if his ultimate decision is too candidly forecast. Whenever he makes an appointment it is an aphorism of politics that the President has made twenty disappointed enemies and one appointed ingrate. Naturally, he seeks to hold out to all the disappointed the hope of some later recompense.

One characteristic of F.D.R. which created serious confusion and inefficiency was his reluctance to delegate much authority to any one person. He knew from long experience that the greater the authority, the greater the possibility of an abuse of power. It was also a certainty that anyone who was greedy for authority would use it to increase his individual power. To minimize such abuses of power and tendencies to self-aggrandizement, F.D.R. employed two devices: first, he avoided a very clear definition of the authority granted; then he provided a further check by creating an overlapping or counteracting authority in someone else.

For example, the vague grant of authority I received as executive director of the National Emergency Council must have been in conflict with many grants of authority to others. Indeed, I did not realize until long after the event that I had also been given a sort of supervisory authority over the administration of NRA. In the same way, when the President made me director of the Industrial Emergency Committee, I did not realize that this implied a certain indefinable power over the policy determinations of the Cabinet members of the committee. I may add, however, that the Cabinet members, particularly my old friend, the Secretary of the Interior, were quite aware of the possibilities of my irritating intervention in their affairs.

Another instance of Roosevelt's system of safeguarding his appointments was my difficult and embarrassing assignment in the NRA. Although nominally appointed general counsel by the administrator, General Johnson, I actually undertook the work only at the special request of the President and for the specific purpose of providing him with a personal representative in whose discretion he seemed to have more reliance than in that of General Johnson. Events subsequently proved that, however misguided or inefficient I may have been, I did not conduct public business like a man playing with fire in a powder magazine—to use a metaphor extremely appropriate to the activities of the brilliant but unpredictable General Johnson.

An equally interesting but also worrisome characteristic of President Roosevelt was his occasional high appointment of a man for whose opinions he did not have a particularly high regard. If he wished to administer an office personally, he would tend to appoint someone who, he felt, would never take an important action without first getting F.D.R.'s approval. A notable example of this was the appointment of Henry Morgenthau, Jr., as Secretary of the Treasury.

President Roosevelt's first Treasury appointee, the intelligent and very charming Mr. Woodin, had a mind of his own. And so had Dean Acheson, who was appointed Under Secretary. Mr. Woodin early developed the serious illness from which he soon died. Acheson disagreed so thoroughly with the President's gold policy that he resigned. The President, who was determined to manage the Treasury (as well as the State Department), then appointed his old friend and neighbor, Henry Morgenthau, Jr. He was an admirable administrator of Treasury operations. But he was not a man whom Roosevelt would have selected if this had been a department in which he was willing to allow the Secretary to shape the fundamental policies and programs.

F.D.R.'s insistence on deciding all major Treasury questions himself was made painfully evident to me one day when I was with him in his study at Hyde Park. A call came in from the Secretary of the Treasury and I rose to leave the room, but he motioned me back to my chair. "I want you to hear this," he said. In the ensuing conversation he laid down the law in no uncertain terms about the exact program he wished to have followed.

This relationship between the President and Secretary Morgenthau caused a great many jealousies among other Cabinet officers. A Monday luncheon with Morgenthau became practically a standing engagement, much to the annoyance of others who had no fixed dates and who often had to wait for some time for a conference with the President on matters with which they were vitally concerned. But it seemed obvious to me that the Secretary of the Treasury felt it necessary to have a regular appointment so that he could be certain of the President's continuing approval of current actions. This was also desirable from the point of view of the President who wished to keep his finger on the pulse of the Treasury.

F.D.R.'s attitude toward Morgenthau was a constant source of surprise to me because of the frankness with which he indicated not only his unwillingness to follow, but his determination to lead the Secretary of the Treasury even in minor matters.

I remember one day when the President interrupted a discussion of more important matters to ask. "Have I told you the latest story about Hen?" It seems that Henry had telephoned that he had received the first of a new issue of stamps and would send a sheet of them over to F.D.R. who was, of course, an avid stamp collector. F.D.R. told him to inscribe a sheet and send it over, whereupon Morgenthau said, according to F.D.R.: "What do you mean about inscribing them?" The President answered: "Just write some appropriate sentiment across them and sign your name." Whereupon Morgenthau said he guessed he had better bring the sheet of stamps over himself, and when he arrived he asked: "What shall I write on them?" F.D.R. said: "Oh, just write 'From one co-conspirator to another.'" Henry started to write, then asked: "How do you spell co-conspirator?" F.D.R. said: "Just follow me and write it down. I'll spell it. C-o-n-s-t-i-p-a-t-i-o-n." Henry, writing diligently, looked up and said: "But that doesn't spell co-conspirator."

In justice to Morgenthau I cannot testify to the accuracy of this episode, but I do know that was the way F.D.R. told it to me, ending in a burst of laughter. And I know from other experiences that sometimes anecdotes which F.D.R. took great pleasure in reciting became much more amusing in the telling. Like all inveterate storytellers, he always liked to make a story a good one.

On another occasion the President said to me: "Henry is very much exercised over receiving identical bids for so many supplies procured through the Treasury. He thinks this is clear evidence of collusion." I replied that this was no evidence of collusion, because under the NRA codes we generally required publicly announced prices, known as posted prices, which manufacturers were required to maintain for all customers. Where prices were posted, naturally, no one would bid higher than his competitors unless his bid included some compensating advantage such as better service. Even such a bid would be exceptional because of the general requirement that the government contract should be awarded to the lowest bidder. Hence, a manufacturer who was able to post a lower price than his competitors was pretty sure to eliminate them before the bidding started.

The President asked me to explain this to Morgenthau. I made an appointment to lunch with him at the Treasury and tried my best to disabuse him of the concept that identical bids meant collusion. I was not very successful. And I am afraid I became rather didactic, for I remember saying to him at one point: "Now this Treasury business is your business and I don't pretend to know anything about it. The NRA codes are my business and I do think I know something about them." At the end of our discussion Morgenthau, with a touch of humor which was rare with him, replied, when I thanked him for a pleasant luncheon, "And thank you for an interesting lecture."

These incidents I have recounted indicate the way in which F.D.R. handled public business for which he felt, whether wisely or unwisely, that he had a particular competence. They are not recounted to reflect on Morgenthau who handled Treasury business very effectively and carried out the policies of the President with meticulous care. I should add, however, that after the development of the so-called Morgenthau Plan for the destruction of Germany's industrial capacity, I had such grave doubts of his political wisdom that I felt the President was well justified in maintaining tight personal control over the Treasury. I had little sympathy with Germany after its people had tolerated and supported the Hitler regime and I expressed this point of view vigorously after the end of the war. But I felt that the policy of trying to exterminate the industrial power of the German people was a tragic mistake for which we and the rest of the world would have to pay dearly. Subsequent events have done nothing to change my mind. To whatever extent Henry Morgenthau, Jr., may have shaped the formulation and execution of such a policy, I think he had a most unfortunate influence upon Roosevelt.

High in the list of F.D.R.'s admirable personal qualities was his attitude toward his own crippled condition. He often seemed extraordinarily insensitive to this physical handicap, which must have been a continual source of embarrassment and annoyance, as well as positive suffering. I never realized until long afterward the physical strain he endured when his leg braces were locked to allow him to walk forward with the aid of a cane and a friendly arm, and appear like a man of normal vigor. The horrible weight of some thirty pounds of steel, and the effort of swinging along on his practically helpless legs, made every public and formal appearance a heavy burden. Around the White House and in the Executive Offices he could be lifted from a wheel chair and into his desk chair and sit in comparative comfort. But to rise and walk he had to assume this heavy harness and then, despite actual pain, stand or walk in smiling disregard of his acute discomfort. But, in the years in which I saw so much of him, he always treated his incapacity with a careless jesting comment which made one feel that somehow it was not distressing him.

I happened to attend a sort of family luncheon prior to the second inaugural, when I was spending a great deal of time in the White House. Mrs. Roosevelt raised a question about the problem of receiving all the guests at the major inaugural reception. There would be a great crowd and it would be difficult for the President to greet and talk with everyone. In the midst of the discussion, the President spoke up: "I'll tell you what we'll do. We'll arrange to have me carried into the East Room and put up on the mantel where everyone can see me and I can greet everybody." The gay humor of his attitude in a difficult situation impressed me deeply.

On various occasions I had the pleasure of swimming with F.D.R. in the White House pool. The minute he lowered himself into the pool there was no evidence whatsoever of physical weakness. He had a magnificent torso and swam strongly, so we could proceed up and down the pool chatting, pausing now and then to rest against the edge. Then he would lift himself up to the floor and be carried into a nearby room for the customary massage. Since we were usually in the middle of a discussion, he would invite me in to talk with him during the massage. Again I felt a great admiration, not only for his cheerful fortitude but for his lack of embarrassment at the stark revelation of his pitifully shrunken legs.

Many examples could be given of the adroitness of Franklin D. Roosevelt in handling political controversies, particularly within the circle of his intimate associates. I do not know how many Cabinet officers and other important officials threatened to resign nor how frequently. I do know that so much of this went on that I once said to Steve Early: "If I ever submit my resignation to the President it will be because I intend to resign. It won't be just a huff in the hope of getting my own way." I made this remark one time when I was thoroughly fed up with many difficulties which I thought the President could have resolved by clear and definite action. Apparently I was so vehement that Steve reported the conversation to F.D.R. The next time I entered the President's office, still stewing over my troubles but not intending to threaten a resignation, he looked up at me with a grin, and as he held out his hand he said, in the gentlest imaginable fashion: "You aren't going to let the old man down, are you, Don?" Now I ask, how could one remain angry under such circumstances?

On a later occasion, when I was harassed with worries and illnesses, I did write F.D.R. a letter stating the difficulty of my continuing in government service. In reply he wrote: "I am terribly sorry that you are still feeling so wretchedly and all I can do is to give you a definite order from old family Doctor Roosevelt." Then followed a prescription to forget about problems until I had a chance to talk them over with him, which ended: "If you are really able and feel completely fit by Saturday or Sunday call me up and we can talk about the Message to Congress, the Budget, etc. My affectionate regards."

The calming influence of such a communication as this can be imagined. During the last six months of my service when I was heavily embarrassed by financial problems and felt that antagonisms which I had aroused were seriously impairing the value of any service I could render, we frequently discussed, without any truculence on my part, my desire to resign.

There were times when he would resort to satire or raillery to shame a recalcitrant subordinate. Some months prior to my leaving, I went through an angry mood, aggravated by some ill health, in which I had confided to some associates that I was seriously considering submitting my resignation. Word of this came to the President, and late one evening the telephone bell rang at my bedside. I found, to my surprise, the President on the wire, and he started in at once, talking somewhat as follows: "I have just had some bad news, Don. Secretary Hull is threatening to resign. He is very angry because I don't agree with him that we ought to remove the Ambassador to Kamchatka and make him third secretary to the Embassy at Svodia."

He went on in this way for some time and I quickly realized that he was not talking about Secretary Hull at all, but was making fun of me for getting all wrought up over things of insufficient importance. Of course I tried to respond in style, for it would have been impossible to attempt a serious discussion of my grievances under the circumstances. So I endeavored, through some fanciful replies, to indicate that the imaginary Secretary Hull was behaving very foolishly and showing signs of either office holder's importance or headaches of the morning after. But I must admit that I felt thoroughly chastened after this conversation and very grateful that the President had betrayed only friendly amusement instead of the stern displeasure which a Chief Executive with a poorer understanding of human nature or less of a sense of humor might well have shown.

During several years I had many opportunities to observe F.D.R. closely; while working with him both in the stress of crowded days and in the comparative calm of long evenings, while lunching with him at his desk or on the terrace outside his office, swimming in the pool at the White House or Warm Springs, or traveling with him by train or on the Presidential yacht. This apparent intimacy might seem to provide ample basis for at least a partial understanding of the inner man whose purposes, ambitions and prejudices motivated the actions of the outer man who occupied what became in Roosevelt's time the most powerful public office in the world.

But I would be the last to claim that I ever became well acquainted with that inner man. In fact, from my own experience in self-analysis I doubt how well acquainted anyone is with his own inner being. One cannot judge another or one's self without using words, which are at best imperfect, to express one's ideas. The effort to appraise the conscious and unconscious motives which determine human behavior is constantly frustrated by the mechanics of trying to put into words the subtleties of feeling that are so hard to define.

No biographer can be relied upon to present a wholly reliable portrait of any man, particularly one with a complex personality who has been required to deal with affairs of vast moment and great uncertainty.

It was plain to everyone who knew him at all well that primarily Franklin Roosevelt "played by ear." He had to do an enormous amount of reading and studying, but the more one reads and studies issues of vast consequence the more difficult it is to simplify them down to the point where any one decision seems to be clearly the right one or the best one. The major issues presented to a President lie in the fields of economics, law and political science. In none of these are the fundamental principles so clear and everlasting that one can turn to them as to a religious creed to find the proper measure or weight to be given to conflicting ideas.

F.D.R. did not claim to be an economist or a skilled lawyer. In fact, he would often listen patiently to the discussion of some question of economics or law and then, when the issue shifted to one of politics, he would interject with a sudden burst of energy: "Now that's a question of politics and as to that I claim to speak with some authority."

He was, indeed, a master politician. He had an extraordinary sense of what would influence public opinion. He had also a most exceptional ability to simplify issues for public statement. Part of this came from his habit, which was almost a necessity, of simplifying large issues for himself. It was plain that he made up his mind over and over again by comparing a complex program with an oversimplified situation. Time and time again in the midst of a complicated problem he would reminisce about something which had happened to one of his ancestors, or to himself, or to a friend or neighbor, or to some person with whom he had had a casual acquaintance.

He had a long-range vision of an historical character, but his major interest appeared to lie in the immediate effect of what was to be immediately done. Fears of ultimate consequences he would often brush aside, unless they happened to present a good argument against doing something he did not wish to do!

It is an old expression that a man is just a boy grown old and in many ways F.D.R. appealed to me as a boy who did not grow old, who was continually interested in the same things which stirred his interest as a boy—for example, in a stamp collection, a habit which many boys outgrow. He loved boats and sailing as a boy, and he never changed or lost his interest in them.

On many occasions this latent boyishness spurted out of F.D.R. He took a natural pleasure in discovering a neat evasion of a difficult question, a stinging retort to some criticism, or a devious way to avoid the immediate decision of a vexatious problem. But his candid expression of his delight was surprising in a mature man of vast responsibilities. He would chuckle and exclaim, "Clever, eh?" with all the unblushing candor of a child showing off before company.

Also, like a youngster, he would contrive to avoid opposition to something he had decided to do. On the day of one of his fireside chats he took a little party of "speech writers" for a sail down the Potomac. As I recall it, the group consisted of McIntyre, Early, Moley, Rosenman, Morgenthau and myself. The President approved the final draft at about 2:30 P.M. and dispatched it by a speedboat back to Washington for mimeographing. There followed an afternoon of relaxation, chatting and, for a time, poker, a game which F.D.R. enjoyed. I joined the game with a certain reluctance, explaining as I sat down at the table: "I am one of the world's worst poker players, Mr. President, but I'll sit in for a time. My wife is the poker player in our family."

For once in my life I had extraordinary luck not only in drawing cards, which I am sure I played and bet very badly, but also in holding just a little better cards than the man who bet most strenuously against me. I recall vividly the extraordinary situation of holding four jacks over four tens. At the end of the session the President, who was the banker, and a fairly large winner (at very small stakes), observed with a grin: "I'm not going to play poker with your wife."

As the afternoon waned, the President directed our course in such a way that when we turned around to go back to Washington it would be impossible to reach there more than half an hour before the time for him to go on the air. He explained this mischievously by observing that Louis Howe, back in the White House, would be sure to have a lot of suggestions to make but that he himself liked the speech as it was and did not want to argue about it. So we would arrive too late to have any changes made in the script.

Howe had been F.D.R.'s political mentor from early days and the President still valued his counsel. But the President felt that he had grown up and was entitled to his own judgment. Nevertheless, he hated to have a contentious discussion with Howe. As he remarked to me once: "I am going to talk this over with Louis. He has forty ideas a day and sometimes a few good ones." I had the feeling that his attitude toward Howe was like that of a middle-aged son who still appreciated his father's wisdom but was also a little impatient at father's efforts to keep him under parental guidance.

Perhaps living in constant association with the paternalistic Howe and a very fond but strong-minded mother gave him something of the feeling of so many mature and successful men that their parents never quite realize that they have grown up. It may also have served to accentuate the boyishness of some of his reactions and particularly his impish pleasure in circumventing attempts to influence his actions contrary to his desire. However, it was one of his peculiarly attractive and interesting qualities that many of the characteristics of the boy remained influential in the man. It is clear from stories of his youth that he very early arrived at unbounded political ambitions which were never completely satisfied. Ahead of him there were always new political worlds emerging. For him, unlike Alexander, there were always more worlds to conquer. So he, unlike Al Smith, was always the "happy warrior."

CHAPTER XXVII

Truman Arrives

IN COMMON with many millions of other people, I was greatly shocked when the word came on April 12, 1945, that President Roosevelt had died at Warm Springs, Georgia. It was, however, not the surprise to me that it would have been if I had not seen him at close range within the previous month. This last view was at the dinner of the White House Correspondents' Association, at which he presented the first Raymond Clapper award to another old friend of mine, Raymond (Pete) Brandt of the St. Louis *Post-Dispatch.*

After the tragic death of Ray Clapper in the South Pacific a large number of his friends had joined in establishing a small foundation to perpetuate his memory and the ideals of journalism which he had exemplified in his long and successful career. Sufficient funds had been obtained to provide for an annual award to the Washington correspondent whose public service best maintained the Ray Clapper standards. As one of the trustees of this fund, I was invited to the dinner and had a seat at a table only a few yards away from the center of the speaker's table where the President sat. I had not had so close a view of him for some time and his haggard, exhausted appearance distressed me. In the course of the dinner a distinguished New York physician sitting next to me asked whether in my experience Roosevelt had been inclined to show obvious signs of nervous strain. I replied that, on the contrary, it had always amazed me to see how cheerful and almost carefree he had appeared on many occasions when one would have expected him to look exhausted from long-continued effort to deal with problems of terrific difficulty. My medical companion frowned and shook his head. "Of course I am in no position to make a diagnosis," he said, "but I would say that man is very ill, not merely tired out; there is something organically wrong." What distressed me particularly was that while F.D.R.'s face lit up and he showed his customary animation in conversation, the moment he was in repose his entire face seemed to sag, his mouth dropped open, as though he were short of breath, and he had the look I have seen on the face of runners at the end of a long, killing race. Yet the next moment, when someone spoke to him, the old animation would reappear, making the contrast between that flash of fire and the dead, ashy appearance of his face in repose all the more disturbing.

The unbearable load suddenly imposed on Harry S. Truman brought him universal sympathy, particularly because of the humility and almost despair with which he undertook his great task. I did not rush to offer him any aid that I might render because the disinterestedness of such an offer is always open to question. But before long a difficult situation arose in connection with labor relations of the railroads wherein I thought I might be of help. There were few people in the country who had had my long and intimate association with railway labor problems. But I recognized that if I volunteered any intervention it would not be particularly agreeable either to the railway managements or the labor organizations. Accordingly, I obtained an appointment to see President Truman, with the express request on my part that I should come and go through the White House proper, thus avoiding the publicity of a scheduled conference. When I met him, I told the President I was sure that if he thought well of my suggestions it would avoid misunderstanding by both management and labor if I were not credited with making them.

Whether my suggestions were used or useful I cannot say; but at least they did no harm since that particular controversy was peacefully adjusted. However, it is worth while recalling some details of that conference. I had assured the President that my main interest was in trying to preserve the effectiveness of the Railway Labor Act, under which the railroads had enjoyed industrial peace for a longer period than any other major industry, despite the incidence of, first, the Great Depression and then the Second World War. The President assured me that he shared my faith in the principles of the Railway Labor Act. He added emphatically that he thought it was the best law concerned with labor relations that had ever been enacted and provided a model for all such legislation. It is important to record this opinion in view of his subsequent attitude on similar legislation.

When I was leaving I referred to the difficulty which he had publicly expressed of getting the best man for a specific job to accept the responsibilities and burdens of public service. Again he responded emphatically, walking to the door with me as I was leaving and telling me of disappointments he had encountered in his efforts to persuade certain men to accept public positions. I had a profound sympathy with his attitude because I had seen over the years how increasingly difficult it had become for the President to command the services he needed.

In the early days of the Roosevelt administration it seemed that anyone who was tapped by the President for a public responsibility would accept it. Over and over again in 1933, 1934 and 1935, I had been able to persuade men to sacrifice private comfort and profit and even to endanger their future careers by taking on a public job. I recall the great pressure which I had put on Clay Williams of the Reynolds Tobacco Company to accept the chairmanship of the NRA Board and then to remain long after his promised term of service had expired. I also recall how many times Arthur D. Whiteside, President of Dun and Bradstreet, took on a public job despite strong opposition in his organization. I could name offhand a score of other men of high quality in business and in educational fields who rendered valuable public service, many of whom were repaid only by their own satisfaction in having performed their duty despite rancorous criticisms which received far more publicity than the good work they did. But as the partisanship of the Roosevelt administration for certain special interests, such as those of labor, increased, it became more and more difficult to persuade disinterested men to accept ungrateful tasks of public service.

Any administration long in power encounters this difficulty. More and more the political necessity of satisfying pressure blocks alienates not only those of opposing interests but also men who desire only to weigh fairly all special interests against the general interest. It was disheartening to learn from my next experience with President Truman how quickly political considerations had come to outweigh his desire to render disinterested public service.

Through the activities of a self-organized committee, independent of any special interest, we had devised a sort of code of industrial relations modeled on the Railway Labor Act which was introduced in Congress by Senators Ball, Burton and Hatch, a bipartisan group of three men not unfriendly to labor and actuated by high ideals of public service. The bill was immediately greeted with a raucous chorus of opposition from the heads of organized labor who hardly had time to read the bill before they denounced it. The proposal at once became the subject of a widespread public debate in the course of which I happen to know that Senator Hatch, a Democrat, discussed the bill with President Truman and received his encouragement to continue in its advocacy.

Then a vacancy occurred on the Supreme Court. To everyone's surprise, including his own, Senator Burton was offered the appointment which, of course, he accepted although, as he assured me, with great regret that he could not carry on the fight for the industrial relations bill. It will also be recalled that Senator Hatch was later appointed a federal judge by President Truman, while Senator Ball's staunch advocacy of the bill earned him the bitter opposition of the labor organizations which managed to bring about his defeat when he came up for re-election.

This effort to enact a comprehensive labor relations act was, of course, a part of the movement to amend the Wagner Act, which had established the National Labor Relations Board.

During President Roosevelt's administration I had worked from time to time for the amendment of the one-sided Wagner Act and on one occasion this had brought me into an unhappy conflict with the President. In the fall of 1938 I was having a conference with F.D.R. in the White House Executive Offices with regard to the Mexican oil problem. I wanted to avoid any public discussion of the Mexican situation in the White House. Accordingly, when the newspaper men gathered around me after I had left the President, I was so anxious to avoid any inquiries about Mexico that I unfortunately seized on a question from one of the reporters as to whether I had discussed amendments of the Wagner Act with the

President. I said I had not, but that it so happened that a Washington afternoon newspaper was publishing that day a statement I had written about amending the Wagner Act. I suggested that if they wanted to know my opinions they would find them all recorded there.

The result of this indiscretion should have been anticipated by me. The story was promptly published that I had been discussing amendments of the Wagner Act with the President and my opinions were publicized with the wholly unjustified implication that the President was at least receptive.

Unfortunately, just at that time Senator Wagner was running for re-election from New York and was being both severely attacked and strongly defended because of his authorship of the Wagner Act. The President was deeply incensed that he had been apparently placed by me in the position of giving comfort to Senator Wagner's opponents. This was, incidentally, also distressing to me because, although I did not approve of the Wagner Act, the Senator was a close friend with whom I had worked in harmony on many matters and whom I certainly had no desire to injure.

I called up Secretary McIntyre the next day and said I wanted to explain my faux pas to the President and do what I could to make amends for it. Mac, with his usual candor, said: "I don't think I'd try to see him now or for some time, Don. He's very angry about the whole business." As a consequence, my friendly relations with the President were seriously weakened for some time. It was something that I think continued to fester in his memory, for although later I saw him on various occasions it seemed to me that his confidence in me had been seriously impaired. Indeed, I would say that at no time thereafter, so far as I can recall, did I ever participate in that intimate work of speech writing in which I had played a considerable part during the preceding five years.

Unfortunately the Wagner Act had acquired the sanctity of a great charter with organized labor and it was made plain that any encouragement for its amendment by legislators or by the President would arouse the bitter hostility of labor. This, of course, President Truman soon learned and he was most careful not to give any *public* support to any such heretical proposals as were involved in the Ball-Burton-Hatch bill. But the movement for amendment of the Wagner Act grew in force until finally the Case

Bill (so named from its sponsorship by Representative, later Senator, Francis Case) was enacted.

Among many others I had contributed my services to the formulation of this bill, and when it became evident that President Truman was seriously considering a veto, I went to Clark Clifford, his legal counsel in the White House. I spent a couple of hours going over the bill with him and arguing that the President, if he was faithful to his expressed convictions, could not possibly veto the bill. I did not feel that Clifford was very sympathetic. Hence I stressed my point that I knew the President must be personally sympathetic with the mild reforms proposed by the Case Bill and that a veto could only be a purely political submission to pressures from the labor unions.

In the end, the President vetoed the bill and thereby fixed my opinion as to the wholly political character of his ultimate decisions. Perhaps I did him an injustice, but I was never again able to feel any assurance that he would place the public interest above party interest. I must concede that he made many momentous decisions which took courage and showed devotion to such ideals as he held. But in matters of public policy, where apparently a voting majority was lined up on one side of an issue, I cannot recall an instance where he espoused a minority program and took the risk of attempting to convert a majority to its support.

The Case Bill was followed in time by the Taft-Hartley Act, which was also vetoed by President Truman. This act, presumably to his great surprise, was immediately passed over his veto. After that time there never came from President Truman any constructive proposal to enact an adequate labor relations law. On the contrary, he relied steadfastly on the concentrated power of organized labor to deliver votes to the Truman party in exchange for his support of labor's indefensible hostility to any revision of the Wagner Act.

By this time it had become quite apparent that Harry Truman, the politician, had definitely adopted the Roosevelt formula to maintain the Democratic Party in power. He would continue farm support and various welfare projects appealing to the self-interest of large groups of voters. He would maintain the continued allegiance to organized labor so as to appeal to the industrial voters in the Northwest and East. Regardless of the antipathy to New

Dealism in the more conservative elements of the Southern states, he would assume they could be kept in line by the self-interest of all Southern politicians in maintaining a national Democratic administration, giving to senior Democrats the control of Congressional committees and the control of patronage in the Southern states. Indeed, Harry Truman moved so enthusiastically to advance the New Deal that he had to give it a new name. His super New Deal he called the Fair Deal.

In his enthusiasm President Truman went beyond the diplomatic efforts of Roosevelt who avoided, as far as possible, giving undue offense to reasonable conservatives particularly in the South. Truman established a President's Civil Rights Committee which reported a program that could hardly have been better devised to alienate Democratic support in the Southern states. This program included anti–poll tax and anti-lynching legislation and the establishment of a permanent federal commission empowered to prevent and punish any discrimination in employing workers on the ground of race, color, religion or ancestry.

This committee was shrewdly organized with many apparent moderate liberals, including Charles E. Wilson, President of General Electric, as chairman. But all such large commissions, composed essentially of volunteers in public service, are actually run by a staff and a few zealous members who are strongly inspired by prejudice or self-interest to advance causes in which they are partisan.

In discussions following the report of the President's Civil Rights Committee, I became convinced that the entire investigation and report had been controlled by representatives of the extreme Left and had been used effectively to advance the Communist program of creating a revolutionary Negro-dominated party in the South. While this seems an absurd and utterly impractical project to most Americans, there is no question today but that at one time this was a definite part of the Communist program for the eventual overthrow of our constitutional form of government.

The so-called Civil Rights Program advocated by the Committee was immediately officially adopted by President Truman and embodied in a message to Congress.

I believed then, as I still do, that all three proposals were not only unconstitutional but, even more important, were maliciously designed to do much more harm than good to the civil rights of American citizens.

The poll tax is wholly a matter of state law with which the national government has so little right to interfere that a large percentage of its opponents have come to advocate a constitutional amendment rather than the passage of an invalid federal law.

The anti-lynching law agitation is to me a particularly obnoxious form of political playing to class prejudice. Since lynchings have become so rare that the Tuskegee report shows recently only one or none a year, it becomes a manifest absurdity for the federal government to pass a law to take over state punishments of this form of murder when thousands of murders each year are punishable only by state law.

The Fair Employment Practice scheme is one of the cleverest devices ever designed to ruin private business by subjecting it to constant supervision and interferences from political bureaucrats. At the request of the Senate Labor Committee which was considering the bill, I submitted an extensive brief showing the unconstitutionality of the proposal. Various organizations have distributed uncounted thousands of copies of this brief, from which I quote:

> If the Fair Employment Practice program had not been originally devised by communist strategists, they would have been ashamed of their stupidity. As a matter of fact, it was a logical outgrowth of their orthodox plan. At the root of communist ideology is the delusion of discrimination. A lot of people are miserable (they are told) not because of their own inherent or cultivated weaknesses, but because other men use their inherited or acquired power to oppress them. The remedy (they are told) is to have the state (a deceptive name for a tyrannical ruling class) control all power and divide up the proceeds of state enterprises without discrimination. The program proceeds logically. The first step is to appeal to the least prosperous to fight "discrimination."
>
> The communists preach anti-discrimination and so appeal to every element of society that suffers any disadvantage because of racial or religious prejudice.
>
> Government, by the enforcement of political controls over

> private management, can make inevitable the failure of a private enterprise system and thus make inevitable state ownership and control of all essential enterprises. This is the objective of communism; and the Fair Employment Practice legislation would furnish incalculable aid to communists in their effort to attain that objective.

At this time Senator Taft was chairman of the Senate Labor Committee. He had not made up his mind as to his position, but with his usual fairmindedness he arranged for an executive meeting of the committee which sat an entire day listening to an argument on the constitutionality and wisdom of the proposed legislation. Charles H. Tuttle of New York, a lawyer of outstanding ability, argued for the legislation which had been introduced by Senator Ives of New York. I opposed it. After lengthy deliberations, the committee, always pro-labor in its general composition, voted six in favor, six opposed, and one member in favor of a noncompulsory law. I am happy to report that Senator Taft became and remained an opponent of such legislation.

This was not my first association with Senator Taft, but it was one of many in which he demonstrated over and over again his fundamental liberalism, his consistent fairness in dealing with opponents as well as friends, and the unswerving integrity of his convictions, which were always based on intensive study and an ability to eliminate personal prejudice that I found extraordinary. I had intended to write little about him as a living statesman whom I did not wish to flatter and in whom I could find little to criticize. Since he died during my writing of this book, I wish to repeat the tribute which I paid to him during the Presidential campaign of 1952 when I introduced him to a Virginia audience with the simple words: "A great American."

From my review of what was called the President's Civil Rights Program it will be easily understood why I found myself early in his administration a confirmed opponent of President Truman and his policies. It will also be understood why I felt an irresistible urge to make a campaign which I shall describe hereafter as "My Personal Crusade for Liberty." But in all fairness I should make it plain that there were qualities in Truman and his administration which I could almost admire. The humility with which he took his oath of office persisted as a mark of many things throughout his administration. He was willing to take counsel from those whom he regarded as having greater intellectual power and learning than he possessed. In one way, this was a weakness because he notably yielded to the judgment of men for whom he had a great admiration, such as Dean Acheson and General George Marshall. To my mind, the very intellectual power of these men contained the seeds of weakness. Their judgments were sometimes so refined that men of more simple mind might have seen more clearly and acted more wisely.

President Truman acted with real courage on big issues. It took courage to decide that the atom bomb should be used against Japan; it took courage to enunciate the so-called "Truman Doctrine" which arose out of the Greek situation; it took courage to go to war against aggression in Korea; Heaven knows it took courage to insist on his renomination against the wishes of most of his party leaders and most of the other leaders of American thought! Without indicating that I agree with any one of these decisions, I must pay tribute to the courage of the man who made them.

That same courage was evidenced in many petty things, such as standing by friends who ought to have been discarded, and expressing himself crudely on various occasions. Again, the courage but not the action is commended.

Harry Truman had a fundamental candor which made discussion more pleasant with him than with other statesmen whom I felt never were willing to reveal what they really thought. A most amusing example of this candor occurred one evening when my wife and I were at the home of former Representative Joseph E. Casey. The small party included Lord Halifax, the British Ambassador, and his wife, Justice William O. Douglas and his wife, and Vice President and Mrs. Truman. There was talk about the inadequacy of the salaries offered American politicians of high rank, Lord Halifax pointing out that in Great Britain men of high position were not only paid large salaries, but also had assurances of pensions and other emoluments which relieved them of some of the economic cares of high office.

Truman responded very briskly that Halifax was quite right; that no senator could live on his salary, then ten thousand dollars, and meet all his obligations at home and in Washington; that those without private means had to supplement their salaries. He mentioned that many of them took to the lecture platform, some practiced law, others wrote articles, and went on to say, in substance: "When I was chairman of the Committee on Expenditures during the war, I had all kinds of offers to make speeches and write articles which would have been very helpful. But I could not do this because the minute I began to make money out of our investigations I would be destroying the impartiality of my position. I would be trying to make something personal out of investigations instead of simply trying to save the government money. But," he ended, "of course I could not live on my salary. So I just put my wife on the payroll."

Now here was Harry Truman, the Kansas City politician, speaking with absolute candor. I can't think of any other senator of my acquaintance who, if he mentioned his wife's employment at all, would not have said something to this effect: "Fortunately my wife has always been of great assistance to me and could handle a lot of my correspondence and other chores, so I was able to engage her services and at the same time help the family income." I admire Truman's candor and I tell the story to his credit.

One can understand, however, the scorn with which this same Harry Truman would regard a lot of the attacks upon other office holders for using family aides or otherwise finding some way to supplement their incomes. I think it would be hard for him to feel that a politician who used his influence to get public contracts for a friend and was willing to take a small percentage profit out of the transaction, was guilty of any serious wrongdoing.

Indeed, I shall go so far as to say that until we are at a much higher level of common morality than we have yet reached, I shall continue to find a good deal of hypocrisy in public complaints against politicians who manage to make a little money out of what Tammany would call "legalized graft." I do not defend making money out of political influence. Certainly I do not defend an office holder who seeks or accepts any profit from his decision or action as a public official. But in commenting on a great many political exposés I think that I would join Harry Truman in citing the Gospel according to St. John, Chapter 8, verse 7: "He that is without sin among you, let him first cast a stone." My feeling is that these hypocritical attacks on minor sins of politics destroy half the force of attacks on major sins against which the public conscience should be aroused.

Let me conclude my vignette of Harry Truman by quoting some verses I included in a speech which I made in 1949. At that time, in deference to the Presidential office, I thought it more courteous to use the name "Hally G." in place of "H.S.T." but the verses were originally written as they appear here.

H.S.T.

In this land of the brave and the free
We are ruled by the great H.S.T.;
He was raised on a bottle by Doc Aristotle;
He learned from old Plato how not to deflate—oh,
By Socrates guided, with billions provided,
A miracle worker is he.

How to make the payor a payee,
No one knew till we found H.S.T.;
In budgeting speed he's a new Archimedes;
You'll hear Euclid gurgle when he squares the Circle;
With Einstein reacting, he adds by subtracting,
And makes two less one equal three.

From the quicksands of debt do not flee,
For you cannot depress H.S.T.;
Canute had a notion to push back the ocean;
Bold Ajax said lightning was not really fright'ning;
And Joshua tried proving he'd stop the sun moving,
But they weren't as smart as he.

To conquer the world we'd agree
Quite a difficult project might be;
The Greek Alexander, he turned out a gander;
J. Caesar, he tried it, but couldn't divide it;
Napoleon would take it, but he didn't make it;
And now comes the super-recouper-hoop-looper
To beat all creation, include our own nation,
So all may be saved by the great H.S.T.

We will save everything, but we won't save our cash;
We will mix everyone, so we hope you like hash;
We will soar up so high we'll be dead when we crash;
And so, from the world of the brave and the free,
Mankind shall be saved by the great H.S.T.

CHAPTER XXVIII

The Double Martini Club and Other Associations

SOCIAL and business organizations play a considerable part in influencing one's opinions and activities, and I have been associated with my fair share of organizations of a professional, convivial or scholarly character. I have belonged to a variety of Bar associations, city clubs, country clubs and fraternities. I also had a unique association with the American Iron and Steel Institute as an administrative member of the Code Authority for the steel industry. (This was an experience which the Institute may prefer to forget, but which I find pleasure in remembering.) Of all these organizations the Double Martini Club stands out as one of the most enjoyable and stimulating and, at the same time, productive of a valuable if intangible public service.

The exceptional feature of the Double Martini Club was that, unlike every other organization to which I belonged, it never had a constitution or bylaws; but its unwritten laws provided cohesion and flexibility in its activities. Its origin was obscure, but it grew out of a friendship of three men, Major Carl Spaatz (later General Spaatz), Henry A. Berliner (later Colonel Berliner), and Milton W. King, a well-known Washington lawyer, onetime president of the District of Columbia Bar Association.

Some years before the Second World War these men inaugurated a series of Saturday luncheons, the theme of which was the expansion of America's air power. They gathered round them informally from time to time most of the men who were later to be famous leaders of the American Air Force, men like Generals "Hap" Arnold, "Jimmy" Doolittle, George Kenney, "Rosie" O'Donnell, Elwood Quesada, Barton Yount, Eric Nelson and "Monk" Hunter. They also brought in a few outstanding newspaper men, such as Lyle Wilson (United Press), Turner Catledge (*New York Times*). Two other members were Edgar J. Goodrich, a Washington lawyer who had been an air observer in the First World War, and Professor Bruce Hopper, historian of the Air Force. My own attendance developed partly out of personal friendship and partly, probably, because at the time my intimacy with the President may have been regarded as possibly helpful to the objectives of the group, although my contribution here was microscopic. Indeed, my principal contribution seems to have been to write occasional verses for its meetings.

As a week-end luncheon club, it seemed appropriate to start with a martini. But the interruption of exciting discussions to order another round of drinks inspired me to suggest starting with double martinis, which eventually became traditional at all gatherings.

One amusing feature of Double Martini Club meetings was the occasional presence of representatives of airplane manufacturers who, since they were operating on expense accounts, were usually permitted graciously to pick up the check. In their absence, we usually rotated this privilege, so that it made considerable difference as to whether there was a large and thirsty attendance or a small gathering of limited consumption.

It seems incredible today that a few years prior to the Second World War the Army Air Force was the most woefully inadequate division of the armed services. When the United States entered the First World War in 1917, the Aviation Service, as it was called then, had only 55 planes and 65 officers, of whom 35 were fliers. Despite the obvious development of airplanes as an instrument of war and the expansion of appropriations for the Army Air Force in subsequent years, we had less than 3,000 planes suitable for combat service when the Japanese attacked Pearl Harbor on December 7, 1941. By contrast we had over 43,000 combat planes in March 1944. I might also record that our aviation expenditures in

1938 were less than $51,000,000, rose to $600,000,000 in 1941, and reached over $13,000,000,000 in 1944.

In the light of these figures, it should be evident why the pioneers in military aviation, such as Arnold, Spaatz and Doolittle, regarded national neglect of the Air Force as a tragic error, which haunted them night and day. I knew a little of the long, exasperating hours which the air men put in, trying to force recognition of the needs of the Air Force from conservative military leaders and uninspired, shortsighted politicians. But the weekly discussions in the Double Martini Club gave me a lively understanding of that lack of vision which was responsible for our inadequate program. I recall the shock with which we heard a report from Henry Berliner, whose factory produced airplane parts during the Second World War, regarding the terrific production of airplanes in Germany. There he had actually been permitted to see vast establishments preparing to turn out the fighting and bombing planes with which the Nazis were intending to demonstrate the obsolete defensive power of Maginot Lines, and massed infantry.

After America was forced into the Second World War by the attack at Pearl Harbor, there was no difficulty in arousing the American people to the need for tremendous air power. They had not only seen what air power was doing in Europe, but they had received a terrible wound from Japanese air power. The demand of Roosevelt for 50,000 planes, which had been ridiculed a year before, seemed all too moderate. Not only the fighting equipment but the personnel of the Air Force expanded beyond all previous expectations until there were nearly 2,500,000 officers and men in the Army Air Force in 1944. Colonel Arnold and Major Spaatz became four-star generals; and lieutenants and captains became brigadier and major generals.

Watching this transformation from afar, I was impressed by the extraordinary ability of so many of these men to fulfill enormously increased responsibilities. It was comparable to the promotion of a small business man to the management of a billion-dollar corporation. Perhaps it was the courage, vision and decisiveness of the kind of man who was attracted to aviation in the early years that was responsible for their amazing achievements.

The civilian members of the Double Martini Club continued to meet intermittently through the war, now and then with some of the military men available for a few hours of relaxation. For one such meeting in December 1943 I wrote:

Now it's seldom there's a meeting
Of the Club, Double-Martini,
Though our hearts are fondly beating and our stomachs still are strong,
But the war pulls us asunder
And we sometimes sadly wonder
If the Club had started sooner, would the war now last so long?
All our plans are in production,
But they came a little slowly,
And it might not cost so much in lives if they had come before;
More Martini men a-rooting,
More airmen prepared for shooting . . .
Well, I wonder if we would have been invited to the war!

Despite the tremendous hazards to which even the highest officers among our friends were constantly exposed, despite numerous hairbreadth escapes, none was struck down, although one suffered a lifelong injury. Colonel Berliner, as a member of the staff of General Spaatz, went on many bombing expeditions, particularly for the purpose of discovering possible structural weaknesses. After one of these dangerous expeditions he was being briefed in England in a crowded room where he was subjected to an icy draft from an open window. He came down with pneumonia and developed an embolism in his right arm, which necessitated its amputation, a particular tragedy for a good athlete, skillful at many games, and a marvelous guitarist, who knew and sang hundreds of songs and played accompaniments to any that might be suggested —one of the three musical lights of the Double Martini Club.

The other two guitarists were Spaatz and Goodrich. Thus at our occasional long evening meetings the three, by changing off, could maintain a steady stream of music for five or six hours. The loss of his right arm to such a man as Berliner was much more than an ordinary tragedy. As I have indicated, we were most blessed in the lack of other great tragedies during the war, although the sudden deaths of General Arnold and General Yount some time afterward showed the lasting effects of the terrific strains imposed upon such men.

During the war General Spaatz passed a ten-day period reporting in the United States, which included one extra social interlude. On the Friday before he was leaving, we arranged for a dinner of the Double Martini Club members and their wives at our house in Spring Valley. There were naturally many difficulties involved in getting everyone together at the last moment, but since everyone was anxious to have this one evening with "Tooey" and Ruth Spaatz, all the obstacles were finally surmounted. Everything was all happily arranged until an episode Friday morning almost upset the whole program.

Mrs. Helm, the White House social secretary, called up Mrs. Spaatz from the White House and informed her magisterially that Mrs. Roosevelt wished General and Mrs. Spaatz to have dinner with the President that evening. With an amazing assurance (considering, of course, that she knew better) Ruth Spaatz said: "Oh, I'm so sorry we can't possibly come because a dinner has been arranged for the General with a lot of out-of-town friends. All the arrangements have been made and I am sure the President won't mind because he is having lunch with General Spaatz today."

Mrs. Helm said with great dignity: "Oh, that is most unfortunate," and there the conversation ended.

Ruth told my wife what had occurred, but kept it from Tooey, which was certainly wifely discretion. Florence and I decided that, knowing F.D.R.'s even disposition, Tooey's career would not be ruined by this failure to respond to a command dinner. However, we chuckled a good deal during the course of the evening, realizing that this was probably the only time in our lives when we would take a ranking guest away from the White House. That evening is, in fact, one of my choicest recollections. Everyone was gay and so happy to forget for a few hours all thoughts of the war while we sat around in the living room playing guitars and singing. I can still see Tooey sitting on the floor at half past one in the morning, twanging his guitar to his favorite "This is love," with Ruth, who had a beautiful singing voice, snuggled up and caroling beside him.

Since the end of the World War the Double Martini Club has lived on as a purely convivial institution. As long as General Spaatz remained in service, completing his work as commanding general, there were many problems of current interest to enliven the club meetings. Since his retirement, meetings are less frequent, although at least an annual reunion has been maintained. It seems appropriate to quote here the short verse I wrote in commemoration of Tooey's retirement, April 1948.

Farewell to Spaatz!
Ah! Many a pilot's heart is sore
For old hot Spaatz he'll see no more.
A tear falls from his bright blue eye,
Double Martini Club runs dry,
But far away in Kaiserplatz
You'll hear them say: "Out! Damnèd Spaatz!"

Among other associations in which I have been particularly active have been, naturally, Bar associations. It would require too much space to review a lot of work as a member, and sometimes chairman, of various Bar association committees. Also I think my most useful service has been in making addresses at various Bar meetings, which would fill a small volume. Three received wide circulation and, from extensive subsequent correspondence, evidently had some influence: "The New Look of the Constitution," [1] "Should We Revive the Constitution," [2] and "Headaches of the Bar." [3]

Throughout my life I have been most fortunate in having missed very few speaking engagements; but the fear that I might have to cancel a speech because of a sudden illness has always been with me, and has become more acute in recent years. One narrow escape that was amusing to my audience occurred in January 1947 when the New York State Bar Association staged a discussion at its annual meeting of "The Plan of Judge John C. Knox for a Federal Labor Court." Judge Knox of the U.S. District Court, Justice Jackson of the U.S. Supreme Court and I were the scheduled speakers and I was naturally anxious to be in good physical shape.

[1] Delivered at the annual meeting of the Virginia State Bar Association in 1949; reprinted later in the Proceedings and in the Virginia Law Weekly.

[2] Delivered at the annual meeting of the Arizona Bar Association in 1951; reprinted later by the Association and in the *American Bar Association Journal*, January, 1952.

[3] Delivered at the annual meeting of the Chicago Bar Association in 1952; reprinted later in the *Association Record* and, in part, in other publications.

A few days before the meeting a heavy cold laid me low. Sulfa drugs brought no relief and were followed by penicillin. When I arrived at my New York hotel the evening before the meeting I was feeling groggy, but still able to speak. Early in the evening my upper lip began to swell and, in a foolish moment, I put on an ointment which apparently aggravated the condition. When I looked in the mirror the next morning my face was truly "a sight." The upper lip was covered with lumpy sores which distorted every attempted smile or frown.

Nevertheless I could still talk; so I went late to the meeting, avoiding most of the preliminary reception, and on the platform concealed my face as far as possible by hand and kerchief until I had to rise and speak. Then I assured a large and almost giggling audience that this was not my customary appearance and that behind this ghastly front there was normally—not a handsome, but an ordinary face! My embarrassment on this occasion was nearly as great as that of a well-known lawyer who, in a vehement argument before the Supreme Court, suddenly ejected his upper plate of teeth—which he fortunately caught in mid-air.

Of scores of amusing and embarrassing incidents in the course of a long speech-making career, two stand out as typical of countless others. The most aggravating experience for any principal speaker is to have one or more speakers on the program injected ahead of him who tire out his audience before he is given a chance to speak. I recall particularly one Bar meeting at which I was assured that only one or two brief speeches would precede my featured address. Actually over one and a half hours were used up in a series of dull talks that left the audience completely worn out, and forced me, in pity and self-protection, to condense my thirty-minute talk into less than fifteen minutes.

Another most exasperating experience came, during the NRA, when I went to Detroit to make a speech of considerable importance. Advance interest was so great that the committee had moved the dinner from hotel to hotel as attendance increased and finally had to resort to an assembly room which accommodated (I believe) 1,700 people.

When we sat down I was informed for the first time that the committee had engaged a professional humorist to precede me. Their reason was, they told me, that there would be a lot of drinking (which was true) and they wanted to quiet the crowd down so that my serious talk would receive proper attention. It seemed that this was a smart idea until the humorist hit his stride. He was so delighted by the response from this huge audience of "Motor City" celebrities to his well-delivered "corn," that he lost all sense of time. His "fifteen minutes" became twenty, thirty, forty, and then he launched into a serious exordium about "loyalty," "enthusiasm" and "fair play" in business. This finished him and the now very quiet audience at the end of fifty minutes.

As the humorist sat down, sweating profusely he whispered to me that he hoped he hadn't talked too long! I replied that he had reminded me of a story which I could use to appease the audience. It was an old story, but most apt—the tale of the speaker at an intercollegiate banquet who responded to the toast of "Yale"—and talked for ten minutes on "Y—which stands for Youth," ten minutes on "A—which stands for Ambition," ten minutes on "L—which stands for Loyalty," and finally ten minutes on "E—which stands for Enthusiasm." The toastmaster, prior to introducing the next speaker, observed drily that they had all enjoyed the eloquence of the previous speaker, but were glad that he had not graduated from the Massachusetts Institute of Technology!

I think this story should be told at every dinner where someone, whether a bore or an entertainer, insists on talking far beyond his allotted time. In a word, the story should be told at almost every public dinner. And this chapter of my reminiscences should end with a comment on one of my speeches by my wife. The occasion was one of importance, and I had worked hard to keep my address down to thirty minutes. When we were returning home Florence said to me: "Oh, you were wonderful!—the first fifteen minutes! I do wish you had stopped there." The trite phrase: "She is my best critic," really applies to my wife.

CHAPTER XXIX

A Personal Crusade for Liberty

As THE Second World War came to its end the question arose strongly in my mind as to whether, after the war was won, we were going to lose the liberties for which we had sacrificed our blood and treasure.

Throughout the First World War there had persisted the usual partisan opposition to the leadership of President Woodrow Wilson. Of course this had been submerged in an apparent nonpartisan support of war measures, but as soon as the war was ended with the Armistice of November 11, 1918, the smoldering opposition to Wilson's leadership increased its heat. President Wilson had practically invited such opposition by his unfortunate demands in the Congressional elections of 1918 for a Democratic Congress. Then, when in the peace conferences he failed to invite Republican participation, the partisan opposition was given further stimulation and justification.

There should not have been a partisan Republican opposition to Wilson's advocacy and successful efforts to create a League of Nations. One of the earliest outstanding sponsors of such a program had been Theodore Roosevelt. Although he had a deep and quite personal hostility to Woodrow Wilson, the Republican Party, under his leadership, could hardly have made a major issue of the formation of a League of Nations, although it might well have opposed specific provisions of the covenant.

Most unfortunately, to my mind, Theodore Roosevelt died in 1919, at a time when his rising influence both in the Republican

Party and among the people as a whole presaged his nomination as the Republican candidate for President in 1920.

The original Republican opposition to the League of Nations program was confined to a few notable Republicans, such as Senator Hiram W. Johnson, Robert M. La Follette, Henry Cabot Lodge and others in the Congress whom Wilson had previously denounced as "a little group of wilful men." My law partner Harold L. Ickes was at that time a very close adviser and aide to Senator Johnson and, indeed, undertook the management of Senator Johnson's campaign for the Republican nomination in 1920. For this reason, I know from many intimate experiences how limited in the early stages was the Republican opposition to Wilson's League of Nations program. But, to the considerable surprise of the early opponents, this opposition spread and grew with amazing rapidity. At the same time, President Wilson exhausted himself in his campaign to gain popular support of the League, suffered a stroke and became an invalid. This so impaired his capacity for leadership (and really for administering the Presidency) that the public demand for a change in the national administration soon developed to the point where it became evident that the next President of the United States would be a Republican committed to a reversal of many Wilsonian policies.

The people generally had lost the spiritual elation which had made our participation in the war a crusade "to make the world safe for democracy." All classes of citizens were infected with an intense desire to get back to what the Republican nominee, Senator Harding, described as "normalcy." They did not want to be called upon for further sacrifices. They did not want to be further involved in the quarrels and conflicting interests of European nations. They wanted to concentrate all their efforts on re-establishing the material prosperity of the United States and insuring the manual workers and business men of the nation unrestrained freedom to improve their fortunes, unencumbered with any obligations to contribute to the welfare of the peoples of other nations.

In company with many other Roosevelt Progressives, this reaction seemed to me likely to go too far in reversing the programs of social justice which Roosevelt had espoused and which Wilson had carried forward. But, I had grave doubts as to whether membership in the League of Nations by the United States would advance the best interests of our people. I had considerable sympathy with the sentiment expressed by Clarence Darrow who opposed our participation in the League on the ground that it might be an effort to "put a lid on the world." In other words, there was a reasonable fear that a combination of ultra-conservative governments might be strong enough to repress the aspirations of many peoples in many lands who would be struggling to get rid of established hierarchies that sought to perpetuate ancient special privileges at the expense of improvement in the conditions of masses of the common people.

It was all very well for the advocates of the League to insist that we had fought the war to save democracy from such imperialist programs as had been espoused by Germany. But the Wilsonian ideals had received little encouragement from the European statesmen participating in the peace conference, even though Wilson himself had been hailed by the masses throughout Europe as their savior from despotism.

Our local band of Roosevelt Progressives in Chicago was sorely perplexed as to whether they ought to support the Democratic candidate, James M. Cox. He was pledged to carry forward the Wilson policies which, at least in the domestic field, were generally approved. The Republican candidate wanted to lead the country back to the "good old days," which apparently meant the days before the Progressive demands for social justice had accomplished a revolution in popular thinking.

In this perplexity we had commissioned Raymond Robins as our representative to obtain a personal interview with Senator Harding and report to us his conclusions. They may be summarized in the vivid phrases in which he reported his personal opinion as to Senator Harding. He said that meeting and talking with him could be compared with the experience of a man walking down the street and coming to a house with a magnificent and imposing façade. Then, he said, you went up the steps and opened the front door—and found yourself in the back yard! Most of us decided that, under the circumstances, we would prefer to support Governor Cox, even though it would be fighting in a losing cause. To carry forward the progressivism of Theodore Roosevelt, Robert M. La Follette and Woodrow Wilson seemed still to be a losing cause even after the election of President Hoover in 1928. Although, as I have heretofore explained, his careful and gradual programs for a moderate progressivism warranted a more sympathetic understanding than he received from the Republican progressives.

Then came the Great Depression, followed by the tremendous resurgence of the old progressivism in the early years of the administration of President Franklin D. Roosevelt. In his administration, however, and particularly in the war years, the evolutionary policies of the old progressivism became gradually transformed into revolutionary policies. The national government began to exercise such far-reaching and detailed controls of all living and working conditions, and even of private morals, that the resemblance of our government to a centralized rule of national socialism became alarming.

Increasing dissent developed among many of the survivors of the old Progressives in both the Democratic and Republican parties.

We found our national government committed at the end of the Second World War to domestic programs of paternalism and international programs that were moving steadily in the direction of a world government. All this was quite intolerable to persons deeply convinced of the everlasting values of individual liberty and a minimum of governmental coercion. We became fearful of domestic programs whereby, in exchange for individual freedom of action, citizens were to be assured of economic security. This the government could only provide by undertaking to regulate and control all private enterprises.

We became fearful that, in attempting through international agreements and legislation to preserve peace and to advance the economic welfare of peoples throughout the world, we would find that we had abandoned our powers of self-government. We could see plainly that the interests of many other peoples in other parts of the world would be in conflict frequently with our own. Although it might be altruistic and noble to subordinate our selfish immediate interests to the ultimate interests of mankind, there would be grave danger that we would only succeed in subordinating our own selfish advancement to the selfish advancement of other peoples.

These doubts and fears, which were beginning to oppress me long before the end of the Second World War, became intensified when it became evident that the "creeping socialism" of the later years of the Roosevelt administration was becoming a galloping socialism under the administration of President Truman. The limited internationalism into which we had been forced by the necessities of the Second World War was becoming a boundless internationalism, under which the government of the United States would soon become the instrument of an international socialism. Thus the individual liberties of American citizens and their powers of self-government would soon be submerged in obligations and responsibilities to the welfare of all the rest of the world. The vast increase in the expenditures of the federal government in the few years following the end of the Second World War presents irrefutable proof that these doubts and fears were in no way exaggerated.

Not only have billions of dollars been spent in unprecedented appropriations for military and economic aid to foreign nations, but civil expenditures for domestic services have increased steadily far beyond prewar appropriations. It is startling to realize that, whereas in 1940 a group of civil departments and offices spent about $3,500,000,000, these same offices in the year 1950, five years after the end of World War II, received appropriations amounting to about $11,250,000,000.

I have reviewed briefly the development of new theories and obligations and powers of the federal government from the close of the First World War to the end of the Second in an effort to make clear why, in the early years of the Truman administration, I became convinced that we must begin a new crusade for the preservation of individual liberty and self-government in the United States.

Any broad attack upon national policies is ineffective for the creation of popular opposition. The average citizen may disagree with a political theory while favoring certain measures in support of that theory. He may be opposed to socialism in the sense that he believes in individual free enterprise, property rights and freedom from political dictation. But he may at the same time strongly support subsidies for agriculture, pensions for the aged, public health services, federal aid to education and similar measures because of concrete immediate benefits which he expects to receive. He may not realize that the ultimate result of the total of such measures will be the dependence of the entire population upon government aid and the abrogation of his right to spend his own income.

There is another weakness in seeking to affect public opinion by broad arguments in favor of fundamental political theories and policies. The masses of the people have little interest in reading serious articles and speeches dealing with fundamental principles of political science or political economy. Indeed, it is no criticism of popular intelligence to state that masses of the people lack the ability to comprehend such discussions. We know how profoundly scholars and students disagree upon either the formulation or application of laws of political science and political economy. It would be asking too much of men and women without training to spend their time in heavy reading and hard thinking in an effort to make up their own minds as to what broad policies they wish to support.

On the other hand, it is possible to take a specific political proposal and to educate masses of people to an intelligent opinion as to what they are for or against.

An impressive amount of popular opposition to the Roosevelt Court packing plan was developed by an intensive campaign to convince masses of people that their safety and freedom depended upon the maintenance of an independent judiciary. In recent days, to cite another example, it has been possible for politicians, aided enormously by the support of the medical profession, to convince masses of people that they do not want the private practice of medicine destroyed or even subordinated to any kind of political control. As a result, the term "socialized medicine" has become a recognized term of reproach and even those who are actually working to bring it about have been forced to disavow their attempt and to abandon the initial programs through which they planned to convert the people to an acceptance of the ultimate program.

My own extensive experience in politics and reform movements long ago convinced me that to be effective the attack on a bad political program had to be made on its details, linking them up one by one to the fundamentals of political wisdom or folly involved. For this reason, when I decided that the policies which later became identified as Trumanism threatened the destruction of

American institutions of government and industry and the fundamental liberties of the American people, I began to devote myself to attacks upon specific measures which would have such immediate harmful results that reasonably intelligent people could be expected to listen.

I need not amplify my discussion previously of the wrongheadedness of the Truman "Civil Rights Program."

My desire to carry on a personal crusade for individual liberty against an advancing socialism happily coincided with a strong determination to retire gradually from the active practice of the law, which grew upon me during the year 1947. A man who has been engaged in the practice of a profession for over forty years should begin to think about at least a semi-retirement, if that be possible, before he is forcibly retired by ill health. Like many another lawyer, I had wanted all my life more time in which to write.

Furthermore, as a lawyer who had engaged in far too many reform movements, I was interested in feeling completely free to speak on public non-political occasions either for or against whatever cause concerned me.

Strangely enough, my freedom of expression had never been restrained by the necessity of conforming to the ideas of important clients. This was partly because those who disagreed with my fairly notorious opinions would not be likely to seek me out as legal counsel. Nevertheless, the personal attacks which have been made on me in recent years because of my espousal of conservative political and economic policies had been more amusing than annoying when they ascribed my opinions to subservience to big business clients.

It is a fact that I have represented a great variety of large business interests ever since I retired from government service in 1935. But it happens that these business interests engaged my services because of my particular familiarity and experience with the problems which concerned them. Among my clients there was considerable quiet dislike for my vigorous expression of my own political and economic views.

It is amusing to recall one occasion when the chairman of the board of my best-paying client heard that I was to make an address at a social occasion honoring a federal commission before which we were carrying on continuing and extensive proceedings.

The president of the company observed somewhat dubiously that he thought probably my forthcoming address would not do the company any harm. The chairman of the board replied that he did not know whether anyone could annoy the commission more than they were already annoyed by us, but he said grimly: "If anyone can I am sure Don will." I was never sure whether my address, satirizing none too gently some of the methods and policies of the Federal Power Commission, did any harm; but certainly no one could say that my remarks were dictated by the primary purpose of advancing my client's interest.

Another time, when I was attacking vigorously the closed-shop policies of labor organizations, a principal client negotiated and signed a closed-shop agreement with a labor union. Later he sent me a copy, red-penciled with a notation: "What do you think of me now?"

As an even larger example of this same lack of subservience, I may mention that throughout the Truman administration it was very much to the interests of most of my clients to maintain harmonious relations with the national administration. Yet I was constantly engaged in efforts to create public opposition to the major policies and programs of the Administration. Nevertheless, I had to question myself frequently whether loyalty to the business organizations who were paying me substantial fees did not call for more discretion in the public expression of antagonisms to politicians who had a great deal of power to affect favorably or adversely the fortunes of my clients.

Throughout the year 1947 Florence and I discussed at great length the desirability of moving our residence from Washington to California, in the area southeast of San Francisco. This locale attracted us particularly because of our common affection for that city and for many friends in that region, and our liking for the equable climate. Such a change of residence would provide a complete break with many business and social conditions. It would also permit us to reduce our scale of living to the modest proportions necessary if we were to live on a small income from investments supplemented by a small amount of earnings from writings or advisory work as a legal and industrial consultant.

When our minds were fairly made up I explained the prospect

to the chief executive officer of my principal client, which was the United Light and Power System, a public utility holding company going through the complicated reorganization required by the Securities and Exchange Act. I was flattered but disturbed to find that the chairman, Mr. William G. Woolfolk, regarded the continuance of my services for a few years as gravely important.

In 1939 when Mr. Woolfolk was made the chief executive officer of this holding company system, he was faced with the long and difficult process of disintegration and reorganization to comply with the law. I had met Mr. Woolfolk when I was special counsel for the city of Chicago and he was, as a consulting engineer, the principal representative of Samuel Insull, whose activities I was opposing from 1915 to 1927. Mr. Woolfolk and I, starting from the basis of a suspicious antagonism inevitable between representatives of public and private interests, had gradually reached an understanding. This was possible largely because of Mr. Woolfolk's fundamental philosophy that the private interests of public utility owners are best served when they themselves undertake to give the best possible public service, and my own recognition of the fact that the best public service can only be obtained from public utilities which are permitted to protect and promote the reasonable private interests of their stockholders and creditors.

Out of this mutual understanding Mr. Woolfolk and I were able to arrive at the agreement for the settlement of the extensive controversies between the city of Chicago and the Insull-controlled Gas Company which as I have told was embodied in an ordinance enacted by the City Council with only three dissenting votes. When this settlement was repudiated by Insull, Mr. Woolfolk and I continued our association in Chicago as vigorous, but as mutually respectful, opponents. After a few years in this relationship our paths had diverged and in the years preceding 1939 we had had very few contacts and no business relations.

Naturally I was very much surprised when he came to my office in 1939 to tell me that he had taken over the management of the United Light and Power System and he wanted to engage me to act as chief counsel in handling the reorganization proceedings before the Securities and Exchange Commission. This was the beginning of a long series of litigations before the Commission and in the courts, resulting in the disintegration of the original system and the reorganization of some of its companies into a new system known as the American Natural Gas Company.

But when I talked about retiring to California, Mr. Woolfolk assured me that we had ahead of us still a few years of difficult decisions and harassing litigations in which he felt that I should continue my services. We had been very fortunate, to put it mildly, in the many complicated and hazardous litigations of the previous years. In fact, at one directors' meeting, a fellow director had turned to me and said, just after we had won a vital victory: "I think maybe you ought to resign, Don." To this I replied: "I hope your reason is the same as mine for agreeing with you." He said: "It is. We have won without interruption ten major victories in litigations, any one of which, if it had been a defeat, might have been disastrous. I think the law of averages is running against you and we had better get another lawyer." This good fortune will explain, at least in part, the desire of Mr. Woolfolk to have me continue when my departure, if one were superstitious, might seem like the losing of a luck piece.

As a result of these discussions, I told Mr. Woolfolk that Florence and I had also considered the possibility of a semi-retirement to Charlottesville, Virginia, a city we had often visited, situated in a countryside and climate that we greatly enjoyed. It was far enough from Washington so that I could keep out of my Washington office most of the time and yet be able to use it when necessary. If the utility executives would be tolerant of more long-distance telephones than personal conferences, I would be able to attend to their important business in New York, Detroit, Chicago and Washington. The conclusion of this new arrangement made it possible for Florence and me to avoid that abrupt lowering of a standard of living which we privately admitted would not be easy, and to establish ourselves in a new home in which we would be willing to live out our lives. Staying in the East would also be advantageous to our daughter who was to graduate from Wellesley in 1948 and had a host of friends in Washington and along the Eastern seaboard.

Thus it came about that after several months of scouting we located and purchased a home on the grounds of Farmington Country Club, two miles west of Charlottesville. During this transition period I had been indulging myself frequently in the pleasure of making speeches from California to Massachusetts. More and more I had become possessed of the idea that my ordained job was to analyze and expose the trend of what was commonly regarded as political progress, but which was actually retrogression to socialism.

During our first year in Charlottesville I found myself with much more time and opportunity to work in comparative peace upon articles and speeches which I found myself producing in large quantities. At the same time, I was becoming more and more concerned with educational institutions. In 1947 I had accepted election as a trustee of the American University in Washington and had become deeply interested in its problems and in its success under the dynamic leadership of President Paul Douglass.

In the spring of 1949 I was invited, much to my surprise, to join the faculty of the University of Virginia Law School and in the fall of that year I began conducting a seminar in Constitutional Law. The choice of this course had been left to me. I chose it because I had been concerned throughout my active practice with questions of constitutional law and had argued—and, incidentally, had won—several landmark cases in the Supreme Court of the United States. Recent years, teaching constitutional law, arguing cases in the Supreme Court and carrying on a public campaign for recognition and maintenance of fundamental constitutional principles, have combined to give me more satisfaction in my public life than I had ever previously enjoyed.

CHAPTER XXX

Life in Charlottesville, Virginia; Teaching Law; Arguing in the Supreme Court

THERE IS a definite attraction in a project to retire gradually from active business. There is the hope of easing the strain of always trying to do too much in too short a time. There is the coincident hope of being able at last to read the books one has never found time to read, to have tranquil discussions of interesting questions with friends, and above all, if one has a literary bent, to be able to write a few articles and books.

But the theory of a gradual retirement is about as impractical as the theory of gradually reducing one's consumption of tobacco or alcohol. Many a man has learned that tapering off is likely to be a failure and that it is easier to quit altogether a lifelong habit.

Nevertheless, by moving to Charlottesville, one hundred and twenty miles from my office in Washington, I have been able to avoid the daily immersion in the routine of a busy office. But the project of retiring gradually from active practice seems more remote today (1953) than it did when I first developed this illusion. In the intervening five years I have briefed and argued many cases in many courts, including such major events as arguing, and happily winning, four cases before the Supreme Court, in which the Court sustained the constitutionality of the Federal Sugar Act; the validity of state regulation of the distribution of natural gas;

the constitutionality of state "right-to-work" laws; and the constitutional rights of a free press to resist improper Congressional investigation.

It seems almost impossible for a lawyer to talk about any case except a criminal one without boring his audience, although of course any legal brethren present may maintain a show of polite interest. For this reason I have decided to say comparatively little about the many litigations in which I have been engaged in nearly fifty years of active practice of law. The constitutional cases to which I have just referred, however, all had sufficiently important effects upon life in America to warrant discussion. But before boasting of my more notable successes, I shall humble myself by recounting an early case which reflected no glory whatsoever on me.

In the first trial by jury in which I had chief responsibility, I was assisted by a classmate of equal inexperience. It was actually a "horse and buggy" case. Our client, driving down a street in South Chicago, was run into by the drunken driver of another horse and buggy. He received a broken arm, among lesser injuries, and sued for damages. The defendant was a local undertaker whom my client knew personally and had clearly recognized when the accident occurred. But at the trial the defendant produced eleven witnesses to testify that he was in attendance at a funeral a couple of miles away at the time of the accident!

All the witnesses, including the defendant, testified through an interpreter, claiming they could not speak English sufficiently well. This made cross examination doubly difficult. I therefore decided to bring out nothing except the somewhat significant fact that each of the defendant's witnesses was a relative. Our hope lay entirely in the jury believing my client and a friend who was driving with him, both of whom swore they knew the man very well and recognized him clearly. We had to trust to the argument that our client would hardly pick out the wrong man to sue, and to the implication that there was something strange in the testimony of witnesses all claiming not to speak English, all being related to the defendant and all testifying to an unbelievable story.

At the noon recess, when apparently all the testimony was against us, one of the jurors came up to my client while they were all waiting for the elevator and said: "Your lawyers are very young." Our embarrassed client admitted that they were. The juror said: "Why don't you get a good lawyer?" This incident was observed by opposing counsel who, when the court reconvened, demanded that the offending juror be excused. The judge refused to do this without our consent. This we would not give, on the ground the other jurors might think we had tampered with one of their number. The judge offered to declare a mistrial, but stipulated that if we went on with the jury, the defendant's attorneys must agree to accept the verdict. Since apparently the prejudice was all in their favor, opposing attorneys preferred to go ahead. My associate and I anticipated that we were about to lose our first case. But apparently our strategy of showing only contempt for the opposing alibi succeeded, because the verdict was in favor of our client.

It is a long way from fighting a little damage suit in a local court to arguing constitutional cases in the Supreme Court of the United States. But I always felt that the experience of petty cases, dealing with judges and juries in matters of only private concern, provided a valuable foundation for work in the higher courts which I have found much more interesting.

My experience in the Supreme Court began very early, although I was not actually admitted to practice in the Court until 1922. It happened, however, that one of the first cases in which my father turned over brief-writing to me (a work which I enjoyed and he found very arduous) went all the way to the Supreme Court where, by the way, we did not win. But in the last twenty-five years, there has almost always been some case either on its way to the Court or actually pending there.

Soon after I moved to Charlottesville a new case called for a Supreme Court appearance. Sugar refiners in Puerto Rico had challenged the limits on sugar refining fixed by the Secretary of Agriculture under the federal law and were joined by the government of Puerto Rico in attacking the whole law as unconstitutional. The law was strongly supported by American sugar refiners, since it gave considerable stability to the sugar market and afforded a definite protection to the very large but none too profitable business of refining sugar in this country. If the law could be overthrown and the allotments made by the Secretary of Agriculture set aside, the result would be to increase the refining of sugar in other countries to the definite injury of the industry in the United States. Despite a good deal of argument in the Supreme Court about the desirability of a different legislative policy, the Court took the eminently proper position that this was a matter for the judgment of Congress and not for any super legislative activity by the Supreme Court. The constitutionality of the Sugar Act and the allotments made by the Secretary of Agriculture were sustained.

Following the sugar case, my next appearance in the Supreme Court was to uphold the state regulation of the local distribution of natural gas. It was clearly provided in the federal law that the function of the Federal Power Commission in regulating interstate commerce should not be extended to interfere with state regulation of rates and services for local natural gas distribution. Yet there was sufficient basis for an argument that a state could not impose its law upon a company operating interstate commerce, so that the favorable decision of the Supreme Court supporting state regulation was only obtained over the dissent of two justices.

A year later a labor case of great importance moved into the Supreme Court where I had the honor and pleasure again to represent the state of Arizona, which I had served many years before in the train limit cases. Arizona and many other states had enacted a so-called "right to work" law which provided that no man should be compelled either to join or to refrain from joining a labor organization by any action of an employer, or by any contract made between an employer and a labor organization. Such a law made the closed shop or the so-called "union" shop (which is a variety of closed shop) illegal within the state. The constitutionality of these laws was challenged in three states—Arizona, Nebraska and North Carolina—and when the cases arrived in the Supreme Court they were consolidated for argument, thus providing six hours of argument instead of the customary allowance of two hours a case; that is, one hour for each side.

It was my good fortune that the attorney general of Arizona and other interested parties were willing to give me their entire time of one hour for argument. In the other two cases the time was divided between the attorney general and attorneys for various business associations interested in supporting the law, with the result that the arguments were so split as to make it difficult for any one attorney to cover adequately his case. In contrast to this, I had the opportunity of presenting a complete argument covering substantially all the questions raised by counsel for the American Federation of Labor who were attacking the laws as unconstitutional.

This case provided an interesting example of how difficult it is to prognosticate Supreme Court opinions. I had told my clients that I thought we had a fair opportunity to gain a favorable decision from at least a bare majority of the Court, or even a six-to-three majority. Among the Justices who I thought might be expected to sustain the constitutionality of the law was Justice Black, concerning whom most of my associates had grave doubts. For my part, I felt strongly that the law was in our favor and that Justice Black, among others, would uphold the legal principles involved and not be swayed by the ill-founded opposition of organized labor. Of course I hoped for a unanimous Court, but I feared that predilections in favor of organized labor might sway some of the justices from a sound legal position. It therefore not only gave me great personal pleasure but also increased my confidence in the intellectual integrity of the Court as a whole when the Court handed down a unanimous opinion written by Justice Black with a strong concurring opinion by Justice Frankfurter. (Justice Murphy dissented without opinion—or any good reason—in the Arizona case.)

The most recent case which I have had in the Supreme Court was the Rumely case, involving the right to sustain the freedom of the press against abuse of power by a Congressional investigating committee. Edward A. Rumely, executive secretary of the Committee for Constitutional Government, had refused to testify before a Congressional committee as to the names and addresses of persons to whom his organization had sold books which it had published as a major part of its activities. He had stalwartly insisted that this question was an invasion of the freedom of the press, that the transactions between a publisher and the purchasers of his books were private transactions.

Dr. Rumely had been held in contempt of the committee by a narrow partisan vote in the House of Representatives. He had been prosecuted in the United States District Court and, under erroneous instructions of the judge, he had been convicted on the ground that the questions asked him were pertinent to the inquiry and were not an invasion of his constitutional right. He had been fined a thousand dollars and sentenced to jail for one year, the sentence being suspended on account of his age.

The appeal from this conviction I argued first in the United States Court of Appeals in the District of Columbia. The conviction was reversed by a vote of two to one, the majority opinion being a powerful argument in favor of freedom of the press written by Justice Prettyman. The government appealed the case to the Supreme Court where the Solicitor General argued that the conviction should be sustained. On March 9, 1953, the Supreme Court handed down its unanimous opinion, written by Justice Frankfurter, denying the authority of the Congressional committee to compel Dr. Rumely to answer the inquiries made of him. This opinion was supported by a very strong concurring opinion by Justice Douglas affirming the fundamental constitutional right involved.

Looking back upon these four cases, I take considerable satisfaction as a lawyer in having been able to make a successful argument; first, in behalf of the legislative authority of the federal government; second, in behalf of the right of a state to regulate purely local business despite the possibility of an overriding federal regulation; third, in behalf of the state's right to protect the freedom of labor and the right of men to work; and, finally, in behalf of a single citizen's right to rely upon the guarantees of the Bill of Rights to preserve his individual freedom against interferences by an all-powerful federal government.

But even more than personal satisfaction, I take comfort in a renewed sense of confidence that I have in the administration of justice and its ultimate integrity as vested in the Supreme Court. It was customary among the Progressives of the Theodore Roosevelt era to criticize vigorously the ultra-conservatism of what was called the "old Supreme Court." It has been customary for conservatives in the radical Franklin D. Roosevelt era to criticize the new Supreme Court for its ultra-liberalism. I have joined at different times in my life in both these criticisms.

However, I have always had an underlying belief that when men were placed in positions of such high responsibility as those of justices of the Supreme Court, they would do their best in the long run to lay aside their personal predilections and to play faithfully their parts in upholding an administration of justice as organized and established under the Constitution and laws of the United States. My personal experience has justified this confidence. The "old Supreme Court" rendered decisions in favor of liberal arguments which were most surprising to conservative lawyers. Conversely, the new Supreme Court has rendered decisions favoring conservative arguments which were equally surprising to liberal lawyers. Judges are human beings, swayed by human emotions. But a good judge, and one worthy of a place on the High Bench, will have greater respect for legal principles that have stood the test of time than for the emotional arguments which arouse the applause of the passing day.

During the years in Charlottesville, I have continued to serve as senior counsel for a very large public utility system, constantly studying and advising regarding issues of importance to stockholders and consumers. I have represented a large number of railroads in the determination of legal issues arising out of labor relations. I have responded to the flattery of requests from senators and representatives to testify before Congressional committees or to aid in the drafting of legislation . . . all, of course, without compensation. (As Senator Homer Ferguson said when we ended an exhausting task of drafting a bill which was the foundation of a subsequent law: "We appreciate your help although you will have to look for the reward of your services in heaven." He was kind enough not to add: "If you ever get there.") Of course any lawyer is called upon frequently to give voluntary services to relatives and friends; and when he is "semi-retired" such demands are likely to be more frequent than when he is assumed to be up to his ears in daily work for remunerative clients.

Although it is plain that my "gradual retirement" has been more of an illusion than a reality, there has been, on the whole, a definite slackening of the pressures of an active metropolitan practice.

One of the main reliefs resulting from our residence in Charlottesville has been that social life is much less active. The number of social engagements—dinners, luncheons and cocktail parties—in which one can get involved in Washington becomes oppressive as advancing years make it harder to sustain this constant drain on one's energies. On the other hand, the social life of Charlottesville is sufficiently brisk and varied so that one need never feel lonesome; but the pace of life is much slower, more like walking, or occasionally trotting, instead of dashing from one festive occasion to another.

There is also the possibility of a leisurely participation in local affairs. In Charlottesville a few hours or days of attention to such public concerns as the Community Chest and other welfare organizations contrast favorably with the burdensome demands for similar services in a city such as Washington. It was no great labor, but real enjoyment, to make a little talk on Jefferson's birthday at his tomb at Monticello. Little speeches to small audiences of local associations have been likewise a pleasure rather than a burden. Even service on a committee directing the University's Institute of Public Affairs, although somewhat onerous, was enjoyable. I mention these activities merely to indicate that no one able to make a contribution to community activities is going to be freed from such tasks merely by moving to another and smaller center of population. But there is a definite decrease of strain; and the mere ease of transportation, now a major problem in any large city, eases the obligations of community service to a considerable degree.

In this peaceful, unhurried and simplified environment it has been much easier to find the time to write occasional articles and to work on one or two long-anticipated book projects. I found particular satisfaction in being able to gather together the poetic efforts of a lifetime into one volume, *Old Faith and Fancies New.* This I had the satisfaction of publishing myself, because I knew very well it would not meet the standards of either serious or frivolous verse which would warrant a publisher investing hard dollars in it. But it was most comforting to select out of a crowded file those verses of mine reflecting many moods of my varied experiences and philosophies which seemed to me worthy of preservation at least for my descendants. Despite my admiration for the "grand old masters" and my affection for many "humbler poets," it is not wholly egotism that has caused me to reread my own verses more frequently than those of any other writer! The fact is that there is both satisfaction and amusement in reviewing one's own emotional output in order to recapture now and then something of the enthusiasm or thrill of bygone days, noting from time to time either how sensible or how foolish one appears to be in retrospect.

Of continuous interest to me in Charlottesville has been my observation of the philosophy of men like myself who have come here to live in a partial or complete retirement from their lifelong activities. It has been quite evident that most of them realize the necessity to keep on doing something. If they had once had the illusion that retirement to a life of eating, sleeping, reading and playing games would be enjoyable, that illusion for most of them has disappeared. A considerable number of these men retired from a strenuous business life to the anticipated joy of running a farm. This has usually meant raising cattle, or perhaps turkeys, or merely running a gentleman's farm for pleasure rather than profit. Others have found opportunity either to indulge in an old hobby or to experiment with a new one. There is, for example, the department store owner who began raising orchids as a hobby but, true to his fundamental instincts, found his ultimate satisfaction in raising them for commercial sale. His philosophy was a sound one for a man with a deep faith in the personal and social values of private enterprise. He told me that he felt any enterprise should be put on a profitable basis in order to justify the time and attention put upon it and to prove its social value. To give money to a charitable undertaking was one thing, but to invest money in a fundamentally commercial project only justified itself when the project became fully self-supporting. This is the fundamental philosophy of individualistic enterprise, the exact opposite of socialism.

A retired general, with a record of long and valuable service in the armed forces, has found his pleasure in woodworking, producing tables, chairs, desks and other articles to add to the comfort and beauty of his home. Others find satisfaction in raising vegetables and flowers for personal use and enjoyment. My own wife has found her steadily increasing enjoyment in cultivating her gardens and beautifying our small acreage. I am sure she gets more daily pleasure out of her activities than semi-retired city housewives find in mere social doings.

Thus, from my life in Charlottesville I have arrived at the strong conviction that a life of leisure is an absurdity. To be happy, man must keep doing something that either benefits others or satisfies his own ambitions.

My experience in teaching constitutional law for three years was one of the most enjoyable and satisfying of my life. It is quite a common aspiration among lawyers as they grow older to become judges. A judicial position gives one not only an honorable standing in the community and in the profession, but also the opportunity to administer the justice which every practicing lawyer is presumably seeking in behalf of his clients.

It was probably fortunate for me (and many may say that it was fortunate for the Court) that the opportunity to sit on the Supreme Court, which at one time seemed very near, did not come to me. But as a consolation prize I regard my opportunity to teach constitutional law to top-grade students in a first-grade law school as quite satisfying.

Teachers of constitutional law do not write the judicial opinions which shape that law, but they can educate and stimulate the active minds of some of the influential lawyers of the future who, as advocates or judges, may ultimately shape the law. As general counsel of the NRA and as an active legal adviser in the early years of the Roosevelt administration, I had been both pleased and distressed by the attitudes of young lawyers whom I had to employ in large numbers and with whom I had worked intensively. As an early exponent of what the 1912 Progressives regarded as a "liberal" construction of the Constitution, I had been worried more and more by the influence exerted in the 1930's by the new "liberal" members of the Bar and the "liberal" educators in the law schools. It seemed that they were converting a new generation of lawyers, not to the liberalism of the writers of the American Constitution, but to the radicalism of the disciples of Karl Marx.

We of 1912 had preached the "social responsibility" of the government so successfully that the next generation had been converted easily to the idea that the government was responsible for much more than maintaining conditions in which self-reliant men and women could take care of themselves. Now it was being urged that the government must go on to assume a direct responsibility for the care of the people. The new doctrine appeared to be that the government must impose a responsibility upon all citizens to provide economic security for all other citizens and accept the ultimate responsibility itself of assuring economic security for all.

The key to a sounder public opinion, and a better understanding of the necessity of limiting the powers and responsibilities of government, seemed to me to lie in a liberal but not a loose interpretation of the Constitution.

When I conducted my first seminar in constitutional law I soon learned that my fears as to the trend of thinking among recent graduates of the Law schools were not exaggerated. It would be expected that there would be more conservatism in a law school at the University of Virginia than at, for example, the law school of Harvard or Yale. But it was evident that some of the best minds, even in this moderately conservative environment, had been strongly impressed with what they regarded as "modern thinking." They were inclined to view interpretations of the Constitution based on the obvious intentions and philosophies of its framers as bringing in "dead hands" to hold back progress. They could recognize, as intelligent, thinking students, that the framers of the Constitution intended to confine the federal government's power to regulate commerce to commerce actually "among the several states." They knew full well that, despite this supposedly limited authority, the federal government was now regulating business transactions wholly within one state. They knew that the Supreme Court, in tolerating such exercises of federal power, had gone to the extreme of asserting that, in order to regulate interstate commerce, the federal government could also regulate all local commerce that "affected" interstate commerce.

These students knew full well that this meant that the Constitution had been revised, not by amendments approved by the people, but simply by acts of the Congress approved by the Supreme Court. Some of them were responsive to the suggestion that the Constitution ought not to be amended except by the votes of "the people," by whose votes the Constitution was originally enacted. But others were strong in their conviction that it was quite right, as conditions changed and it became desirable in the opinion of many to extend the powers of the federal government, to accomplish that result by the short cut of "interpreting" the Constitution to authorize that which it did not authorize.

Against this type of thinking it seemed to me that young minds should be made aware that there were virtues in fundamental principles and in adherence to the plain meaning of plain words. This "conservatism" was more important for the preservation of free institutions than the "liberalism" of setting legislatures free from constitutional restraint to do whatever seemed at the moment desirable in the public interest. Our youth needed a re-education in the evils of big government and unrestrained political authority. Our youth had grown from childhood to citizenship maturity in the years when the world had been moving through the substitution of fascist autocracies for democratic government into wars that had forced a temporary socialization of government and industry. As a consequence, in the post-war period some form of socialism of a benevolent character had come to be regarded as the "wave of the future." Our youth did not understand that this alleged wave of the future was only a retrogression toward those political tyrannies which had dominated all nations until the later years of the eighteenth century. Then the doctrines of self-government and individual liberty, rising in England, France and the American Colonies, had blossomed into the new form of government first adequately expressed in the Constitution of the United States.

As an old lawyer, but a fledgling teacher, I had to come to an early decision on a problem that must vex every teacher of semi-mature minds. How far should one seek to be objective and impartial in expositions to students? How far should one seek to influence their opinions in the direction of what seems to the instructor to be sound thinking?

Presumably the object of education is to teach young people to think for themselves and to learn how to utilize the wisdom of our forebears. At least this must be the object of advanced courses in a law school.

From my early experiences in Harvard Law School, studying under a faculty of extraordinary ability and educational force, I had become convinced that classroom controversies provided the best method of teaching law and encouraging students to think for themselves. A teacher with positive convictions who did not try to conceal them might have an undue influence over the less robust minds in his class. But at the same time he would arouse enough opposition from strong-minded students so that even those inclined to accept the instructor's ideas would be led either to question them or seek to support them by their own reasoning powers.

Moved by this philosophy, it seemed to me that a teacher should definitely take sides on controversial issues of constitutional law and arouse the belligerent opposition of those who disagreed. Debate should be encouraged with the assurance that marks would be based, not on the extent of agreement with the teacher's opinions or with majority opinions of the high courts, but upon the ability shown by the student to reason out his own opinions and then stand by them regardless of the weight of authority in favor or against them. My attitude was expressed to a class of students somewhat as follows:

"You may think that I am trying to indoctrinate you as, for example, a Communist would in teaching political science or political economy. But there is this difference: I do not assume my opinions are necessarily correct and I am not interested in indoctrinating you with them unless by virtue of your own hard thinking you agree with them. If, on the other hand, you disagree, you must be prepared to fight for and to justify your opinions. You are going to be graded on the basis of the evident amount of real study which you have given to important issues and the mental capacity which you show in arriving at conclusions regardless of whether I agree or disagree with them."

Within a term or two I think I was able to establish among the students in the Law School an understanding that I meant what I said. The best proof of this lay in the fact that students who differed with me most vigorously received better marks than students who manifested something in the nature of parrot-like agreement. As a result, I found an increasing stimulus to my own thinking from the students, and I had a feeling that I was more effectively stimulating them.

An acid test of the reaction of the Virginia Law School students is obtained through an annual performance called the *Libel Show* in which the students, with a surprising and happy lack of inhibitions, satirize the teaching and the teachers in the Law School. To an unduly sensitive man some of these satires verge upon the cruel, but they certainly provide a valuable indication to the professors of the impress they are making on their students. For my part, I found pure amusement and some gratification in the satiric indication that I might be regarded as a little crazy, but certainly not uninteresting.

There is a rigid rule in the University requiring the retirement of professors at the age of seventy and this is applied, not only to the full-time members of the faculty but also to lecturers like myself who give only one advanced course. Two of the lecturers in the Law School who approached this deadline in the spring of 1951 were Judge Dobie, of the United States Court of Appeals for the Fourth Circuit, and myself. It happened that Judge Dobie reached the age of seventy before the end of the school year, whereas my birthday, occurring in July, permitted me to teach for another year. I thought it most unfortunate for the Law School that Judge Dobie should be retired, inasmuch as he had an extraordinary background for his course on Federal Practice and Procedure. He had taught in the Law School and had been its dean before he went on the bench. With this teaching experience and his judicial service, his seminar was of exceptional value.

An interesting example of his stimulating influence is the story by now traditional in the Law School. In reply to a question he had posed, a much-embarrassed student had replied: "God knows. I don't." Judge Dobie had answered: "God gets 100. You get zero."

There was a strong resentment, almost indignation, among the first- and second-year students that they would not have the privilege in their senior year of taking the course with Judge Dobie. Then it became a matter of common knowledge that my teaching also would end the next year. The second-year students of 1951 could take my course (for which the regular course in constitutional law was a prerequisite), but the first-year students would not have that opportunity in my final year—1952–53. For my own part, I was beginning to feel that the obligation of conducting a seminar once a week throughout the fall, winter and spring was a trifle burdensome, largely because of the fact that I could not take any extended winter vacation. So I was not unhappy at the prospect of retirement. But I did join in the opinion, quite generally expressed, that it was unfortunate that a rigid rule would deprive the students of the continuing volunteer services of Judge Dobie.

One day when I was working in the library a second-year student came to me and with considerable indignation said in effect: "Now they retire Judge Dobie and next year they are going to retire you and we feel that is most unfair to us." Of course I was pleased at the compliment and agreed that they would suffer a real loss in Judge Dobie's retirement. Somebody else could conduct a seminar in constitutional law and probably do a better job than I did. But I was pleased at the fact that the student body evidently had a high regard for my course. As I remarked to Dean Ribble, it was entirely possible that my popularity might arise out of the apparent fact that my markings were a bit above the average! But I had justified those higher grades by the fact that my small course included most of the cream of the class and the average marking ought to be higher.

However, I was particularly impressed by the fact that students came to me and asked if I would not continue to give the course even though they got no credit for it. They even offered to raise the money themselves to pay me a compensation, although I assured them that I would be glad to give the course without any compensation. (The fact was that I had privately returned my compensation every year in the form of a donation to the Dean's Special Fund out of which expenses could be met which were not provided for in the ordinary budget.) But I did not think it would be fair to have them do the work necessary to carry an extra course and get no credit for it.

The final result of these discussions was surprising and quite pleasing to me. In the last course which I gave in the spring of 1952, 61 students registered for a course which was limited to 16, which is plenty large for a seminar. But, I could not face the idea of refusing to take such a large group of students who wanted to take the course the last time it would be given. So I announced that I would not cut the registrations down and finally, after all the conflicts with other courses, etc., had been resolved, I found myself with a class of 46 students, entirely too large for the ordinary process of a seminar. So I changed it to a "lecture and major thesis" course, which put a heavy burden on me.

I was both surprised and pleased when, in the final session of the class, I was presented with a bronze humidor inscribed "With appreciation" from the members of the class. I assured them that this was a great mistake on their part because they could not wisely establish the practice of giving a remembrance to each teacher at the conclusion of the course. To this they responded almost with one voice: "That doesn't bother us. We're all graduating." I answered that as far as I was concerned they could be assured that they *were* graduating, because happily I had marked all their papers before this final session, since the marks of the graduating class had to be promptly recorded. I also assured them that my judgment had not been and would not be affected by their unexpected action, as there would be no revision of the grades already recorded!

In thus recounting the conclusion of my teaching adventure I should add that I had an enormous advantage over many teachers of constitutional law in that many of the cases we discussed were cases which I had argued before the Supreme Court, although not always successfully, as for example the NRA case. But many of these cases had helped to determine the direction of constitutional law and there was, therefore, present in the minds of the students the same feeling that a student of military history might have had in discussing famous battles with a general who had actually led the forces in combat.

Indeed, my long experience in the Supreme Court gave authenticity to the philosophy, which I sought to impress upon my students, that constitutional law is never static. The course of opinions and decisions in the Supreme Court moves in the line of historical trends, and is constantly affected by changing economic and political conditions. So I endeavored to impress upon my classes an understanding of the fact that the dissents of yesterday were often the majority opinions of today and the majority opinions of today might become the dissenting opinions of tomorrow.

For an interesting and easily understood example of how changing conditions change constitutional law, one can consider the preservation in the Supreme Court of the guarantees of free speech and a free press written in the Constitution. Long ago it was recognized that these are not absolute, as in Justice Holmes's famous comment that freedom of speech would not permit a man to cry "Fire!" in a crowded theater. So the Supreme Court, in seeking to safeguard and at the same time sustain the necessary limitations upon free speech and a free press, established the rule that these freedoms could only be limited when there was a "clear and present danger" to vital public interests in their unrestrained exercise. For a time there appeared to be no such "clear and present danger" in tolerating propaganda for communism. But, as the modern menace of international communism developed, with deliberate and far-reaching plans to undermine and corrupt free government and free institutions, the Court was compelled by the logic of events to find that legislative and executive action restraining subversive activities could be constitutionally enforced because of the "clear and present danger" to the maintenance of our constitutional form of government.

Many other examples could be given to show how changing conditions have compelled new interpretations of powers granted by the Constitution and their application to conditions unknown when the Constitution was written. It is sufficient to point out how transportation, once limited to horsepower, manpower or sail power on land and water, has now come to include steam power, electric power, and gasoline power on land and water and in the air. And how communication, once limited to voice, pen and type, is now carried on by telegraph, telephone, phonograph, radio, television, moving pictures and related devices.

My experience in teaching and practicing law during the first four years of my residence in Charlottesville combined to give me more solid enjoyment in the practice of my profession than I had found in all the previous years. There was, most of the time, a pleasant lack of that sense of pressure and hazardous decisions which made the earlier years so full of excitement and straining interest.

Burning the candle at both ends may, in the poignant phrase of Edna St. Vincent Millay, "give a lovely light" through youth and middle age, but it becomes more obviously an exhaustion of one's candle power in later years. To me it has become more important to have more time to think, more time to study, to reflect and to enjoy some of the simpler pleasures than to feel the urge to accomplish at once some project which may seem immediately of great importance. As the years go on the difference between things of immediate and ultimate importance grows. What seems to be of ultimate importance is not so much the winning of a particular argument or the success of a particular project, but rather if, in looking backward, one can feel that what one did was a good way to spend one's time and energy in the light of what faith one may have in what is good.

Much of the increasing comfort which I have enjoyed in recent years has come from a feeling that, regardless of what use I might have made of my life and what things might have been accomplished, and regardless of inevitable mistakes and follies, for which I can still blush, I have been exceedingly fortunate in having my course largely determined by conditions which I could not have affected substantially by any personal decision.

Those decisions in which I take the most pride seemed inevitable when one took the time to consider alternatives with due care. One of these decisions was that of moving from Washington to Charlottesville. I had no idea at the time what a profoundly intelligent decision that was. It seemed to be forced upon me by pressures that were compelling me to move out of a whirlpool of activities into quieter waters. But the selection of Charlottesville itself, although a reasoned choice, was demonstrated to be so sound that an exposition of life in Charlottesville has been necessary to an understanding of why I came to a final understanding that I would never be or find my hero.

CHAPTER XXXI

In Conclusion—No Hero

As I come to the conclusion of these rambling reminiscences I return to the purpose of writing them which I indicated in the first chapter. It was not a pessimistic desire to explain my own disillusionment with the achievements of the political and social leadership of my times. It was a desire to provide an explanation for the apparent failure of social leadership to keep pace with the terrific material progress of mankind.

In contrast to this material advancement of human beings there has seemed to be a retrogression in the ability of men to adjust the conflicts of interest between classes, communities and nations. As a result, after two World Wars of unprecedented devastation, mankind, instead of learning the way to peace, seems to have been driven more and more into an ultimate reliance upon brute force to end conflicts. Solutions are sought, not by measures of improved cooperation but through the ancient feudal method of compelling masses of men to submit to domination by the most successful organizers of force. In other words, there has been a retrogression from the ideals of voluntary cooperation to programs of involuntary servitude.

What have I as an individual learned about the weaknesses of political and social leadership in which I have found no heroes comparable to those men of science who have been responsible for material progress and even spiritual advance by the devotion of their lives to a search for truth?

One lesson I have learned, in common with multitudes of elders everywhere and in every time: each human being is born with a few instincts and nothing which can be called knowledge. He must learn from the beginning what mature people have spent many years in learning. The phenomenal child is not born with a knowledge of how to play a musical instrument, or how to express interesting ideas. The prodigy simply learns with amazing speed. If he had not been taught something by somebody he would have remained an ignorant animal.

Thus it follows that the accumulated knowledge of the centuries is the essential basis for living well in the present and playing a part in bettering human life in the future. The zeal of youth, selfishly or unselfishly, to achieve a better life than his parents, or to improve the lives of others, is admirable but a little pathetic and often tragic because it is not well grounded on an understanding of how men have lived, what they have sought to accomplish, where they have failed and where succeeded, in past centuries.

It is quite obvious that no such understanding of industry or politics or morality can be quickly gained even in the course of an education that may lead through school and college up to the accolade of a professional degree. Learning must be related to the individual experience of the student before there can be any real grasp of the meaning and possibilities of human existence. I am reminded here of the eminent professor of law who remarked that the opinions of a learned member of the Supreme Court were "more notable for their reach than for their grasp." This was, I think, merely another and more trenchant way of saying that the judge had been concerned all his life with the theory of law, but had never come to grips with the actual practice in which logical theory is continually overcome by illogical facts.

Another justice of the Supreme Court, of much broader experience illuminated by a keen philosophy, wrote, "The life of the law is not in logic but in experience." There is no substitute for experience in gaining an understanding of how human life progresses and how human beings will behave, how they can be educated in social adaptability and become either useful servants or enemies of the common good.

About twenty-five years ago, I arrived at the conclusion that the commercial and financial leaders of my time had been as I then put it: "improving the production and distribution of almost everything except law and justice."

My feeling was that an enormous amount of hard work and hard thinking had gone into planning *how* things *could* be done. But there had been no comparable effort to plan *what* things *should* be done. Hence I assumed that the next generation of "progressives" would undertake this sort of planning and thinking. Since I published these conclusions at the time, I may claim a trifling gift of prophecy. Heaven knows that the progressives of recent years have devoted a great deal of time to planning what things should be done! But I regret to say that they acted on the assumption that this planning should be done by government, which really means by politicians with their ears to the ground in a continual effort to ascertain what their constituents want. Let me submit that this is a totally different method of planning progress from what I had in mind.

A scientist may be moved, in the study of tuberculosis or cancer, by the need of a great many people for protection against these diseases. A research chemist may be moved, in developing new textiles or plastics, by the need for better materials of common use. A business man may drill oil wells, build pipe lines, devise new machineries of production and distribution and improve or cheapen products, because there are large needs which it will be profitable to serve.

But the scientist or business man is not selected for his task on the basis of his promise to see that someone else satisfies a public need. Nor is he, like a politician, given the power to tax those who select him in order to pay for his services and the cost of trying to carry out his promises. The scientist or business man, if working for himself, is risking his own time and money in the hope that he may serve his fellow men in such a way that they will reward him with either money or honors or both. If he is employed by another, he is employed on the basis of *his* own ability to achieve desired results, not on the basis of his promises to see that other people produce these results.

If the scientist or business man plans badly, he suffers the consequences of his own incompetence. He has no compulsory power to make other men pay for his mistakes. If the politician, on the other hand, plans badly, he will lay the blame for his failures on others, still demanding confidence and employment on the basis that his objectives are always noble. Furthermore, because of his compulsory powers, he may continue to make mistakes and to fail in his objectives for a long, long time while still compelling support for his program, instead of being forced promptly to acknowledge failure and confess bankruptcy.

A major vice of all political planning is that it starts with an undertaking to satisfy a popular demand which it may be absolutely impossible to satisfy if one proceeds on the principle that the beneficiary should pay for the benefits received. But that principle is the first essential basis of any business plan. Something is to be produced for which the anticipated beneficiary will be expected to pay the full cost.

We have seen in recent years a hundred plans of government to satisfy the needs of a great many people. But somehow or other government planning usually produces a program of satisfying some people at the expense of other people, a merry-go-round of robbing Peter to pay Paul.

Farmers should be able to sell their products profitably in order to keep on raising them. So the government underwrites the farmer's business and taxes everybody to protect him against losses. Industrial workers cannot in competition obtain what they regard as satisfactory wages and working conditions. So the government aids organized labor to establish monopolies of employment whereby they can force wages above a competitive level. This produces an increased cost of living and a steady depreciation in the purchasing power of money, whereby everybody is taxed to maintain these artificial levels of wages. Any wage level that is not established by competition must be established by compulsion and hence is artificial and unsound.

There is a great need of protection against the hazards and misfortunes of existence. So we have the government planning and enforcing a "social security" program whereby everybody is taxed to provide the illusion of a social security to be provided by dollars of constantly declining value.

These are only a few examples of the virtuous objectives of political planning and of the manner in which government uses its compulsory powers to put these plans in effect with a somewhat careless disregard of the underlying problem, which is, who is going to pay in the end for the benefits received? Only one thing is certain: the masses of beneficiaries are not expected to pay, but in the end they will have to pay.

The fundamental virtue in private planning for progress is that the beneficiaries must be able and willing to pay for the goods or services they receive. The fundamental evil in so much political planning is the perpetual promise that a lot of people will get something for nothing. In other words, all of us will get more out of the total community output than all of us put in—which is impossible.

It was far from clear to me twenty-five years ago how planning for progress should be carried on. It often seemed, in the anarchy of what the socialists called "ruthless competition," that some organization, remote from the greed and selfishness of the market place, should undertake it. We saw in conservation policies an example of long-range planning by government: the forests must be preserved; they should not be ruthlessly destroyed for the temporary benefit of a few generations. But we should have seen a vast difference between the imposition by government of restraints on private enterprise in the public interest and a taking over by government of all the forests with subsequent government operation of the lumber business.

We saw the need for government intervention in banking and finance to protect people from irresponsible handling of money and the reckless financing and sale of securities. But our experience in government financing has proved again that there is a healthy disinclination on the part of private managers to invest private money except where there is a reasonable prospect of not losing it. On the other hand, it has appeared that the major reason for investing public money has been because the investment was so undesirable that no private investor would make it.

I well remember my experience in presenting a proposition to Jesse Jones, then head of the Reconstruction Finance Corporation, for the investment of $75,000,000 in a huge construction project which would employ a large number of workers at a time when unemployment was still a major problem. Mr. Jones observed that if we could obtain half of the amount from private sources he felt the RFC could properly invest the other half. "But," I said to him, "the reason this is presented to you is because it is not the type of loan which the banks and private investment houses will make." Whereupon he indicated that that was a very good reason why the government should not make the investment. I cite this as an exceptional example of a banker's judgment which should prevail in the loaning of public as well as private funds. But it will be noted that such a banker's judgment is not common, but ordinarily is deprecated, in the handling of public money.

In recent years we have been taught the great difference between a program of political protection and a program of political promotion or direction.

In protection the government is dealing with an appropriate subject for reasonably competent government action—the prevention or elimination of evils of a positive and proved character. In promotion and direction the government is taking over the natural function of private enterprise. It is undertaking to substitute the judgment of a personally irresponsible monopolist for the judgment of a personally responsible competitor in private industry.

As a political monopolist, the government must adopt an arbitrary political morality. What is good for people is determined, not by their free choice of what they want and are willing to pay for, but by an imposed choice of what someone else thinks is good for them. We see politicians resorting to public opinion polls in order to try to find out what the people want. The best public opinion poll ever devised is the free market in which people demonstrate what they want by the simple process of paying for what they want most and doing without the things they want less.

It is no accident that communism has been spreading from a land of notorious illiteracy and mass ignorance and has gained most of its adherents among the more illiterate and ignorant masses of other lands. The fact that communism has also found adherents in many men who are highly literate and others of great native intelligence can be ascribed to two reasons. In the first place many men of intellectual attainments who have achieved eminence in a specialized field, such as one of the natural sciences, are often thoroughly uneducated in history and the social sciences, or are dominated by the false theory that men can be made good or efficient or even "free" by disciplines imposed by master minds. In the second place some strong, intelligent men are drawn to the communistic theory through a profound faith in the desirability of a master class which will dominate either for its own selfish benefit as a "chosen people," or for the benefit of "lesser breeds" whom they regard as incapable of ruling their own lives.

The philosophy and theories of communism are among the oldest of the discredited theories of government. No one could have read the long history of communistic experiments and paternalistic governments without having learned that when a government (which is simply organized force) undertakes to regulate the lives and work of its citizens, they become the victims of a depressing external compulsion instead of the beneficiaries of an exhilarating internal propulsion.

The choice of any human being must be whether he will submit to a destiny fixed by his masters or make his life, so far as he can, the instrument of his self-developed ambitions. The argument can be perpetual as to whether those of physical or mental strength should rule their weaker brethren, or whether "the kingdom of heaven is within you" and the object of each life should be to accomplish its own salvation. If the former is the divinely ordained way of life then the rule of humanity by successively rising classes of master men is right. But, if, as I believe, it is divinely ordained that men and women should be free and individually responsible for the conduct of their individual lives, it is clear that the less control of their lives by the organized force of government, the better. The supreme necessity, as I see it, of human progress is the freedom of the individual mind and body from any coercive control except those imposed by natural laws, or by the least practical number of human laws necessary to protect the individual from the violence or fraud of other men. That there has come to be almost universal recognition of this natural law of life seems clear from the fact that even those who seek to nullify it by governmental force try to justify their program by the insupportable claim that in the end, when government is all-powerful, there will be no further need of government, and mankind will become really free.

One of the difficulties in maintaining free competition in the modern world is the extent to which the wicked influence of monopoly controls has permeated industrial and political life as civilization has advanced. The concentration of industry and all social activities in huge communities makes inevitable the rise of monopoly powers in large organizations. In the last seventy-five years we have seen how the expansion of industrial enterprises originally gave to big business organizations monopoly powers over employment and over the production and distribution of necessities. To restrain these powers we saw the rise of big labor organizations; and then, as the arbiter of the resulting economic conflict, the rise of big government organizations. Finally, we saw in the clash of national interests the rise of great military organizations.

It is not surprising that, in view of this trend, socializing fanatics reached the conclusion that individualism, free competition and individual self-service had become impractical as a way of life in a world wherein enormous organizations of power seem inevitable.

Against the class domination of business executives or labor executives there was an obvious appeal in placing the overriding power in the hands of political executives, since, under democratic processes and universal suffrage, political executives are assumed to be the choice of the people and kept subservient to their will. But those who understand the limits of any effective control which a people can exert over a government know that big government monopolies soon become as evil and oppressive as the business or labor monopolies from which people sought relief. In addition, we have seen that the powerful government of one nation is not likely to satisfy its own citizenship without extending its monopoly powers over other nations.

Prior to the First World War it was quite evident that in Germany the national government had gone further than any other government in socializing the lives of its people. The German people had accepted the intimate control and regimentation of their lives with a pride based on the assumption that Germany would become the most powerful nation on earth and thereby able to exploit the peoples of weaker nations. To implement this pride, it was necessary to create armed forces through which the will of the rulers of Germany could be imposed first upon their neighbors and then throughout the world.

Despite all cynical criticisms, the gathering of forces against German ambitions was a war "to save democracy." But nothing could have demonstrated more clearly the difficulty of resisting coercive power with a greater coercive power than the ultimate failure of the fight to save democracy. Out of the First World War were generated the forces that produced, first, the Russian Revolution; then the revival of Germany's expansive ambitions and accumulation of power that brought about the Second World War. Out of the Second World War developed the Russian Communist ambition and power to attempt world dominion through a Third World War in which, in one way or another, the entire world is now being engulfed.

Despite the obvious insanity of the Communist program for "one world" ruled by Communists, there has developed in the anti-Communist areas an equally insane program for "one world" ruled by another variety of socialists. The most widely advocated alternative to the Communist program is the development of a hybrid sort of world government through an alliance of individual nations of supposedly free people who will be willing to delegate a part of their national sovereignty to an international organization. The high purpose of this organization is to preserve the peace of the world by organizing an overwhelming military power to compel non-peaceful nations to be peaceful either by threat or actual use of irresistible force.

Whether this expanding control of our lives from big business to big labor, to big national government, to big international government, can be checked and reversed before ultimate disaster disintegrates the mammoth structures of power and re-establishes the small structures of local self-government as a necesary preventive of universal anarchy, is too large a question to debate in this volume.

What should be evident is that, as we move from local to national to international activities, we move inevitably from local to national to international moralities. In small communities individual freedom and rights, and individual duties to one's self and one's family, if not paramount, were at least of primary importance. But as the communities enlarged, rights of, and duties to, the community were enlarged. The legal concept was well stated by Justice Brandeis in the famous opinion wherein he said: "All rights are derived from the purposes of the society in which they exist; above all rights rises duty to the community."

As our nation has grown and the national government has enlarged its dominion, we have found national moralities and duties tending steadily to reduce and obscure individual moralities and individual freedom to live life according to one's own conscience. Now as the concept of "one world" has been spreading we have been moving steadily into the concept of complete individual subordination to collective programs for the progress of mankind.

But who is to decide what is good for all mankind? The answer to this question is the development of what is essentially a religious hierarchy which establishes political moralities that are imposed by political rulers. These rulers are so far beyond individual control that their edicts, unless resisted by the counter organization of huge numbers, must be accepted. The result is the development of what is essentially a state religion which is oppressive in even a small state, but would be quite intolerable if imposed by a world government.

It is also impractical, in view of the diversity of opinions and interests in many areas of the world's population, to impose an international morality by any peaceful means. If we look carefully at what has been happening in the last fifty years we shall see why the political morality of any government is transformed inevitably into an unmorality as the size of the government grows. In collective action we behave worse as human beings than we could or would behave individually. We do much less good for others and for ourselves than we could or would do individually.

As a government, we plan and fight wars wherein mass murders and destruction are justified as the necessary means to accomplish some laudable end. But when an individual kills and destroys, his fellow men generally condemn his acts, no matter how strong the provocation. Individually, we do not tolerate in ourselves or in others cruelty, treachery and beastliness. Collectively, we seek to impose our will on others by terror, suffering and death. In collective sinning we soak ourselves in a moral degradation that would drive us as individuals into suicide or insanity.

As a government, we plan and carry out projects for the proclaimed benefit of masses of people. But in the end we benefit others and ourselves much less than the good we could accomplish by individual kindness and self-sacrifice. We may drop our money into the political contribution plates reluctantly or cheerfully. But in either case we will seek in vain for the satisfaction of a good deed and the glow of virtue that would come from giving aid and comfort directly to a fellow man in distress. We know we do not make our lives nobler or happier by paying someone to do good for us. Even a conscript soldier can find no pride, but only shame, in hiring a substitute to fight for him. There is so little virtue in collective charity, goodness and kindness that a sanctimonious mask eventually debases the face of every collective reformer.

There lies the perpetual weakness of socialism. Compulsory collective action to improve society will never elevate but always degrade the individual. Men and women have been given the lifelong task of saving their own souls. They may achieve success by voluntarily rendering services that will be welcome to their fellow men, but when, in self-righteous assurance of their own superior morals, they undertake to compel others to serve under their command, they become enemies of themselves, of mankind, and of their God, who made a man able to see, to hear, to speak and, above all, to think for himself, with an everlasting desire to be the master of his own fate and the captain of his soul.

The salvation of the divinity of human life lies in the faith that the individual should be free to rule his own life. We are told that the complications of modern life have made it necessary to increase the powers of government and the restraints of government upon individual freedom. To some extent this is true; but we seem frequently to forget that the complications of modern life only make it more imperative to preserve individual liberty against more tyrannies whether by private organizations or by extension of public powers.

The sole object of government should be protection of the individual against oppression by individual or collective action. The commonest form of such oppression is a monopoly control. Competition is the way of freedom. The high objective of government, to keep the individual free from the oppression of monopoly powers, cannot be reached by concentrating monopoly power in the government itself. That is the way to tyranny and slavery.

We have had many heroes in other centuries who have achieved greatly because they fought and died for liberty. Where shall we find such a hero in the twentieth century? Men and women of noble intentions have fought valiantly for what they called the common good, for collective progress and reform. Who have fought for individual liberty? If I had seen this great issue and sacrificed my life for it, I might now be a hero to myself if to no one else! But it took me a lifetime to see the issue clearly. Then it was too late to become a hero. I was not only too old but too soft.

Every comfort and ease of living tends to soften the tough fiber of the self-reliant individual, to induce him to seek pleasure in a synthetic existence. In the twentieth century, instead of living dangerously and bravely, most people get a vicarious pleasure out of the adventures and courage of synthetic heroes. These portray synthetic emotions and perform synthetic deeds which are recorded by cameras which reproduce them for the amusement of millions of slothful people watching moving pictures in theaters or on television. There is a demand of the multitude for less arduous work, less risk of failure in self-service, a demand for more leisure, not as an opportunity to work for one's self, but more leisure to be amused or to waste time in inconsequential games.

So I come at the end of this chronicle to the question of who could be my hero in this or the coming generation? He could not be a zealous paternalist. Yet all of the political leaders since 1900 have been moving in the direction of a more and more paternalistic government, unless we assume that President Eisenhower's administration marks the turn of the tide. As I have tried to make clear, the objective of "social justice" which inspired the earlier leadership of Theodore Roosevelt, William Jennings Bryan, Robert M. La Follette and Woodrow Wilson was not to establish a democratically controlled socialism.

These early leaders were convinced that a modern government must assume a larger social responsibility than previous governments. But in essence that meant that the owners and managers of industry must accept a larger responsibility for the welfare of the workers employed and for the service to be rendered to consumers. They must include in the price of products not only a "depreciation charge" to replace worn-out or obsolescent machinery. They must also include an adequate wage to maintain the workers (the human machines) in a healthy condition, including a "depreciation charge" to provide for their protection against the hazards of accident and disease and the inevitable incapacities of old age. The idea of early progressivism was that these obligations should be imposed upon the owners and managers of private business and met out of the charges for goods or services imposed upon consumers.

In addition to imposing an obligation of social responsibility on private business, the early Progressives came slowly to see the need for government to accept now and then a direct responsibility for the general welfare in times of national or community disaster. Such aid might only be available from government itself in the event of devastating floods, unusual drought, or spreading epidemics. Then with the Great Depression of 1929 came a further demand for expansion of government powers to meet an economic sickness too widespread and overpowering to yield to private or local relief.

Here is where the need for emergency action, which could only be met by the extraordinary powers and strength of government, insidiously prepared the way for the argument that government should not only relieve an emergency but should take steps to make sure that it did not recur. Consequently it was easy for the worried individualist to become a convert, or to be overborne in his natural resistance, to the apparent necessity of a permanent expansion of government powers and the assumption by government itself of a direct responsibility for the economic welfare of its citizens. Thus the progressivism of the first quarter century became lost in the socialist movement of the second quarter.

If there is to rise a hero in this or the coming generation, he will be no young, enthusiastic paternalist. He will be a mature political leader who will raise the banner of Divine Freedom and wage war against every form and project of collective action that is not aimed at establishing and preserving the liberty of the individual human being to elevate and to save his own life—his liberty even to do that which in common judgment may degrade and destroy his own life.

Even those who may not accept Thomas Jefferson as an outstanding hero of the age of the American Revolution may be willing to accept the heroism of his proclaimed purpose: "I have sworn upon the altar of God eternal hostility against every form of tyranny over the mind of man." Tyrannies over the bodies and minds of men go hand in hand. He who has a faith in the divinity of human life must have faith that, if individual freedom is maintained, those who, with instinctive wisdom, are seeking to elevate their individual lives will survive, and those who, with instinctive folly, are seeking to degrade their lives will perish; and thus the destined uplift of humanity will be fulfilled. It requires this faith to leave other men and women free to injure themselves despite our "superior" views of what might be good for them.

One of the inevitable results of the socialization of government, so that it becomes directly responsible for the economic welfare of the people, is the necessity placed upon the government to establish moral standards and to enforce them with the responsibility of a parent over its children. It becomes necessary for the government to accept the tremendous responsibility of helping all its people avoid the hardships that come, not merely from misfortune, but from physical or mental or moral incapacity to take care of themselves.

From ancient times there has been some responsibility accepted in any civilized community for the care of those physically crippled or mentally incompetent. Those morally incapable have been usually dealt with by punishments, perhaps ineffective to reform the individual but helpful to protect the community.

In a small community, among neighbors, the physically crippled may be aided and the mentally incompetent protected. Both may be made somewhat self-serving through intelligent personal treatment, but without any hopeless or extravagant effort to lift them to the same level of enjoyment and comfort of life as their more fortunate neighbors. But, by a government such sensible and humane treatment is impossible. A government must either be as ruthless as a great wind that destroys all weak and rotting trees; or it must seek to save and serve all the weaker citizens at the expense of all the stronger. How can a government, with bureaucratic rules and regulations, make fine distinctions between the halfwitted and the imbecile, the partially crippled and the malingerer? Only the crude, but on the whole just, judgments of one's neighbors can make such distinctions.

Government is peculiarly unable to deal with the variations of moral incapacity which in private enterprises may permit a petty grafter to work in a machine shop, where there is not much of value which can be easily stolen, but will deny him a place behind the counter of a bank.

Big government cannot help being an utterly incompetent dispenser of charity. How hard it is to distinguish between an altruistic effort to help people help themselves and a moralistic tyranny to make other people better and happier! We can see the difference between the "friendly" and the "sanctimonious" activity of an individual, but the distinction becomes completely obscured in a political project.

Nevertheless, we must expect that every generation of eager, inexperienced children will produce a crop of coercive reformers who will insist on trying to make the world over in short order. Their good intentions may be admired. They may reawaken the consciences of their elders which have been dulled by either success or failure. But they will produce no heroes until the lessons written down in history have been illuminated for them by experience and they have reached an actual maturity. If it be a maturity of cynicism and disillusionment, that will be their personal misfortune. If it be a maturity where they find a faith in which they wish to serve, but do not wish to govern, the lives of their fellow men—they will be fortunate. Those of the oncoming generation who find this idealism will be fortunate, indeed, because that is not the idealism which has been dominant in the first half of the twentieth century. The descendants of my generation will not inherit, but must rediscover, a faith in individual liberty and responsibility.

Such happens to be my faith today. In it I have found an increasing happiness in living, even though in the service of that faith I have found no hero.

Index

Acheson, Dean, 191, 287, 305
Adair case, 143
Addams, Jane, 50, 51, 66-67
Allen, Robert, 191
Allen, William, 167, 168
American Federation of Labor, 116, 138, 142, 163
American Iron and Steel Institute, 309
American Natural Gas Company, 326
American University, 327
Angell, Norman, 79
Antwerp, 229-30
Armour, J. Ogden, 93-94
Army Air Force, 310-11
Arnold, General "Hap," 310, 311, 312
Assistant to the President, 178, 183
Association of State Public Utilities Commissioners, 122
Atomic Energy Commission, 127
Atterbury, General, 115, 130

Baker, Newton D., 80, 97, 235
Ball, Senator, 299
Ball-Burton-Hatch bill, 300
Barkley, Alben, 128-30
Baruch, Bernard M., 164, 165, 176
Beck, James M., 196
Bemis, Edward W., 105, 107
Benton, John E., 122
Benton, Thomas H., 98
Berle, Adolph, 155-56
Berliner, Henry A., 309, 311, 312
Beveridge, Albert J., 55, 57-58
Biddle, Francis, 274
Biggs, Crawford, 159
Black, Hugo, 163, 225, 227, 332
Blair, Harry, 203, 225
Blodgetts, Thomas, 225
Boettiger, John, 92
Borah, William, 223
Bowen, Mrs. Joseph T., 50
Brain Trust, 155, 160
Brandeis, Louis, 80, 120, 124, 191-92, 224, 354
Brandt, Raymond, 296
Brantley, Judge, 122
Bridges, Harry, 180
Brussels, 230
Bryan, William Jennings, 10, 21, 23-24, 27, 42, 45, 80, 82, 114, 119, 121, 357
Bryce, Cornelia, 68
Bull Moose Party, 44, 60-77
Burling, Edward B., 47, 48
Burton, Senator, 299
Butler, Justice, 223
Byrnes, James, 274, 276

Cárdenas, President of Mexico, 249, 251, 252, 254, 255-62, 265, 266
Cardozo, Benjamin, 191
Case, Francis, 301
Case Bill, 300-01
Casey, Joseph E., 305
Castillo Nájera, Ambassador, 254, 259, 261, 262, 265, 267
Catledge, Turner, 310
Chamberlain, Neville, 233
Charlottesville, Virginia, 326-27, 328-45

Chenery, Christopher T., 105
Chicago, Illinois, 9-10, 26-41
Chicago Fire of 1871, 9
Chicago *Tribune,* 27, 34, 65, 92
City of Paris, 229
Clapper, Raymond, 296
Clark School, Chicago, 13
Cleveland, Grover, 49, 83, 160
Clifford, Clark, 301
Cochems, Henry F., 51
Constitution, U.S.S., 9
Coolidge, Calvin, 43, 130-32, 134, 135-36, 138, 139, 153
Coolidge, Mrs. Calvin, 132
Copley, Representative, 52
Coppage case, 143
Corcoran, Tommy, 206, 281, 285
Costigan, Senator, 158, 163
"Court packing" plan, 203-05, 220-27, 322
Cox, James M., 319
Cruice, Daniel, 28
Cuernavaca, Mexico, 258
Cummings, Homer, 113, 158, 179, 193-94, 198, 221, 225, 226, 238
Cutting, Senator, 163

Daniels, Josephus, 80, 254, 257
Darrow, Clarence, 28, 214, 319
Daugherty injunction case, 117-19
Davies, Dienie, 230
Davies, Joseph E., 61, 228-31
Davies, Marjorie, 229
Davies, Morgan, 61, 62, 228
Davies, Ralph K., 239
Davies, Richberg, Beebe, Busick and Richardson, 229
Davies, Richberg, Tydings, Beebe and Landa, 229
Davis, John W., 136, 138, 139, 232
Dawes, Charles G., 149
"Democratization of Industry," 94
Depew, Chauncey, 23
Depression period, 147, 320, 358
Dern, Secretary of War, 238
Dever, Mayor, of Chicago, 119
Dickinson, Assistant Secretary, 164
Dilli, Reginald, 124
Dobie, Judge, 340-41
Doolittle, James, 310, 311
Double Martini Club, 309-14
Douglas, Lewis W., 164, 237-38, 246
Douglas, William O., 226, 305, 333
Douglass, Paul, 327
Dowd, Peggy, 285
Dowie, John Alexander, 20-23
Dunne, Mayor, 28
Dutch Shell Company, 248, 255

Early, Steve, 63, 239, 240, 271, 274, 291, 294
East Clinton, Tennessee, 10
Eastman, Joseph B., 160
Eckels, James H., 160
Edison, Charles, 276
Eisenhower, Dwight D., 357
Electric Light Company, Chicago, 104
Elliott, Miss, 167
Emery, James, 130
Executive Council, 177, 183
Ezekiel, Mordecai, 92

Fairbanks, Mrs. Kellogg, 51
Fairbanks, Vice President, 131
Fair Employment Practice program, 303-04
Farley, James, 236, 238
Federal Emergency Relief, 238
Federal Power Commission, 127, 324, 331
Federal Reserve System, 80
Federal Sugar Act, 330-31
Federal Trade Commerce Bill, 65
Federal Trade Commission, 65, 80, 193, 228
Ferguson, Homer, 334
Fisher, Walter L., 123
Fitch, Clyde, 208
Frankfurter, Felix, 126, 159, 224, 332, 333
Franklin, Jay, 234

Garfield, James R., 51
Garner, John Nance, 155, 238

George, David Lloyd, 231-32, 269
Goodrich, Edgar J., 310, 312
Green, William, 186, 187, 191
Gridiron Club, 172
Guilty! The Confession of Franklin D. Roosevelt, 269-70

Halifax, Lord, 305
Hamilton, Walton H., 187, 276
Hand, Learned, 191
Harding, Warren G., 43, 83, 134, 137, 153, 318, 319
Harlan, John M., 60
Harper, William Rainey, 24
Harriman, W. Averell, 186-87, 238, 276
Harrison, Carter H., 9
Harvard Glee Club, 20
Harvard Law School, 11, 19-20, 60, 126, 209, 210, 339
Hatch, Senator, 299
"Headaches of the Bar," 314
Hearst, William Randolph, 13
Helm, Mrs., 313
Heney, Francis J., 51, 69
Herrick, Elizabeth, 207-11
Herrick, Robert, 31, 208
Hillman, Sidney, 186, 187, 275, 276
Hitler, Adolph, 4, 229, 233, 270
Holmes, Oliver Wendell, Jr., 125, 191, 343
Hoover, Herbert, 43, 83, 139, 143, 149-53, 228, 319
Hopkins, Harry L., 151, 238, 239, 240-43
Hopper, Bruce, 310
Howe, Louis, 155, 295
Howell, Robert, 128-30
Hughes, Charles Evans, 86-91, 143-44, 198, 225
Hull, Cordell, 166, 179, 238, 250, 262, 271, 292
Hunter, "Monk," 310
Hurley, Patrick J., 265-66
Hutcheson, Joseph C., Jr., 143
Hyde Park, New York, 181-83, 287
Hylan, John, 119

Icaza, Justice, 251
Ickes, Harold L., 37, 60-64, 89, 109, 151, 156, 157, 158, 238-39, 241, 244, 318
Illinois Progressive Service Board, 50-51
Illinois State Council of Defense, 106
Illinois Utilities Commission, 106-07, 110
"Imprisonment of Criminal Corporations," 33
Industrial Emergency Committee, 183, 286
Insull, Samuel, 72, 102-11, 113, 325
Interstate Commerce Commission, 114, 119, 120, 121-22, 123
Interstate Trade Commission Bill, 65

Jacobs, District Judge, 146
Jefferson, Thomas, 358
Jewell, Bert M., 116, 117
Johnson, Hiram W., 69, 88-89, 156, 157, 158, 318
Johnson, Hugh S., 163, 165-66, 167, 173, 174-76, 178-79, 180, 181, 183, 184, 185, 239, 247, 287
Jones, Jesse, 350-51

Keeley, James, 34
Kennedy, Joseph P., 231, 232
Kenney, George, 310
Kent, Frank R., 3
Kent, William, 119
King, Mackenzie, 94
King, Milton W., 309
Kipling, Rudyard, 212
Kirchwey, George W., 51
Knox, John C., 314
Knox College, 9, 98
Knoxville, Tennessee, 10

La Follette, Phil, 126
La Follette, Robert M., 36, 38, 42, 43, 45, 67, 114, 119-20, 121, 123, 128, 136-40, 318, 357
La Follette, Robert M., Jr., 138, 157, 158, 163

Lane, Secretary of the Interior, 80
League of Nations, 82, 317, 318-19
Lehman, Herbert, 183
Lend Lease Act, 272
Lewis, David, 230
Lewis, J. Hamilton, 28-29
Lewis, John L., 181, 186, 187, 235-36
Lewis, William Draper, 35, 51, 52-53, 69
Lilienthal, David E., 126-28, 217
Lindbergh, C. A., 51
Lindbergh, Charles, 51
Lindsey, Ben B., 51, 69-70
Lodge, Henry Cabot, 88, 318
London, 231, 232
Longworth, Nicholas, 128
Lord, John S., 61
Louis, Joe, 240
Lovett, Robert Morss, 31
Lundin, Fred, 70

Marshall, George C., 305
Marshall, Leon, 187, 276
Marshall, Vice President, 131
Marx, Karl, 337
McAdoo, William G., 43, 80, 113, 115, 136, 149
McCaskill, O. L., 23
McCormick, Medill, 65-66
McCormick, Mrs. Medill, 29, 50
McCormick, Robert R., 27-28, 65
McDowell, Mary, 50
McGrady, Edward F., 180
McIntyre, Marvin, 161, 178, 179-80, 227, 239, 294, 300
McKinley, William, 23
McReynolds, Justice, 125, 194-95
Mellett, Lowell, 240
Merriam, Charles E., 36-38, 51, 60, 72-76
Metropolitan magazine, 94
Mexican oil negotiations, 248-63
"Mexican Oil Seizure," 264
Mexico City, 253-58, 261
Michelson, Albert A., 4, 24, 31
Millay, Edna St. Vincent, 344
Miller, John S., 104
Millikan, Robert A., 4, 24, 31
Mitchell, William D., 123
Moley, Raymond, 155, 156, 159, 163-64, 166, 294
Moody, William Vaughn, 31, 34-35
Morgen, J. P., and Company, 53
Morgenthau, Henry, Jr., 287-90, 294
Morgenthau Plan, 289
Mulholland, Frank, 118
Mullen, Senator, 158
Murdock, Victor, 35, 51, 58, 69
Murphy, Justice, 332
Murray, Philip, 187, 276
Mussolini, Benito, 5

National Association of Manufacturers, 130, 131
National Conference on Valuation of Railroads, 112, 114, 119-23
National Emergency Council, 63, 177, 183, 187, 274, 286
National Industrial Recovery Act, 164-65, 185, 188, 189-96, 199, 247
National Labor Relations Board, 299
National Progressive League, 157
National Progressive Service, 51-59, 67
National Recovery Administration, 162-69, 171, 173-75, 177, 178, 184-88, 189-96, 197-202, 236, 243, 286, 287
Nelson, Eric, 310
New Dealers, The, 234-35, 237-38
"New Look of the Constitution," 314
New Republic, 94
New York *Journal,* 20, 22, 208
New York State Bar Association, 314
Norris, George W., 123, 156
North German Lloyd, 78

O'Donnell, "Rosie," 310
O'Fallon case, 121-22, 124
Old Faith and Fancies New, 335
Orr, Dr., 205
Owen, Senator, 121

Palmer House, Chicago, 62, 217
Panama Canal, 78-79

Paris, 231
Parker, Congressman, 129
Patterson, Joseph M., 27
Peace Conference, 82
Pearl Harbor, 273, 310, 311
Pearson, Drew, 190
Pendergast, Jim, 39, 54
Penn Medical College, 11, 12
Peoples Gas Light and Coke Company, 72, 102-11, 212, 325
Perkins, Frances, 164, 165, 175, 179, 180, 238, 246, 273
Perkins, George W., 36, 51, 53-54, 55, 68
Phi Gamma Delta fraternity, 80, 131, 207
Pierian Sodality, 20
Pinchot, Gifford, 36, 51, 57, 67-68, 181
Plumb, Glenn E., 73-74, 113-14
"Plumb Plan," 114, 115
President's Civil Rights Committee, 302, 323
President's Re-employment Agreement, 184-85
Prettyman, Justice, 333
"Progressive Congressional Program," 52-58
Progressive movement, 35-39, 358
Progressive Party, 42-59, 61, 136-40

Quesada, Elwood, 310

Railway Labor Act, 126-33, 141, 142, 149, 277, 297-98, 299
Railroad Labor Board, 115
Railway Labor Executives Association, 141-42, 162
Railway Valuation Bill, 120
Rainbow, The, 189, 202
Randall, Eloise, 10, 11, 12-15, 91
Randall, George C., 12
Randall, Marenda, 11-12
Randall, Nathaniel, 11-13
Reader's Digest, 271
Reconstruction Finance Corporation, 350
Reed, Stanley, 123, 193, 194, 221, 222
Rehoboth Beach, Delaware, 202, 229
Ribble, Dean, 341
Richardson, Seth, 228
Richberg, Eloise (daughter), 217, 253
Richberg, Ickes, Davies and Lord, 61
Richberg, Ickes and Richberg, 61
Richberg, John C. (father), 9-11, 13-15, 28-30, 32, 61, 71, 91, 98, 209
Richberg, Louis, 8-9
Richberg, Lynette, 212-14
"Right to work" law case, 331-32
Roberts, Justice, 223, 225
Robins, Raymond, 58-59, 64-65, 319
Robinson, Joseph, 224, 225
Rogers, Walter S., 149
Rogers, Will, 174
Roosevelt, Anna, 92
Roosevelt, Eleanor, 155, 223, 290
Roosevelt, Franklin D., 4, 62-63, 76, 111, 127, 136, 139-40, 147, 151, 153-55, 157, 159-61, 163-67, 174-76, 177, 181, 182-83, 187-88, 197, 199-201, 203-06, 220-27, 230-31, 237, 241-43, 246, 254, 269-74, 276, 279-95, 296-97, 320
Roosevelt, Quentin, 98
Roosevelt, Theodore, 4, 34, 35, 38, 40, 42-59, 67, 70, 80, 82, 83, 84-88, 89-91, 94, 96-98, 99-101, 109, 114, 232, 281, 317, 357
Roosevelt and Hopkins, 247
Roosevelt I Knew, The, 246
Roper, Secretary of Commerce, 238
Rosenman, Judge, 222, 240, 246, 275, 294
Rumely, Edward A., 332-33
Rumely case, 332-33
Russian Revolution, 95, 354

St. Louis *Post-Dispatch,* 296
St. Sure, District Judge, 146
Saltillo, Mexico, 260, 261
San Antonio, Texas, 260
San Francisco, California, 14
San Francisco strike, 179-80

Saturday Evening Post, 55
Schechter case, 188, 189-96
Schecter Poultry Corporation, 189
Sea Cloud, 229-30
Securities and Exchange Commission, 325
Seneca, 76
Sexton, Roy, 205
Shadow Men, The, 40, 210
Sherman, Larry, 59
Sherman Anti-Trust Act, 53
Sherwood, Robert, 242, 247
Shipstead, Senator, 119, 123
Shopmen's strike of 1922, 115-16, 125
"Should We Revive the Constitution," 314
"Sick Chicken" case, 189-96
Sinclair Oil Company, 248, 255, 259, 265-66
Smith, Alfred E., 43, 136, 139, 150, 295
Smith, Blackwell, 168-69
Smith, Herbert Knox, 51, 68-69
Smoot, Senator, 132
Southampton, 232
Spaatz, Carl, 309, 311, 312, 313-14
Spaatz, Ruth, 313
Springfield, Illinois, 14
Stagg, Amos Alonzo, 24
Stalin, Joseph, 239
Standard Oil of California, 248, 255, 259, 267
Standard Oil of New Jersey, 248, 255, 259, 264, 267
Stone, Harlan, 192, 223-24
Stone, Warren, 114, 119
Strouss, Assistant Attorney General, 146
Sullivan, Roger, 59, 108
Supreme Court, 330-34
Swanson, Secretary of Navy, 238

T. & N.O. Railroad case, 142-43
Taft, Lorado, 216
Taft, Robert A., 304
Taft, William Howard, 36, 42, 43, 49, 120, 123
Taft-Hartley Act, 301
Tarbell, Ida, 36
Tariff Commission, 80
Taxco, Mexico, 258
Teagle, Walter, 248
Tennessee Valley Authority, 127
Thom, Colonel, 129, 131
Thompson, William Hale, 70, 72
Thomson, Charles M., 51, 70
Toledano, 251
Torrison, Judge, 104
Transportation Act of 1920, 115
Truman Doctrine, 305
Truman, Harry S., 140, 277-78, 297-99, 301-08, 321, 323
Tugwell, Rex, 155, 156, 164
Tully, Grace, 285
Tuttle, Charles H., 304
Tydings, Senator, 230, 231

United Light and Power System, 325
United States Naval Academy, 9
United States Steel Corporation, 53
University Club of Chicago, 40-41
University of Chicago, 11, 18-19, 21, 23, 31, 60, 207
University of Virginia Law School, 327, 337-45

Vanderbilt, Cornelius, 107
Vandeventer, Justice, 225
Van Hasselt, B. Th., 254
Vinson, Fred, 277
Von Bülow, Busso, 78-79, 98
Vrooman, Carl, 119

Wagner Act, 299-300
Wagner, Robert, 164, 204, 236-37, 247, 300
Walker, Frank, 183
Wallace, Henry A., 92, 151, 156, 243-45
Warm Springs, Georgia, 296
Watson, Senator, 129
Weed, Florence, 214-19, 225, 226, 227, 258, 313, 316, 324, 326
Welles, Sumner, 166, 250, 262

Weyl, Walter E., 51
Wheeler, Senator, 123, 136
White House Correspondents' Association, 296
Whiteside, Arthur D., 186-87, 298
Whitney, Richard, 279-80
"Why No Third Term?" 271
Wickersham, George W., 123
Wilbur, Circuit Judge, 146
Wilkerson, Judge, 117, 118
Willard, Daniel, 116, 117, 147
Willcox, William R., 88, 89
Williams, Clay, 184, 186, 298
Wilson, Charles E., 302
Wilson, Lyle, 310
Wilson, Woodrow, 36, 42, 45, 46, 49, 66, 67, 76, 80, 81-86, 90, 91, 94, 96-97, 113, 114, 115, 140, 165, 232, 317, 318, 357
Wisconsin Public Service Commission, 126
Witherow, W. P., 187, 276
Woodin, Secretary of the Treasury, 287
Woods, Muir, 119
Woodstock, Vermont, 11-12
Woolfolk, William G., 105, 325-26
Working With Roosevelt, 246
World War I, 42, 78-101, 113, 135, 149, 310, 317, 354
World War II, 152, 229, 252, 263, 266, 270-78, 311, 321, 354

Yount, Barton, 310, 312

Zion City, 21
Zionism, 21-23